Religion and the Law

A Dictionary

CONTEMPORARY LEGAL ISSUES

Religion and the Law

A Dictionary

Christopher Thomas Anglim

ABC-CLIO

Santa Barbara, California
Denver, Colorado
Oxford, England

Library of Congress Cataloging-in-Publication Data
Anglim, Christopher.
    Religion and the law : a dictionary / Christopher Thomas Anglim.
        p.   cm.—(Contemporary legal issues)
    Includes bibliographical references and index.
    ISBN 1–57607–028-X (alk. paper)
        1. Church and state—United States—Dictionaries. 2. Freedom of
religion—United States—Dictionaries. 3. Religion and law—United States—
Dictionaries. I. Title. II. Series.
    KF4865.A68A54 1999
    342.73′0852′03—dc21   99–32889
                                                                            CIP

05 04 03 02 01 00 99   10 9 8 7 6 5 4 3 2 1

ABC-CLIO, Inc.
130 Cremona Drive, P.O. Box 1911
Santa Barbara, California 93116-1911

This book is printed on acid-free paper ∞.

Manufactured in the United States of America

Contents

Preface

Americans are a remarkably religious people. Virtually every poll on the state of religious belief in the United States reports that at least 90 percent of Americans have some form of religious faith. Of the 90.7 percent of Americans who profess to have a religion, an overwhelming majority (83.8 percent) identify their religion as either Protestant (55.2 percent) or Catholic (28.6 percent). Despite the steady growth of non-Christian religions in America, most Americans still describe themselves as Christian.

Today, there is considerable disagreement on the roles of religion and law in contemporary American society. Indeed, the controversies over Christianity's role in shaping the nation's law and public policy, especially the restrictions placed on that role by the doctrine of the separation of church and state, have been among the leading issues in America's debate on how its destiny should be shaped.

Religious freedom and the nonestablishment of religion on a federal level have been embodied within the First Amendment of the U.S. Constitution since the ratification of the Bill of Rights in 1791. These important constitutional guarantees were uncommon in the world of the late eighteenth century and are not universal even today. The interpretation of the First Amendment's Establishment and Free Exercise Clauses is primarily a function of the judiciary, and the final decision on First Amendment issues comes from the U.S. Supreme Court. The late Chief Justice Warren Burger both described the process the Court used in explaining the meaning of these constitutional provisions and summarized their boundaries in *Walz v. Tax Commission* (U.S. 1970):

> The general principle deducible from the First Amendment and all that the Court has said is this: that we will not tolerate either governmentally established religion or governmental interference with religion. Short of those expressly proscribed governmental acts there is room for play in the joint product of a benevolent neutrality

which will permit religious exercise to exist without sponsorship and without interference.

In developing its position of "benevolent neutrality," the Court has produced a crucially important body of caselaw that became a vital part of American constitutional jurisprudence. In the past two decades, legal scholars have produced a large body of literature on church and state issues. This phenomenon is due to several factors, including the debate over the role of original intent in constitutional interpretation, the Court's difficulties in applying the *Lemon* test, and the emergence of the chronological sequence in which cases where decided.

Surprisingly, it was not until the 1940s that the Supreme Court began developing a jurisprudence of the Religion Clauses of the First Amendment. Since then, most Supreme Court justices have written opinions expressing their deeply held views on the proper relationship between law and religion, and between church and state. Often, the views expressed by one justice will sharply conflict with the views of the other justices.

In interpreting current issues involving religion and the law, this dictionary includes entries necessary to establish historical context such as Thomas Jefferson's Bill for Establishing Religious Freedom and James Madison's *Memorial and Remonstrance Against Religious Assessments*. These documents were critical in the development of religious freedom in this country. The Supreme Court has also repeatedly referred to both documents in its various majority, concurring, and dissenting opinions. Primarily, this dictionary focuses on current developments in the field. For example, it will cover issues such as the Religious Freedom Restoration Act (RFRA) of 1993, which was enacted to reverse the U.S. Supreme Court's interpretation of the Free Exercise Clause in *Employment Division v. Smith* (U.S. 1990).

Second, a bibliography lists many important monographs and articles that form a representative part of the vast literature on the relationship between religion and the law.

Third, the work contains an alphabetical table of the cases from the U.S. Supreme Court, lower federal courts, and state courts that are discussed in the book. Because the entries frequently cite many leading cases, the table of cases is the only place where full citations are found, to conserve space and to minimize distraction for the reader.

The dictionary focuses on terms involved with the constitutional theory and interpretation of religion and the law; terms providing a historical explanation of the ways in which America's ever increasing ethnic and religious diversity contributed to our current understanding of the mandates of the First and Fourteenth Amendments; terms and concepts describing the development of religion clause jurisprudence; an analytical examination of the distinct vocabulary used in this area of the law; the means by which American courts have attempted to balance religious liberty against other important individual and social interests in a wide variety of physical and regulatory environments (including the classroom, the workplace, the courtroom, religious group organization and structure, taxation, the clash of "secular" and "religious" values, and the relationship of the generalized idea of individual autonomy to the specific concept of religious liberty).

Unlike many other current treatises on First Amendment law, this dictionary focuses strictly on religion and the law as its primary subject, rather than also focusing on the Free Speech and Free Press Clauses.

I would like to thank Doherty Library, especially James Pi and Mark Landingham, for their support in this endeavor. I would also like to thank Professor Collett of South for advice, support, and encouragement.

Religion
and the Law

A Dictionary

Introduction

The broad religious freedom found in the United States is a distinctly American creation that has evolved throughout American history. Pure religious liberty is one great contribution that this country has given the world.

The Bill of Rights, as the first 10 amendments to the United States Constitution are called, has long been the chief guarantor of freedoms for individual Americans. The cornerstone of the Bill of Rights is the First Amendment. First among the rights guaranteed to all Americans in the First Amendment are those expressed in the religion clauses. Indeed, the First Amendment begins with the words: "Congress shall make no law respecting an establishment of religion, or prohibiting the free exercise thereof." The First Amendment sets forth the two major principles of constitutional law regarding religion: (1) the state may not establish a religion or religions and (2) the people may practice whatever religion they choose.

THE RELATIONSHIP OF RELIGION AND STATE
IN THE WESTERN WORLD

To appreciate the significance of American contributions to religious freedom, one must understand how the relationship of church and state in the Western world evolved over time. In general the Christian religion has influenced law in the Western world in at least five distinct ways that have also influenced American law. It has done this:

1. By influencing the natural law theory
2. By directly supplying rules that are enacted into the secular laws
3. By reinforcing ethical principles and providing an underlying justification for statutes or common law traditions
4. By influencing law in a humanitarian direction
5. By justifying and emphasizing the maintenance of moral standards, notions of honesty, good faith, and fairness.

1

The most common single example of Christian influence on the law is the oath; for example, elected officials and government employees swear to uphold the Constitution, judges swear to administer the law justly, and—most commonly—witnesses swear to tell the truth.

Religious beliefs, particularly the belief in a God who reveals morally correct conduct, greatly influenced the medieval idea of natural law. God's law, law revealed by reason, and the law determined by nature, were hardly distinguishable in medieval thought. Beginning in the twelfth century with the scholastics and continuing in the thirteenth century with Thomas Aquinas, a belief arose in the law of nature as the law of God; the sharing in the eternal law by a rational creature is natural law. Later Spanish jurist theologians, notably Domingo de Soto in the mid-sixteenth century and Francisco Suarez in the early seventeenth century, found a religious basis for legal systems, both on a national and international level.

Although spiritual and secular authorities in Europe in the Middle Ages for the most part complemented and strengthened each other, they nevertheless clashed several times. Notable among these quarrels was the investitures contest that involved a power struggle between the papacy and the Holy Roman emperor during the late eleventh and early twelfth centuries. It began with a dispute about the lay investiture of bishops and abbots. Such prelates held land and often exercised secular as well as ecclesiastical functions; for this reason, lay overlords had an understandable interest in their appointment and frequently invested (formally presented) them with the symbols of their various offices.

Because Pope Gregory VII's condemnation (1075) of lay investiture immediately preceded his dispute with the German king and Holy Roman Emperor Henry IV (who reigned 1056–1106), historians have referred to the quarrel and its aftermath as the "Investiture Controversy." The real conflict, however, between Henry IV and Gregory, the main disputants, involved the issue of whether the pope or the emperor should dominate the church. A compromise to this controversy was reached in the Concordat of Worms (1122), in which the emperor renounced the practice of investing prelates, and in return, the church conceded that homage to the Emperor would precede episcopal consecration.

Religions develop their own laws governing not only the organization of ritual, practice, and belief, but large parts of the secular lives of their adherents. When a religion has secured a controlling hold on state authority, law dictated by the state religion shares total social control with law dictated by the secular state. In western Europe, for example, the canon law became a major part of the legal system of every Christian country. Canon law is the body of law constituted by ecclesiastical authority for the organization and government of the Christian church. A canon is a rule or norm and the church, as much as civil society, has found it necessary to prescribe rules setting standards and norms for conduct in many situations, and the body of these is the canon law. Even after its formal authority was abolished in many countries during the Reformation in the sixteenth century, canon law continued to exercise a powerful influence on the law of marriage and wills, and on the attitude of the courts.

In the sixteenth and seventeenth centuries Europe produced a few advocates of religious tolerance and the individual's right to worship freely according to conscience, but the prevailing policy was one of close cooperation between church and state to maintain religious and political orthodoxy. Establishment was the order of the day: the state was the defender and sponsor of the church and the church was a bulwark of the existing political order. In the name of religion, European governments frequently persecuted domestic dissenters and engaged in bloody foreign wars.

The notion of both freedom of religious exercise and nonestablishment of religion was truly revolutionary and was to find its first official expression in the nation that was developing across the Atlantic.

THE RELATIONSHIP BETWEEN CHURCH AND STATE IN AMERICA

From the time of Columbus's first voyage in 1492 until 1607, Roman Catholicism was the predominant influence of European Christianity in the New World. Roman Catholic beliefs were imported by explorers, conquerors, and missionaries from the Iberian peninsula, chiefly Spain. This influence shifted after permanent British settlements were established in Virginia in 1607 and in New England after 1620. The beginnings of the Puritan colonies at Plymouth and Massachusetts Bay presaged what was to become the strongest influence in American religiosity: Protestantism.

The exact role religion played in the settlement of the English colonies in America is difficult to determine. Nonetheless, the British North American colonies that eventually formed the United States were settled by many people who refused to compromise deeply held religious convictions in the face of persecution in Europe and risked the perilous crossing of the Atlantic to practice their religious faith as they believed the Scriptures commanded. Diverse individuals of many faiths—Puritans, Quakers, Mennonites, Roman Catholics, Brethren (Dunkers), and others—came in search of "Zion in the Wilderness" where they could practice their religious beliefs without fear of persecution. The missionary spirit also led many to make the sojourn.

The New England colonies in particular, as well as New Jersey, Pennsylvania, and Maryland, were conceived and established "as plantations of religion." A large majority of the settlers of these colonies enthusiastically supported the efforts of their leaders to build "a city on a hill" or a successful "holy experiment" to prove to the Old World that God's plan for his churches could be realized in the American wilderness.

The Puritans who came to New England in 1620 were not particularly concerned with politics or law as such, but as political issues were often involved in religious issues, politics was handled through religious law. In early New England intellectuals wrote extensively on the nature of law and governance. Among these was a group of highly educated philosophers who had grown to adulthood in England and believed in the principles of English Puritanism. In England during the seventeenth century many accepted the law of God (identified with the law of reason) as the fundamental law of the kingdom, which no parliamentary act could contravene. Not only did New England's political thinkers maintain the supremacy of the law of nature and its identity with the law of God, but they believed in the Bible as the source of their law. The theory of Richard Hooker that "laws human must be made according to the general law of nature, and without contradiction to any positive law of Scripture otherwise they are ill made" was literally placed into practice by the Puritans. Calvinist jurists in America followed their acceptance of the law of God as the fundamental law to identify law with morality and sin with crime. This was possible in New England because of the homogeneous character of the community, the dominant position of the New England clergy, and the close relationship between the church and the courts. Criminal offenses in these colonies included unmitigated lying, scolding, idleness, and drunkenness.

The Massachusetts General Laws and Liberties, a legal code adopted in 1648, contributed to a decline in Puritanism. This code retained some features of English common law but rejected others, and took the novel step of declaring basic human rights and freedoms, such as the right of all to equal protection under the law, the right to bail, the right to appeal from adverse judgments, freedom from double jeopardy, the privilege against self-incrimination, and the freedoms of speech, travel, and judicial dissent. Most of these principles were eventually incorporated in the Bill of Rights or elsewhere in American law.

Even the colonies not principally founded for religious reasons gave at least some nominal acknowledgment to religious objectives. The royal charter of 1607 granted to the commercial corporation that colonized Virginia emphasized a commitment to the propagation of the Christian faith to the aboriginal peoples "who yet live in darkness and miserable ignorance of the true knowledge and worship of God." It expressed the hope that in time those who were already enlightened might "bring the infidels and the savages, living in those parts, to human civility, and to a settled and quiet government."

Although economic considerations may have been the paramount objective of the effort, it is still significant that in practically every statement of purpose, appeal to settlers, and charter issued in Virginia, religious purposes were given a prominent position. Also, the entrepreneurs who planned these ventures considered themselves "militant Protestants" and worked diligently to promote the prosperity of the church.

Not all those who appealed for religious tolerance and Christian love while persecuted in their homelands practiced those virtues when they assumed political power in the New World. Too often their concept of religious freedom proved to mean freedom for their own particular beliefs and practices only, and they began to reproduce the European model of establishment and oppression. This occurred repeatedly in the colonies.

In Massachusetts Bay, Plymouth, Connecticut, and New Hampshire, Congregationalism was the established church, despite the protest of Protestant dissenters. Rhode Island, founded by the pioneer in religious freedom, Roger Williams, stood in sharp contrast to the rest of New England because it strictly respected the religious liberty of all Protestants, and to some extent, that of Roman Catholics and Jews. In North and South Carolina, Georgia, and Virginia, the Church of England was the official church. With the exception of Virginia, however, its power to influence law and society was relatively weak. Virginia, of all the southern colonies, had the most entrenched establishment, as the Church of England enjoyed such privileges as tax support. Individuals who did not believe in the Anglican faith were punished as criminals if they did not attend the services of that church and dissenters were driven from the colony.

New York, Maryland, and Georgia went through various stages of establishment and disestablishment of religion during the colonial period. The status of New Jersey is still debatable: it is unclear whether there was ever formal establishment of an official religion or just an informal understanding. Only Pennsylvania, Delaware, and Rhode Island never designated an official church. Of the 13 colonies, Massachusetts and Virginia had the closest relationship between law and religion.

The fate of dissenters in most of the early colonies was little different from what it would have been in England, except perhaps even harsher. Such fellow Congregationalists as Roger Williams, Anne Hutchinson, and John Wheelwright, were banished from Massachusetts because of their failure to conform to the prescribed orthodoxy of the dominant church leadership. Roman Catholics were forbidden to enter the colony under threat of death. Baptists and Quakers were regularly fined, imprisoned, whipped, and banished, and at least four Quakers were executed. The settlement of Rhode Island, Connecticut, and New Hampshire can be attributed primarily to the intolerant actions of Massachusetts authorities. One of the greatest ironies of the entire colonial period occurred in 1662 when King Charles II wrote to the legislature of the Massachusetts Bay

Colony, blaming the Colony's officials for excessive acts of persecution against religious dissenters and demanding that worship in the Church of England be permitted.

Although physical persecution was never as prevalent outside Massachusetts, similar religious intolerance existed in most other colonies, as evidenced by several repressive legislative acts and executive proclamations that appear in early colonial records. Even the more secular southern colonies had repressive laws that were often enforced. For example, many Quakers were arrested, fined, and ordered to leave Virginia under a law passed by that colony's legislature in 1663. This repression was repeated a hundred years later on the very eve of the American Revolution.

From 1768 to 1770 Baptists were persecuted because they refused to comply with a requirement that meeting houses be licensed and for their outspoken criticisms of the established church. In Virginia, when some 30 Baptist ministers were imprisoned, an outraged Patrick Henry rode 50 miles on horseback to make a successful dramatic appearance for three of the defendants in a Spotsylvania County trial.

Roger Williams in Rhode Island and William Penn in Pennsylvania, as well as Maryland in its early years, were striking exceptions to the societies that demanded religious conformity. These colonies soon became havens for the religiously persecuted of both the Old and New Worlds. Penn, George Calvert (the first Baron Baltimore), and Cecil Calvert (the second Baron Baltimore) were rightly commended for their practice of toleration. Roger Williams, however, argued not for mere toleration, but rather for complete religious freedom and the disestablishment of official religions based on the natural rights of man as well as biblical authority.

Although Williams's concept of religious rights was far ahead of his day, the success of his "livlie experiment" inevitably affected the rest of the colonies. As persecution gradually subsided in all the colonies, many different Christian sects began to appear, which foreshadowed the eventual demise of any single established church. Also, steadily increasing numbers of people without church affiliations obviously did not favor either persecution or establishment. William Warren Sweet has estimated that even in stern New England only one in eight persons was a church member by the end of the colonial era.

In addition, many Deists came to positions of prominence and added their influence to that of Baptists, Presbyterians, Quakers, and other opponents of establishment and oppression. Deism signifies a belief in a single God and in a religious practice founded solely on natural reason, rather than on supernatural revelation.

The religious pluralism of colonial America required some kind of unique accommodation when the United States was created as a government. Indeed, religious establishment—the designation of a particular religious group or denomination as favored by civil authorities and therefore eligible to receive public revenues—was impractical in most of the colonies outside of New England. Protestant leaders such as Isaac Backus and William Livingston joined Thomas Jefferson and the Enlightenment Deists in an unlikely alliance to ensure religious toleration and disestablishment.

By the time of the American Revolution conditions were right for the enunciation of religious liberty and the separation of church and state. Each colony had its own specific experience, but there was not a clear consensus as to whether to incorporate separation of church and state in the newly drafted state constitutions. Popular opinion was more tolerant, notwithstanding the severity of the code under which the colonists lived. The religious movement known as the Great Awakening, which swept the country just before the Revolution, resulted in new alignments. It placed greater emphasis on individual conversion and thus tended to make church membership more a matter of personal decision and less a matter of family inheritance. Many Americans, while accepting the principle of nonestablishment, nonetheless expected the state to do nothing harmful to the churches and to religious life. Indeed, the state was expected to forge a comfortable relationship with religion. An examination of early state constitutions somewhat supports this conclusion.

Virginia adopted a Declaration of Rights in June 1776 that contained a stirring and comprehensive statement of religious freedom: "[A]ll men are equally entitled to the free exercise of religion, according to the dictates of conscience; and that it is the mutual duty of all to practice Christian forbearance, love, and charity towards each other." Supporters of the Episcopal Church fiercely resisted the combined efforts of Thomas Jefferson and James Madison to disestablish it. Despite the Declaration of Rights, it would be several years before all of the vestiges of the established church would be removed. Indeed, Jefferson would remember the struggle as the most severe contest in which he had ever been engaged.

In December 1776 the Virginia legislature passed a bill that exempted dissenters from supporting the established church. In June 1779 Jefferson presented his Bill for Establishing Religious Freedom, but Virginia did not enact it into law. After several sessions of legislative inaction, the forces of establishment counterattacked by introducing a bill in 1874 providing for a general assessment for the teaching of religion. James Madison, who assumed the primary leadership role upon Jefferson's departure to France, finally—but narrowly—defeated the Assessment Bill by circulating his celebrated *Memorial and Remonstrance Against Religious Assessment*. He then reintroduced Jefferson's Bill for Religious Liberty, which became law in January 1786, the year before the Philadelphia Convention, at which Madison would come to be known as the "Father of the Constitution."

RELIGION AND THE CONGRESS OF THE CONFEDERATION

The Continental-Confederation Congress, a legislative body that also exercised executive power, governed the United States from 1774 to 1789 and left an impressive list of accomplishments, not the least of which was winning independence from Great Britain, the greatest military power of the age. This Congress, composed of many men who were deeply religious, was convinced that the "public prosperity" of a society depended on the vitality of its religion. As a result, the Congress invested substantial energy in encouraging the practice of religion throughout the new nation, exceeding that expended by any subsequent American national government. Nothing less than a "spirit of universal reformation among all ranks and degrees of our citizens," Congress declared to the American people on 19 March 1782, would "make us a holy, that so we may be a happy, people."

RELIGION IN THE FRAMING OF THE CONSTITUTION

The faith in which each colony was founded gave the new nation a religious orientation that remained strong after the government of the United States was created in 1776. Nonetheless, after the American Revolution, it was obvious that if a single nation was to replace the 13 colonies, the Congress dared not attempt to choose which church to establish or which faiths to privilege. Yet 10 of the original 13 colonies (the exceptions were Rhode Island, Pennsylvania, and Delaware) continued to prefer and support one religion over all others.

Because of the nation's history up to that time, it seemed natural that the framers of the United States Constitution would devote substantial attention to the issue of religion. Actually, there was remarkably little discussion of the question, due largely to the practical needs of the time. Shortly after the Constitutional Convention began in 1787, Charles C. Pinckney of South Carolina submitted his draft of a proposed constitution, which provided that the "[l]egislature of the United States shall pass no law on the subject of religion." This draft was not accepted, but toward the end of the convention he submitted another, more limited proposal. It passed on 30 August 1787. Ultimately, Pinckney's proposals became Clause 3 of Article VI of the Constitution, which provides that, while all state and national officers are bound by oath or affirmation to support the U.S. Constitution, "no religious test shall ever be required as a qualification to any office or public trust under the United States." Only Roger Sherman of Connecticut spoke against this single reference to religion in the original Constitution. He thought it unnecessary, "the prevailing liberality being a sufficient security against such tests."

In the state ratifying conventions for the new Constitution some complaints arose because of the omission of any reference to God, and in at least two conventions fear was expressed at the inclusion of Pinckney's "no test oath" clause. In Massachusetts Major T. Lusk said that he "shuddered at the idea that Roman Catholics, Papists, and pagans might be introduced into office, and that Popery and the Inquisition may be established in America."

The strongest and most persistent criticism of the Constitution throughout the ratification struggle, however, involved the absence of a bill of rights containing specific guarantees of religious liberty as well as other fundamental rights. From his diplomatic post in France, Jefferson wrote to his friend Madison on 20 December 1787, "I will now add what I do not like. First the omission of a bill of rights providing clearly and without the aid of sophisms for freedom of religion."

Supporters of the Constitution responded to the criticism by contending that the inclusion of a bill of rights was not only unnecessary but that, if included, it might prove dangerous to the rights of the people. The national government, they reasoned, was one of delegated authority only; it possessed no powers except those given to it by the Constitution, and no such grant of power to impinge on the rights of individuals had been made. The danger of inclusion of a bill of rights lay in the fact that no listing of such rights could possibly be all-inclusive, and that inadvertent failure to include a particular right could be taken to mean that it was not protected. As Alexander Hamilton warned in *The Federalist No. 84*, such a bill of rights "would contain various exceptions to powers not granted; and on this very account, would afford a colorable pretext to claim more than was granted. For why declare that actions shall not be done which there is no power to do?"

THE ISSUE OF RELIGION AND THE DRAFTING OF THE FIRST AMENDMENT

Despite their own assurances, many advocates of the Constitution shared the apprehensions of the people. Various state conventions urged adoption of a bill of rights by constitutional amendment after the new government was established.

In his inaugural address President George Washington called for a congressional response to the suggestions for a bill of rights, and on 8 June 1789 James Madison, now a congressman from Virginia, submitted a series of amendments prepared largely from those suggested by the ratifying conventions of his own and other states. Madison's initial proposed amendment to prevent the infringement of religious freedom by the federal government read: "The civil rights of none shall be abridged on account of religious belief or worship, nor shall any national religion be established, nor shall the full and equal rights of conscience be in any manner, or on any pretext, infringed." The House of Representatives altered the language to read: "Congress shall make no law establishing religion, or to prevent the free exercise thereof or to infringe the rights of conscience." The committee appointed to consider Madison's proposals, and on which Madison served with Pinckney as chairman, had rewritten the religion section to read: "No religion shall be established by law, nor shall the equal rights of conscience be infringed." After some debate, during which Madison suggested that the word "national" might be inserted before the word "religion" as "point[ing] the amendment directly to the object it was intended to prevent," the House adopted as a substitute reading: "Congress shall make no laws touching religion, or infringing the rights of conscience." On 20 August 1789 Fisher Ames of Massachusetts moved that the proposed amendment be adopted as worded. There is little doubt that Madison wrote this. In the Senate the section adopted read: "Congress shall make no law establishing the articles of faith, or a mode or worship, or prohibiting the free exercise of religion." It was at this point that the religion clauses were joined with the Freedom of Expression Clauses.

In the conference committees of the two bodies, chaired by Madison, the present language was written with its somewhat indefinite "respecting" wording. The Congressional debate lends little assistance in interpreting the religion clauses. Madison's position, as well as that of Jefferson who influenced him, is fairly clear, but the intent, insofar as there was one, of the others in Congress who voted for the language and those in the states who voted to ratify it is subject to speculation.

After extended congressional debate, the Senate approved the Bill of Rights and submitted 12 amendments to the states for ratification. During the next two years, 10 of the 12 proposals received requisite state legislative approval and were added to the Constitution by proclamation on 15 December 1791. Significantly, the First Amendment begins with the religion clauses: "Congress shall make no law respecting an establishment of religion, or prohibiting the free exercise thereof . . ." In these brief but emphatic statements the long and bitter struggle for constitutionally protected freedom of religion was brought to fruition. Of these clauses, Justice Wiley Rutledge wrote: "No provision of the Constitution is more closely tied to or given content by its generating history than the religion clause of the First Amendment. It is at once the refined product and the terse summation of that history." [*Everson v. Board of Education* (U.S. 1947)]

Far from crippling religious expression, as the Congregationalists of New England had feared, disestablishment instead created a salubrious religious climate in America. The First Amendment, with its proscription against religious establishment and its guarantee of religious freedom, fostered a nation where different religions were able to compete for popular followings in the religious marketplace of ideas.

Some churches came with new waves of immigrants; others developed from renewed versions of older faiths (for example, Methodism out of Episcopalianism; the Baptists out of Congregationalism; Disciples of Christ (Christian) out of Presbyterianism); still others arose from completely new religious movements (for example, the Shakers, Latter-Day Saints, Seventh-Day Adventists, Christian Scientists, and Jehovah's Witnesses).

Even George Washington, in his Farewell Address on 17 September 1796, advised his fellow citizens that "religion and morality" were "great pillars of human happiness, these firmest props of the duties of Men and citizens." "National morality," he added, could not exist "in exclusion of religious principle." "Virtue or morality," he concluded, as the products of religion were a "necessary spring of popular government."

INTERPRETATION OF THE RELIGION CLAUSES IN THE NEW NATION

The First Amendment protects personal belief and opinion, as well as actions emanating from personal belief and opinion. It addresses freedom of religion as one of the four basic freedoms deemed imperative to a free society. The other three freedoms are freedom of speech, freedom of the press, and the dual rights to peaceable assembly and petitioning of the government.

The two provisions that protect freedom of religion are the Establishment Clause, which prohibits the government from establishing a religion, and the Free Exercise Clause, which ensures the freedom to practice one's religion. By implication, a right of association also flows from the First Amendment. These rights are not absolute; the U.S. Supreme Court has generally held that a balance is required between First Amendment freedoms and the powers of a government to govern effectively.

The drafters of the Bill of Rights included the Establishment Clause because they remembered the colonial experience with European state churches. At a minimum the Establishment Clause prohibits the government from showing favoritism to a particular church or sect. To understand the meaning of the phrase "separation of church and state," one must realize that modern U.S. Supreme Court case law has interpreted it as implying more than merely forbidding an established church.

Since World War II, the U.S. Supreme Court has broadly construed the First Amendment's prohibitions against establishment of religion. It has attempted to create standards by which it can distinguish prohibited church and state involvements from those that are permitted. For a government policy to withstand the limitations imposed by the Establishment Clause, it must (1) have a secular purpose, (2) have a primary effect that neither advances nor inhibits religion, and (3) not excessively entangle church and state authorities. The court has interpreted the neutral position to be occupied by the state applies both to spiritual practices, such as devotional exercises, and to the allocation of public monies for the benefit of religion.

The Free Exercise Clause prevents the government from interfering with religious practices. That Clause protects absolutely a person's right to believe. The line-drawing problem for the courts exists when some kind of conduct accompanies religious belief. As Justice Felix Frankfurter observed in the first so-called flag salute case, conscientious scruples are insufficient to relieve an individual from "[o]bedience to a general law not aimed at the promotion or restriction of religious belief." [*Minersville School District v. Gobitis* (US 1940)] Thus, a law that has a legitimate secular purpose may impinge upon the ability of a person to act out of a religious belief.

More recently the Court has held that laws or regulations interfering with religious practices are valid only if there is no reasonable alternative to accomplish their legitimate secular objectives. And even more recently it has abolished this "compelling interest" test in *Employment Division v. Smith* (US 1990).

EXTENDING FIRST AMENDMENT PROTECTIONS TO THE STATES

Important as the religious guarantee of the First Amendment was when it was adopted in 1791, the circle of protection drawn around the individual was not yet complete. Although the First Amendment denied the national government the power to interfere with the free exercise of religion or to establish religion, it did not prohibit such actions by the states.

To be sure, all of the states had either bills of rights or other specific constitutional provisions assuring religious freedom. Except for Louisiana, every state constitution adopted between 1776 and 1895 had a provision guaranteeing freedom of worship and conscience. Furthermore, additional provisions often augmented this guarantee by prohibiting compulsory religious attendance and compulsory citizen support of churches and ministers. Many states had proscriptions against religious tests for public office, and proscriptions against enlarging or diminishing an individual's civil rights because of religious beliefs. In short, state constitutions contained rather extensive provisions guaranteeing religious belief and worship. These were strengthened as the states amended their original constitutions or adopted new ones. The last establishment provision was removed from a state constitution in 1833 in Massachusetts. As new states applied for admission to the Union, Congress insisted on adequate constitutional guarantees of freedom of religion and a disestablishment clause. Nevertheless, state judges sometimes failed to apply vigorously the protective guarantees of the state constitutions and, because no federal question was involved, there was no recourse to the U.S. Supreme Court from their decisions.

In 1810 Chief Justice John Marshall suggested that the Supreme Court might be prepared to extend the provisions of the federal Bill of Rights to the states when he said: "The Constitution of the United States contains what may be deemed a Bill of Rights for the people of each state." [*Fletcher v. Peck* (U.S. 1810)] In 1833, however, Marshall decided otherwise, removing any question as to the applicability of the Bill of Rights when he wrote: "These amendments contain no expression showing an intention to apply them to the State governments. This Court cannot so apply them." [*Barron v. Mayor of Baltimore* (U.S. 1833)]

Eleven years later in *Permoli v. First Municipality of New Orleans* (U.S. 1845), the Court again refused to expand its jurisdiction when it held specifically with respect to the Free Exercise Clause of the First Amendment: "The Constitution makes no provision for protecting the citizens of the respective States in their religious liberties; this is left to the state constitutions and laws; nor is there any inhibition imposed by the Constitution of the United States in this respect on the States."

Here the question rested until 1868 when the Fourteenth Amendment to the Constitution was adopted. It did unquestionably apply to the states, and prohibited them to "make or enforce any law which shall abridge the privileges or immunities of citizens of the United States" or to "deprive any person of life, liberty, or property without due process of law." Almost from the time of its adoption there were persons, sometimes members of the Court itself, who contended that the purpose—or at least the effect—of the Amendment was to "incorporate," "absorb," or "nationalize" the federal Constitution's Bill of Rights, thus making its guarantees applicable to the states.

Despite the historical evidence supporting this contention, the Court consistently rejected the argument in several cases until 1925. Then, in a landmark decision, *Gitlow v. New York* (U.S. 1925), which involved questions of free speech in the press, Justice Sanford opened the door to "selective incorporation" when he wrote, "for present purposes we may and do assume that freedom of speech and press—which are protected by the First Amendment from abridgment by Congress—are among the fundamental personal rights and 'liberties' protected by the due process clause of the 14th Amendment from impairment by the states."

This assumption heralded what has became one of the most significant movements in American constitutional law. Although the argument was made with great force by such justices as Black and Douglas for "in toto incorporation," this concept has not been accepted by a majority of the Court. The Court, however, has applied virtually all provisions of the Bill of Rights to the states in *Palko v. Connecticut* (U.S. 1937). In 1940 the Free Exercise Clause of the First Amendment was specifically incorporated in one of the leading Jehovah's Witnesses cases, *Cantwell v. Connecticut* (U.S.

1940). In *Everson v. Board of Education* (U.S. 1947), also known as the *New Jersey Bus Case,* the Court similarly applied the Establishment Clause to the states under the Fourteenth Amendment.

In a democracy it is necessary for the people themselves and all agencies of government to see that these constitutional provisions are respected and implemented. Ironically, for a country that rightfully boasts of its democratic institutions, the United States has most often imposed this awesome burden upon its least "democratic" institution—the nonelected, life-tenured U.S. Supreme Court.

Constitutional provisions such as the Free Exercise and Establishment Clauses are obviously not self-defining. They are emotion laden and susceptible to varied and contradictory definitions. The conflicts that result must eventually be submitted to a recognized arbiter if they are to be resolved peacefully. In large part because of its power to decide the constitutionality of the actions of other government agencies, this role of an arbiter has fallen to the Supreme Court. An arbiter must defend, as well as interpret, constitutional guarantees of fundamental religious rights, and the Court fortunately has assumed this role. Although the idea is now generally accepted that the Court is a political as well as judicial institution, its more insulated position often permits its members to make necessary but unpopular decisions that the more politically vulnerable legislative and executive branches cannot, or think they cannot, afford to do.

Many decisions have been heavily criticized. Presidents have called for corrective actions; literally hundreds of constitutional amendments designed to modify Supreme Court rulings have been introduced by angered members of Congress. Still, compliance—though sometimes grudging—has eventually been forthcoming, likely because, as Justice Robert Jackson wrote in his work, *The Supreme Court in the American System of Government* (1955): "The people have seemed to feel that the Supreme Court, whatever its defect, is still the most detached, dispassionate, and trustworthy custodian that our system affords for the translation of abstract into constitutional commands." (Jackson 1955, 23)

More than their counterparts in the elective branches of government, judges are expected to articulate and to justify their decisions in coherent written opinions not only for the benefit of the parties to the immediate litigation but also for the enlightenment and guidance of other judges, lawyers, and laymen of this and subsequent generations. Even those judges whose arguments do not then prevail frequently feel a duty to offer alternatives for the future as dissenting and concurring opinions. These, too, make up the subject matter for the continuing national constitutional seminar that the educational function of the Court requires it to conduct.

RECONCILING THE RELIGIOUS FREEDOM CLAUSES

The First Amendment requires the government to remain neutral on the subject of religion. The Free Exercise Clause forbids government from discriminating against religion or disfavoring religious practice. On the other hand, the Establishment Clause forbids government from favoring one or more religions, or religion over nonreligion. Thus, the religion clauses function as two sides of the same coin: one side forbidding intentional governmental suppression of religion, the other side forbidding intentional government support of religion. In practice, however, the clauses often appear to conflict. For example, exemption from generally applicable laws that burden a particular religion may serve the interests of religious freedom. Such exemptions, however, may be perceived as government support for religion and thus, a violation of the Establishment Clause. Similarly, the proscription against religious establishment may bar government support for religion and religious institutions, but denial of public benefits and services (especially given the important role played by government in our lives) may impose hardships on religion, thus presenting free exercise problems. A persistent problem is how to reconcile these potentially conflicting constitutional demands.

Although some have argued for the primacy of free exercise when the two clauses conflict, the Court has not yet clearly accepted this approach. At present the law appears to require accommodation of religion where doing so does not seriously threaten an important governmental interest. Thus, the government may not benefit a religion unless (1) the benefit is an exemption from an otherwise applicable ban or other regulatory restraint that would otherwise substantially burden the practice of the religion, and (2) the exemption does not seriously compromise an important public interest. The Rehnquist Court is much less insistent on the strictness with which government must maintain neutrality in religious matters and is much more willing to entertain government accommodation of religion. This has been particularly true of the Supreme Court Justices Kennedy and Scalia.

HOW MUCH SEPARATION SHOULD THERE BE BETWEEN CHURCH AND STATE?

The United States has never had a solid wall of separation between church and state. For instance, by granting a tax exemption to the property of religious organizations, the state and national governments in effect are favoring religious institutions and arguably granting them a financial benefit. The vast majority of citizens support such a policy. Similarly, there are tax-supported military and legislative chaplaincies. Still, despite the inevitable blurring of the line, most citizens want church and state to be separate, even as the government shows what one justice called "wholesome neutrality" with respect to the churches.

On the other hand, for many it is only natural that people associating politically for their common good would consider religion an appropriate subject of public regulation, perhaps even that religious association would precede and produce political bonds. This is the crux of an intense debate between those known as separationists and those known as accommodationists.

Separationists, including supreme court justices and many legal commentators believe that history forms the basis for the paradigm of mutual abstention by religion and law. They argue that the framers of the religion clauses of the First Amendment to the federal Constitution between 1789 and 1791 sufficiently warranted the relegation and isolation of religion. For many years the Supreme Court has followed a separationist interpretation, observing that the nation's founders self-consciously and deliberately erected a wall of separation between church and state and that the Constitution's framers declared religion a private matter entirely distinct from public life, effectively holding that the concerns and competence of religion and of government are at opposite ends of a linear construct and that the Constitution—or at least the Court—intends to keep them there.

The accommodationists, however, believe that the religion clauses of the U.S. Constitution permit various forms of nonpreferential government support for religion. They argue that government may aid all religions, as long as it does not prefer one religion over another. Justice Reed, in dissenting in *McCollum v. Board of Education,* set forth an accommodationist approach to interpreting the Establishment Clause. Justice Reed maintained that although the state could "make no law respecting an establishment of religion," the meaning of that phrase does not call for strict separation in light of past precedents, customs, and practices of the federal government. Furthermore, accommodationists believe that government accommodation is necessary because action by the government, although neutral on its face, hinders the free exercise of religion, especially because the pervasive nature of modern government and the prominent position of religion in American society inevitably results in contact between the state and the spiritual practices of its citizens. Accommodationists criticize the rationale for separationist judicial decisions as both intuitively and historically unsound. Nonestablishment, accommodationists believe, merely means a neutrality among sects. Current government interaction with religion, they believe, should be based on this understanding of the Establishment Clause.

How Does the Nature of Religion Influence the Believer's Attitude toward the State?

Religion involves belief in and conciliation of powers deemed superior to mankind that are believed to regulate and control the course of nature and of human life. It involves elements of belief, a body of dogma, acts of conciliation or worship, and ritual. Religious beliefs and practices are very widespread among humans and are found from very primitive stages of development upwards.

What persons believe to be ultimately true forms the core of their religion and influences—if not controls—every significant decision they make. Besides directing the purely spiritual life, religious beliefs influence such acts as choosing a spouse, selecting a profession, performing familial duties, deciding upon family size, and determining the type of education for one's children. More important, what people believe to be ultimately true invariably results in some kind of moral code that determines how they treat others. Religiously grounded morality often supersedes society's own assignments of duties as contained in the secular law. The U.S. Supreme Court has made this primacy of conscience the crucial element of its definition of religion as a "faith, to which all else is subordinate or upon which all else is ultimately dependent." [*U.S. v. Seeger* (U.S. 1965); *Wisconsin v. Yoder* (U.S. 1972)] If a person believes that God is the ever-present basis of all existence, then necessarily such person's very being and his or her every activity will involve a religious dimension. Religious adherents therefore perceive their fate, and the fate of their society, through the interpretive medium of faith.

The collective political activity of Americans, including their political beliefs and voting behavior, have been greatly influenced by religious belief. It is difficult to disentangle great nonpartisan political movements like the abolition of slavery and the creation of a free public school system in the nineteenth century, and the push for temperance, female suffrage, prison reform, and the civil rights and antiwar movements of the twentieth century, from their proponents' religiously based vision of the United States. More recently, the prominent participation of clergy and religiously motivated laypersons in the abortion, sanctuary, and antiapartheid controversies has raised the issue of how religious people and institutions should affect public policy.

Although atheism, agnosticism, and a decline in religious beliefs have somewhat reduced religion's influence on late twentieth-century American society, the simultaneously declining influence of political parties has accentuated the religious content of politics. Without the moderating and aggregating influence of parties, single-issue believers enter the public realm unrestrained by entangling political alliances so that the religious substance of their political program is closer to the surface.

A

ABINGTON SCHOOL DISTRICT V. SCHEMPP (U.S. 1963) A 1949 Pennsylvania statute compelled public schools to begin each day with a reading of 10 Bible verses. Teachers ordered students to rise and recite the verses reverently and in unison, or, as in the Abington School District, students in broadcasting class read the verses over a public address system. Teachers could be fired for refusing to participate, and students were occasionally segregated from others if they did not join in the daily reading.

The statute brought a challenge from the Schempps, who objected because the Bible readings contradicted the religious training they wanted for their three children.

Although hardly the first lawsuit on this issue—Bible reading cases in state courts had yielded contradictory rulings since 1910—the Schempps's challenge was the first to reach a federal court. In 1958 a special three-judge federal court heard the case and ruled that the Bible-reading statute violated the First Amendment's Establishment Clause ("Congress shall make no law respecting an establishment of religion") and interfered with its Free Exercise Clause ("or prohibiting the free exercise [of religion]"). Local and state officials immediately appealed to the U.S. Supreme Court.

The Supreme Court agreed to hear the appeal along with a case from Maryland, *Murray v. Curlett* (Md. 1962), as a single consolidated case that would henceforth be known as *Abington School District v. Schempp*. The *Murray* case involved Madalyn Murray and her 14-year-old son, William, who were atheists. They had challenged a 1905 Baltimore school board rule requiring each school day to start with Bible reading or the Lord's Prayer, or both. The Murrays' suit alleged that the rule violated the Establishment Clause by discriminating against atheists. The Murrays originally lost in state courts and on appeal.

When the U.S. Supreme Court heard oral arguments for the consolidated cases, the nation was still debating the previous year's ruling in *Engel v. Vitale* (U.S. 1962). In that case the Supreme Court held that a

19

school prayer written by New York state officials was unconstitutional. *Abington* gave advocates of school prayer a chance to argue that the Court had been wrong in *Engel.*

Attorneys representing Pennsylvania and Maryland denied that Bible reading or prayer had a religious nature, and claimed that requiring it therefore did not violate the Establishment Clause. In any case, they argued that the Establishment Clause was designed only to prevent an official state religion. They alleged that the Bible readings advanced a legitimate, secular state interest in maintaining order and providing a proper moral climate for students. The attorneys for the states also distinguished this case from *Engel,* because in neither school had government officials written the prayers that were recited. The states also argued that the forbidding of organized prayer in the schools would be antireligious, and would, in fact, amount to the establishment of a "religion of secularism."

Attorneys for the Schempps and the Murrays maintained that the Establishment Clause, which was made applicable to the states by the Fourteenth Amendment in *Cantwell v. Connecticut* (U.S. 1940), prohibited states from requiring that passages from the Bible be read or that the Lord's Prayer be recited in the public schools, even if individual students could be excused from attending or participating in such exercises upon written request of their parents.

Justice Thomas C. Clark wrote the opinion for the Supreme Court. He concluded that the Pennsylvania exercise was as much a violation of the Establishment Clause as the New York prayer involved in the *Engel* case. Clark's opinion in *Schempp* was the first separationist opinion of the Supreme Court. The Court for the first time articulated two prongs of the present three-prong test for determining whether governmental action violates the Establishment Clause. In order to be constitutional (1) the purpose of the government action must be secular, rather than to advance or inhibit religion; and (2) the primary effect of the government action must not be to advance or inhibit religion.

The Bible readings in *Abington* were clearly "religious exercises," Justice Clark concluded, and thus failed at least the "primary effect" prong of the test. Because of this primarily religious effect, it was no defense for the state to argue (even if accurately) that its purposes were the secular ones of promoting order and morality. The Court also disagreed that prohibiting prayer would be "antireligious," finding that such a prohibition merely accomplished the constitutionally required neutrality of the government concerning religion.

The test for constitutionality set out in *Abington* clearly explained its limits. Study of the Bible or religion was acceptable in public schools, said Justice Clark, but only so long as it was "presented objectively as part of a secular program of education." Religious practices in public school were indefensible under the First Amendment. "While the Free Exercise Clause clearly prohibits the use of state action to deny the rights of free exercise to anyone," Justice Clark observed, "it has never meant that a majority could use the machinery of the State to practice its beliefs."

Justices William O. Douglas and William J. Brennan concurred separately in opinions reflecting an even stricter separationism than Clark's. (Brennan's opinion comprised 74 pages.) Justice Arthur J. Goldberg also filed a brief concurring opinion.

Justice Potter Stewart dissented, as he had in *Engel*, arguing that religious exercises as part of public ceremonies were permissible as long as children were not coerced to participate. In his view, a completely noncompulsory scheme of Bible reading that provided alternative activities for nonparticipating students would not violate the Establishment Clause.

Abington concluded the initial round of the Supreme Court's prohibiting organized prayer in the public schools. The issue, however, remains an issue of public concern more than 30 years later.

ABOLITION In U.S. legal history, abolition generally refers to the eighteenth- and nineteenth-century movement to abolish the slavery of African Americans. As a significant political force in the antebellum United States, the abolitionists greatly affected the legal and political landscape. They developed comprehensive but conflicting theories about the place of slavery in the American constitution. Abolitionists, who took their stand on religious grounds, attacked the moral impropriety of the institution. Although these ideas did not positively influence political and legal debate until the 1850s, they exercised profound influence over subsequent constitutional development, merging with constitutional aspirations of nonabolitionist Republicans after the Civil War to provide the basis for what one writer has labeled the Third Constitution: the Thirteenth, Fourteenth, and Fifteenth Amendments. Their consistent efforts to end the institution of slavery culminated in 1865 with the ratification of the Constitution's Thirteenth Amendment, which outlawed slavery.

The abolitionists' ranks included many different factions and people of different backgrounds and viewpoints, including European and African Americans, radicals, and moderates. The motives of the abolitionists ran a broad spectrum, from those who opposed slavery as unjust and inhuman, to those whose objectives were purely economic and focused on the effects that an unpaid Southern workforce had on wages and prices in the North. The abolitionist movement resulted from social and moral impulses that, in time, were aggravated by political and economic factors. New England-based churches, such as the Unitarian Church and the Congregationalist Church, were almost totally antislavery in character.

The Roman Catholic Church in the United States would not agree that slaveholding was necessarily forbidden to Catholics, and thus, opposed antislavery programs. This was despite the fact that from the fifteenth century forward, Catholic missionaries, theologians, and statesmen continuously sought the end of the slave trade. The Catholic Church officially condemned the slave trade in 1838.

The Methodist and Baptist churches were strong factors in the growth of the antislavery movement because they were the largest Protestant denominations in the United States and were strong both in the North and in the South. The Reverend Orange Scott, a Methodist abolitionist leader, wrote "An Appeal to the Methodist Episcopal Church" in 1838 that opened a struggle within the church itself. In 1845, it resulted in a church schism and the organization of the Methodist Episcopal Church, South. The Baptists had a similar history of differences on the slavery issue, which also resulted in a schism and the emergence of the Southern Baptist Convention.

The Quakers, beginning in the 1760s, began to work as a church for the end of slavery. Although conservative in other respects, opposing antislavery agitation that could disturb their proslavery business associates and neighbors, they engendered a relatively high proportion of antislavery pioneers.

Many abolitionist leaders were clergymen. The Reverend George Bourne's effort to preach in Virginia the principles he expressed in *The Book and Slavery Irreconcilable* (1816) resulted in his having to leave the South. The Reverend John Rankin, who worked with the well-known abolitionist Elihu Embree in creating the Manumission Society of Tennessee and publishing the *Manumission Intelligencier,* in 1822, on the banks of the Ohio River, set up the best-known "underground station" for fugitive slaves. Rankin also wrote *Letters on Slavery* (1826), which prepared the way for more famous abolitionist writings.

Beginning in the 1830s evangelical Christian groups, particularly in New England, brought a new radicalism to the cause of abolition. They focused on the sinfulness of slavery and sought to end its practice by appealing to the consciences of European Americans who supported slavery. Rather than endorsing gradual emancipation, these new abolitionists called for the immediate and complete emancipation of slaves without compensation to slave owners. Leaders of this movement included William Lloyd Garrison, founder of the abolitionist newspaper, *The Liberator,* Frederick Douglass, a noted African American writer and orator; and the sisters Sarah Moore Grimké and Angelina Grimké, lecturers for the American Anti-Slavery Society.

Support for "immediate abolition" arose as a result of being proposed by Elizabeth Heyrick in *Immediate Not Gradual Emancipation* in 1824. The religious leaders who supported immediate emancipation included Reverend Samuel J. May and Reverend Theodore Parker. A significant proof that the antislavery cause had ceased to be limited to radicals and sectarians was the conversion of the Unitarian leader, the Reverend William Ellery Channing to antislavery, although he deplored the antagonism between the factions. His *Slavery* (1835) advocated a firm stand on the moral impropriety of the institution and influenced many Northerners who were reluctant to join the antislavery cause.

During what was called the "Martyr Age" in the 1830s, a domestic missionary named Reverend Elijah P. Lovejoy published the St. Louis *Observer* in which he denounced slavery. His antislavery sentiments incited a vengeful mob that vandalized his office. Lovejoy moved across the Mississippi River to Alton, Illinois, where he continued to issue the *Observer*. Three times his press was removed and destroyed. While defending it a fourth time, in November 1837, he was shot and killed. Lovejoy's violent death led many Americans to become abolitionists.

John Brown, an itinerant preacher, belonged to no antislavery faction. Some radical abolitionists may have known that he planned an insurrection, although they were unwilling to help him. On 16 October 1859, Brown led 21 men into Harper's Ferry, Virginia (now West Virginia), where they seized the federal arsenal and collected some local hostages. In several actions, several local persons as well as members of Brown's company were killed or wounded. The local slaves refused to rebel, and Brown and some of his men were captured by Colonel Robert E. Lee. Brown's own serenity as he approached his death, and his eloquence in court and in correspondence, won many Northerners to his cause.

ABORTION   Abortion is the expulsion of the human fetus from the womb before it has reached a state of development sufficient to permit it to survive independently, a state reached between the twenty-first and twenty-eighth week of pregnancy. It may occur accidentally or spontaneously (when it is usually called a miscarriage) or may be induced.

Abortion is one of the most controversial legal, social, and religious issues in American life in the late twentieth century. Because it touches on fundamental questions of gender, personhood, and community, one's view of abortion is inexorably linked to one's religious and philosophical commitments.

Advocates for and against legalized abortion focus on two major issues: (1) the moral status of the fetus, or (2) the bodily rights of the pregnant woman. Those who oppose legalized abortion justify their position based on the fact that: (1) the fetus is a person and ought to have a right to life, and (2) the fetus is a completely innocent and defenseless person. Prolife (or antiabortionist) advocates argue that individual human life begins at conception, that is, when sperm and ovum cease to exist as individual entities, a new human being with its own genetic code comes into existence. No new genetic information is added from this moment until natural death.

Prochoice advocates see the abortion issue as related to what degree government should intrude on the reproductive rights of women and men. Prochoice advocates argue that the fetus, although a human being from conception, is not a person until some decisive moment after conception. Some argue that personhood does not arrive until brain waves are detected (40 to 43 days). Others define a person as a being with certain functions, such as consciousness and the ability to solve complex problems, which would put the arrival of personhood after birth.

Prochoice advocates argue that even if the fetus is a human person from conception, abortion is still morally justified. Some argue that the fetus's physical dependence on the pregnant woman's body entails a conflict of rights if the pregnant woman did not consent to the pregnancy. Consequently, the fetus cannot use another's body without her consent. Thus, a pregnant woman's removal of the fetus by abortion, although it will result in its death, is no more immoral than an adult person's refusal to donate her kidney to someone who needs one, although this refusal will probably result in the death of the person who needs the kidney.

Induced or artificial abortion has extensive legal implications. Formal ecclesiastical legislation punishing abortion was enacted in the Western Church by the Council of Elvira around the year A.D. 300, and in the East by the Council of Ancyra in A.D. 314. English common law generally allowed abortion before the "quickening" of the fetus (that is, before the first recognizable movement of the fetus in the uterus), which occurred between the sixteenth and eighteenth week of pregnancy. After quickening, however, common law was less clear about abortion.

After American independence, Pennsylvania and North Carolina held that at common law both abortion and attempted abortion was a felony at any stage of pregnancy. This caselaw was similar to an English Statute of 1803. American state legislatures began enacting abortion statutes in the nineteenth century. Beginning in the mid-nineteenth century every American state criminalized abortion by statute, mainly to protect women from unsafe medical procedures. Most state legislatures enacted statutes similar to those of Pennsylvania and North Carolina. Connecticut in 1821 enacted the first U.S. abortion statute making quickening an essential element and providing for no justifications.

Despite the illegality, many thousands of women every year sought abortions. Under a heavy cloak of shame and secrecy, many had abortions performed in unsafe conditions, and many died or suffered complications from the procedures.

The abortion laws of the late nineteenth century remained largely unchanged until the 1960s and 1970s, when several different circumstances combined to cause a movement for their reform. Women's rights groups, doctors, and lawyers began an organized abortion reform movement to advocate changes, in part because many of them had witnessed the sometimes deadly complications resulting from illegal abortions. Women's organizations also began to view abortion reform as a crucial step toward the goal of equality between the sexes. The prochoice movement argued that women must be able to control their pregnancies to secure an equal status with men in American life. In addition, new concerns regarding explosive population growth and its effect on the environment increased public awareness of the need for birth control. Simultaneously, other countries enacted far more permissive laws on abortion. In Japan and Eastern Europe, abortion was available on demand, and in much of Western Europe, abortion was permitted to protect the mother's health.

Public awareness of the abortion issue also increased through two incidents in the early 1960s that caused many children to be born with physical defects. In 1960 the drug thalidomide, used to treat nausea during pregnancy, was found to cause serious birth defects, such as stunted, flipperlike limbs or no limbs at all. And a 1962–1965 German measles epidemic caused an estimated 15,000 children to be born with defects. Pregnant women who were affected by these incidents could not seek abortion because of the strict laws then in existence.

Reacting to these and other developments and inspired by the success of the civil rights movements of the 1950s and 1960s, women's rights organizations—including the National Organization for Women (NOW), formed in 1966—sought to reform abortion laws through legislation and lawsuits. They hoped to educate a largely male-dominated legal and judicial profession about issues important for women. Their work, supported by such groups as the American Civil Liberties Union (ACLU), quickly began to have an effect. Between 1967 and 1970, 12 states adopted abortion reform legislation. Abortion activist groups, however, began to see the abortion issue as a question of social justice and pressed for more than reform. Under the rallying cry of reproductive freedom, they demanded the outright repeal of existing state laws and unobstructed access for women to abortion.

The increase in abortion-related cases before the courts eventually resulted in the need for clarification of the law by the U.S. Supreme Court. After considering many abortion-related cases, on 31 May 1971 the Court agreed to decide two cases, *Roe v. Wade* (U.S. 1973) and *Doe v. Bolton* (U.S. 1973).

Although the two cases before the Court appeared by their titles to involve two individuals, *Roe* and *Doe*, in reality both suits were brought by many people representing many different interests. As a class action lawsuit, *Roe v. Wade* was argued for all women of the state of Texas. Thirty-six abortion reform groups filed briefs with the court on Roe's behalf. They included civil rights, medical, public health, legal, welfare, church (including socially liberal Protestant denominations), population control, and other groups. The antiabortion side of the case included representatives from seven different antiabortion groups and the attorneys general of five states. The antiabortion position was shared by the Roman Catholic Church, the Church of Jesus Christ of Latter-Day Saints, Orthodox Jews, and fundamentalist Protestant denominations.

The plaintiffs in *Roe* sought to have the Texas abortion statute declared unconstitutional as an invasion of the right to privacy as guaranteed by the First, Fourth, Fifth, Ninth, and Fourteenth Amendments. The abortion reform movement attached two other cases to Roe's in an attempt to represent a wider range of the interests involved in the issue. A physician, James Hallford, who was being prosecuted under the statute for two abortions he had performed, also filed suit to challenge the Texas law, as did a childless couple, the Does. The Does claimed a personal stake in the right to an abortion, because Mrs. Doe's physician had advised her to avoid pregnancy for health reasons. The Does claimed that Mrs. Doe might become pregnant due to possible failure of her contraception. If this occurred, she might need an abortion to avoid the health impairment that would arise from a pregnancy. The Court denied standing due to the speculative nature of this claim.

In *Roe v. Wade* (US 1973), the U.S. Supreme Court held that for the period of approximately the first three months of pregnancy "the abortion decision and its effectuation must be left to the medical judgment of the pregnant woman's attending physician." If a doctor performs an abortion during the first three months of pregnancy, the state is powerless to interfere or punish. During the last six months of pregnancy, the state may regulate abortion procedures "in ways that are reasonably related to maternal health." The only time that the state can protect the fetus is after the fetus has reached viability, and not even then if a doctor judges an abortion necessary for the preservation of the life or health of the mother. The states are free, however, to require that all abortions, at any stage of pregnancy, be performed only by licensed physicians.

Both *Roe* and *Doe* were decided by votes of seven to two. The majority relied on the basic legal principle that people have a constitutional right not to be interfered with by government in decisions that profoundly affect their whole lives unless government has a compelling reason connected with the public welfare for such interference. In the Court's view, no such reason exists during the first three months of pregnancy; discouraging abortions will not discourage illicit sex; abortions during the early period of pregnancy are reasonably safe medical procedures; and the medical, philosophical, and theological experts are greatly divided about exactly what degree of human development is involved in the fetus during that period. Since there is no compelling reason to justify governmental interference, the Court held that the woman's "right to privacy" must be respected. If she can find a doctor who will perform an abortion during the first three months of pregnancy, the state can do nothing.

The court went on to say, however, that the reasons for state interference grow more compelling as the pregnancy progresses. Abortions during the last six months of pregnancy become increasingly more dangerous for the mother, and the state has the right to protect the life of the mother, even against her wishes. Moreover, at some point, the fetus becomes "viable," capable of independent life outside the mother's womb. From that point on, the Court declared, the state may protect the fetus against the mother unless a doctor judges an abortion necessary for the life or health of the mother.

The most difficult question for the Supreme Court to resolve in these cases was whether a fetus is a "person" within the meaning of the Due Process Clause, which forbids governmental deprivation of any person's life, liberty, or property without due process of law (Fifth and Fourteenth Amendments to the U.S. Constitution). After reviewing legal history, the majority of the Court concluded that "the unborn have never been recognized in the law as persons in the whole sense."

One distinct criticism of the Court's decision in Roe concerns not the legitimacy of judicial activism but the soundness of the Court's answer to the political-moral question it addressed. Because many people believe that the Supreme Court's decision in Roe was wrong, in the decades following various attempts were made to overrule Roe legislatively—either by taking away the Court's jurisdiction to review state abortion law, or by constitutional amendments, or even simple congressional legislation to the effect that a fetus is a person within the meaning of the Fourteenth Amendment and thus that states may ban abortion to protect its life. The proposals to limit the jurisdiction of the Court and to override Roe by simple congressional legislation—as opposed to a constitutional amendment—became subjects of vigorous political and constitutional controversy.

The vigor of the political controversy over abortion cannot be fully comprehended—indeed, the Court's decision to constitutionalize the matter of abortion cannot be fully comprehended—without reference to an important development in American society that gained momentum in the 1970s and 1980s: a fundamental shift in attitudes toward the role of women in society. Many of those who opposed abortion and the "liberalization" of public policy on abortion did so as part of a larger agenda of profamily legislative objectives. Many of those on the other side of the issue were seeking to implement a different vision—a feminist vision in which women are free to determine for themselves what shapes their lives will take, and therefore free to decide whether, and when, they will bear children.

Not surprisingly, this basic shift in attitude toward women—from patriarchal to feminist—resulted in a deep division in American society. "Abortion politics" was merely one manifestation of that division (although an important one). Thus, a controversy that sometimes seemed on the surface to consist mainly of a philosophical-theological dispute over the question, "When does 'life' begin?" actually involved much more. The complexity of the abortion controversy was dramatically evidenced by the fact that even within the Roman Catholic Church in the United States, which was the most powerful institutional opponent of abortion, attitudes toward abortion were deeply divided, precisely because attitudes toward women were deeply divided.

As a result of its decision in *Roe v. Wade,* the Court has had to resolve many other controversial issues regarding abortion. For example, in *Planned Parenthood of Missouri v. Danforth* (U.S. 1976), the Court ruled that a state may not require a woman to obtain the consent of her spouse before she terminates her pregnancy. The Court's positions with respect to parental consent and parental notification requirements have been unclear, in part because the rulings have been fragmented. In *Bellotti v. Baird* (U.S. 1979), for example, in an eight-to-one decision striking down a parental consent requirement, the majority split four to four as to the proper rationale. What is clear, however, is that state governments may not require *every* minor, whatever her level of independence or maturity, to obtain parental consent before she terminates her pregnancy.

Undoubtedly, the most controversial issue concerning abortion that the Court has addressed since *Roe v. Wade* involved abortion funding. In *Maher v. Roe* (U.S. 1977), the Court ruled that a state government that spends welfare funds to subsidize medical expenses incident to pregnancy and childbirth may decline to subsidize medical expenses incident to nontherapeutic abortion, even if its sole reason for doing so is to discourage abortion. In a companion case, *Pioelker v. Doe* (U.S. 1977), the Court extended this ruling to hold that public hospitals may also decline to provide nontherapeutic abortions for the sole reason of discouraging abortion. Three years later in *Harris v. McRae* (U.S. 1980), the Court sustained the Hyde Amendments (to appropriations for the Medicaid program), which prohibited federal funding of abortion, including therapeutic abortion, even though the sole purpose of the amendment was to discourage abortion.

▆▆▆▆ ACCOMMODATION OF RELIGIOUS BELIEF   Gener-

ally, an accommodation is an arrangement or engagement made as a favor to another. Under both state and federal employment discrimination laws, an employer is obligated to make a reasonable accommodation to the religious beliefs of an applicant or an employee. The test of what is reasonable is whether the accommodation will place an "undue burden" on the employer. Although what constitutes an undue burden is open for interpretation and may vary depending on the size and resources of the employer, it is clear that the employer must at least consider and make some effort to accommodate an employee's religious practices. The employer has the burden of showing that he or she made a reasonable accommodation or was unable to do so without incurring an undue burden.

The reasonableness of an accommodation is determined on a case-by-case basis. In assessing undue hardship, courts have been careful to examine whether the employee desiring accommodation performs an "essential" job for the employer, whether the employee can easily be replaced, and whether the employer must pay higher wages in order to hire a replacement. Courts also have looked at noneconomic factors, such as safety and health concerns, the effect upon morale of fellow employees when an accommodation is made to one employee, whether the employee has fully exhausted an employer's already existing procedures for accommodation, and whether accommodating an employee would result in violating a state or federal statute. All noneconomic factors, however, must be shown to have an "adverse impact on the conduct of the business." [*Palmer v. Board of Education* (7th Cir. 1979)]

Because Congress did not define either the terms "reasonable accommodation" or "undue hardship" there has been considerable litigation interpreting these terms, the bulk of which has involved applying the duty of reasonable accommodation to the desires of employees not to work on Saturdays or Sundays for religious reasons or on religious holidays. [See *Estate of Thornton v. Caldor, Inc.* (US 1985); and *Trans World Airlines v. Hardison* (US 1977)] Another focus of litigation has been the right of employees to wear particular clothes, hairstyles, or beards for religious reasons. In *Wilson v. U.S.W. Communications* (8th Cir. 1995) the court of appeals held that an employer could not require a woman who wore a large button depicting a fetus because of her religious opposition to abortion to cover the button when outside of her cubicle at work without violating its duty to reasonably accommodate the religious practices of its employees.

The issue of reasonable accommodation for religiously dictated attire was recently considered in a federal case out of Pennsylvania. [*Reid v. Kraft General Foods, Inc.* (E.D. Pa. 1995)] In March 1991 Priscilla Reid, a member of the Church of the Apostolic Faith, accepted a position as a production worker for the Kraft company. At an orientation meeting the following month, Reid discovered for the first time that she would be required to wear pants on the job. Reid notified Kraft that her religious beliefs prohibited her from wearing pants and requested that she be able to wear a dress or a skirt as a substitute. She even offered a letter from her pastor confirming the church doctrine against women wearing pants. Kraft turned down her request. It was only after Reid filed a religious discrimination complaint with the Pennsylvania Human Relations Commission that Kraft—in August 1991—notified Reid that she would be permitted to wear a dress to work. Reid failed to report to work, and Kraft subsequently terminated her employment.

In a subsequent suit in federal court Kraft sought to have Reid's discrimination claims dismissed because the company had reasonably accommodated her religious practice by allowing her to wear a dress to work. Reid countered that her hiring had been delayed nearly 15 weeks after she first notified the employer of her religious practice. The court agreed with Reid.

This case is instructive regarding the duty to make "other" reasonable accommodation and, in particular, the need to act in a timely fashion to satisfy that duty. If the employer awaits the filing of a complaint or lawsuit before extending a reasonable accommodation, it may be too late to avoid liability.

A second type of reasonable accommodation involves an employee's absence from work for religious observance. The Ninth Circuit Court of Appeals recently ruled that because an employee failed to show that a temporal mandate—in this case, that she was required to be in Yugoslavia at a definite and certain point in time—was part of her protected religious belief, she could not maintain a suit for religious discrimination. [*Tiano v. Dillard Department Stores* (9th Cir. 1998)] Mary Tiano worked for an Arizona department store. She was a devout Roman Catholic. The department store terminated Tiano after she departed on an unapproved religious pilgrimage to Yugoslavia. Tiano contended that the store had violated Title VII of the Civil Rights Act of 1964 when it terminated her and failed to make reasonable accommodation of her religious beliefs. In this case, the Ninth Circuit Court of Appeals established a two-part test to analyze whether a valid Title VII religious discrimination claim exists. First, a plaintiff must establish a prima facie case; that is, he or she must show enough evidence of religious discrimination that, if the employer could not rebut this evidence, the court would be justified in ruling in the employee's favor. To establish this prima facie case, the employee must show that: (1) he or she had a bona fide religious belief, the practice of which conflicted with his or her employment duty; (2) he or she informed the employer of the belief and conflict; and (3) the employer threatened or subjected the employee to adverse treatment, including discharge, because he or she failed to fulfill the job requirements. If the employee proves a prima facie case of religious discrimination under these criteria, the second part of the test comes into play: now the burden of proof shifts to the employer to show either that it initiated good faith efforts to reasonably accommodate the employee's religious practices or that it could not reasonably accommodate the employee without undue hardship to itself.

In Tiano's case, the Ninth Circuit Court of Appeals found that because her religious belief was not limited to participation in the pilgrimage, her religious belief did not conflict with her employment duties at the department store. She had other opportunities to practice her religious beliefs. Because Tiano could not establish that she had to be in Yugoslavia at a certain time as part of a bona fide religious mandate, she could not satisfy one crucial element of her case—the conflict between religious belief and employment duty. Judge Charles Wiggins wrote, "There is no evidence upon which one could rely except for Tiano's lone statement that she 'had to be there at that time.' That statement is insufficient to prove that the temporal mandate was part of her religious belief." Thus, Tiano could not show a prima facie case (that is, initial evidence of a violation that is sufficient to allow the case to continue) of religious discrimination.

The courts have repeatedly held that "reasonable accommodation" is not open ended. A policeman's request for accommodation of his religious beliefs, which prevented him from standing duty outside of an abortion clinic, were satisfied by the police department's offer to transfer him—with no reduction in pay or benefits—to a district that did not have abortion clinics. [Rodriguez v. City of Chicago (7th Cir. 1998)] The court rejected the officer's contention that he preferred to stay in his current district, and that granting him an exception to the abortion clinic duty would not constitute an undue hardship for the employer. The court noted that the need for reasonable accommodation does not require satisfaction of an employee's every desire. Provided it has accommodated an employee's religious needs in some reasonable manner, the employer need not prove that each of the employee's suggested alternative accommodations would result in undue hardship to it.

The federal Equal Employment Opportunity Commission (EEOC) has developed a list of possible accommodations an employer can use to meet its obligation to accommodate an employee's religious practices. Among these are:

1. Voluntary substitutes and "swaps," requiring an employer to "promote an atmosphere in which substitutions are favorably

regarded," and to provide a central location to facilitate posting of requests for substitution

2. Flexible scheduling, so that employees requesting accommodation can be served by permitting them flexible arrival and departure times, flexible work breaks, and use of lunch, personal, or vacation time in exchange for early departure; staggering work hours, or allowing an employee to make up lost time due to observing religious practices, and

3. Arranging lateral transfers or changing an employee's job assignment.

ACCOMMODATIONIST (OR NONPREFERENTIALIST)

An accommodationist is one who believes that government may assist religion if it assists all religions equally. Accommodationists (also called nonpreferentialists) believe that the framers of the Constitution did not intend the Establishment Clause of the First Amendment to absolutely prohibit government aid to religion in general, but only to prohibit the government from favoring any one religion over another. The accommodationists dispute the separationist conclusion that the federal government is absolutely prohibited from granting nondiscriminatory aid to religion.

In interpreting the historical evidence behind the writing of the First Amendment, accommodationists assert several important facts, including:

- The grammar of the phrase "Congress shall make no law respecting an establishment of religion." The use of "an" rather than "the" indicates that the drafters of the First Amendment were concerned with official favoritism toward religion rather than irreligion.

- The issue of federalism. Madison's original proposal for the First Amendment prohibited the establishment of a "national" religion, and the debate was largely framed in terms of what Congress could not do. Therefore, the meaning of the language ultimately adopted must be read in light of the fear that the federal government might otherwise interfere with actions properly within the authority of the states. Additionally, the phrase "respecting an" does not just prohibit Congressional actions "tending toward" an establishment, but also respects the division of powers between the federal and state government by barring Congress from interfering with state establishments.

- Contemporary actions by the first Congress that exhibit an affinity for—or at least a lack of objection to—state-sponsored religious activities. These included appointing chaplains, requesting President Washington to issue a thanksgiving proclamation, and reenacting the Northwest Ordinance (in which the U.S. government provided for the Old Northwest territory, now encompassing the midwestern states east of the Mississippi River). All these actions argue against a separationist interpretation of the language of the Establishment Clause.

- Activities of early presidents involved in drafting the Constitution. For example, President Thomas Jefferson signed a treaty agreeing to build a church and supply a Catholic priest in exchange for land owned by an Indian tribe. Surely, some would argue, aiding only a Catholic priest would violate a rule against nonpreferentialist treatment.

Believing religion to be integral to our nation's heritage, accommodationists argue that the government should adjust where necessary to allow religious adherents to practice their faith. Accommodationists are divided on questions such as whether it is appropriate for the courts to fashion constitutionally required religious exemptions from general laws. Some accommodationists argue that there should be exemptions from general laws for religious adherents if those laws impose a hardship on the believers. The Free Exercise Clause, however, does not authorize judicial exemption for religious objectors from conformity to a religiously neutral law.

ADOPTION   Adoption involves the creation of the relationship of parent and child between individuals who are not naturally so related. An adoption order transfers all rights, duties, and obligations of the adopted child's natural parents to the adoptive parents, as though the adopted child were born to them. For the purposes of marriage, family allowance, claims of damage on death, and intestate succession, an adopted child is deemed a child born in wedlock to the adopter.

Because adoption was not recognized as common law, all adoption procedures in the United States are regulated by statute. Adoption statutes prescribe the conditions, manner, means, and consequences of adoption. In addition, they specify the rights and responsibilities of all parties involved.

Courts are constitutionally required to maintain a posture of neutrality in religious matters as they relate to adoptions, but are bound at the same time to give paramount consideration to the welfare of the child. Courts have generally taken the position that the religious beliefs and affiliations of the parties to adoption proceedings, while not controlling, should properly be considered in determining what will best serve the interests of the child.

There are two principle aspects of religion as a factor in adoption proceedings: (1) the significance of the religious background and belief or nonbelief of the adoptive parents, and (2) the effect of a difference in the religious faiths of the adoptive parents and the child or the child's natural parents, or between the adopting parents themselves.

Several courts have regarded the religious background and convictions of those seeking to adopt to be relevant considerations in determining their suitability as parents.[*In re H.* (Mo. Ct. App. 1980); *In re Adoption of "E"* (N.J. 1971)]

The concern evident in this area seems to reflect a judicial attitude that religious belief and church affiliation on the part of the adoptive parents are significant indicators of their interest in, and capabilities with respect to, the spiritual and moral development of the child. Thus, several courts have considered the regularity with which prospective parents attend church to be a relevant factor in the determination of whether the best interests of the child would be served by the proposed adoption, pointing out that church attendance plays an important role in the moral training of the child.

Despite these policies, in actual practice many courts pay little attention to religious matching, in part due to the great need of hard-to-place children to have permanent homes. Some judges do not consider religion as an important factor at all if a family seeking to adopt a child will give that child a stable home.

ADULTERY   Adultery is the violation of the marriage vows through sexual intercourse between a married person and another to whom one is not married. Throughout history, most societies have been concerned with adultery, treating it variously as a crime, a moral wrong, a private matter, an infringement of the husband's rights, or a threat to family stability and orderly succession. Adultery is widely considered to be an offense against morality. Religious institutions have regulated sexuality and its expression throughout time. The Ten Commandments forbade adultery, even the desire for it. [Ex. 20:14, 17; Deut. 5:18, 21] The New Testament reiterated the condemnation. [Matt. 5:27–28, 19:18; Mark 10:19; Luke 18:20] Jesus, however, showed clemency to the woman taken in adultery in John 8:1. Adultery was a capital crime under Mosaic law. Under Muslim law, a wife who engages in adultery may be killed with impunity by her husband, and mere suspicion of adultery is acceptable grounds for divorce.

Christian canon law adopted and contained the view that adultery is a violation of the moral code and is thus sinful. At first, adultery was dealt with by ecclesiastical courts. In turn, English common law prohibited such behavior, not only in its effort to embody community values, but also because of the possible threat to the integrity of the family and the danger of illegitimate offspring. British statutes made adultery a crime.

Most American states have followed suit, not so much to criminalize consensual relations between adults as to obviate harmful public results. Beyond its moral considerations, adultery is viewed as a possible source of discord (for example, when a wronged spouse seeks revenge), or prejudicial to the couple's children in the case of public scandal, or as an affront to community standards.

Opposition to these laws has grown on the grounds of evolving mores and the widespread violation of traditional moral codes. Infrequent and inconsistent enforcement of laws prohibiting adultery has led to charges of discrimination and arbitrariness, and thus, contempt for the law. Regardless of whether there is a criminal prosecution, proven adultery is legal grounds for divorce or separation in civil courts. State laws against adultery have survived the constitutional challenge that they infringe in the right of privacy. Several U.S. Supreme Court justices have indicated in dicta (observations that are not part of the holding in the case) their assumptions that adultery statutes are constitutional. [*See, e.g., Bowers v. Hardwick* (US 1986)(indicating assumption that adultery statutes are constitutional); *Griswold v. Connecticut* (US 1965)(Goldberg, J.)(asserting that constitutionality of criminal adultery laws is "beyond doubt"); *Poe v. Ullman* (US 1961)(Harlan, J., dissenting)("I would not suggest that adultery, homosexuality, fornication, and incest are immune from criminal enquiry, however privately practiced.")]

AGUILAR V. FELTON **(U.S. 1985)** In 1985 the U.S. Supreme Court considered a First Amendment challenge to a New York program that sent public school teachers into parochial schools to provide remedial education. The program had been established pursuant to a federal statute: Title I of the 1965 Elementary and Secondary School Act. The program employed guidance counselors, psychologists, psychiatrists, social workers, and other specialists to teach remedial reading, mathematics, and English as a second language, and to provide guidance services. The participants in the program worked part-time on parochial school premises, using only materials and equipment supplied by secular authorities. They were forbidden to participate in religious activities at the schools and worked under supervision similar to that in public schools; that is, the city supervisory personnel made unannounced "occasional" visits. Almost three-fourths of the educators in the program did not share the religious affiliation of the schools in which they taught. The Second Circuit Court of Appeals, following a series of decisions premised on *Lemon v. Kurtzman* (U.S. 1971) declared the New York program unconstitutional.

The Supreme Court, in a five-to-four decision, applied the three-part *Lemon* test and found that the program entailed "excessive entanglement of church and state in the administration of those benefits." Justice William Brennan, writing for the majority, made an analytical stretch to find infirmities in the city's program. He expressed concern that the program might infringe on the religious liberty of its intended beneficiaries. He saw government "intrusion into sacred matters" and the necessity of an "ongoing inspection" to ensure the absence of inculcation of religion in the instruction. The need for "a permanent and pervasive State presence in the sectarian schools receiving aid" infringed the values protected by the Establishment Clause.

Thus, according to the majority, if government fails to provide for surveillance of participating educators in order to prevent inculcation, its aid unconstitutionally advances the religious mission of the church schools. If government, however, does provide for monitoring—even if only periodically—it gets excessively entangled with religion. Justice Sandra Day O'-Connor dissented, declaring that the conclusion that auxiliary services provided by the public would advance the religious mission of the schools was "not supported by the facts of this case." The 19-year record of the program showed not one allegation of an attempt to indoctrinate religiously at public expense. O'Connor believed that the majority's decision would adversely affect disadvantaged parochial school children who needed special auxiliary services not provided by their schools. On remand, a permanent injunction was issued barring any use of Title I money for services at sectarian schools in New York City.

Almost 10 years later, parents of parochial school students filed motions seeking to end the injunction because the law had changed since 1985 and the present law no longer barred use of Title I money for parochial schools. The Supreme Court, again in a five-to-four decision, held that the Court's understanding of the law had also changed as to "the criteria used to assess whether aid to religion has an impermissible effect." Justice O'Connor, now writing for the majority, stated that recent cases indicated that shared-time programs like those in New York City did not advance or promote religion, nor create any excessive entanglement between the government and religion.

The earlier *Aguilar* decision had "presumed that full-time public employees on parochial school grounds would be tempted to inculcate religion." This is no longer a presumption. Simply stated, under the new standards, "this carefully constrained program . . . cannot be viewed as an endorsement of religion."

There were two dissenting opinions in this case, one by Justice David

Souter (in which Justices Stevens and Ginsburg joined, and in which Justice Breyer joined in part) and the other by Justice Ruth Bader Ginsburg (in which Justices Stevens, Souter, and Breyer joined). In his dissenting opinion, Justice David Souter denied that the standards for application of the Establishment Clause have changed sufficiently to warrant such a complete reversal. In his view, there has been a "flat ban on subsidization [that] antedates the Bill of Rights and has been an unwavering rule in Establishment Clause cases." By mixing responsibilities for teaching secular subjects with religious ones, there is an implied approval or endorsement of religion by the schools that is prohibited by the First Amendment.

Justice Souter also criticized the majority for disregarding the doctrine of stare decisis—the importance of precedent and certainty in the law: "Constitutional lines have to be drawn [and] . . . constitutional lines are the price of constitutional government."

Justice Ruth Bader Ginsburg, in her dissent (joined by Justices Souter, Stevens, and Breyer), continued on this theme of judicial consistency. At a minimum, she argued, the Court should not reconsider the original *Aguilar* decision and should wait until another unrelated case is presented to address a possible change in the law.

In response Justice O'Connor, for the majority, stated that stare decisis reflects a policy judgment that "in most matters it is more important that the applicable rule of law be settled than that it be settled right." Nevertheless, that policy is "at its weakest" when dealing with constitutional interpretation.

In overturning *Aguilar*, the U.S. Supreme Court concluded that changes in Establishment Clause law allowed the provision of Title I services on the premises of private schools.

ALLEGHENY COUNTY V. AMERICAN CIVIL LIBERTIES UNION (U.S. 1989)

Each year Allegheny County, Pennsylvania, had set up several exhibits to commemorate the holiday season. Inside the county courthouse a nativity scene was displayed on the grand staircase. Outside the courthouse stood a Christmas tree and a menorah, the latter a symbol of Hanukkah. The outside display was accompanied by a sign describing it as part of the city's salute to liberty. A splintered Supreme Court ruled that the nativity scene violated the Establishment Clause, but the menorah did not.

Justice Harry A. Blackmun delivered the opinion of the Court with respect to the nativity scene. He argued that the scene violated the second prong of the *Lemon* test [from *Lemon v. Kurtzman* (U.S. 1971)] because it expressed a patently religious message, as indicated by an accompanying banner with the words, "Gloria in Excelsis Deo!" ("Glory to God in the

Highest!"). Under the *Lemon* test, for a statute to be constitutional, it must meet the following conditions: (1) It must have a secular purpose; (2) its primary effect must neither advance nor inhibit religion; and (3) it must not foster an "excessive entanglement" of government with religion. Justice Blackmun, however, argued that the menorah did not endorse religion because, in context, it was devoid of religious significance. The menorah and Christmas tree together merely symbolized the different facets of the "same winter-holiday season, which has attained a secular status in our society."

Justice Sandra Day O'Connor rejected Blackmun's reasoning with respect to the menorah, although she concurred in the Court's judgment. Unlike Blackmun, O'Connor readily acknowledged the religious meaning of the menorah, but argued that its display was permissible because in context it "conveyed a message of pluralism and freedom of belief" rather than endorsement. Justices William Brennan, John Paul Stevens, and Thurgood Marshall disagreed. They contended that both the Christmas tree and the menorah were religious symbols and that their display effected a dual endorsement of Christianity and Judaism.

Four justices on the Court—William Rehnquist, Antonin Scalia, Byron White, and Anthony Kennedy disagreed with the ruling on the nativity scene. Writing for the minority, Justice Kennedy argued that the guiding principle in Establishment Clause cases should be government neutrality toward religion—but neutrality must be properly understood. Given the pervasive influence of the "modern administrative state," said Kennedy, complete government nonrecognition of religion would send a "clear message of disapproval." Hence, some government recognition of religion may actually further the goal of neutrality. As applied to this case, for the government to recognize only the secular aspects of a holiday with both secular and religious components would signal not neutrality but "callous indifference" toward the religious beliefs of a great many celebrants. Such hostility is not required by the Constitution according to Kennedy. As long as holiday displays do not directly or indirectly coerce people in the area of religion and the displays do not tend toward the establishment of state religion, then they should be constitutional. Under this standard, the nativity scene, Christmas tree, and menorah would all be permissible.

AMERICAN CIVIL LIBERTIES UNION   The American Civil Liberties Union (ACLU) is often called the nation's foremost advocate of individual rights. Its single purpose is an uncompromising protection of civil liberties for all, no matter how unpopular, outrageous, or despicable the cause or individual. Founded in 1920 by distinguished individuals such as Roger Baldwin, Jane Addams, Felix

Frankfurter, Helen Keller, Scott Nearing, and Norman Thomas, the private nonprofit organization today is a multipurpose legal group of 300,000 members. With involvement in dozens of Supreme Court cases and thousands of state and federal rulings behind it, the ACLU is a firmly established force in U.S. law. It has championed racial and religious minorities, the right of labor to organize, and equal treatment for women, and it has opposed arbitrary treatment of persons in closed institutions. The ACLU also has influence beyond the courts. Monitoring legislators, it frequently issues public statements on pending national, state, and local legislation, and campaigns for and against laws.

The ACLU has been involved in many of the most important and controversial cases of the twentieth century. By 1926 the ACLU joined the so-called Scopes monkey trial, arguing against a Tennessee law that forbade teaching the theory of evolution in public schools. [*Scopes v. State* (Tenn. 1925, Tenn. 1927)] Besides bringing the group to worldwide attention, *Scopes* set the ACLU on a course from which it has never veered, taking a strong separationist stand on church and state issues. It has opposed both official help and hindrance to religion. In a 1962 challenge originally brought by the ACLU, the Supreme Court ruled that prayer in public schools is unconstitutional. [*Engel v. Vitale* (U.S. 1963)]

Strict separation of church and state to the ACLU means absolute opposition to the most bland organized prayers in public schools and to the display of any religious symbol on public grounds or documents. Its strong devotion to these concerns is one factor that makes it highly controversial. Some critics label the ACLU as "anti-God, anti-American, and anti-life." Other conservatives argue that in the defense of an abstract principle, ACLU members have become inflexible, rigid absolutists. Even some who support its positions have criticized the ACLU for asking courts to hold unconstitutional every cooperative relationship between government and religion. These critics believe that such rigidity could actually damage the cause of separation between church and state by making it appear absurdly uncompromising.

AMERICANS UNITED FOR SEPARATION OF CHURCH AND STATE

Since 1947 the group known as Americans United for Separation of Church and State has worked to protect the constitutional principle of church-state separation, which it holds as a vital cornerstone of religious liberty. The organization believes that "Our forefathers fought, bled, and died to keep us from a state church and a church state. We must continue to hold high the torch of liberty they have passed on to us." [*See* Americans United for Separation of Church and State website]

Americans United for Separation of Church and State opposes mandatory prayer in public schools, public support for parochial schools, government intrusion into religious affairs, and partisan political involvement by religious groups as threatening the protective wall between church and state.

The organization is regularly involved in litigation, setting legal precedents on behalf of church-state separation. The group initiates lawsuits, provides legal counsel and support in other cases, and serves as a partner in joint lawsuits.

Americans United serves as a liaison between its members and the U.S. Congress, White House, and state legislatures.

Working closely with allied groups, Americans United has successfully prevented political attempts to require prayer and religious activities in public schools. Simultaneously, the organization has supported legal protections of truly voluntary student religious exercises. In Congress, state legislatures, and public referenda, Americans United has consistently opposed efforts to provide public support for parochial schools based on the principle that the government oversight that accompanies government aid would harm religious freedom.

AMISH EXCEPTION   The U.S. Supreme Court has allowed an exemption for the Amish from a neutral Wisconsin law that required school attendance until age 16, because a fundamental tenet of the Amish religion forbids secondary education. The Amish maintain that learning beyond that which can be acquired in neighborhood elementary schools tends to generate values that alienate their children from God. The Amish faith counsels its members to reject the competitive spirit, deemphasize material success, and insulate its youth from the modern world. In *Wisconsin v. Yoder* (U.S. 1972) the Supreme Court found that the Amish are productive and law abiding, and that their right to educate their own children and the Free Exercise Clause outweighed Wisconsin's interest in demanding a certain education level for its citizens. In this case the Court held that Amish children could not be compelled to attend high school even though they were within the age range of Wisconsin's compulsory attendance statute.

The primary importance of *Yoder* is that it elevates religion to a special constitutional status that must be given particular consideration by the courts when parents and students contest state action. Importantly, it requires that the state bear the burden of showing that a compelling reason justifies government interference in citizens' religious practices. Generally, education is considered an important, if not compelling, interest. But, in the unique case of *Yoder* and the Amish religion, the state was unable to meet its burden of proof on this issue.

ANTI-DEFAMATION LEAGUE The Anti-Defamation League (ADL), founded in 1913 by the Jewish fraternal organization B'nai B'rith, is the world's leading organization fighting anti-Semitism through programs and services that oppose hatred, prejudice, and bigotry. In 1913 Leo Frank, a Jewish factory owner in Atlanta was arrested and charged with the murder of a female employee. After his trial and conviction, he was kidnapped from jail and lynched. Shortly thereafter, Frank was fully exonerated. This incident led B'nai B'rith to form the ADL to counter defamatory statements about Jewish people and to secure fair treatment for all people.

The ADL is a leader in the development of materials, programs, and services that build bridges of communications, understanding, and respect among diverse racial, religious, and ethnic groups.

The League carries out its mission through the work of a skilled professional staff and dedicated lay leadership across the United States and abroad. In civil rights issues, the ADL works to oppose prejudice and discrimination. The Legal Affairs Department fights discrimination and bigotry in the courts and defends the constitutional separation of church and state. The ADL probes the origins of anti-Semitism and extremism and serve as public resources on hate crimes and bigotry for the media and law enforcement agencies. The *ADL Audit of Anti-Semitic Incidents* measures and analyzes anti-Semitic sentiment in communities across the country. ADL reports alert the public to the dangers of anti-Semitism, racism, and bigotry. ADL staff help individuals around the country who face religious and other discrimination. The ADL provides educational programs to assist in eliminating prejudice, including antibias training and diversity awareness programs for schools, corporations, colleges, and communities.

The ADL is involved in international affairs by monitoring and counteracting anti-Semitism and promoting the security of Jews throughout the globe and in the state of Israel. The ADL plays a leading role in educating Christians to avoid anti-Jewish attitudes.

The ADL advances its policy objectives in the nation's capital through information and education, and as a liaison to the federal government, foreign embassies, and nongovernmental agencies.

ASYLUM In international law asylum is the offer of shelter and protection given by a nation to a person who is not a citizen. The granting of asylum is guided by national laws and international laws and treaties. Asylum is an ancient practice. Early Hebrew and Greek societies offered it under certain circumstances. The Romans recognized a more limited form of asylum. The tradition of asylum was most frequently offered in consecrated places of worship, such as temples, churches, or mosques. Political asylum became more common in the twentieth century.

Asylum may be territorial or nonterritorial. Territorial asylum is the protection granted within a nation's boundaries. Nonterritorial asylum, commonly called diplomatic asylum, is the protection given in diplomatic missions, such as in embassies and on ships. The granting of asylum remains the prerogative of the individual state. Conventional states rights (based on notions of sovereignty and the obligation to protect one's "community") are being challenged by arguments from human rights and humanitarian law, but the debate has yet to conclude that individuals or groups in need have an absolute right to asylum. Outside of Latin America, the right primarily exists because of treaty law protecting the inviolability of diplomatic premises, such as that established by the Vienna Convention. But even then, the practice is rare.

According to the United Nations, refugees may seek asylum if they fear persecution based on race, religion, nationality, or social or political beliefs. No person, however, has a right to asylum. Political persecution is the main reason nations grant asylum. In the United States, a person who wishes to receive asylum must prove a "well-grounded fear of persecution within the meaning of the United Nations Convention and Protocol." [*Chu v. INS* (9th Cir. 1989)] To qualify for asylum, an alien must establish that he or she meets the statutory definition of a "refugee," which requires a showing either of past persecution or a "well-founded fear" of future persecution because of race, religion, nationality, membership in a particular social group, or political opinion. Granting asylum is solely a matter of discretion for the U.S. attorney general. [8 U.S.C. § 1158(b)] In contrast, however, withholding deportation is mandatory if the alien can meet the threshold showing of a "clear probability of persecution due to one of the five noted grounds of future persecution if returned to his or her country. [*INS v. U.S.* (U.S. 1984)]

Religion is not exclusively a matter of private, inner conviction, but also entails a social concern arising within a community of faith and imposing religious duties on believers. These duties must be exercised within religious communities and in other social contexts. Often, a person's political opinions and affiliations are shaped by his or her religious beliefs. For example, the political differences in Northern Ireland are widely known to have their roots in the religious conflicts between Irish Catholics and Irish Protestants. Likewise, much of the current political turmoil in Kosovo is driven by religious differences between Orthodox

Christians and Muslims. Because political differences are often based on religious differences, only one test should be applied for determining when actions amount to persecution on account of either religious or political opinions. One issue is what constitutes persecution on account of mere membership in a religious community. It is often given a narrow interpretation. In *Minwalla v. INS* (8th Cir. 1983), a Pakistani member of the Zoroastrian faith claimed persecution on account of his religious membership based on his systematic removal from government jobs and other economic punishments. The court found that mere economic punishments did not amount to persecution and consequently denied him refugee status. In *Youkhanna v. INS*, an Iraqi Christian asserted that he was persecuted on account of his membership in the Kurdistan Democratic Party. The court found that the applicant had not proved that he had been singled out for prosecution despite being in the religious minority. The Seventh Circuit Court of Appeals questioned this finding, but affirmed denial of refugee status and thus denied the petition for asylum.

In some cases, asylum for religious persecution based on mere membership has been granted. In *In re Solmani* (BIA 1989), an Iranian Jew asserted that she would be persecuted because of her religious membership if she returned to Iran, and the immigration judge agreed. Likewise, in *In re Chen* (BIA 1989), a Chinese Christian asserted that he had suffered persecution in the past because of his religion, and the immigration judge agreed that the past persecution led to a well-founded fear of future persecution because religious persecution in China had not been eliminated.

The international community accords absolute protection to religious beliefs. [Universal Declaration of Rights, Art. 18, 1951] An example of persecution for religious beliefs is not allowing an individual to change religious convictions. Fear of persecution for changing religious beliefs was the basis for claiming refugee status in *Bastanipor v. INS* (7th Cir. 1992). Bastinipor was an Iranian Muslim in the United States who claimed to have converted to Christianity, an action for which the penalty is death in Iran. Bastanipor was granted refugee status based on his fear of religious persecution.

Religious persecution is seldom used successfully in the United States as a basis for claiming refugee status. This is true in part because courts exhibit a bias against claims of persecution "on account of religion" by placing onerous burdens on applicants claiming it, including proof of an antireligious motivation of the alleged persecutors. Courts tend to favor political claims over religious ones. An applicant for asylum on the basis of religious persecution is more likely to prevail if he or she can present evidence of religious persecution on a nationwide basis in the country in question. When a government has been supporting policies increasing discrimination and religious intolerance throughout the nation and there is no evidence that these actions of the government were localized, the United States is more likely to grant asylum to those fleeing that country. [*Abdel-Masieh v. U.S.* (5th Cir. 1996)]

B

▟▟▟▟ *BAEHR V. LEWIN* (HAW. 1993)   Three couples challenged Hawaii's refusal to provide marriage licenses to same-
sex couples under § 572–1 of the Hawaii Revised Statutes, which restricts
marital relations to a male and a female. The Hawaii Supreme Court
ruled that because the Hawaii constitution forbids discrimination on the
basis of sex, Hawaii could justify § 572–1 only by showing a compelling
state interest for barring same-sex marriages that was narrowly drawn to
achieve those ends. On remand to the Circuit Court of Hawaii, Judge
Kevin Chang ruled decisively in favor of the plaintiffs on 3 December
1996.

The unprecedented ruling in *Baehr* was partly the impetus for federal
legislation known as the Defense of Marriage Act (DOMA). Section 7 of
DOMA defines *marriage* as "a legal union between one man and one
woman as husband and wife" and defines *spouse* as a person of the opposite sex of the party in the marriage. Technically, DOMA forbids "same-
sex marriages," gay or otherwise. Two same-sex heterosexuals are
equally barred by DOMA from marriage. In practice, however, the majority of the beneficiaries of the right to same-sex marriage would be homosexuals. "Gay marriage" subsequently becomes the focus, with the attitudes toward homosexuals thereby emerging as the predominant issue.
DOMA advocates vocally opposed gay marriages, and pointed to their
private religious faiths as the source of that opposition.

DOMA was enacted because proponents feared that large numbers of
gay and lesbian residents from other states would travel to Hawaii and
get married. Upon their return, the newly wedded couples would sue for
recognition of their marriages and those state benefits deriving from their
legal marriage in Hawaii. The anticipated tool for these judicial challenges would be the federal constitutional provision that "full faith and
credit shall be given in each state to the public acts, records, and judicial
proceedings of every other state." [Art. IV, sec. 1] DOMA was designed to
prevent this by prohibiting any requirement compelling states to validate
same-sex marriages performed beyond their borders in other states.

Many states have passed legislation explicitly forbidding the recognition of extrajurisdictional same-sex marriages.

In the second appeal of the *Baehr* case, *Baehr v. Miike* (Haw. 1998), the Hawaii Supreme Court made the state the first in the nation to approve gay marriages. However, in November 1998 voters in Hawaii and Alaska joined 29 other states in passing prohibitions against same-sex marriages. This effectively was a legislative overturning of the *Baehr* decision. It remains to be seen whether this legislation has effectively squelched the movement for recognizing same-sex unions, or whether the legislation itself will now be subject to constitutional challenge.

BAKER V. FALES (MASS. 1821)   This case involved an early attempt to deal with the legal claims of churches undergoing religious schisms. It illustrates what can happen when the apparatus of church and state are intertwined, as was the situation in Massachusetts in the early 1800s.

In 1818 the pastor of the Congregational Church in Dedham, Massachusetts, resigned to accept the presidency of Middlebury College. By that time a rift had developed within the church, in Dedham and elsewhere in Massachusetts, between orthodox Congregationalists, or Trinitarians, and Unitarians. The Unitarians, unlike the Trinitarians, rejected the doctrine of the Trinity as unscriptural, believing that Jesus performed a divine mission but was a mere human being, not at all divine in his person. Because the political system established 200 years earlier had mandated that all members of the community also be members of the church, no legal distinction had been drawn between members and nonmembers in assigning responsibility for the church. Consequently, the selection of a minister was a civil function in which all community members were eligible to participate. By the time of this controversy, Unitarianism had grown in strength in Massachusetts. It spread quickly, capturing the venerable Pilgrim Church in 1800, and within eight years controlled the Harvard Divinity Department and all of Boston's colonial churches except one. Thus, Unitarians now constituted a majority of the electorate and they promptly selected one of their own as a minister, leaving the Trinitarian members no alternative but to form a separate church. Although a general assessment was in effect, and the deposed Trinitarians were not compelled to continue supporting their former church, they also lost all state support, along with the buildings and property of their former church.

A legal question thus worsened profound religious hostilities: Which body constituted the true church when divided loyalties resulted in a schism? The question was passionately contested because the victor's prize included the name, records, and property of many a wealthy "first church." The controversy affected political control of the state and its establishment of religion.

When the Trinitarians sought to undo this turn of events by bringing a lawsuit in 1820, the Supreme Judicial Court of Massachusetts distinguished between the *church*, consisting of its members, and the *church society*, which it considered a *civil* body consisting of the voters of the parish. The court held that under the Massachusetts constitution, the church and its property belonged to the parish, which could select the minister.

As a result of the *Dedham* decision, as this case is often called, the Orthodox Congregational church in Massachusetts was compelled to surrender about 80 churches to the Unitarians, with a property value estimated by the Trinitarians to be in excess of $600,000. However, by the early 1830s, support for an established church in Massachusetts had greatly diminished, and in 1833, article XI of the amendments to the 1780 state constitution was adopted and ratified by the voters by a ten-to-one margin. This article disestablished the church and terminated all state support for it. The *Dedham* case was decided long before the Fourteenth Amendment to the United States Constitution imposed the requirements of the Bill of Rights on the states, including the First Amendment's proscription of "established" religion. Thus, it should be remembered that states were free to have established churches at that time.

BECKER AMENDMENT Widespread public outrage aroused by the U.S. Supreme Court's decisions forbidding organized school prayer and school-sponsored Bible reading in *Engel v. Vitale* (U.S. 1962) and *Abington Township v. Schempp* (U.S. 1963) provoked the introduction in Congress of more than 160 proposed constitutional amendments. When the chairman of the House Judiciary Committee, Emmanuel Celler (D-NY), bottled them up in committee, proponents united behind a compromise measure drafted by Representative Frank J. Becker, a Republican member from New York.

The Becker Amendment was intended as a guide to interpretation of existing constitutional provisions rather than as new law. It had three parts. The first two provided that nothing in the Constitution should be deemed to prohibit voluntary prayer or scripture reading in schools or public institutions or the invocation of divine assistance in government documents or ceremonies or on coins or currency. The third part declared: "Nothing in this article shall constitute an Establishment of Religion."

Under the pressure of parliamentary maneuvering, Celler conducted hearings in 1964 at which many denominational leaders and constitutional scholars expressed opposition to the Becker Amendment. Opponents raised issues such as the separation of church and state, and many questioned the wisdom of altering any part of the Bill of Rights. As a result, the Judiciary Committee never reported any proposal to the House of Representatives. Amendments similar to Becker's have been introduced in subsequent Congresses, but none has come close to the majority votes needed for submission to the states.

Some proponents of greater religious freedom retain the hope that the U.S. Supreme Court will resolve this issue by officially sanctioning some existing moment-of-silence laws (that is, laws that allow government sponsorship of moments of silence in schools or other public institutions). In 1995 President Clinton stressed that a prayer amendment was not necessary because of the religious rights that school children already enjoy under the Equal Access Act. Some versions of a proposed Religious Equality Amendment specifically provide for reinstitution of public prayer in schools.

BELIEF-CONDUCT DICHOTOMY   The U.S. Constitution provides in the First Amendment that Congress "shall make no law respecting the establishment of a religion, or prohibiting the free exercise thereof." However, the First Amendment principle of religious freedom does not necessarily extend to protection of the practices and conduct associated with the protected beliefs.

Generally, in evaluating Free Exercise Clause challenges to legislation or governmental policy the Supreme Court applies the same tests used in Establishment Clause cases; that is, the challenged law must have a secular purpose and effect and, presumably, excessive "entanglement" of the government with religion must be avoided. However, there are some necessary differences. While legislation may impermissibly "respect" an establishment of religion without actually affecting persons in their religious beliefs or practices, the effect of a law or a governmental action upon an individual's beliefs or conduct is the gravamen of a free exercise complaint. The familiar distinction between belief and conduct—the belief-conduct dichotomy—has varied in legal interpretation over the years.

As the Supreme Court has noted, the Free Exercise Clause "embraces two concepts—freedom to believe and freedom to act. The first is absolute, but in the nature of things, the second cannot be." [*Cantwell v. Connecticut* (U.S. 1940)]

In its first free exercise case involving the power of government to prohibit polygamy, the Supreme Court invoked a hard distinction between the two, saying that although laws "cannot interfere with mere religious beliefs and opinions, they may with practices." [*Reynolds v. United States*

(U.S. 1878)] *Reynolds* thus was the first case in which the Supreme Court distinguished between belief and action. The Court in *Reynolds*, in focusing its inquiry on which religious freedoms are actually guaranteed by the First Amendment, concluded that Congress has no power to restrict religious opinions and beliefs, but is "left free to reach actions which [are] in violation of social duties or subversive of good order."

A later Court held that "[c]rime is not the less odious because sanctioned by what any particular sect may designate as 'religion.'" [*Davis v. Beason* (1890)] In another context, Justice George Sutherland in *United States v. MacIntosh* (U.S. 1931) suggested a plenary governmental power to regulate action in denying that recognition of conscientious objection to military services was of a constitutional magnitude, saying that "unqualified allegiance to the Nation and submission and obedience to the laws of the nation, as well those made for war as those made for peace, are not inconsistent with the will of God."

The rule, as it was developed and propounded, protected only belief: religiously motivated action was to be subjected to the police power of the state to the same extent as similar action originating from other motives. And although the rules were applied in several cases, more recent cases have established that religiously grounded conduct is not always outside the protection of the Free Exercise Clause. Rather, the Supreme Court will balance the secular interest asserted by the government against the claim of religious liberty asserted by the affected person. Only if the governmental interest is compelling and if no alternative forms of regulation would serve that interest is the claimant required to yield. The "compelling state interest" test for religious action, as this is known, was first articulated in *Braunfeld v. Brown* (U.S. 1961). The U.S. Supreme Court had consistently adhered to the distinction between belief and action for 85 years, until the free exercise doctrine was abruptly changed in *Sherbert v. Verner* (U.S. 1963). In *Sherbert*, which involved the denial of unemployment compensation to a Seventh Day Adventist who was discharged by her employer for refusing to work on Saturday, the Supreme Court found that the indirect burden on the appellant's free exercise of religion could not be tolerated. In determining whether a state could constitutionally infringe on the religious practices of an individual, the *Sherbert* Court developed a three-pronged analysis: (1) After an initial showing that a challenged state action impairs a complainant's religious freedom, (2) the burden then shifted to the state to demonstrate that it had a compelling interest that justified such a burden on religion, and (3) the state had to show that there was no less restrictive means of furthering that interest than the challenged action.

The *Sherbert* balancing test was reaffirmed in *Wisconsin v. Yoder* (US 1972), which is the leading free exercise case that attempts to break through the belief-conduct paradigm. *Yoder* represents a break with the

U.S. Supreme Court's longstanding observance of the "belief-conduct" dichotomy in its Free Exercise Clause cases, whereby religious beliefs are accorded constitutional protections that are usually denied to religiously motivated conduct covered by laws of general applicability.

Except for *Yoder* and cases on unemployment compensation laws, the U.S. Supreme Court, from the *Sherbert* decision in 1963 to the *Employment Division v. Smith* decision in 1990 (known as the "balancing era," based on the idea that the Free Exercise rights were balanced against the duties of the government in order to find whether a compelling state interest exists for the government regulation burdening religious exercise), ruled in favor of the government in every case in which an individual sought a Free Exercise Clause exemption from a government regulation of the actions of persons within its jurisdiction.

The "compelling state interest test" for religious action for the free exercise of religion analysis was the law until it was abolished by the Supreme Court in *Smith v. Employment Division* (U.S. 1990).

BIBLE DISTRIBUTION AT PUBLIC SCHOOLS   The

U.S. Supreme Court has held that Bible reading as a daily classroom exercise in public schools is unconstitutional. [*Abington School District v. Schempp* (U.S. 1963); *Stone v. Graham* (U.S. 1980); *Lynch v. Donnelly* (U.S. 1984)] Many courts nonetheless have been confronted with a variety of other questions on the distribution and use of Bibles in public schools. These questions include not only challenges to public school policies or regulations permitting the use or distribution of Bibles, but also challenges by Bible proponents to school policies and regulations prohibiting the use and distribution of Bibles. In *Berger v. Rensselaer Central School Corp.* (N.D. Ind. 1991) a federal district court held that the Establishment Clause of the U.S. Constitution was not violated by a school district's policy of permitting the distribution of books and other publications in the schools, even though the Gideon Society distributed Bibles in the schools pursuant to this policy. The court noted that the Bibles did not come from a teacher, but from a private party who did not engage in a proselytizing recitation of scripture and verse, but merely invited each student to take a Bible.

Other cases also support the view that it is constitutionally permissible to distribute Bibles to students in public schools under certain circumstances. [*Gregoire v. Centennial School District* (3d Cir. 1990)] In 1998 the Fourth Circuit Court of Appeals rendered a controversial ruling upholding the constitutionality of a school policy allowing the passive distribution of religious material to secondary school students. Key to the court's decision was the fact that the policy was necessary to prevent discrimination against religious speech, and that the school board implemented various procedures to minimize Establishment Clause concerns. [*Peck v. Upshur County Board of Education* (4th Cir. 1998)]

The court's opinion began with a recitation of the evolution of the Upshur County, West Virginia, school board's religious distribution policy. Historically, the board permitted only nonstudent, private groups to distribute literature to secondary school students. Groups falling into this category included Little League, the Boy Scouts, the 4-H Club, and the Women's Christian Temperance Union. In 1989, however, several members of the Gideon Society distributed Bibles to, and conversed with, students in the classroom. This incident prompted the school board to adopt a formal policy prohibiting the distribution of religious or advocacy materials to students in the county's schools.

Five years later a local minister requested permission to make Bibles available to Upshur County students one day during the year at predetermined locations in the schools. In response, the school board reexamined its 1989 policy and determined that language prohibiting the distribution of religious material did not preclude private groups from making Bibles and other religious material available to students on tables located in the schools. Accordingly, the school superintendent and minister consented to select an appropriate time to conduct the passive Bible distribution, and to establish guidelines on the manner in which Bibles would be distributed.

At the district court level the plaintiffs' request for a permanent injunction to halt the scheduled Bible distribution was denied. The district court did, however, issue an order requiring the school board to post a disclaimer sign on the Bible display tables indicating that the board neither sponsored nor endorsed the materials provided.

The policy also survived the scrutiny of the Fourth Circuit Court of Appeals. Consistent with the district court's decision, the circuit court found that the policy maintained the First Amendment principle of neutrality. Under the neutrality test, a government policy will be upheld if it was enacted "for some purpose other than advancing religion," and "if, when [government] opens a forum for private speech, it respects the distinction between government speech and private speech endorsing religion by refraining from encouraging any mistaken impression that the private speakers speak for the government."

The court noted that the school board's policy neither coerced participation in religious activity nor impermissibly "endorsed" religion. Students were not encouraged to obtain Bibles, and the distribution of the Bibles did not constitute a formal classroom activity or a requirement of the schools' curriculum. Consistent with U.S. Supreme Court precedent, the court further found that "secondary school students are capable of distinguishing between a school's equal access policy and school sponsorship of religion."

The federal Equal Access Act, passed in 1984, makes it unlawful for any public secondary school that receives federal financial assistance and has a limited open forum to deny equal access to any students wishing to conduct a meeting within that limited open forum on the basis of the religious content of the speech at the meeting. Thus the Act may protect prayer groups, Bible readings, and other worship services. Courts have held the Equal Access Act to be violated when school authorities fail to recognize a Bible club as a student organization, thereby denying it equal treatment with other student groups at a high school in a limited open-forum setting. [*Westside Community School District v. Mergens* (U.S. 1989); *Pope v. East Brunswick Board of Education* (3d Cir. 1993)] A limited open forum exists when the school grants an opportunity for one or more noncurriculum-related student groups to meet on school premises during nonclass time. The Equal Access Act does not violate the Establishment Clause of the Constitution because it does not mandate that schools require or encourage participation in religious activities, it just requires that they allow student-initiated religious activities to occur on the same basis as other student activities. State-sponsored Bible distribution or devotional readings are still prohibited, however.

BIBLE, READING OF   Throughout much of early American history, public schools had a distinctly religious foundation. Clergy often served as teachers, Bible reading was a regular event, and prayers were often a part of the school day. Indeed, religious instruction was one of the primary purposes for which schools were founded in the British colonies.

Today, however, organized Bible reading in public schools, or devotional Bible reading as a classroom exercise, is impermissible as an establishment of religion in violation of the First Amendment to the U.S. Constitution. [*Engel v. Vitale* (U.S. 1962); *Abington School District v. Schempp* (U.S. 1963)] It does not matter whether participation is voluntary or involuntary, and neither does it matter that the prayer period is designated as a period of silent prayer or meditation. [*Wallace v. Jaffree* (U.S. 1985)] The Supreme Court, however, has made clear that the "Bible is worthy of study for its literary and historical qualities." The Court has allowed the study of the Bible or religion in public school when information about it is objectively presented.

Two Supreme Court cases in which parents and their school-age children challenged the validity under the Establishment Clause of requirements that each school day begin with readings from the Bible helped establish this principle. [*Abington School District v. Schempp* (U.S. 1963); *Zorach v. Clausen* (U.S. 1952)] Scripture reading, like prayers, the Supreme Court found, was a religious exercise. Rejected were contentions by the state that the object of the programs was the promotion of secular purposes, such as the expounding of moral values, the contradiction of the materialistic trends of the times, the perpetuation of traditional institutions, and the teaching of literature, and that to forbid the particular exercises was to choose a "religion of secularism" in their place. Though the "place of religion in our society is an exalted one," the Establishment Clause, the Court in *Schempp* continued, prescribed that in "the relationship between man and religion," the state must be "firmly committed to a position of neutrality."

BILL OF RIGHTS   The first 10 amendments to the U.S. Constitution are known as the Bill of Rights. They were proposed by Congress in 1789 at the insistence of James Madison and ratified in 1791. The Bill of Rights is the Constitution's most concentrated statement of civil liberties. This document describes the fundamental liberties of the people and forbids the government to violate these rights.

The main rights entitled to legal protection under the Bill of Rights are those usually considered inherent in societies following the English legal traditions. The concept of a bill of rights as a statement of basic individual freedoms derives in part from the English Bill of Rights, enacted in 1689. This document, which was created after the Glorious Revolution of 1688, established the terms by which William and Mary were accepted as king and queen of England. It forbade the monarchy to suspend laws, raise taxes, or maintain an army without the consent of Parliament. It also declared that freedom of speech in Parliament could not be challenged, protected those accused of crimes from excessive bail and cruel and unusual punishment, and provided several other privileges and freedoms. The English Bill of Rights had no provisions on religious freedom, however.

As a fundamental guarantee of individual liberty, the Bill of Rights forms a vital aspect of U.S. law and government. Scholars have described the Bill of Rights as protecting three different types of human rights: (1) rights of conscience, including the First Amendment's freedom of speech and religion; (2) rights of those accused of crimes, such as the Eighth Amendment's protection against excessive bail and cruel and unusual punishment; and (3) rights of property, such as the Fifth Amendment's provision that no one may be deprived of property without due process of law.

The opening words of the Bill of Rights, "Congress shall make no law respecting an establishment of religion [the Establishment Clause] or prohibiting the free exercise thereof [the Free Exercise Clause]," provide the primary basis for religious freedoms in the United States. The U.S. Supreme Court has incorporated both the Establishment and the Free Exercise Clauses into the Fourteenth Amendment. Incorporation means that the actions of state and local governments are also subject to the Free Exercise Clause and the Establishment Clause, as well as the actions of the federal government. The Establishment Clause was incorporated in the case of *Everson v. Board of Education* (U.S. 1947) and the Free Exercise Clause was incorporated in the case of *Cantwell v. Connecticut* (U.S. 1940). Of all the sections of the Bill of Rights, the provisions of the First Amendment were the first to be incorporated under the Due Process Clause of the Fourteenth Amendment.

BIRTH CONTROL   *See* CONTRACEPTION

BLAINE AMENDMENT   Representative James G. Blaine (R-ME), with the support of President Ulysses S. Grant, introduced in December 1875 a constitutional amendment to prohibit state financial support of sectarian schools. The amendment was intended to prevent public support of Roman Catholic schools, which educated a large percentage of the children of European immigrants.

The first clause of the proposed amendment provided that "no State shall make any laws respecting an Establishment of Religion or prohibiting the free exercise thereof." This is an indication that Congress did not believe that the Fourteenth Amendment incorporated the religion clauses of the First Amendment.

The second clause would have prohibited the use or control by a religious sect or denomination of any tax money or land devoted to public education. Together with the first clause this prohibition suggests the connection between support of church-related schools and the establishment of religion recognized in twentieth-century U.S. Supreme Court opinions beginning with *Everson v. Board of Education* (U.S. 1947).

The Blaine Amendment was approved by the House of Representatives by a vote of 180 to 7; but even a heavily amended version failed to carry two-thirds of the Senate, so the proposal failed.

In an effort to stop public funding of sectarian schools, Justice Felix

Frankfurter later used the Blaine Amendment as evidence that by 1875 "the separation . . . of the state from the teaching of religion, was firmly established in the consciousness of the nation." [*McCollum v. Board of Education* (1948)]

BLASPHEMY   Generally, blasphemy is any expression of insult or contempt maliciously cast upon God or irreverent behavior toward objects that are held sacred. Blasphemy has been made a crime in many cultures and religions. In Christianity, blasphemy has been regarded as a sin by moral theologians. Thomas Aquinas regarded it as a sin against faith. For the Muslims, it is blasphemy to speak contemptuously of either God or Mohammed. Mosaic law decreed the death sentence by stoning for blasphemy.

In England, blasphemy became both a statutory and common law offense. It became a common law offense in the seventeenth century. In early English law, blasphemy was regarded the offense of speaking matter relating to God, Jesus Christ, the Bible, or the Book of Common Prayer, intended to wound the feelings of mankind or to excite contempt and hatred against the church by law established, or to promote immorality.

Even in the seventeenth century, when the rate of North American blasphemy prosecutions was at its highest, such prosecutions were unusual. At the peak, there were 11 cases in the 1660s, six in the 1670s, and six more in the 1680s, nearly all in New England. In most of these cases, a statute criminalizing blasphemy was the basis of the charges. In Massachusetts blasphemy was a capital crime under the Body of Liberties of 1641 and under the Laws and Liberties of 1672. It became punishable by a variety of alternative lesser sentences (including "boaring throw the Tongue, with a red hot Iron") in 1697. A few seventeenth-century blasphemy prosecutions were without any statutory basis, a circumstance that apparently caused no more controversy in the colonies than in England.

Only 10 prosecutions for blasphemy occurred in the entire eighteenth century, spread over 10 colonies (states), all of which had statutes prohibiting blasphemy. Thus, even if eighteenth-century American criminal defendants had been disposed to question whether blasphemy was punishable at common law, no opportunities presented themselves.

By the nineteenth century, prosecutions for blasphemy were extraordinarily rare. They also had become more controversial for two reasons. First, nearly every state had a constitutional provision with an establishment clause, so defendants had a plausible argument that what was once considered blasphemy was now protected by the constitution. Second, nearly every state had a reception statute adopting only so much of the common law as suited the state's situation. Defendants could now claim that the common law status of blasphemy in England did not necessarily resolve the issue at home. *People v. Ruggles* (N.Y. 1811) was the first reported blasphemy case under this new judicial thought. Thus, it provided the first occasion to discuss these issues. Nonetheless, the *Ruggles* court upheld an indictment for blasphemous utterances against Jesus Christ. In so doing, the chief justice observed that "[w]e are a Christian people, and the morality of the country is deeply ingrafted upon Christianity." The decline in blasphemy prosecutions was part of a broader decline in the prosecution of religion-based offenses.

In the leading American blasphemy case, *Commonwealth v. Kneeland* (Mass. 1838), Chief Justice Lemuel Shaw of Massachusetts rejected arguments based on freedom of the press and on religious liberty when he sustained a state law against blasphemy and upheld the conviction of a pantheist who simply denied belief in God, Christ, and miracles. In all the American decisions, the courts maintained the fiction that the criminality of blasphemy consisted in the maliciousness with which the words were spoken or the intent to insult, rather than mere difference of opinion.

There have been very few reported cases on the constitutionality of blasphemy statutes and ordinances. The claims most commonly advanced in those cases are that the statutes or ordinances under which the prosecution was brought violated the constitutionally guaranteed freedoms of religion, of speech, or of the press.

Early cases generally upheld blasphemy statutes or ordinances under the rationale that Christianity was the religion of the majority of the people in the United States [*State v. Mockus* (Me. 1921)]; that it "played a significant role in the development of our governmental institutions and common law" [*Updegraph v. Commonwealth* (Pa. 1824)]; and that to permit the malicious reviling of this religion would be to risk the danger of public vengeance in the form of breaches of the peace. [*State v. Chandler* (Del. 1839)] The courts also reasoned that any word or deed that would expose the Christian religion to contempt or ridicule would rob official oaths of any of their sanctity, thus, undermining their binding force. [*Mockus*, above]

The U.S. Supreme Court has never decided a blasphemy case. In *Burstyn, Inc. v. Wilson* (U.S. 1951) the Court relied on the freedom of speech to void a New York statute authorizing the censorship of "sacrilegious" films. Justice Felix Frankfurter, concurring, observed that *blasphemy* was a far vaguer term than *sacrilege* because it meant "criticism of whatever the ruling authority of the moment established as the orthodox religious doctrine." In 1968, when the last prosecution for blasphemy occurred in the United States, an appellate court of Maryland held that the prosecution violated the First Amendment's ban on the establishment of religion and its protection of the freedom to exercise one's religion. The court, in examining the history of the statute at issue, concluded that it had no secular purpose, but was patently intended to perpetuate the Christian religion, and that it thus violated the requirement of the First Amendment that states assume a "neutral position" with respect to religion. [*State v. West* (Md., 1970)]

BLOOD TRANSFUSIONS   Some religious faiths oppose the use of blood transfusions to treat medical conditions. For example, the Jehovah's Witnesses decline blood transfusions based on biblical injunctions against the "eating of blood." They further believe that undergoing transfusions could deprive them of eternal life.

In cases in which a person has refused a blood transfusion on the basis of religious beliefs, courts have based their decisions of whether to order treatment on the age or mental competency of the patient.

When the person needing treatment is a minor or mentally incompetent, courts have ordered life-saving blood transfusions despite the religious beliefs or wishes of the patient or his or her family. [*Application of the President and Director of Georgetown College* (D.C. Cir. 1964); *Winters v. Miller* (2d Cir. 1969)]

When the person is a mentally competent adult, the cases are split as to whether the life-saving treatment may be ordered. A patient's right to refuse medical treatment takes priority over a hospital's interest in preserving life, the Connecticut Supreme Court ruled in *Stamford Hospital v. Vega* (Conn. 1996). After entering the hospital to deliver her baby, Nelly E. Vega refused blood transfusions because they violated her religious beliefs as a Jehovah's Witness. After her condition worsened, the hospital received a court order directing doctors to administer the transfusions. After her recovery, Vega appealed the order. Upholding her "common law right of bodily self-determination," the court stated that the hospital "had no common law right or obligation to thrust unwanted medical care on a patient who, having been sufficiently informed of the consequences, competently and clearly declined that care." The court also rejected the hospital's claim it was protecting the long-term interests of the newborn child.

Cases holding that a person may refuse blood transfusions based on religious objections include *Fosmire v. Nicoleau* (N.Y. 1990); *Public Health Trust v. Wons* (Fla. 1989); *In re Brown* (Mass. 1965); *State v. Perricone* (N.J. 1962); and *Martin v. Industrial Accident Commission* (Cal. 1956).

Cases holding that a person may not refuse blood transfusions despite religious objections include *United States v. George* (D. Conn. 1965); *Raleigh Fitkin-Paul Morgan Memorial Hospital v. Anderson* (N.J. 1964), *cert. denied* (U.S. 1964); and *Powell v. Columbia Presbyterian Medical Center* (N.Y. 1965).

▦ **Blue Laws**   *See* SUNDAY CLOSING LAWS

▦ *BOARD OF EDUCATION V. ALLEN* **(U.S. 1968)**

New York's Education Law required local public school authorities to lend textbooks free of charge to all students in grades 7 through 12, including those in private schools. Certain school boards opposed the law, seeking a declaratory judgment from the courts that the statutory requirement was unconstitutional as violative of the prohibition against establishment of religion. After the New York Court of Appeals, the state's highest authority, found that the law was valid, the case was appealed to the United States Supreme Court.

The Supreme Court agreed that the New York statute did not violate the Establishment or the Free Exercise Clauses of the First Amendment. Justice Byron R. White, speaking for the majority, relied heavily on the "student benefit theory," purportedly derived from *Everson v. Board of Education* (U.S. 1947). The student benefit theory holds that a governmental aid program may be permitted, provided that its beneficiaries are principally school children, and not religious institutions.

The New York scheme of providing secular textbooks to parochial school students also passed the "purposes and effects" test used by the Supreme Court to decide Establishment Clause challenges. The New York textbook law provided that only books for secular studies could be lent to students and that the books had to be either ones used in public schools or ones approved by the public school boards as being secular in nature. The Court accepted the state's position that the program was designed to aid the secular education of students and had no religious purpose.

The *Allen* majority also found that the program did not have a primary effect of advancing religion. Noting that religious schools must also teach secular subjects, a majority of the justices refused to assume that the sectarian schools were so permeated with religion that even classes in secular subjects advanced religion. Thus the Court found that the books were used only for the secular teaching component of such religious schools.

Justice Hugo L. Black, the author of *Everson*, dissented. *Everson*, he recalled, held that the transportation of students to church-related schools went "to the very verge" of what was permissible under the Establishment Clause. Justices William O. Douglas and Abe Fortas also dissented.

The decision in *Allen* stimulated efforts to aid church-related schools in many state legislatures. However, the *Allen* case represented the outermost reaches of permissible aid to parochial school students. The Supreme Court after *Allen* become increasingly strict in the scope of aid that may be afforded to sectarian schools. Later opinions of the Court have invalidated many such aid programs and limited *Allen*'s precedential force to cases involving textbook loans.

BOARD OF EDUCATION V. GRUMET (U.S. 1994)

Often called the *Kiryas Joel* case, *Board of Education v. Grumet* was another case involving the separation of church and state in a public school context.

Adherents of the Satmar Hasidic sect of Judaism believe in a literal interpretation of the Scripture and the Torah; they speak Yiddish, wear special clothes, avoid television and radio, generally segregate the sexes, and look to their Grand Rebbeh for his advice and blessing before buying a house, marrying, changing jobs, and making other decisions. In the 1970s a Satmar Hasidic community was formed in the town of Monroe, about 30 miles north of the Bronx, New York. After a bitter fight between the town and the Satmar Hasidim over zoning regulations, the town supervisor allowed the Satmar to incorporate as a village. About 320 acres were carved out of Monroe for the Village of Kiryas Joel.

Most of the children in Kiryas Joel attended the community's own religious schools, but about 200 were special-needs children who required programs too costly for the village's private schools to offer. Many of these children took special classes from the Monroe-Woodbury public schools in an annex to one of the yeshiva schools. But in 1985 the U.S. Supreme Court ruled that public school teachers could not work at private religious schools in *Aguilar v. Felton* (U.S. 1985). The annex program was terminated and some Satmar parents enrolled their disabled children in the Monroe-Woodbury public schools.

Disputes quickly arose over the educational services provided by the public schools. Some Satmar parents felt the services were not meeting the unique language needs of the children. They also felt the children were traumatized by their experiences in attending schools outside of the village and insisted that their children's needs be met within the confines of a "neutral site" within the village.

In 1989 New York passed a law that created a separate public school district, the Kiryas Joel Village School District, essentially for the sole purpose of serving disabled Satmar children. Shortly after the district was created, Louis Grumet, executive director of the New York State School Board Association, filed a lawsuit, claiming that the statute violated the Establishment Clause of the First Amendment. The Satmar Hasidim lost at each court level, including in New York's highest court, the New York Court of Appeals. The United States Supreme Court agreed to hear the final appeal.

By this time, every Establishment Clause case is brought up for review, expectations rise that the Supreme Court would take the opportunity to enunciate a new formula to replace the so-called *Lemon* test, developed in *Lemon v. Kurtzman* (U.S. 1971), which allows the government to do little to accommodate religion without crossing the constitutional line, and which is the modern standard for judging whether governmental involvement in parochial school education is in violation of the Establishment Clause. Under the *Lemon* test, to be valid a law (1) must have a secular purpose, (2) that neither advances nor inhibits religion, and (3) that does not result in excessive "entanglement" between government and religion.

In the post-*Lemon* era, the Supreme Court has repeatedly decided religion cases without directly applying the three-part test originally articulated in *Lemon* and without setting forth any other objective standard against which governmental action is to be judged. As Justice O'Connor said in her concurring opinion in *Kiryas Joel*, like the opinions in *Lee v. Weisman* (U.S. 1992), *Zobrest v. Catalina Foothills School District* (U.S. 1993), and *Larson v. Valente* (U.S. 1982), the Court's opinion in *Kiryas Joel* did not rest on the *Lemon* test. Rather the Court analyzed the facts using a neutrality analysis.

The major issue in neutrality analysis is whether the law under investigation is truly neutral with respect to religion, that is, whether the law either advances or inhibits religion. [*See Allegheny County v. ACLU* (U.S. 1989)] The Supreme Court has interpreted the First Amendment to demand not only a prohibition of government-sponsored religion, but also equal treatment among religions. The Supreme Court has recognized that absolute, total separation is not possible and that some interaction between church and state is inevitable. Nevertheless, in evaluating church-state interaction, the Court has emphasized that the federal and state governments should maintain a position of neutrality. To maintain this neutral role, the state need not be hostile toward religion, but instead is encouraged to assume a posture of neutral accommodation.

In an analysis relying primarily on *Larkin v. Grendel's Den* (U.S. 1982), Justice David Souter asserted that there was little difference between granting a franchise over traditional government authority to a religious organization, as in *Larkin*, or to a collective of individuals who all share in the same religious following. Justice Souter stated that the act that created the special Kiryas Joel Village School District departed from a constitutional requirement of neutrality toward religion by "delegating the State's discretionary authority over public schools to a group defined by its character as a religious community, in a legal and historical context that gives no assurances that governmental power has been or will be exercised neutrally." In discussing the state's creation of this school district, "following the lines of a religious community," Justice Souter suggested that the district can be treated as a "reflection of a religious criterion for identifying the recipient of civil authority," since its creation constituted a deviation from "customary and neutral principles."

The Supreme Court also declined to uphold the act under the Free Exercise Clause. The school district sought to have the district declared constitutional on the grounds that to do so would allow them to "pursue their own interests free from governmental interference." To this end, Justice Souter declared that the Court has "never hinted that an otherwise unconstitutional delegation of political power to a religious group could be saved as a religious accommodation."

In finding that the formation of the Kiryas Joel Village School District violated the principle of neutrality, the Court implicitly employed the status quo as the baseline against which it judged the New York legislature's action. Some commentators argued that the Supreme Court erred in its *Kiryas Joel* decision by employing the status quo as the baseline against which to judge legislation enacted to aid a minority religious sect. According to some, the use of the status quo to judge the actions of a legislature responding to the unique concerns of a minority religious sect amounts to an establishment of the status quo, and thus to an establishment of dominant religious groups. They argue that state action that results in the isolation or segregation of schools based on religious beliefs or practices must be measured against the constitutional mandate that states not engage in state-authorized, state-sponsored, or state-facilitated religious "line-drawing."

BOARD OF EDUCATION V. MERGENS (U.S. 1990)

The U.S. Supreme Court decided the constitutionality of the federal Equal Access Act in this case. The Equal Access Act requires public secondary schools to allow student-initiated religiously oriented clubs to use their facilities during nonschool hours on the same basis as secular groups. Two questions were raised in *Mergens*. The first was whether the Equal Access Act prohibited the Westside High School in Omaha, Nebraska, from denying a student religious group permission to meet on school premises. The second issue was whether the Act violated the Establishment Clause of the First Amendment.

The U.S. Supreme Court answered the first question in the positive: Yes, the school was prohibited from denying the student religious group access to school premises. The second question the Court answered in the negative: No, the Equal Access Act does not violate the Establishment Clause. The Court said that a "limited open forum" exists whenever a public school "grants an offering to or opportunity for one or more non-curriculum-related student groups to meet on school premises during noninstructional time." The statutory reference to "noninstructional time" means "time set aside by the school before actual classroom instruction begins or after actual classroom instruction ends."

The Court found that a school's obligations under the Act are triggered even if it allows only one noncurriculum-related student group to meet. A noncurriculum-related student group is a group that "does not directly relate to the body of courses offered by the school." A French or a Latin club, for example, would directly relate to a French or Latin course offered as a planned part of the curriculum. However, an ethnic dance club, or a branch of the Young Republicans organization probably would not relate directly to the school's curriculum. If even one such noncurriculum-related club is permitted to use school premises during nonschool hours, then the school is considered to have a "limited open forum" and religious and other student-initiated clubs must have equal access to the school premises.

In deciding that the Equal Access Act itself is constitutional, the Court referred back to *Widmar v. Vincent* (U.S. 1981) in which it had ruled that "an open forum policy" did not violate any of the three parts of the test enunciated in *Lemon v. Kurtzman* (U.S. 1981). Under the *Lemon* test, a statute must meet the following conditions to be constitutional: (1) it must have a secular legislative purpose; (2) its primary effect must be one that neither advances nor inhibits religion; and (3) it must not foster an excessive entanglement with religion. In this case, the Court found that allowing the religious speech of noncurricular, student-sponsored groups did not "confer any imprimatur of state approval on religious sects or practices." Thus, the secular purpose part of the *Lemon* test was met. In addition, to allow all to speak equally maintained the necessary government neutrality, neither inhibiting nor advancing religion.

▉ *BOARD OF TRUSTEES V. MCCREARY* (U.S. 1985)

The issue in this case was whether citizens could erect a public display of a Christian nativity scene on public land contrary to the orders of the town government. The Supreme Court decided that they could. The Village of Scarsdale, New York, refused to allow a private group to erect a public display of a Christian nativity scene on public land, which did not abut a government building, throughout the holiday season. The proposed manger scene was to stand alone, without a Santa Claus, reindeer, or other seasonal figures. The park had been used to display manger scenes from 1956 until 1980. In 1981 and 1982, the village denied the Scarsdale Creche Commission permission to place a manger scene in the park. The U.S. Supreme Court's four-to-four tie vote in the case left standing a decision by the Second Circuit Court of Appeals against Scarsdale on the grounds that the town had denied free speech in a public forum. The Supreme Court made a summary decision without a written opinion. Justice Powell took no part in the result. The Court in *McCreary* followed the reasoning of *Widmar v. Vincent* (U.S. 1981), providing all religious groups equal access to public forums and hypothesizing that allowing equal access to a religious display could constitute an acceptable purpose of public land.

The argument of those advocating the display was that, if wearing black armbands and burning flags are symbolic speech worthy of constitutional protection, so too is a nativity scene at Christmas time in a public park. The opponents of the display argued that a nativity scene on public property during a religious holiday and without Santa Claus and other similar characters is a sacred symbol that has a religious significance, and thus, violates the Establishment Clause. According to the opponents, the status of a public park as a public forum cannot justify its unconstitutional use.

Following *McCreary*, the next major Establishment Clause challenge to seasonal religious displays produced five opinions and a mixed result. [*See Allegheny County v. ACLU* (U.S. 1989)] In *Allegheny County* a narrowly divided Court forbade a private organization to erect an unattended, isolated manger scene on public property, even though accompanied by signs disclaiming official sponsorship. But the Court, again, by a narrow margin, allowed the Pittsburgh city government to place an unattended Christmas tree, menorah, and sign saluting liberty directly in front of the government courthouse. Five of the justices agreed that the critical question as to the holiday displays was whether the displays could suggest to the reasonable observer that the government was endorsing the symbols' religious message. Because the staircase where the creche was placed was not open to all religious expression on an equal basis, the Court in *Allegheny County* determined that the county was favoring certain sectarian religious expression (in this case, the Christian faith) in violation of the Establishment Clause. Thus, the Court deemed the display to be unconstitutional governmental "endorsement" of the communication of a particular religious message. The court noted that had the physical setting been different, such as that in *McCreary*, the display would have been permissible.

BOB JONES UNIVERSITY V. UNITED STATES (U.S. 1983)

The Internal Revenue Service adopted a policy in 1969 of denying a federal income tax exemption, available to educational and religious institutions, to schools that practice racial discrimination. Two of the schools denied the exemption were Bob Jones University and

Goldsboro Christian Schools. Bob Jones University had a multiracial student body but restricted interracial socializing. Goldsboro Christian Schools practiced racial segregation. Both institutions claimed that their practices were based on religious conviction, and sought to have their tax-exempt status reinstated. They contended that denial of the tax exemption provided for by § 501(c)(3) of the Internal Revenue Code violated the Free Exercise and Establishment Clauses of the U.S. Constitution. Their claims were rejected by federal district courts and by the Fourth Circuit Court of Appeals.

On appeal the United States Supreme Court also rejected the schools' arguments. In an opinion by Chief Justice Warren E. Burger the Court, in an eight-to-one vote, held that the Internal Revenue Service had the authority to deny tax exempt status to private schools that practice racial discrimination on the basis of religious doctrine. The Court noted that the denial of "tax benefits will inevitably have a substantial impact on the operation of private religious schools, but will not prevent those schools from observing their religious tenets." Moreover, "the Government has a fundamental, overriding interest in eradicating racial discrimination in education" and this interest "substantially outweighs whatever burden denial of tax benefits places on petitioners' exercise of their religious beliefs."

Justice Burger said that the history of the statute made it clear that entitlement to a tax exemption depends on meeting certain common law standards of charity, "namely, that an institution seeking tax-exempt status must serve a public purpose and not be contrary to established public policy." Undoubtedly, racial discrimination in education violates deeply and widely accepted views of elementary justice, the chief justice said, and in enacting Titles IV and VI of the Civil Rights Act of 1964, Congress clearly expressed its agreement with that position.

At a minimum, the Thirteenth and Fourteenth Amendments represent values that should prevent the government from actively aiding these schools, continued the chief justice. Because the schools represent values opposed to the constitutional rights of racial minorities, only accommodation of their existence and the provision of such general governmental services as police and fire protection might be required.

Justice William Rehnquist dissented, arguing that the history of § 501(c)(3) of the Internal Revenue Code indicated that Congress did not intend to deny tax-exempt status to organizations that practice racial discrimination.

BOERNE, CITY OF V. FLORES (U.S. 1997)   In a six-to-three decision, the Supreme Court ruled in this case that the Religious Freedom Restoration Act (RFRA) was unconstitutional, holding that the law exceeded congressional authority under the Fourteenth Amendment to enact "remedial" legislation. (Remedial legislation ensures that persons injured by violations of existing statutes have an effective remedy under those laws.) The Court also held that the law intruded on state authority and on the powers of courts to interpret the meaning of the Bill of Rights.

In 1990 the U.S. Supreme Court ruled that the Free Exercise Clause of the First Amendment no longer affords special protection for religious conduct against a generally applicable, religiously neutral law. [*Employment Division v. Smith* (U.S. 1990)] Prior to this the Supreme Court had held that even those laws and policies that do not single out religion for disparate treatment had to accommodate religious conduct unless the government could show a compelling reason why an exemption could not be given. In *Smith*, however, the Court reversed itself, effectively lowering the level of protection provided under the Free Exercise Clause (and making it easier for government to inadvertently infringe upon religious liberty).

In response to the *Smith* holding, a broad coalition of denominations and religious and civil rights groups (ranging from Americans United for Separation of Church and State and the American Civil Liberties Union on one side to the National Association of Evangelicals and the Home School Legal Defense Fund on the other) was formed to lobby for a new law that would raise the legal standard (and the protection afforded religious conduct) back to the pre-*Smith* standard. After several years of work, Congress enacted the Religious Freedom Restoration Act (42 U.S.C § 2000bb) in 1993. The constitutionality of the RFRA was challenged, and eventually one case, *City of Boerne v. Flores*, which involved landmark restrictions on a historic church, was heard by the U.S. Supreme Court.

In *Flores*, the conflict was over whether a municipality could prohibit a congregation from modifying or demolishing its house of worship because it was in a designated historic district. St. Peter Catholic Church in Boerne, Texas, near San Antonio, was built in the Texas mission style in 1923. Because the parish population had outgrown the church, the archbishop of San Antonio approved alterations to enlarge the structure.

Before the project began, however, the Boerne City Council empowered the municipal Historic Landmark Commission to prepare a preservation plan for the central city. Concluding that the church facade fell within the historic district, the city in 1993 refused to issue a building permit for the church expansion.

Archbishop Patrick F. Flores sued the city in U.S. district court, alleging that the refusal to grant the permit violated the Religious Freedom Restoration Act.

At that point, the dispute between the diocese and the city over whether the church could be expanded intersected with the ongoing national debate over the *Smith* case and the reach of the Free Exercise Clause.

The Fifth Circuit Court of Appeals considered the *Flores* appeal and ruled that Congress had the authority under the enforcement clause of the Fourteenth Amendment to enact the RFRA. The court also determined that the RFRA did not violate the separation of powers doctrine even though it imposed a stricter standard than the standard set forth in *Smith*, finding that by enacting RFRA, Congress did not usurp the judiciary's authority to decide when a statute impermissibly burdened a person's free exercise of religion, but rather exercised remedial power to reach conduct that only threatened the free exercise of religion. The RFRA did not advance religion any more than other legislatively mandated accommodation of the exercise of religion, the court declared, adding that the RFRA's prohibition against the placing of substantial burdens on the exercise of religion did not amount to the government coercing religious activity through its own activities and influence. The court further held that the RFRA did not violate the Tenth Amendment, because it did not intrude upon state sovereignty any more than a myriad of other federal statutes that preempted state regulation.

The case then was appealed to the U.S. Supreme Court and attention was focused on the key provision of the RFRA that reversed the holding in *Smith*. Specifically, this was that the government may not "substantially burden" a person's exercise of religion unless that burden "is 1) in furtherance of a compelling governmental interest; and 2) is the least restrictive means of furthering that compelling government interest." This provision was responsible for a substantial amount of litigation. An amicus curiae brief filed with the Court in *Flores* for 13 states claimed that the RFRA, between its passage in 1993 and mid-November 1996, had resulted in reported decisions in 189 lawsuits just by prison inmates who claimed denial of their religious rights. These claims included demands for the distribution of drugs to prison members of the Church of Marijuana, and requests for swords as well as material for burnt offerings. In the end, 16 states had urged the Court to strike down the law, which they said was being used by prisoners to make outlandish claims, supposedly based on religion.

Critics attacked the constitutionality of the RFRA from several different perspectives. Some claimed the RFRA infringed on judicial authority by directing courts to apply a particular legal standard in free exercise cases, and violated the separation of powers between the branches of government. Others claimed that the law offended notions of federalism (infringing on state powers), while others asserted that the law violated the Establishment Clause by affording preferential treatment to religious conduct. The most damaging argument, however, was that the RFRA exceeded the authority of Congress under the Fourteenth Amendment to protect existing rights by enacting remedial legislation. Critics claimed that the RFRA did not protect an existing right but actually created a new right, or at least fundamentally changed the interpretation of the Free Exercise Clause.

A majority of the Supreme Court, in an opinion written by Justice Anthony Kennedy, agreed with this latter argument, as well as with the federalism and separation-of-powers criticism. Congress's enforcement power under Section 5 of the Fourteenth Amendment is limited to preventive or remedial action, Kennedy held, and does not extend to legislation that alters the meaning of the First Amendment. "Congress does not enforce a constitutional right by changing what the right is." In *Smith* the Court had determined the meaning of the Free Exercise Clause, RFRA sought to give it a new meaning. Thus, Congress had gone beyond enforcing an existing right to creating a new one.

The majority also found that the RFRA's scope was too broad to be considered "remedial." The RFRA applied to every federal, state, and local action, and had a "[s]weeping coverage [that] ensure[d] its intrusion at every level of government, displacing laws and prohibiting official actions of almost every description and regardless of subject matter." As such, it was "so out of proportion to a supposed remedial or preventive object that it [could] not be understood as responsive to, or designed to prevent, unconstitutional behavior." Finally, the majority held that the legislative record lacked substantial evidence that such comprehensive legislation was necessary.

By invalidating the RFRA, the Supreme Court reaffirmed its holding in *Smith* that the Free Exercise Clause does not preempt facially neutral laws of general applicability, even if they incidentally affect a religious practice.

Justices O'Connor, Souter, and Breyer filed dissenting opinions, arguing that *Smith* was wrongly decided or should be reconsidered. It appears from the majority opinion, however, that six justices still adhere to the *Smith* rationale.

Although all people of faith will be affected by *Flores,* the decision will have its greatest impact on those religious practices that either are unusual or are out of the mainstream. Government agencies and officials will no longer be required to accommodate religious practices (such as exempting Amish from certain traffic regulations), even if such could be done without undue cost.

The issue of what degree of protection religion should receive under the law is likely to continue to be a matter of contentious debate. Congressional supporters of the Religious Freedom Restoration Act vowed to write a narrower version for passage. Some RFRA supporters announced an effort to reenact it as a constitutional amendment. Even without a constitutional amendment, the *Flores* decision does not close the door to all future legislative remedies. The Supreme Court's objections over the RFRA's breadth, and the lack of evidence supporting its need, can be addressed through more directed and better substantiated legislation. Also, Congress may still have the authority to enact a scaled-down version of the RFRA that is limited to the federal government. Finally, nothing in the decision prevents states from enacting statutes that will obtain the same result or interpreting their own constitutions more protectively. Thus, although the *Flores* result disappointed supporters of the RFRA, other avenues remain open to them in the effort to protect religious expression.

BOWEN V. KENDRICK **(U.S. 1988)**   In this case, the Supreme Court sustained the constitutionality of the federal 1981 Adolescent Family Life Act against a claim that it violated the Establishment Clause of the First Amendment. The statute authorized federal funds for services that related to adolescent sexuality and pregnancy. A federal district court found that the statute was unconstitutional on its face, and that, as administered, it impermissibly advanced religion by subsidizing and allowing sectarian organizations to preach their message to adolescents. The district court also found that the statute unduly entangled the government with religion by requiring official monitoring to ensure that religiously affiliated grantees did not promote their religious missions.

On appeal the Supreme Court, by a five-to-four vote, reversed the lower court's decision. It found that the Act was constitutional in its express terms. However, it remanded the case for a determination of whether the statute was applied unconstitutionally.

Chief Justice William H. Rehnquist, writing for the majority, observed that the statute neither required grantees to be religiously affiliated nor suggested that religious institutions were specifically qualified to provide the services subsidized by the government. Congress merely assumed that religious organizations as well as nonreligious ones could influence adolescent behavior. Congress impartially made the monies available to achieve secular objectives, regardless of whether the funds went to sectarian or secular institutions. This was not a case in which the federal subsidies flowed primarily to pervasively sectarian institutions; moreover, the services provided to adolescents, such as pregnancy testing or child care, were not religious in nature. The majority also held that the type of government monitoring required by the statute did not necessarily entangle it excessively with religion. Conceding, however, that the law could be administered in such a way as to violate the Establishment Clause, the Court returned the case to the district court for a factual finding on that issue.

The four dissenters, speaking though Justice Harry A. Blackmun, may have been influenced by the fact that the statute banned grants to institutions that advocated abortion. Blackmun, as devoid of doubts as was Rehnquist, confidently deplored a decision that allowed federal monies to be provided to religious organizations, thereby enabling them to promote their religious missions in ways that were pervasively sectarian and contradictory, and requiring intrusive oversight by the government to prevent that objective. The majority, Blackmun reasoned, distorted the Court's precedents and engaged in doctrinal missteps by treating the statute as if it merely subsidized a neutral function, such as dispensing food or shelter, instead of pedagogical services that impermissibly fostered religious beliefs.

IIII *BOWEN V. ROY* **(U.S. 1986)** A federal statute requires state agencies administering the Aid to Families with Dependent Children (AFDC) program to use the Social Security numbers of applicants and recipients when processing claims. In this case a parent, Stephen J. Roy, claimed that obtaining a Social Security number for his two-year-old daughter, Little Bird of the Snow Roy, would violate the family's Native American religious beliefs. Although Roy disclosed at a lower court trial that his daughter in fact had a social security number (obtained shortly after her birth by Roy's wife), he asserted that agency use of the number would deprive his daughter of her ability to have greater power.

Roy appealed the lower court's decision requiring use of the number to the Supreme Court. The justices ruled that the use of Social Security numbers by the state agency in accordance with the statutory requirement did not violate Roy's rights under Free Exercise Clause of the First Amendment. Writing for the majority, Chief Justice Warren Burger said that "[t]he Free Exercise Clause simply cannot be understood to require the Government to conduct its own internal affairs in ways that comport with the religious beliefs of particular citizens." Distinguishing between freedom to believe, which is absolute, and freedom of individual conduct, which is not, the chief justice ruled that the use of the Social Security number did not impair Roy's freedom to believe or to exercise his religion.

The Roys had argued that it violated their religious beliefs to be required to provide their daughter's Social Security number in order to obtain money from the government's Aid to Families with Dependent Children program. A plurality of the Court held that this indirect free exercise burden on the Roys did not violate the Free Exercise Clause.

BRADFIELD V. ROBERTS (U.S. 1899) In this case the U.S. Supreme Court upheld government grants to church-affiliated hospitals. The lawsuit challenged an agreement between a private hospital in the District of Columbia operated by a monastic order, the Sisters of Charity (an order of Catholic nuns), and the Commissioners of the District of Columbia and the U.S Surgeon General. Under the agreement, a federal grant was provided to the hospital for building construction and the care of indigent patients without regard to the patients' religion. The plaintiff, a U.S. citizen and taxpayer, brought the suit on the grounds that the agreement in question violated the Establishment Clause of the First Amendment by giving public funds to a religious organization.

The U.S. Supreme Court found the agreement constitutional and upheld government grants to church-affiliated hospitals. The Court found that the purpose of the appropriation was not to establish religion, but rather to enable the hospital to provide quality medical services. The Supreme Court held that, despite the "sectarian character of the hospital," the agreement did not violate the Establishment Clause because the case was one of a "secular corporation being managed by people who hold to the doctrines of the Roman Catholic Church, but who nevertheless are managing the corporation according to the law under which it exists." The Court thus held that the religious affiliation of the hospital was "wholly immaterial" to its right to receive government funds to advance the secular purpose of the hospital: treating patients regardless of their religious affiliation. Thus, despite the "controlling influence" of the Roman Catholic Church, the secular nature of the incorporated hospital removed any constitutional infirmities that might have otherwise arisen. So long as the hospital aided is not so "pervasively sectarian" as to subsume its role as a hospital in its religious mission, its secular medical function may receive government aid. This case was cited with approval as recently as 1976 by the U.S. Supreme Court in *Roemer v. Board of Public Works* (U.S. 1976).

BRAUNFELD V. BROWN (U.S. 1961) In this case the Supreme Court considered the constitutionality of applying Sunday closing laws to Orthodox Jews whose beliefs required them to observe Saturday as their Sabbath. A majority of the justices held that the economic burden placed on a Sabbatarian did not violate the Free Exercise Clause, although no opinion garnered a majority vote. The Sabbatarians' claim for an exemption was based on the fact that their religious beliefs required them to abstain from commercial activity on Saturday. Thus the statutory prohibition of shopping or selling on Sunday placed an added economic burden on them because of their religious practices. Chief Justice Earl Warren, writing for four members of the Court, found that this law placed a severe burden on Sabbatarian retailers. However, the chief justice held that, because the burden was the indirect effect of a law with a secular purpose, it would violate the Free Exercise Clause only if there were alternative ways of achieving the state's interest. He then employed a test of validity that essentially was a two-part balancing test. First, the plaintiff had to show that there was some real burden placed on the exercise of his or her religion by the regulation. Second, this burden would be permissible only if the state was pursuing an overriding secular goal by the means that imposed the least burden on religious practices. The plurality opinion by Chief Justice Warren found that the state had an overriding secular interest in setting aside a single day for "rest, recreation and tranquility." Although some states exempted Sabbatarians from the closing laws, Warren's opinion found that an exemption for those whose beliefs required them to close on another day might undermine the state's goal. Additionally, the chief justice noted that the state could choose to avoid a system whereby it would have to examine the good faith of those who claimed a religious exemption in order to make effective its laws.

▥ *BURSTYN, INC. V. WILSON* (U.S. 1952)

The U.S. Supreme Court in this case ruled that motion picture films are expression included within the Free Speech and Free Press Clauses of the First Amendment and protected against state abridgment by the Fourteenth Amendment. The Court thereby overruled *Mutual Film Corp. v. Industrial Commission* (U.S. 1915), which held that movies are a business "pure and simple," and "not entitled to constitutional protection as a medium for the communication of ideas."

Burstyn involved provisions of the New York Education Law that forbade the commercial showing of any motion picture film without a license and authorized denial of a license on a censor's conclusion that the film was "sacrilegious." The Supreme Court held the provision void as a prior restraint on freedom of speech and freedom of the press. Justice Thomas C. Clark, who wrote the Court's opinion, declared that the state had no legitimate interest in protecting any religion from offensive views. He added that it cannot be doubted that motion pictures are a significant medium for the communication of ideas. Moreover, their importance as a means of public opinion is not lessened by the fact that they are designed to entertain as well as to inform. The fact that the production, distribution, and exhibition of motion pictures was a large-scale business conducted for private profit also did not prevent motion pictures from being a form of expression, the liberty of which was safeguarded by the First Amendment, the Court held. Even if motion pictures possess a greater capacity for evil, particularly among the community's young people, than other modes of expression, the Court reasoned, it did not follow that they were not entitled to the protection of the First Amendment or could be subjected to substantially unbridled censorship.

On the issue of prior restraint, the Court held that under the First and Fourteenth Amendments, a state may not place a prior restraint on the showing of a motion picture film on the basis of a censor's conclusion that it is "sacrilegious." Although the Constitution does not require absolute freedom to exhibit every motion picture of every kind at all times and in all places, there was no justification in this case for making an exception to the basic principles of freedom of expression previously announced by the Supreme Court with respect to other forms of expression. The Court found that such a prior restraint as that involved in *Burstyn* was a form of infringement upon freedom of expression to be especially condemned. [*Near v. Minnesota* (U.S. 1931)]

Justice Felix Frankfurter, concurring, emphasized the danger to the creative process and to religious liberty from a censorship standard that was so vague that it could be confused with condemning blasphemy.

C

CANON LAW   Canon laws are regulations enacted and promulgated by ecclesiastical authorities for the orderly administration and government of the Roman Catholic Church. Canon law as it developed from early Christian times is binding today upon the world's more than 6 million Roman Catholics. Its development began long before the persecution of Christians had ceased. Since the Reformation, of course, non-Catholics developed their own church legislation, which varies from one denomination to another. The ecclesiastical laws of non-Catholic Christian churches are within the province of national or international conferences.

In reviewing legal matters involving the Catholic Church, each transaction requires a valid canonical act that is implemented in a civilly valid manner. First, the procedures followed by the ordinary (which refers to the bishop and his vicars general and episcopal vicars) must be valid. Generally, a juridic act is valid, under canon law, if the person has proper authority, presents what the act essentially requires, and observes the formalities and conditions required by the law for validity. The second requirement is that there must be a civil law counterpart to the canon law. Canon law requires that church administrators observe the mandates of both canon law and civil law.

For many centuries canon, or ecclesiastical, law consisted only of numerous decretals, or authoritative decisions of the popes on legal matters, which were in no systematic form. During the ninth century, an obscure monk named Isidore compiled a collection of decretals. This was accepted as authentic for six centuries but later was found to contain many forged documents.

In about 1140 a Camaldose monk named Gratian attempted to compile all ecclesiastical legislation in what he called *Concordia Discordantium Canonum*. These *Decretals of Gratian*, as they came to be known, were unofficial but very useful.

Pope Innocent III, who died in 1216 after an 18-year reign, sought to systematize canon law and he issued 3,400 decrees, but did not live to see the completion of his work. His successor, Pope Honorius III, was not as ambitious a legislator. He was succeeded by Pope Gregory IX in 1227.

In 1230 Pope Gregory called to Rome a Dominican priest named St. Raymond of Penafort, who had doctorates in both civil and canon law, in order to systematize the existing ecclesiastical law. He completed this work in 1234 in five books consisting of 2,000 paragraphs.

The *Decretals of Gregory IX,* compiled by St. Raymond, were supplemented in 1298 by the *Liber Sextus,* and in 1317 by the *Clementianae.* In 1500 a learned canonist, John Chapuis, edited all previous compilations in what became the *Corpus Juris Canonici.*

After the Council of Trent, which adjourned in 1563, Pope Gregory XIII appointed a commission consisting of six cardinals and 15 doctors of the law who revised the *Corpus Juris Canonici.* This was the official code until the present century.

In late 1904 Pope Pius X announced his desire for a complete and orderly modern codification of canon law. This was completed only after a dozen years and was promulgated on 27 May 1917, to become effective a year later except for a few canons that were applicable immediately.

The *Corpus Juris Canonici* of 1917 consisted of 2,414 canons or sections divided into seven general groupings. First are general rules, then those relating to the clergy, religious orders, indulgences, marriage, sacred places, and crimes with their ecclesiastical penalties. A commission to revise this code was appointed after the Second Vatican Council.

In June 1972 a commission was appointed to revise the code of Eastern-rite canon law, which governs the Eastern-rite Catholics who are in communion with the pope. The present code consists of 2,555 canons of which about two-thirds were revised during the reign of Pope XII.

CANTWELL V. CONNECTICUT **(U.S. 1940)**   As Jehovah's Witnesses and, by definition, ordained ministers, Newton Cantwell and his sons, Jesse and Russell, were engaged in street solicitation in New Haven, Connecticut, without the certificate for soliciting support that was required by the state. They distributed pamphlets, made statements critical of the Roman Catholic Church, and offered to play for passers-by a phonograph record including an attack on the Roman Catholic religion. The Cantwells were arrested and convicted of violating a Connecticut statute that prohibited persons from soliciting money for any cause without a certificate issued by the state secretary of the Public Welfare Council. Further, Jesse Cantwell was convicted of the common law offense of inciting a breach of the peace. The Cantwells' case reached the Supreme Court.

Justice Owen J. Roberts delivered the opinion of a unanimous court. He began by discussing how the doctrine of incorporation applied in this case. Incorporation is the process by which the Bill of Rights, comprising the first 10 amendments to the federal Constitution, is made to apply to the state governments through the Fourteenth Amendment. In this case Roberts declared that, by virtue of incorporation of the principles of liberty contained in the First Amendment, the enactment by a state of any law respecting an establishment of religion or prohibiting the free exercise thereof is forbidden by the Fourteenth Amendment.

The opinion continued, stating that "[u]nder the constitutional guaranty, freedom of conscience and of religious belief is absolute, although freedom to act in the exercise of religion is subject to regulation for the protection of society. Such regulation, however, in attaining a permissible end, must not unduly infringe the protected freedom."

The Court found that a state statute forbidding any person to solicit for a religious cause without first obtaining a permit from an official who must determine whether the cause qualifies as "religious" is a prior restraint upon the free exercise of religion and a deprivation of liberty without due process of law and violates the Fourteenth Amendment. The Court, therefore, held the Connecticut law invalid as it was applied to persons engaged in distributing literature purporting to be religious, and soliciting contributions to be used for the publication of the literature.

The Court conceded that a state may, by general and nondiscriminatory legislation, regulate the time, place, and manner of soliciting or holding meetings upon its streets, and may in other respects safeguard the peace, good order, and comfort of the community. The statute in this case, however, was not such a regulation. If a certificate was issued, solicitation was permitted without other restriction but if a certificate was denied, solicitation was altogether prohibited.

The fact that an arbitrary or capricious action by the licensing officer was subject to judicial review could not validate the statute, held the Court, noting that a previous restraint by judicial decision after trial is as unconstitutional as restraint by administrative action.

The Supreme Court then considered Cantwell's defense to the charge of breach of the peace. Under Connecticut law, this offense could be committed not only by acts of violence, but also by acts and words likely to produce violence in others.

While on a public street Cantwell sought to interest passers-by in what he believed to be true religion, in part by inducing individuals to listen to a phonograph record that contained vitriolic criticism of the Catholic

Church, of which some of the listeners were members. This provoked their indignation and a desire on their part to strike Cantwell, who thereupon gathered his books and phonograph and left the area. There was no proof that Cantwell was noisy, truculent, overbearing, or offensive, nor was there any evidence he intended to insult or affront the listeners by playing the record, nor was it shown that the sound of the phonograph disturbed persons living nearby, drew a crowd, or impeded traffic. The Court partially invalidated the breach of the peace statute as construed and applied to Cantwell to the extent that it prohibited the peaceful distribution of religious material.

CAPITAL PUNISHMENT   Capital punishment is the infliction of death by an authorized public authority as a punishment for crime. Capital punishment was accepted by ancient legal systems, including the Babylonian, Assyrian, and Hittite. Ancient Hebrew law prescribed death for homicide and for some religious and sexual offenses, including bearing false witness, kidnapping, sexual immorality, witchcraft, idolatry, blasphemy, and sacrilege. Greek law generally regarded homicide, treason, and sacrilege as capital crimes. Roman law recognized the death penalty, but favored hard labor and banishment, both of which resulted in serious loss of civil status. During the Roman Republic death was mainly imposed for military crimes.

In the nineteenth and twentieth centuries attention has increasingly been devoted to the religious and moral justifications for imposing death as a penalty. Cesare Beccaria, an Italian aristocrat and philosopher, who wrote *An Essay on Crimes and Punishments* (1764), provided the impetus for a rejection of the death penalty as unjustifiable and also as cruel and ineffective. In England the work of Jeremy Bentham and Sir Samuel Romilly (who devoted his life to a crusade against capital punishment) led to a great reduction in the number of capital crimes. Every Western industrial nation has stopped executing criminals except the United States. Great Britain conducted its last execution in 1964. Spain and France were among the last Western European countries to abolish capital punishment and did so in 1978 and 1979 respectively. There is no country in Western Europe that still uses the death penalty. Even in countries where the death penalty is retained, many have experienced steep decreases in the numbers of actual executions. While the movement to abolish capital punishment was one of the great reform movements of the early nineteenth century, featuring such notable persons as Jeremy Bentham, Samuel Romilly, and Benjamin Rush, today's human rights advocates oppose capital punishment, citing to both the UN Covenant on Civil and Political Rights (1966) and international human rights law, both of which oppose the use of the death penalty.

The first known infliction of the death penalty in the American colonies occurred in Jamestown Colony in 1608. During the period of the Revolutionary War, capital punishment was widely accepted. One hundred and sixty-two documented executions occurred in the eighteenth century. At the end of the Revolutionary War 11 states wrote new constitutions, and although nine of them did not allow cruel and unusual punishment, all authorized capital punishment. In 1790 the first Congress enacted legislation that implemented capital punishment for the crimes of robbery, rape, murder, and forgery of public securities. The nineteenth century saw a dramatic increase in the use of capital punishment with 1,391 documented executions. The death penalty continued as an acceptable practice in the United States for some time.

In 1967 a national moratorium was placed on capital punishment while the Supreme Court considered its constitutionality. In 1972 it appeared that the Court had put an end to the death penalty in the case of *Furman v. Georgia* (U.S. 1972). That case declared certain capital punishment laws to be unconstitutionally cruel and unusual because juries were applying them arbitrarily and capriciously. Existing state death penalty laws disappeared from the statute books. It appeared that *Furman* would represent the end of capital punishment in the United States.

However, Georgia, Florida, and Texas drafted new death penalty statutes and in 1976 the Supreme Court upheld them in *Gregg v. Georgia* (U.S. 1976). Of the nine Supreme Court justices, only two, William J. Brennan, Jr., and Thurgood Marshall, believed that capital punishment was unconstitutional.

Capital punishment continues to be used in the United States despite controversy over its merits and over its effectiveness as a deterrent to serious crime. A death sentence may be carried out by one of five lawful means: electrocution, hanging, lethal injection, gassing, or by firing squad. As of 1998, 38 states still retained capital punishment as a sentence. Twelve states—Alaska, Hawaii, Iowa, Maine, Massachusetts, Michigan, Minnesota, North Dakota, Rhode Island, Vermont, West Virginia, and Wisconsin, and the District of Columbia—did not.

Decisions on this issue have divided the Court and done little to convince opponents of the death penalty's fairness. Critics have argued that the death penalty is a cruel and unusual punishment, that it is applied in a racially discriminatory manner, that it lacks a deterrent effect, and that it is morally or ethically wrong.

The movement to abolish the death penalty has been supported by many religious groups. Modern Judaism, for example, repudiates capital punishment as degrading and brutalizing of any society that practices it. Many Christian denominations also oppose its use. Their justifications range from the belief that the life of an individual is of infinite worth in the sight of God and that the taking of such life is God's prerogative alone, to a belief that the penalty is contrary to the concept of Christian love. The Christian arguments against capital punishment also include the observation that the institutionalized taking of human life prevents the fulfillment of the Christian commitment to seek the redemption and reconciliation of the offender. They also believe that executions harm society by mirroring and reinforcing violence and the lust for vengeance. In the long run, the use of the death penalty by the state will increase the acceptance of revenge in our society and give official sanction to a climate of violence, according to these religious groups.

In 1995, Pope John Paul II, stated the Roman Catholic Church's position on the death penalty: "It is clear that . . . the nature and extent of capital punishment must be carefully evaluated and decided upon, and ought not go to the extreme of executing the offender except in cases of absolute necessity in other words, when it would not be possible otherwise to defend society. Today, however, as a result of steady improvements in the organization of the penal system, such cases are very rare, if not practically nonexistent." [Quoted in *The Death Penalty: The Religious Community Calls for Abolition*. Washington DC: National Coalition to Abolish the Death Penalty (NCADP), 1996]

Some Christians support capital punishment based on some of the precepts of the Old Testament. Others cite Jesus's admonitions in the New Testament to turn the other check and to love and forgive our enemies as an argument against capital punishment. American Catholic bishops declared their opposition to the death penalty in 1974. Although most Protestant churches have called for the abolition of capital punishment, some Protestant groups, such as the Lutheran Church—Missouri Synod, believe that "capital punishment is in accord with the Holy Scriptures."

Religious controversy over capital punishment appears likely to continue, and any temporary moratorium in its use is typically followed by intermittent reinstatements of executions. Modern religious groups increasingly base their arguments for or against capital punishment less on biblical texts and antiquated philosophical tenets than on civic and cultural concerns for justice, for fairness and equality in application, for the purposes of punishment, and for alternative penalties.

CHAPLAINS   A clergyman officially attached to a unit of the armed services, or to some public institution, for the purpose of performing religious services.

Strict separationists argue that the use of government-supported chaplains violates the Establishment Clause of the U.S. Constitution. The

Supreme Court, while not specifically deciding this issue in *Abington School District v. Schempp* (U.S. 1963), did note the unique circumstances of military service "where the Government regulates the temporal and geographic environment of individuals to a point that, unless it permits voluntary religious services to be conducted with the use of government facilities, military personnel would be unable to engage in the practice of their faiths."

Some argue that while free exercise considerations may justify government provision of an opportunity to worship, the Establishment Clause nonetheless prohibits a government-subsidized ministry. One position is that the governmental interest in avoiding burdens on the free exercise of religion could be satisfied merely by allowing free time for service personnel to seek nonmilitary worship or by giving the religious faiths the right to come into the military environment, at their own expense, to provide the opportunity for worship. Others argue that the government need not necessarily provide chapels and chaplains to military personnel who are not cut off from civilian church facilities.

Despite the principle of separation of church and state, the Supreme Court has held that a state legislature could employ a chaplain and begin each legislative day with a prayer. [*Marsh v. Chambers* (U.S. 1983)] This decision was based on the history of legislative prayer in America. It does not, however, modify the Supreme Court's rulings on religious activities in public schools.

CHARITABLE CORPORATION

A charitable corporation is a nonprofit corporation organized for charitable purposes—that is, for the purpose of promoting the welfare of mankind at large, or of a community, or some class forming a part of it that is indefinite as to numbers and individuals. [*Lynch v. Spilman* (Cal. 1967)] Charitable corporations are created to minister to the physical needs of the indigent or to advance a particular goal, such as the aid of a particular religious group or corporation.

As early as the seventeenth century, the corporation was used in the New World as an organizational form for charitable activities. Almost all colonial corporations had charitable purposes. They were churches, charities, educational institutions, or municipal corporations. Religious societies began to incorporate early in American history. In the early eighteenth century, several colonies, borrowing from an English statute of 1597 that allowed for the automatic incorporation of hospitals and houses of correction, provided for self-incorporation of some religious, charitable, or municipal organizations.

The early colonial corporations were of two kinds. The first was the public corporation—municipal corporations chartered by the towns or a few administrative boards charged with the oversight of public education, charity, and the like on behalf of local units of government. The second kind of corporation was the private corporation. Such corporations included ecclesiastical, educational, charitable, and business corporations. The most numerous in the second category were corporations concerned with religious worship. Next in numerical size were those formed for charitable or educational purposes, although they still might have a religious nature. Business corporations were few and of little importance. Many of the colonial business corporations would be considered cooperatives or quasi-philanthropic today. They were incorporated for the purposes of erecting bridges, buildings, or repairing roads, or promoting ends of general public utility.

From the foundation of the Republic, most states actively encouraged the incorporation of private associations that performed vital public services. Upon independence, several state legislatures passed statutes permitting general incorporation of charitable organizations such as churches, schools, and literary societies.

The rationale motivating the passage of early general incorporation acts included benefits to the public if such incorporations were increased; convenience to individuals desiring to incorporate; relief of legislative workload; and promotion of freedom of religion. Incorporation also enabled the trustees of a charitable organization to receive legacies and bequests, and it provided a less expensive legal process at the local level for property to be defended at law in the name of the corporation.

By the second decade of the nineteenth century, general incorporation statutes existed in New York for several organizations, including Bible and common prayer organizations. Other charitable and benevolent organizations were readily granted incorporation by special legislative charter. Charitable corporations also began to supplant charitable trusts in the mid- and late nineteenth century. The growth in size and complexity of charitable organizations resulted in an increasing abandonment of the charitable trust in favor of the corporate form. Throughout the nineteenth century, charitable trusts remained under a cloud and were construed strictly in many jurisdictions. In their place, the charitable corporation was used for eleemosynary organizations.

Despite the encouragement of corporate status, legislatures tightly controlled corporate purposes and activities. The New York General Incorporation Statute of 1784 for the incorporation of religious societies had limitations upon the amount of an estate these bodies could accumulate and required trustees to render stated accounts to the Chancellor. All of the early general incorporation statutes contained limitations upon the amounts of revenue to be held by such organizations and the purposes for which such revenue was to be applied and requirements for furnishing inventories and reporting any excess property to the legislature. The legislative policy was to enforce, within certain limits, the accumulation of property.

Beginning in 1790 the New York legislature, concurrently with the general incorporation statutes, incorporated by special charter societies for a variety of religious, literary, scientific, benevolent, and charitable purposes. The corporate body thus was kept under tight legislative control and supervision.

In 1840 the New York legislature passed a statute authorizing gifts of real and personal property to any incorporated college or other charitable institution. In 1848 the legislature passed a general incorporation statute for all classes of charitable organizations. A similar movement toward the consolidation of charitable corporations statutes occurred in other states in the mid-nineteenth century.

Corporation statutes evolved similarly in other states. In California in 1850, the first legislature enacted an Act Concerning Corporations that specifically allowed charitable organizations to incorporate. Legislation governing California nonprofit corporations was minimal, outlining purposes specifically permitted, elections of directors, bylaw provisions, and the requirements for holding and mortgaging of property. In 1931, California enacted a General Nonprofit Corporation Law, based largely upon an Ohio act, which in turn had been drafted on the basis of the nonprofit statutes of New York, Maryland, Illinois, and Michigan. The General Nonprofit Corporation Law abandoned many of the restrictions on charitable corporations, and gave nonprofit corporations greater flexibility in internal affairs. Nonprofit corporations were, however, also bound by the General Corporation Law, thereby carrying into nonprofit corporation law an undefined body of business corporate law. In other areas such as the law on standards of conduct of directors, trust principles governed. The General Nonprofit Corporation Law was largely incorporated into the Corporation Code of 1947. In 1980, the current Nonprofit Corporation Law became effective and for the first time treated California nonprofit corporation law as a coherent whole. The American Bar Association's Revised Model Nonprofit Act, completed in 1987, is largely based on the California statute.

Charitable corporations must meet certain criteria to receive tax "exempt" status. When examining an organization claiming a religious character, the primary rule as to religiosity is whether the organization's adherents are sincere in their beliefs. If that question is resolved affirmatively, the rule of *Unity School of Christianity* (B.T.A. 1926) is used to test the use of the profits of the organization and the exclusive purposes of its existence. In addition, an organization must conform to basic principles of charity law to qualify for recognition of exemption under U.S.C. § 501(c)(3). Thus, for example, its organizational documents cannot authorize it to engage, nor can it engage, in activities that are illegal, or contrary to clearly defined public policy.

Ordinarily, charitable corporations have no capital stock and they obtain their funds primarily from private and public charity. These funds are held in trust to serve the charitable objectives of the institutions.

CHARITABLE DEDUCTION   A contribution to a qualified charity or other tax exempt institution entitles the taxpayer to claim a deduction on his tax return. Contributions are tax deductible (subject to various restrictions and ceiling limitations) if made to qualified nonprofit charitable organizations. Generally, a gift for a religious purpose is one for a charitable purpose. As the term *church* implies an organization for religious purposes, a gift to a church or a church society by name, without declaration or restriction as to the use to be made of the gift, is considered a gift for the promotion of the purposes for which the church was organized and, therefore, to be a gift for a charitable purpose.

Provided the beliefs of the particular sect are not averse to all religion, or subversive to all morality, the fact that a gift that is otherwise valid as for a religious purpose is intended to aid or benefit a particular sect or denomination, or to promote the spread of its doctrines does not prevent it from being for a charitable purpose. [*See White v. White,* 2 Ch. 41 (English C.A. 1893)]

The justification for the deduction of contributions to religious, charitable, educational, and cultural organizations is usually the encouragement of socially desirable activities rather than in any allowance for differences in taxable capacity. The contributions that qualify for this deduction vary, and total contributions are usually limited to some percentage of the taxpayer's income.

One issue arising in this context is whether the charitable deduction is available in situations in which the donor receives back from the charity some benefit that is of only spiritual or religious worth. For instance, are deductions available in situations typified by the following: (1) A Catholic makes a donation in exchange for a mass being dedicated to him or his designee; (2) a Jew purchases a seat to pray for the High Holy Days; or (3) a Mormon contributes a tithe to the church, without which he or she would not be able to enter the temple.

Under § 170 of the Internal Revenue Code, a charitable deduction is unavailable when the donor expects some "quid pro quo" for the contribution, even when the expected return is intangible or even spiritual. Interpreting this "quid pro quo" provision in 1989, the U.S. Supreme Court held five to two that fixed payments to the Church of Scientology weren't deductible as charitable contributions because Church members received benefits in return. [*Hernandez v. Commissioner of Internal Revenue* (U.S. 1989)] Scientologists must pay "fixed donations" to participate in auditing and religious training, the Church's only religious rites. The IRS denied Scientologists' charitable deduction, asserting that members made their payments with the expectation of receiving a commensurate benefit in return.

The Supreme Court held that a case for the charitable deduction is not made when the donor expects a quid pro quo, even if it is a religious benefit. The Scientologists claimed that their payments had been singled out for unfavorable treatment, whereas the IRS's published rulings allow deductions for similar payments to other religious institutions (fixed donations for saying masses, pew rents, building assessments, and periodic dues).

CHARITABLE IMMUNITY   The legal doctrine of charitable immunity shields charitable organizations from liability for damages caused by their own negligence or other wrongful acts. Several theories support this doctrine. One is the idea that property is donated to a charity for a particular purpose and that it ought not to be diverted from that purpose to cover debts or liabilities incurred by the recipient charity. Another theory is that, because nonprofit organizations do not profit from the work performed by their employees, liability pursuant to the doctrine of *respondeat superior* (the rule that a master/employer is liable in certain cases for the wrongful acts of his or her servant/employee, or that a principal is liable for the acts of his or her agent) is not appropriate.

In many states, however, the courts have modified the rules governing charitable immunity so as to abrogate or restrict application of the doctrine. Thus it is no longer safe for churches and religious organizations to assume that they are protected from lawsuits simply because of their nonprofit or charitable status.

CHARITABLE TRUST   A charitable trust is an arrangement by which real or personal property given by one person is held by another to be used for the benefit of a class or the general public. The holdings of charitable trusts are intended to support religious organizations, to enhance education, or to relieve the effects of poverty and other misfortunes. [*See Shenandoah Valley National Bank v. Taylor* (Va. 1951)] Charitable trusts, sometimes called public trusts, are recognized for their beneficial social impact and are given certain privileges, such as gift and estate tax deductions, exempting them from the rule against perpetuities, and possibly exempting them from inheritance and ad valorem property taxes. In addition, courts apply liberal rules of construction in order to find a charitable purpose whenever possible.

The concept of the charitable trust was developed by the Romans and became part of English law through the ecclesiastical courts. Charitable giving was popular, in part, because of the belief that gifts to the church were an effective way to atone for sins and attain salvation. The legal protection of charitable uses became part of the common law of England at a very early stage. Such trusts were enforced by the judiciary before the Norman conquest in 1066.

In England, the charitable trust, rather than the corporation, has been the predominant form of organization for charitable activities. While English concepts of charity were adopted by the United States in colonial times, the charitable trust has had more difficulty being implemented in the United States because of history and early ignorance as to its origins. After the American Revolution, many states repealed all British statutes. Judicial support for charities remained somewhat limited after the Revolutionary War because its associations with English rule tainted the custom. In addition, some courts erroneously had charitable trusts invalidated because the state's law did not include the English Statute of Charitable Uses.

During the nineteenth century, the American perception of charitable trusts changed dramatically. In the early nineteenth century, charity was associated with privilege, with established churches, and massive wealth held in perpetuity. All were unpopular at the time. By the late nineteenth century, however, the increased accumulation of private wealth in the United States again made charitable trusts popular. Legislatures began recognizing that using private wealth for community purposes reduced the need for government spending, and statutes were enacted validating charitable trusts.

Contemporary American law favors charitable trusts by according them certain privileges, including an advantageous tax status. Before a court will enforce a charitable trust, however, it must examine the charity and evaluate its social benefits. The court cannot rely on the view of the settlor, the one who establishes the trust, that the trust is charitable.

In order to be valid, a charitable trust must fulfill certain requirements. The maker of the trust (the *settlor*) must intend to create this type of trust. There must be a trustee (the legal owner of this property) to administer the trust, which must consist of some property. The charitable purpose must be expressly designated. A definite class of persons comprised of indefinite beneficiaries within it must actually receive the benefit. The requirements of intention, the trustee, and the property are the same in a charitable trust as they are in any other trust. [*See Agudas Chasidei: Chabad v. Gouray* (E.D.N.Y. 1987)]

The definition of *charitable purposes* is derived from an old English law, the Statute of Charitable Uses, but has been expanded throughout the years as new public needs developed. A charitable purpose is one designed to benefit, ameliorate, or uplift mankind materially, morally, or physically. The relief of poverty, the improvement of government, and the betterment of public health are examples of charitable purposes. Trusts to prevent cruelty to animals, to build a monument in honor of a famous historical figure, and to beautify a designated village are charitable trusts aimed, respectively, at fostering kindness to animals, patriotism, and community well-being.

The class to be benefitted in a charitable trust must be a definite segment of the public. The segment must be large enough that the community overall is affected by, and interested in, the enforcement of the trust, yet it cannot encompass the entire human race. Within the class, however, the specific person to benefit from the trust must be indefinite.

A trust for the benefit of the orphans of American veterans of the Vietnam Conflict is charitable. The orphans of these veterans form a definite class. The indefinite persons within the class are the ones who are ultimately chosen by the trustee to be paid the benefits. The class is large enough so that the community is interested in the enforcement of the trust.

Charitable trusts for the advancement of religion of all types are generally upheld in the United States today. Such trusts are considered charitable. Religion may be advanced in several different ways. Courts have held that the construction, repair, or beautification of a place of worship to advance religion qualifies as a subject for a charitable trust.

Under tax law, the "advancement of religion" component of a charitable trust is applied, for the most part, to activities that support the functions of one or more churches or sects. This would include publishing a church newsletter, or providing materials for a parochial school system. In one unusual case, a settlor attempted to establish a charitable trust to study souls leaving the body and ascending to heaven.

The advancement may be in the form of direct payment to a church or rabbi, minister, or priest or it may be associated with religious work (missions, pamphlets, etc.) or accessories (choir, organs, etc.). A close area is a religious purpose that is connected to the personality of the settlor, for example, the saying of masses or maintenance of a grave. The problem with trusts for masses and other rituals for deceased persons is that they may lack the public benefit usually required to sustain a charitable trust. In defense of finding a trust in these instances, churches suggest that prayers offer a benefit to all members of the public and not just the person for whom the prayers are said or the persons present when the payers are said. Trusts for saying masses have generally been upheld in the United States. However, such trusts are sometimes treated as compensation for the clergy's services in celebrating the masses. In addition, the advancement of religion includes support of whatever organizations are necessary to promote the church's purposes: because prayer is an essential function of churches, trusts for societies and boards, monasteries, and orders of nuns have been upheld.

To be eligible for tax-exempt status under § 501c(3) of the Internal Revenue Code, a given institution must be charitable within the meaning of that term at common law, which indisputably excludes institutions whose activities are contrary to public policy. The IRS has used the general common law of charitable trusts to determine that racially discriminatory private schools are not entitled to tax-exempt status. [See *Bob Jones University v. United States* (U.S. 1983)

Established churches have had less difficulty in gaining acceptance as being for charitable purposes than newer religions. Some denominations, such as the Church of the Latter-Day Saints of Jesus Christ (Mormons), have evolved entirely within the United States from small initial groups. It can be difficult to separate legitimate churches in their initial years from sects that are doomed to be less successful in serving the spiritual needs of their followers (such as Joanna Southcote who declared that she was pregnant by the Holy Spirit and would give birth to a second Messiah). Southcote's trust was upheld by Justice Samuel Romilly in the English Court of Chancery in 1862. Generally, trusts for the benefit of new religious groups are upheld as charitable unless the court decides that the religion is so absurd as to be irrational. This, however, places the beliefs of the judge against the religious convictions of the settlor.

▥▥▥ **CHARITY**　A charity is an organization created for the purpose of philanthropic rather than pecuniary pursuits. Its purpose may be educational, humanitarian, or religious. A charity goes beyond bringing relief to the indigent, extending to the promotion of happiness and support of many worthy causes. A gift given to a charity or for charitable purposes is also known as charity.

The law favor charities because they promote goodwill and lessen the government's burdens. They are therefore ordinarily exempt from paying income or property taxes.

Charities are ordinarily supported by gifts from donors and most states have statutes controlling the manner in which funds are solicited for charities. In addition, charities are required to disclose their financial structure and condition.

The modern law of charities emerged with the adoption of the Statute of Charitable Uses in England in 1601. Prior to the Statute of Charitable Uses, the development of the law of charities took place in common law courts. Common law courts have struggled for centuries to delineate the characteristics of the activities and purposes that should be recognized as charitable.

Because Parliament intended to correct what it viewed as the "misdirection" of property put to charitable use, the courts gave the Statute controlling effect when it applied. When the proposed use provided a public benefit and was otherwise consistent with the public policy of England—including the Statute of Charitable Uses—the judges held the use to be "charitable."

From the beginning of the North American colonies, public and private philanthropy coexisted. The immediate stimulus for the benevolent atmosphere to charity in the colonies was the urgent need to establish public facilities, such as hospitals, churches, and schools. In the immediate post-Revolutionary War era, the favorable attitude toward charity continued. Each state adopted an approach reflective of its local needs and customs. Massachusetts, Pennsylvania, Vermont, and New Hampshire gave constitutional protection to charities. Other states enacted statutes facilitating and reaffirming the benefits of charities to the community. In part, the retention of prior statutes and practices resulted from the general continuation of English law and precedent in the first years following independence.

Today, the test to determine whether an organization is charitable is whether its major purpose is to aid others or to make a profit. The test for determining whether an educational institution is a charitable organization is whether it exists for a public purpose or for private gain.

Although charities may charge a nominal fee for some of their services and still be considered charitable societies, they are organized primarily for the public good and not for profit.

CHILD BENEFIT THEORY   Under this theory it is permissible for the government to render assistance and services to students in sectarian schools without being deemed to be aiding the religious mission of the school in violation of the Establishment Clause of the U.S. Constitution. In order to comply with the doctrine and, hence, within the law, the government's assistance to all schools—public and private—

must be ideologically neutral. However, this test has not been easy for courts to apply.

The child benefit theory was first announced by Chief Justice Evan Hughes in *Cochran v. Louisiana Board of Education* (U.S. 1931), in which the Supreme Court held constitutional a Louisiana statute that provided textbooks to private schools. The child benefit theory was further developed in *Everson v. Board of Education* (U.S. 1947) as a classification within the neutrality principle. The Court explained that the First Amendment requires simply that the state remain neutral, not hostile, in its relations with religious and nonreligious groups alike. Since *Everson*, the Court has recognized the child benefit theory as an important exception to the principle of neutrality and separation in the Establishment Clause cases.

The Supreme Court reaffirmed the child benefit theory in *Board of Education v. Allen* (U.S. 1968). In *Allen*, the Court decided whether a New York statute violated the Establishment Clause because it required public school districts to purchase and loan textbooks to students, including those attending parochial schools. The Court upheld the loan of the textbooks to students attending parochial schools, based on the child benefit theory. The Court compared the direct loan of textbooks to the bus fare reimbursement program in *Everson*. Relying on the child benefit theory, the Court stated: "The law merely makes available to all children the benefits of a general program to lend school books free of charge . . . Thus no funds or books are furnished to parochial schools."

In *Lemon v. Kurtzman* (U.S. 1971), the Court attempted to reconcile and apply its conceptions of neutrality and separation. The resulting *Lemon* test combined the "wall of separation" philosophy and the child benefit theory. Under the *Lemon* test, a government action is constitutional in light of the Establishment Clause only if: (1) it has a secular purpose; (2) its primary effect is neither to advance nor inhibit religion; and (3) it does not result in excessive entanglement of government with religion.

In *Wolman v. Walter* (U.S. 1977) the Supreme Court approved a program by which a state government supplied standardized tests and scoring services to students in parochial schools. Speech, hearing, and psychological diagnostic services were also provided in the private schools, and therapeutic, guidance, and remedial services for parochial students were provided off the premises of the private schools. All the services were provided by public employees and not the employees of the private schools.

The Court thought that the program contained adequate built-in protections against excessive government entanglement with religion. Although the Court adhered to its ruling permitting the states to lend secular textbooks used in the public schools to students attending religious schools, it declined to extend the precedent to permit the loan to students or their parents of instructional materials and equipment, such as projectors, tape recorders, maps, globes, and science kits, although they were identical to those used in the public schools. Nor was a state permitted to expend funds to pay the costs to religious schools of field trip transportation, such as was provided to public school students.

The Court also relied on the child benefit theory in *Mueller v. Allen* (U.S. 1983), which upheld a state statute providing tax benefits for parents of parochial school students because no direct benefit to schools was involved.

The Court reaffirmed the child benefit theory approach to Establishment Clause jurisprudence again in *Zobrest v. Catalina Foothills School District* (U.S. 1993). Although the Court did not specifically refer to the child benefit theory as the basis of its decision, there are similarities between the Court's rationale in the *Zobrest* decision and the child benefit theory cases. In *Zobrest*, the Court found that the provisions of the Individuals with Disabilities Education Act (IDEA) were neutral in offering educational assistance to individuals without reference to religion and, therefore, did not give direct financial benefit to the parochial school that the recipients attended. Where *Zobrest* differs from the previous child benefit theory cases is that, unlike providing secular textbooks, transportation, or diagnostic services, the aid at issue in *Zobrest* was an interpreter who would be translating religious doctrine and messages for the student. Nevertheless, the majority of Supreme Court justices was not concerned with the problem of public funding for an interpreter to translate religious doctrine. *Zobrest* was seen as potentially having a tremendous impact on future legislative enactments because the child benefit theory permits certain types of government aid to religious institutions based on the theory that the aid is only incidental to the direct benefit received by the child or his or her parents.

Although advocates of the child benefit theory argue that it does not breach the wall of separation between church and state because the beneficiaries of government aid are the children themselves and not the parochial schools they attend, separationists criticize the theory because, even if the aid is provided to the student, it ultimately flows to the school. In other words, the argument goes, the indirect aid has the same effect as direct aid in establishing a relationship between the church and state.

CHILD CUSTODY   The court in a child custody proceeding may adjudicate the comparative merits of various religions. [*S.E.L. v. J.W.W.* (N.Y. 1989); *Zummo v. Zummo* (Pa. 1990)] Nevertheless, courts have frequently recognized that a child's spiritual welfare or well-being is a legitimate factor to be considered in determining custody and visitation rights. [*Cushman v. Lane* (Ark. 1955); *Witmayer v. Witmayer* (Pa. 1983); *In re Marriage of McKeever* (Ill. 1983)] Many courts have referred in custody cases to the fact that one choice or another would best provide for the child's religious or spiritual welfare, or that the home chosen would better facilitate the child's church attendance or religious training. One state, however, invalidated a child custody determination that was based on religious considerations, holding that the decision did not meet the requirements of the Supreme Court's so-called *Lemon* test: that is, that the government action (here the custody decision) have a secular intent, a primary effect that neither advances nor inhibits religion, and that does not result in excessive "entanglement" of the government with religion. [*Bonjour v. Bonjour* (Alaska 1979)] Another state's constitution has a provision that forbids courts deciding child custody cases to prefer the religious or theistically religious parent. [*Gould v. Gould* (Wis. 1984)]

CHRISTIAN LEGAL SOCIETY The Christian Legal Society (CLS), founded in 1961, is a nonprofit organization of lawyers, judges, law professors, and law students. The group's mission is to promote high ethical standards within the legal profession, support its members' commitment to Christian professional lives, and advance religious freedom for all American citizens regardless of religious affiliation. The CLS provides resources for research into law and theology, maintains a data bank of commentaries on legal issues, provides a speakers' bureau, lawyer referral service, and mediation and arbitration services. It also publishes *Christian Legal Society—Briefly*, a quarterly newsletter for its members, and *Christian Legal Society—Quarterly*, a magazine that covers issues in line with the society's goals. The Society's legal advocacy arm, the Center for Law and Religious Freedom, promotes freedom of religion and challenges government interference with the free exercise of religion.

In 1993 CLS supported passage of the Religious Freedom Restoration Act (RFRA), a response to the 1990 U.S. Supreme Court decision in *Employment Division v. Smith* (U.S. 1990). *Smith* upheld a denial of employment benefits to Native Americans fired from their jobs for using peyote, a hallucinogenic drug, as part of a religious ceremony. The CLS and several other groups representing several religious and political persuasions lobbied for the RFRA, which required that the government show a "compelling state interest," such as public health or safety before interfering with religious practices.

CLS members successfully argued two important religious freedom cases before the Supreme Court in 1993. In *Zobrest v. Catalina Foothills*

School District (U.S. 1993), the Court held that the Establishment Clause did not prohibit a public school district from paying for a sign language interpreter for a deaf student who attended a Catholic high school. In *Lamb's Chapel v. Center Moriches Union Free School District* (U.S. 1993), the Court held that a school district's denial of a religious organization's application to use school facilities to show a film on Christian values in family relationships violated the organization's First Amendment right to freedom of speech.

CHRISTIAN NATION   In the *Church of the Holy Trinity v. United States* (U.S. 1892) the Supreme Court formally declared that the United States was not founded on the Christian faith. A trade agreement between the United States and Tripoli signed in 1797 plainly stated that the "Government of the United States is not in any sense founded on the Christian religion, as it has in itself no character of enmity against the laws, religion, or tranquility of Musselmen . . . and as the said states never have entered into any war or act of hostility against any Mohammedan nation, it is declared by the parties that no pretext arising from any religious opinions shall ever produce an interruption to the harmony existing between the two countries."

CHURCH AND STATE   The church-state relationship in the United States is primarily governed by the two (sometimes conflicting) religion clauses of the First Amendment of the U.S. Constitution, supplemented by analogous provisions in the state constitutions.

The First Amendment prohibits Congress from making laws "respecting an establishment of religion" (known as the Establishment Clause), or "prohibiting the free exercise thereof" (known as the Free Exercise Clause). The Establishment Clause is the guarantee against a state religion and the prohibition against state participation in religious activities; it is considered the guarantee of freedom *from* religion. The Free Exercise Clause prohibits the state from interfering with religion; it is a guarantee of freedom *of* religion.

One longstanding controversy is which authority in a society—spiritual or temporal—is superior and to which the individual owes greater allegiance. This has been described as the most serious practical problem in politics down to the Industrial Revolution. In Rome, the church was a branch of the state. The problem became more serious with the growth of Christianity, and particularly after Christianity was first tolerated and then established as the official religion of the Roman state by the Emperor Constantine in A.D. 313. This was a concession made by the secular law to a large group united by a common faith and having an extensive organization with disciplinary powers.

In the American colonies the Church of England was established in Virginia, the Carolinas, and Georgia. New Haven, Connecticut was a theocracy. However, in Rhode Island the earliest fundamental legal code ended civil magistrates' authority over spiritual matters. In Pennsylvania there was no established religion, and in Delaware there was religious toleration.

By the time of the American Revolution religious persecution had largely ended and a measure of toleration existed, but in 10 of the 13 colonies there was preference and support for one religion over others. The Constitution, before being amended by the Bill of Rights, guaranteed the freedom of religion only in the sense that Article VI prohibited religious test oaths for public office. Clause 3, section 1, provides that "no religious Test will ever be required as a Qualification to any Office or public Trust under the United States." The Supreme Court, in *Girouard v. United States* (U.S. 1946), declared such oaths "abhorrent to our tradition."

The Bill of Rights struck at any establishment of religion or prohibition of the free exercise thereof. Remnants of the state establishments existed well into the nineteenth century. In the period from 1834 to 1900 there remained in some states religious tests for holding public office. Some of the original states were slow to remove such requirements, but nearly all later states guaranteed such religious freedom from the start. Since 1940 the Supreme Court has in various contexts enforced religious freedom and the neutrality of the state on religious issues.

Although the two religion clauses in the Constitution are couched in absolute terms, there is an internal inconsistency in their application, leading to constitutional conflict or tension. And the U.S. Supreme Court has yet to make a definite statement on resolving such conflict.

The Court announced that it "struggled to find a neutral course" between the clauses in *Walz v. Tax Commission* (U.S. 1970). There, the Supreme Court considered an Establishment Clause challenge to a property tax exemption that was defended on free exercise grounds. The Court decided that the tax exemptions could be upheld as a nonsecular benefit. On the other hand, in *McDaniel v. Paty* (U.S. 1978), the Supreme Court applied a balancing test to weigh the conflicting interests in the two claims. The balance resulted in striking down a Tennessee law prohibiting members of the clergy from being delegates to a constitutional convention (two concurring justices, however, rejected the use of a balancing test).

Although previous challenges had been exclusively based on First Amendment analysis, the new federalism of the Reagan administration focused attention on the Establishment and Free Exercise Clauses of state constitutions. In *California Teachers Association v. Riles* (Cal. 1981) the California

Supreme Court came to the opposite conclusion of the U.S. Supreme Court in *Board of Education v. Allen* (U.S. 1968). Both controversies centered on the validity of lending public school textbooks to students attending nonprofit, nonpublic schools. Such practices had been upheld by the Supreme Court under a "child benefit" theory. The lending program was, however, struck down under the California constitution, which forbids the legislature to grant "anything to or in aid of" any church or religious sect or to "help to support" any school controlled by a church or sectarian denomination.

CHURCH ARSON   During the 1990s many churches were destroyed in deliberately set fires throughout the United States, particularly in the South. These incidences of arson were considered "hate crimes" because it was believed that the perpetrators were motivated by hatred of a group's religion or race.

In early 1996 law enforcement officials were confronted with an increase in the number of reported arsons at houses of worship, especially African-American churches in the South. In 1996 President Clinton formed the National Church Arson Task Force (NCATF) and made the investigation of these fires a top priority of federal law enforcement. He called on all Americans to come together in a spirit of respect and reconciliation. Specifically, the president directed his administration to implement a strategy to: (1) identify and prosecute the arsonists, (2) help communities rebuild the burned houses of worship, and (3) offer assistance to the communities and victim congregations in an effort to prevent more fires.

Federal prosecutors use several statutes to prosecute arson cases. For example, the Anti-Arson Act of 1982 permits the prosecution of defendants who uses fire to destroy property involved in interstate commerce (18 U.S.C § 844(i)). Criminal civil rights statutes permit prosecutors to charge defendants who conspire to deprive persons of their civil rights or who have desecrated religious property or a house of worship (18 U.S.C §§ 241 and 247). Because the majority of church arson cases involve the use of fire or explosives, additional provisions of Title 18, of the United States Code § 844 apply.

A majority of church arson cases have been prosecuted using 18 U.S.C § 844(h)(1) or § 844(i). Section 844(h)(1) applies when a defendant uses "fire or explosives to commit any felony which may be prosecuted in a court of the United States." The underlying felonies most likely to be charged are civil rights conspiracy (§ 241) or damage to religious property (§ 247).

In cases in which a racial or religious motivation has been identified, prosecutors may charge a violation of 18 U.S.C § 247, Damage to Religious

Property. This section provides two approaches for prosecution of church cases, depending on whether the arson or vandalism is motivated by religion (18 U.S.C § 247(a)), or race (18 U.S.C 247(c)). If two or more persons are involved in the commission of the crime, 18 U.S.C § 241, Conspiracy Against Rights, may be used as well.

To prove a violation of § 247(a)(1), the government must show:

- defendant defaced, damaged, or destroyed religious real property;
- defendant acted intentionally;
- defendant acted as he or she did because of the religious character of the property; and
- offense is in or affects interstate commerce.

To prove a violation of § 247(a)(2), the government must show:

- defendant used force or threat of force to obstruct a victim in the free exercise of the victim's religious beliefs;
- defendant acted intentionally; and
- offense is in or affects interstate commerce.

To prove a violation of § 247(c), the government must show:

- defendant defaced, damaged, or destroyed religious property;
- defendant acted intentionally; and
- defendant acted as he did because of the race, color, or ethnic characteristics of any individual associated with that religious property.

To prove a violation of § 247(a), the government must show that the religious property was used in interstate commerce or in activity affecting interstate commerce. The government, however, is not required to prove an interstate connection if the motivation for the crime was race hatred. The law does vary in the different federal circuits concerning sufficiency of evidence for satisfying the interstate commerce connection. The evidence necessary to establish that a church is involved in interstate commerce is evolving. Courts have viewed the extent to which churches are involved in interstate commerce as somewhere between that of residences and commercial properties.

CHURCH AUTONOMY DISPUTES   Because government is prohibited from becoming involved in religious issues

set forth in the Establishment Clause of the First Amendment, an important question in American jurisprudence is how to resolve disputes that involve churches: either those that arise within the churches, or those that are between outsiders to the church and the church itself. Church autonomy principles exist to ensure that no governmental encroachment into the substantially religious activities and purpose of religious entities occurs. Under this doctrine, a church has a right to settle disputes over control of church property, church organization, and entitlement to ecclesiastical office. The U.S. Supreme Court has on one occasion specifically identified a right to church autonomy as a free exercise right. [*Kedroff v. St. Nicholas Cathedral* (U.S. 1952)] Concern for institutional church autonomy dictates that any judicial resolution of an internal dispute conform to the disposition by an authoritative church body or with the disposition mandated by internal church rules. Concern for the rights of church members, however, dictates that any judicial resolution conform to the reasonable expectations of those members. In the church autonomy context, then, there is a strong case for deferring to a religious institution on matters that are genuinely internal to the institution and rest on religious principles. One example of an internal dispute was when the Eleventh Circuit Court of Appeals refused to settle a procedural argument regarding the election of officers within the Southern Baptist Convention, viewing it as doctrinal in nature and beyond the court's jurisdiction. [*Crowder v. Southern Baptist Convention* (11th Cir. 1987)]

Until recently, a line of cases beginning with *Watson v. Jones* (U.S. 1872) seemed to offer some support for a limited doctrine of church autonomy. These cases consistently forbade judicial resolution of issues of religious doctrine, and required deference to whichever authority within the church was empowered by church doctrine to resolve disputes within that body. Although deciding who is legally empowered to resolve disputes within the church may itself involve questions of religious doctrine, such occasions were thought to be infrequent.

In *Jones v. Wolf* (U.S. 1979), the Supreme Court abandoned the doctrine of absolute deference. In its place, the Court expressly sanctioned the application of "neutral principles of law," which do not involve judicial resolution of church doctrine or dogma, to internal property disputes. *Jones* involved disputes over church property and, hence, the Court ruled that the dispute was not internal to the institution. The Supreme Court thus gave the lower courts two alternative methods of resolution when faced with property division disputes: courts could either defer to the "authoritative ecclesiastical body," or examine religious documents themselves to discern legal intent. Although the latter approach precluded courts from resolving questions of religious doctrine, this grant of discretion to civil courts to "substitute this conventional dispute-resolution method in place of deference," significantly undermined any absolute notion of church autonomy.

In *Watson* the Supreme Court recognized two basic types of church polities, or structures: congregational and hierarchical, and articulated rules for use by the courts when dealing with them. A hierarchical organization is one in which the body of officers form an ascending series of ranks or degrees of power and authority, with ones below being subject to the ones above. In the case of the Roman Catholic Church, this would be the pope at the top, then bishops below him, and then priests below them. The hierarchical form, with authority vested in church offices at successive levels, includes presbyterial polities that are representative, authority being exercised by laymen and ministers organized in an ascending succession of judicatures—presbytery over the session of the local church, synod over presbytery, and special assembly over all. In the episcopal form, power reposes in clerical superiors, such as bishops.

The congregational form is that form of church polity with relatively independent and self-governing congregations. Some examples are Congregational, Baptist, and American Judaism. In the case of Christian congregational sects, the form professes to represent the principle of democracy in church government, which is held to follow from its fundamental belief in Christ as the sole head of his church. All the members of the church, being Christians, are "priests unto God."

When a church is found to be congregational, a court is to treat the church just as it would any voluntary association. In other words, in congregational churches, the majority of the members rules. Therefore, the court should defer to the majority's determination.

When the church is found to have a hierarchical structure, the court should defer to the decision of the highest tribunal or authority, because hierarchical churches have their own systems of courts and laws. The *Watson* decision's proscription of judicial review in cases involving hierarchical churches was absolute. While the Court admitted that the church tribunal might violate its own rules and procedures, it refused to sanction judicial review even on this narrow ground.

Church autonomy disputes typically arise under one of three scenarios: (1) internal disputes over church property; (2) tort claims against the church or its officers or employees; and (3) church challenges to governmental laws or regulations.

The first type of church autonomy dispute involves disagreements within the church itself over church property. [For example, *Watson v. Jones* (U.S. 1872)(taking a hands-off approach to internal church dispute based on common law)] Other leading church property cases include *Ser-*

bian Eastern Orthodox Diocese v. Milvojevich (U.S. 1976), in which the Supreme Court held that civil courts are not permitted to review the decisions of ecclesiastical bodies.

The second type of church autonomy dispute encompasses the growing number of tort claims. A tort is a private wrong for which civil courts will provide a remedy. Generally, a religious organization has a duty to use reasonable, or ordinary, care in maintaining its premises in safe condition or to warn those legally on the property of hidden dangers. In cases involving personal injury on church property, courts may determine the liability of the church because the issues involved do not usually touch religious doctrine. Some example of tort cases involving churches are *Guinn v. Church of Christ* (Okla. 1989) (holding that a former member can recover for defamation for remarks made in course of church discipline after she withdrew from membership); *Nally v. Grace Community Church* (Cal. 1988)(holding that clergy acting as nontherapist counselors have no duty of care to refer potentially suicidal persons to mental health professionals); *Gorman v. Swaggert* (La. Ct. App. 1988) (holding that statements to the media as part of church's internal discipline procedure are not protected by the First Amendment from civil court jurisdiction in defamation suit); *Holy Spirit Association v. Molko* (Cal. 1988) (former members were allowed to sue former church for fraud, deceit, intentional infliction of emotional distress, and false imprisonment); *Madsen v. Erwin* (Mass, 1985) (holding a religious organization immune from sexual orientation discrimination lawsuit, but not from related tort lawsuits). While a court may decide a tort claim that arises from the practice of "shunning" in some religious sects [*see Bear v. Reformed Mennonite Church* (Pa. 1975)], shunning has been held to be a constitutionally protected activity, so that a religious organization has the defense of a privilege that permits it to engage in shunning without incurring tort liability. [*Paul v. Watchtower Bible Society*]

The third type of church autonomy dispute involves church resistance to government regulations. Usually churches do not prevail in these cases unless the regulation impinges on areas central to the church's ministry. Some examples of these types of cases include *McClure v. Salvation Army* (5th Cir. 1972) (First Amendment prevented application of Title VII sex discrimination charge brought by female minister); *State v. Whisner* (Ohio 1976) (a religious school successfully resisted requirement that it be accredited by state); but chiefly, *State ex rel. Douglas v. Faith Baptist Church* (Neb. 1981) and *State v. Shaver* (N.D. 1980) (the state prevailed on requiring accreditation for church-run schools). In *Mitchel v. Pilgrim Holiness Church Corporation,* the Seventh Circuit Court of Appeals decided that the Fair Labor Standards Act, which requires equal pay for equal work, could be enforced against a religious organization, in spite of arguments that church doctrine allowed discrimination in pay between men and women. The court held that the Act was a reasonable, nondiscriminatory regulation in the interest of society for the welfare of all workers, and its application to employees of religious corporations who work in activities that touch interstate commerce does not unconstitutionally prohibit the free exercise of religion.

Both the Free Exercise and Establishment Clauses of the First Amendment require governmental neutrality in deciding controversies arising out of religious disputes. Occasionally, a schism (or split) will develop within churches or between a local church and the general church that results in secession or expulsion of one faction. A dispute over which body is to have control of the property of the church will then often be taken into the courts. It is now established that both religion clauses prevent governmental inquiry into religious doctrine in settling such disputes and require courts to look strictly to the decision-making body or process in the church and to give effect to whatever decision is officially and properly made there.

The first such case was *Watson v. Jones* (U.S. 1872), which was decided on common law grounds without explicit reliance on the First Amendment. A constitutionalization of the rule was made in *Kedroff v. St. Nicholas Cathedral* (U.S. 1952), in which the Supreme Court held unconstitutional a state statute that recognized the autonomy and authority of those North American branches of the Russian Authorities Church that had declared their independence from the general church. Recognizing that *Watson* had been decided on nonconstitutional grounds, the Court thought nonetheless that that opinion radiated a spirit of freedom for religious organizations and independence from secular control or manipulation to decide for themselves "matters of church government as well as those of faith and doctrine." The power of civil courts to resolve church property disputes was severely circumscribed, the Court held, because to permit resolution of ecclesiastical disputes in court would jeopardize First Amendment values. What a court must do, it was held, is to examine the church rules: if the church is a hierarchical one that requires determination of ecclesiastical issues in a certain body, the resolution by that body is determinative. On the other hand, if the church is a congregational one that prescribes action by a majority vote, that determination will prevail. The Supreme Court did suggest that a court confronted with a church property dispute should apply "neutral principles of law, developed for use in all property disputes," when to do so would not require the court to decide doctrinal issues. In other words, the court should defer to the governing body of the religious body when the First Amendment would be violated by independent review.

Application of neutral principles is only possible when the case can be decided by a review of nonecclesiastical grounds of dispute. [*Presbyterian Church v. Mary Elizabeth Blue Hill Memorial Presbyterian Church* (U.S. 1969); *Maryland and Virginia Eldership of the Churches of God v. Church of God* (U.S. 1970)] However, the Supreme Court views strictly the limits of the inquiry a court might make, holding that an argument over a matter of internal church government—the power to reorganize the dioceses of a hierarchal church in this country—was "at the core of ecclesiastical affairs" and a court could not interpret the church constitution to make an independent determination of the power, but must instead defer to the interpretation of the body authorized to decide. [*The Serbian Eastern Orthodox Diocese v. Milvojevich* (U.S. 1976)]

In *Gonzalez v. Archbishop* (U.S. 1929) the Supreme Court had permitted limited inquiry into the legality of the actions taken under church rules for fraud, collusion, or arbitrariness. Gonzalez was a layman who sued to recover income from a chaplaincy established in trust by a family member a century earlier. Justice Brandeis determined that it was not arbitrary for the defendant archbishop to apply the rules of a 1917 code of canon law that limited such chaplaincies to ordained priests. Justice Brandeis used a contract rationale to justify judicial acceptance of church decisions in the absence of fraud, collusion, or arbitrariness. This reversal of *Watson's* refusal to countenance any review of church decisions incorporates a requirement of good faith and consistent application of church rules by the church courts.

However, in the *Serbian Eastern Orthodox Diocese* case the Court disapproved of this inquiry with respect to concepts of "arbitrariness," although it reserved its decision on the "fraud" and "collusion" exceptions. The Court in *Serbian Eastern Orthodox Diocese* concluded that any inquiry into internal church administration would require an examination of church doctrine and, notwithstanding the rule of *Gonzalez*, could not be justified on a charge of "arbitrariness" because it is the essence of religious faith that ecclesiastical decisions are reached and are to be accepted as matters of faith, whether or not they are rational or reasonable by objective criteria. The "arbitrariness" exception may have been abolished by *Serbian Eastern Orthodox*.

CHURCH OF LATTER-DAY SAINTS V. AMOS (U.S. 1987)

The Supreme Court in this decision exempted religious organizations from Title VII's prohibition of religious discrimination. Title VII of the Civil Rights Act of 1964 prohibits employment discrimination based on an employee's race, color, religion, sex, or national origin. The Court ruled unanimously that religiously affiliated institutional employers have the right to summarily terminate competent, long-service employees. The Deseret Gymnasium was a nonprofit facility open to the public and operated by the Corporation of the Presiding Bishop of the Church of Jesus Christ of Latter-Day Saints (LDS). Both of these were religious entities associated with an unincorporated religious association—the LDS Church. Arthur Frank Mayson worked at the Deseret Gymnasium for approximately 16 years. He was discharged in 1981 because he failed to qualify for a "temple recommend," a certificate that he was a member of the LDS Church and eligible to attend its temples. Mayson alleged that his discharge was unlawful discrimination on the basis of religion. The church maintained that § 702 of Title VII shielded it from liability. This section provides an exemption for religious groups from Title VII. Section 702 states that, "with respect to the employment of individuals of a particular religion to perform work connected with the carrying on by such [religious groups] of its activities."

Mayson argued that if Title VII permitted religious employers to discriminate on religious grounds in their employment of persons for obviously nonreligious, secular jobs, then § 702 of Title VII would violate the Establishment Clause of the First Amendment.

Without dissent, the Supreme Court reversed the decision of the lower federal court, which had found in Mayson's favor. Specifically, the question before the Court was whether the § 702 statutory exemption for churches from Title VII would have the primary effect of unconstitutionally advancing religion in violation of the Establishment Clause. The Court believed that the section did not violate the Establishment Clause. In *Amos*, the Court held that the religious employer exemption applied to employees performing nonreligious as well as religious activities.

The Court reviewed § 702 using the *Lemon* test's three elements: intent, primary effect, and entanglement. The first element, intent, the Court discounted by reasoning that the legislature was attempting "to alleviate significant government interference with the ability of religious organizations to define and carry out their religious missions." The Court explained that the intent "requirement aims at preventing the relevant governmental decision maker ... from abandoning neutrality and acting with the intent of promoting a particular point of view in religious matters." Thus, the Court found the legislative intent was secular, and the first *Lemon* test element was met.

The second element, primary effect, was slightly more difficult for the Court to analyze. The Court took the defensive position, stating that some laws benefit religion, but the benefit is incidental. In addition, because the nonprofit facility was a gymnasium, the Court could not fathom how it would promote religion. Therefore, the religious exemption under the 1964 Civil Rights Act did not have the primary effect of advancing or establishing religion. The Court did not analyze the entanglement element because § 702 did not involve any government interference with religion. The statute was written to prevent this from happening. Thus, the Court held that the exemption for the 1964 Civil Rights Act did not violate the Establishment Clause.

Subsequent decisions by federal courts of appeals continue to follow the *Amos* decision. Religious employers consequently remain free from government regulation with respect to religious and nonreligious jobs alike.

CHURCH PROPERTY   Church property may be defined as anything that is possessed by the church as a corporation or as a moral person. Any property, moveable or immovable, owned by a moral personality created by a religious organization, such as a parish or a religious house. For purposes of exemption from taxation, church property is that used principally for religious worship and instruction. [*Church of the Holy Faith v. State Tax Commission* (N.M. 1935)]

The use or relation of property to the purposes and activities of a church organization determines whether or not the property is "church property" and thus entitled to an exemption from taxation. [*Petition of the Board of Foreign Missions of Augustana Synods* (Minn. 1946)]

A nursing home operated by a church-affiliated nonprofit corporation for the sick and aged was not "church property" for purposes of tax exemption, but where the substantial and primary use was for charitable purposes, the facility was tax exempt. [*Retirement Ranch, Inc. v. Curry County Valuation Protest Board* (N.M. 1976)]

CHURCH RECORDS AND DOCUMENTS   Church records are writings that furnish information, proof, or support of something else, or written accounts of proceedings or activities pertaining to religious organizations qualify as church documents and records. Church documents and records include church registers. A church register is a church parish record of baptism, marriages, and deaths. In the Catholic Church, canon law requires that every pastor keep five distinct books in which are recorded: baptisms, confirmations, marriages, deaths, and the parish census. Copies of all these records, except the parish census, are sent to the diocesan chancery at the end of each year. Marriages of conscience and other secret matters are recorded elsewhere, ordinations are to be recorded alongside the baptismal name. These records are to be kept in a secured location, in a safe if possible.

An important issue concerning church records is whether they may be disclosed in proceedings in courts of law, whether civil or criminal. In some cases the most basic sort of protection against church document discovery may be provided by the subject matter of the litigation in question, since certain subject matters cannot constitutionally be decided by civil courts because of the First Amendment's Free Exercise or Establishment Clause protections. A civil court's exercise of jurisdiction over several different kinds of issues is circumscribed, whether these issues involve church property disputes, the many variations of clergy malpractice cases, or ministerial selection and removal disputes. The Establishment Clause generally provides that civil courts may not resolve disputes over the appointment of clergy or disputes over religious doctrines or teachings. [*Serbian Eastern Orthodox Church v. Milvojevich* (1976)] When disputed religious issues have been resolved by an authoritative ecclesiastical body, the rule is that courts must defer to the resolution of the doctrinal issue made by the appropriate ecclesiastical body. [*Jones v. Wolf* (U.S. 1979)]

The First Amendment in some instances would protect against discovery of church documents and records. In *Word of Faith Outreach Center Church Inc. v. Morales* (WD Tex, 1992), *reversed on other grounds* (5th Cir. 1993), the Texas attorney general sought to apply that state's Deceptive Trade Practices Act to an investigation focusing on claims and statements made in the center's written and broadcast materials. The Fifth Circuit Court of Appeals decided that the attorney general could not constitutionally conduct such an investigation, or obtain those church records and documents, because to do so would violate the Establishment Clause. The court offered several reasons for its conclusion. First, the attorney general would have been obliged to determine which of the center's publications and activities were religious and which were not. Second, there was a concern on the part of the Fifth Circuit that any such investigation could lead to ongoing state monitoring and regulation of the religious activities of the Word of Faith Outreach Center. Third, the attorney general's activities could lead to evaluation of the legitimacy of religious practices themselves. While the opinion in the case did not specifically strike down any particular document production request, the Fifth Circuit referred explicitly to the problematic potential for the review of internal church documents.

In *Rayburn v. General Conference of Seventh day Adventists* (4th Cir. 1985), *cert. den.* (U.S. 1986), a female plaintiff who had been denied a position as pastor at a Seventh-Day Adventist church claimed sex discrimination, and brought a Title VII claim against her church. The court refused to adjudicate the claims based on the Establishment Clause, explaining that to do so would require the court to decide who could minister for the church, which was an inevitably religious question. The court also spoke directly to the document production issue, and wrote that "church records would inevitably become subject to subpoena, discovery, cross-examination—the full panoply of legal process designed to probe the mind of the church in the selection of its ministers." The court concluded that those inquiries would relate to nonjusticiable questions, would create the potential for pervasive monitoring of a religious institution by public authorities, and would infringe upon "precisely those Establishment Clause values at the root of the prohibition of excessive entanglement."

The most obvious source of protection from disclosure of church documents and records may be the state's law of evidentiary privilege. All states have such privileges in place, although there are limits to the applicability of these statutes. Many are clearly oriented to confessions only. Many are totally silent about protecting documents, and extend the privilege only to preclude a clergy person from testifying about what was said to him or her in confidence or in a confessional situation. Such privilege statutes may be unclear as to whom the privilege belongs. Specifically, they may state, and many do, that the privilege belongs only to the individual who is making the statements, and not to the clergy member to whom they are made. These statutes, however, may establish an additional foundation for clergy to demonstrate a legitimate expectation of privacy, as part the proof of a Fourth Amendment or § 1983 claim under the federal Civil Rights Act.

CHURCH SCHOOLS   See GOVERNMENT AID TO RELIGIOUS INSTITUTIONS

CHURCH TRIBUNALS   Church tribunals are judicial bodies within the structure of a church that are charged with adjudicating disputes of an ecclesiastical nature, which are outside the jurisdiction of secular civil courts.

Unlike a congregational church, which is governed by the majority rule of its membership or the decision of an elected group of officers, in a hierarchical church a system of superior church tribunals controls the local church. The U.S. Supreme Court has ruled that the highest church tribunal must resolve internal church disputes. The civil courts must defer to such church decisions when they involve questions of discipline, faith, custom, or belief. [*Watson v. Jones* (U.S. 1872)] This rule is mandated by both the First and Fourteenth Amendments. If a secular court were permitted to reverse the decisions of a church tribunal, the state would subvert the hierarchy and thus undermine an individual's ability to worship freely within that church structure. The law, however, does allow the potential for "marginal civil court review" in cases in which the decision of church tribunals involves fraud, collusion, or arbitrariness. [*Gonzalez v. Roman Catholic Archbishops* (U.S. 1929)] For example, in one case, a constructive trust was found when a party engaged in fraud or misrepresentation and benefitted from unjust enrichment. [*St. Cyprian's Chapel, Inc. v. Fraternity of the Apostles of Jesus and Mary* (E.D. Pa. 1985)] In another case of alleged fraud, *Bjorkman v. Protestant Episcopal Church* (Ky. 1988), the court described constructive trusts as an equitable remedy imposed to redress wrongful conduct by a titleholder who has deprived another party of beneficial ownership. Constructive trusts are limited to situations of fraud or unjust enrichment.

The *Gonzalez* holding was reaffirmed in *Serbian Orthodox Diocese v. Milvojevich* (U.S. 1986), which involved both a church property dispute and the defrockment of a bishop. The Supreme Court further restricted the standard for marginal civil court review set forth in *Gonzalez*, stating that an "arbitrariness" exception to the *Watson* rule is inconsistent with the constitutional mandate that civil courts must accept as binding decisions of church tribunals on matters of "discipline, faith, internal organization, or ecclesiastical rule, custom or law." The Court reasoned that a civil court's determination of whether a particular action by a church tribunal is "arbitrary" inherently entails either inquiry into the procedures that canon or ecclesiastical law supposedly requires the church judiciary to follow, or into the substantial criteria by which they are supposed to decide the ecclesiastical question. "But this is exactly the inquiry that the First Amendment prohibits; recognition of such an exception would undermine the general rule that religious controversies are not the proper subject of civil court inquiry and that a civil court must accept the ecclesiastical decisions of church tribunals as it finds them." The majority's approach likely would preclude a review of the tribunal's decisions, even though the Court could potentially resolve the dispute in a manner different than the church.

One of the legal issues involving church tribunals still being debated is whether the First Amendment prohibits all clergy malpractice actions (including those involving sexual misconduct) when a church tribunal has spoken. Critics of the Supreme Court's jurisprudence believe that it created an unfair level of immunity for hierarchical churches. Justice Rehnquist in his dissent discussed this argument against the deference rule.

CIVIC RELIGION Civic religion, sometimes referred to as public religion or civil religion, is defined as "a set of beliefs and attitudes that explain the meaning and purpose of any given society in terms of its relationship to a transcendent, spiritual reality, that are held by the people generally of that society, and that are expressed in public." Constitutional law has occasionally been regarded as America's unofficial "civic religion." Indeed, constitutionalism seems potentially capable of performing the function of bonding together a nation of diverse peoples, which is the hallmark of a civic religion. Americans feel a reverence for the Constitution that has been deemed almost "religious."

Civic religion may also encompass a uniquely American blend of law, religion, self-improvement, politics, and nationalism. Examples of civic religious observances include the practices of briefly honoring God on public occasions of patriotism.

The concept of a civic religion has found significant support in caselaw that is based on the fact that they are perceived to represent an acknowledgment by the state of the place of religion in our society. When such government recognition of religion is challenged, the courts generally uphold the governmental practices of what are essentially religious ceremonies and displays by invoking history and tradition. The theory is that the sectarian aspects are subsumed by the secular values that can be marshaled to justify the practice.

An alternative to the Supreme Court's current standard is the neutrality standard, which distinguishes between the government's use of religious symbols and private religious displays in otherwise open public forums. Truly private displays would be per se constitutional because they do not involve a government decision to favor or value one religion over other religions or nonreligion.

Even government-sponsored religious displays are unconstitutional "only if the display is based on the view that one or more religions (or religious practices or tenets) are, as such, better than one or more other religion or than no religion at all." [Perry, Michael J. *Religion in Politics: Constitutional and Moral Perspectives* 1997, p. 21] This kind of formal government neutrality approach to the Equal Protection Clause has been rejected by at least five members of the current court: Justices O'Connor, Stevens, Souter, Ginsburg, and Breyer have each authored or joined opinions that interpret the Establishment Clause to apply in situations involving private religious speech that conveys—intentionally or not—a message of government endorsement of religion. Thus, this neutrality standard as a test for public religious displays has not yet been adopted by a majority of the U.S. Supreme Court as of 1997.

▥ **CLERGY** An individual who has special status to administer spiritual counsel and religious instruction and to perform religious ceremonies in the Christian church is a member of the clergy. Prior to the Reformation, which began in 1517, clergy were divided into the regular clergy, who were subject to the rules of a religious order (particularly abbots, priors, and monks), and the secular clergy, who were not subject to such rules (such as bishops, deans, and parsons). The term now includes persons of all branches of the Christian church who have been ordained to the ministry, and of all ranks in hierarchical denomination. Ecclesiastical law of the various religious bodies confers particular powers or privileges, or impose duties or disabilities on clergy, and much of ecclesiastical law is concerned with the discipline of the clergy.

A state may not exclude clergymen (persons who hold an office or official position in a religious organization) from being elected to the state legislature, or from other governmental positions, because that exclusion would impose a disability on these persons based upon the nature of their religious views and their religious status. [*McDaniel v. Paty* (U.S. 1978)]

▥ **CLERGY, BENEFIT OF** Benefit of clergy refers to a privilege allowed under the common law of England to members of the clergy that provided immunity from prosecution by secular authorities for crimes and misdemeanors of which they were accused. Benefit of clergy also existed in American criminal law and the law of some countries in Western Europe. The principle of benefit of clergy developed from the contest between Henry II and Thomas à Becket in 1164 as to who had jurisdiction over clerics accused of crime. At that time an accused who pleaded benefit of clergy could not be punished by a lay court but had to be handed over to church authorities to be tried. In practice, however, church authorities usually released accused clergy members. Later benefit of clergy was available only in cases of felonies. Statutes in the fourteenth century extended the doctrine to secular clerks and probably to anyone who could read. To satisfy themselves of the validity of a claim to benefit of clergy, judges required the accused to read (or recite) the so-called neck verse (Psalm 51, verse 1) of the Bible. This reading test was abolished in 1707.

It was later decided that only persons actually in orders could claim benefit of clergy a second time. Under King Henry VII (1457–1509) it was provided that anyone convicted of a "clergyable" offense should be branded on the thumb, M for murder, or T for theft. Queen Elizabeth I (1533–1603) provided that laymen who relied on benefit of clergy should be liable to imprisonment for no more than a year. Under the Act of 1576, despite a plea of clergy, a convict could be transported for seven years instead of being branded. Originally, only women who were nuns could take advantage of benefit of clergy, but from 1692 all women could do so.

From the sixteenth century on, statutes made various felonies punishable "without benefit of clergy." The neck-verse test was abolished in 1706, branding in 1779, and the principle of benefit of clergy was altogether abolished in England in 1827.

Benefit of clergy was adopted in most of the American colonies by judicial practice. Although generally abolished soon after the American Revolution, it persisted in the Carolinas until the mid-nineteenth century.

CLERGY MALPRACTICE A claim asserting that a member of the clergy should be held liable for professional misconduct or incompetence in his or her capacity as a religious leader and counselor. For various legal and social reasons, claims of clergy malpractice have been relatively fruitless. Court cases since the 1980s have consistently ruled in favor of the defendants.

The claim of clergy malpractice is based on the premise that members of the clergy owe the same kind of duty to persons they counsel as doctors owe to patients or lawyers owe to clients. Most licensed professionals in the secular world (physicians, lawyers, psychologists, and so on) may be held liable for negligence. Clergy members, however, are not licensed as professional counselors, making them generally accountable only to religious standards. Moreover, because the free exercise of religion is protected by the Constitution, courts remain reluctant to apply secular laws to what they perceive as religious matters.

Nally v. Grace Community Church (Cal. 1988) was an early clergy malpractice case in which the parents of 24-year-old Kenneth Nally argued that pastors at Grace Community Church in Sun Valley, California, were liable for his suicide in 1979. Nally's parents maintained that church pastors should have directed him to seek psychiatric care. Instead, they claimed that the pastors may have actually encouraged Nally's suicide by teaching him that taking his own life would not prevent his entrance into heaven.

The ensuing litigation lasted for more than eight years. The final appeal to the California Supreme Court attracted participation from some 1,500 churches and religious organizations in support of Grace Community Church, seeking protection against tort claims under the Free Exercise Clause of the First Amendment. When the California Supreme Court finally dismissed the lawsuit in 1988, however, it did not directly address the First Amendment issue. In a five-to-two opinion the majority held that the clergy in this case did not hold any licenses as counselors and could not, therefore, be held legally liable for failing to provide proper care for the people they advised. The case established the principle that religious counseling need not meet the same legal standards that apply in other professional areas.

Although several courts have reviewed clergy malpractice claims over the years, plaintiffs have largely been unsuccessful. Exceptions include *Sanders v. Casa Baptist Church* (5th Cir. 1998), in which the court held that the Free Exercise Clause does not prevent a church minister from being liable for misconduct as a marriage counselor. In *Amato v. Greenquist* (Ill. App. Ct. 1997), the court ruled that the plaintiff's claim of intentional infliction of emotional distress was viable. The plaintiff alleged that his church pastor acted outrageously in counseling him and seeking to undermine his marriage while the pastor was having an affair with the plaintiff's wife. In another case a pastor was held liable for psychological counselling that led to sexual relations with a parishioner. [*Dausch v. Ryske* (7th Cir. 1994)] However, that case alleged professional malpractice, rather than clergy malpractice, because no cause of action was available specifically for clergy malpractice.

The plaintiffs felt that the reluctance to allow suits alleging clergy malpractice has allowed blatant and damaging acts of misconduct go unpunished. Courts, however, have generally held firm in ruling that the dictates of the First Amendment and the availability of other forms of relief leave little room for judicial resolution of these claims.

In 1996 a New Jersey appellate court became the first to allow malpractice claims against pastors, priests, rabbis, and members of the clergy. [*F. G. v. McDowell* (N.J. App. Ct. 1996)] The new cause of action would have allowed for lawsuits against clergy for sexual misconduct in the course of counseling congregants. In deciding that a claim of clergy malpractice was viable, the New Jersey appellate division court rejected contrary case law and statutes in at least six other states that a clergy malpractice standard, no matter what the claim, would infringe on constitutional free exercise of religion protections. On appeal the New Jersey Supreme Court reversed. While allowing the plaintiff to sue the priest for a breach of fiduciary duty because she placed her trust in him while he counselled her, the state's high court refused to recognize clergy malpractice as a basis to sue, noting that it would entangle the courts in religion and violate the First Amendment to adjudicate such claims. [*F.G. v. McDowell* (N.J. 1997)]

▥ **COMMITTEE FOR PUBLIC EDUCATION AND LIB-**
ERTY V. REGAN (U.S. 1980)   In this case the Supreme
Court upheld, by a five-to-four vote, a state statute reimbursing private
schools for expenses incurred in administering standardized tests and for
other state mandated record keeping and reporting requirements. Writing for the majority, Justice Byron White found that the program had primarily a secular purpose and that its primary effect neither advanced nor
inhibited religion. In this instance the state retained control over the tests,
which "serves to prevent the use of the test as part of religious teaching."
The state mandated services were "ministerial" and "lacking in ideological content or use." Concerns that the program resulted in excessive government entanglement with religion were dismissed because the services
were "discrete and clearly identifiable," and did not require excessive
governmental monitoring. Thus, the promotion of quality nonreligious
education of students in private schools was once again found sufficient
to pass the first prong of the three-part test enunciated in *Lemon v. Kurtz-*
man (U.S. 1971). Under the *Lemon* test, in order for governmental action
to be valid, it must: (1) have a secular legislative purpose; (2) neither advance nor inhibit religion in its primary effect; and (3) not foster an excessive government entanglement with religion. The Court found that
the program did not have a religious effect because it required repayment
for administrative costs connected to specific state-required functions
and, therefore, had virtually no potential for aiding the propagation of religious beliefs.

▥ **COMMON LAW AND CHRISTIANITY**   The common
law is that body of Anglo-Saxon law that originated and developed in England and later spread to the United States and other nations
sharing a British heritage. It differs from code law, which is derived from
ancient Roman law and forms the basis of the legal systems of many
other countries, such as France. Common law differs from statutory law
in that it is made by judges, who decide cases based on customary resolutions of disputes that over the years have become "common" for all
similar cases.

During the nineteenth century American judges and lawyers often
claimed that Christianity was part of the common law. From well-known
treatise writers such as James Kent and Joseph Story in the early part of
the century to Thomas Cooley and Christopher G Tiedeman toward the
end, the maxim that Christianity is part and parcel of the common law (or
some variant thereof) was heard so often that later commentators could
refer to it as a matter arising repeatedly and one that was adopted by both

the treatise writers and the courts. These nineteenth-century commentators asserted that in adopting the common law of England, the American people made Christianity part of their fundamental laws. The maxim even received what could be considered an endorsement from the U.S. Supreme Court, which in 1844 affirmed that "the Christian religion is part of the common law of Pennsylvania." [*Vidal v. Girard's Executors* (U.S. 1844)]

The idea that Christianity was part of the common law rested in part on a belief widely held in the early nineteenth century that the common law had an existence independent of the statements of judges—that it was discovered, not made. It was also believed that the sources of the common law extended well beyond the confines of the legal system. As ideas of the common law slowly altered over the course of the nineteenth century, so did attitudes toward the maxim that Christianity was a part of it.

In the nineteenth century the idea that Christianity was part of the common law was often supported with two related arguments about the nature of the common law. First, it was argued that the common law was derived from Christian principles. Justice Joseph Story, for instance, believed that Christianity lay "at [the] foundations" of the common law and cited a few examples of what he meant (albeit with pronouns that obscured his meaning):

> It [the common law] repudiates every act done in violation of its [Christianity's] duties of perfect obligation. It [the common law] pronounces illegal every contract offensive to its [Christianity's] morals. It [the common law] recognizes with proud humility its [Christianity's] holidays and festivals and obeys them as dies non juridicit. It [the common law] still attaches to persons believing in its [Christianity's] divine authority the highest degree of competency as witnesses.

This sort of argument in support of Christianity as part of the common law was made a few times at midcentury, but drops out of the case reports entirely after the 1850s. Common at midcentury was a related argument consisting of three steps: (1) the common law is nothing more than custom or natural justice; (2) the principles of Christianity are customary, or are consistent with natural justice; therefore (3) Christianity is encompassed by the common law. The argument rests on a nonpositivist (or in retrospect, a prepositivist) view of the common law. To make this argument, one has to understand common law as having an existence independent of the statements of judges and as being drawn from a range of sources much wider than the commands of authorized government officials.

Because the debate over Christianity as part of the common law engaged only lawyers it is misleading to assume that many cases were decided on the basis of the maxim. It is equally misleading to call the maxim the "cornerstone" of any broader conception of the relationship between church and state. No doubt the idea that Christianity was a part of the common law fit into a large cluster of ideas about law and religion. However, if one has to decide which ideas rested upon which, the maxim was more of a stone somewhere near the top of the pyramid. It stayed in place so long as it was supported by one conception of the church-state relationship and one conception of the common law, but when these were replaced by other conceptions, the maxim began to fade.

Twentieth-century judges and lawyers seldom accept that Christianity is no longer a part of the common law. In most cases, they have simply let the maxim fade into disuse.

CONSCIENTIOUS OBJECTOR   A person who is opposed to all war regardless of its cause on the basis of his or her religious training and moral belief is a conscientious objector. Conscientious objection is a widely respected religious practice recognized by such diverse traditions as Christianity, Buddhism, Judaism, and Hinduism. Historically, conscientious objection has been considered mainly in the context of compulsory military service, and specifically in terms of this issue: Should those whose consciences forbid killing be conscripted for combat? The controversy is the classic dilemma between secular obligation and religious duty. Members of pacifist religious sects were the first to raise conscientious objections to military conscription. Pacifism by the late eighteenth century was a mainstream religious doctrine in America. Pacifist religious sects, such as the Quakers, Mennonites, and Brethren, were well represented in early colonial immigration. Many of these religious pacifists had fled from persecution in England and continental Europe. Not surprisingly, these pacifists considered conscientious objection a fundamental right. This right was secured in the colonies that provided for religious freedom, including Rhode Island and Pennsylvania. Colonial charters, especially the Pennsylvania Charter, were used by the Founding Fathers as models for the Free Exercise Clause of the First Amendment to the U.S. Constitution.

The principle that society should excuse conscientious objectors from military service was widely recognized in the colonies and states prior to adoption of the U.S. Constitution. James Madison's original proposal for the Bill of Rights included a clause that "no person religiously scrupulous of bearing arms shall be compelled to render military service in person." That clause was never adopted, partly because conscription was considered a state function. At the time of the original Constitutional Convention in 1789 and the debates on the Bill of Rights, there was no recognition of a federal power to conscript or draft. Instead, the Founding Fathers understood conscription to be a state power over state militias.

The U.S. Constitution does not address conscientious objection. For most of American history Congress freely decided whether to grant any exemption from military service and how to define the class of persons who would benefit. The Civil War period saw the first examples of national conscription and the first affirmation of the concept of exemption from national military service because of religious-based objections to such service. Individual states had enacted conscientious objector exemptions to compulsory service in the militias that, at least arguably, did not require a religious basis to qualify.

After several years of unsatisfactory experience with draft laws that made no provision for Quakers and others having conscientious objections to military service, Congress passed a new draft act in 1864 containing an exemption for members of religious denominations whose religious tenets forbade the bearing of arms and who had conducted themselves in a manner consistent with such beliefs. Furthermore, the exemption applied to combat military service only. Therefore, conscientious objectors were subject to the draft, but served in noncombat roles only.

In 1917 Congress again authorized a draft to support the United States's efforts in World War I. As in the 1864 Draft Act, the Selective Service Act of 1917 contained exemptions limited to members of religious denominations whose creeds forbade participation in war. The 1917 Act excused objectors only from combat service, but the War Department permitted some of those also opposed to noncombat military service to be released for civilian service. To obtain a noncombat assignment, the registrant was required to show membership in a "well-recognized religious sect or organization" whose tenets forbade "participation in war of any form."

Draft boards responsible for classification of registrants, however, were not furnished with any approved list of sects or organizations meeting the legal requirements for conscientious objector status. Of the 2,810,296 men inducted under this draft law, local boards certified 56,830 claims for noncombat service under the conscientious objector exemption. Ultimately, Congress authorized the military to furlough enlisted men from military control and the secretary of war used this authority to furlough conscientious objectors who were against any kind of military service so that they could work in agriculture and industry.

Although the 1917 draft law limited the noncombat exemption to members of pacifist sects, the secretary of war issued a regulation that authorized exempting those men with "personal scruples against war." This was the first and—until the Supreme Court interpreted the exemption broadly beginning in the 1960s—the only example of the federal government granting an exemption to conscientious objectors whose objections may not have been based on religious belief.

America's treatment of conscientious objectors was more enlightened than that of other belligerent nations during World War I. But only members of pacifistic religious groups, perhaps 5,000 of the 21,000 conscientious objectors inducted, qualified for alternative service. Others took up arms or faced prison sentences ranging up to 25 years. An estimated 400 conscientious objectors went to jail, including Roger Baldwin, head of the National Civil Liberties Bureau, which was the precursor of the American Civil Liberties Union. After World War I America returned to all-volunteer armed forces.

The next mobilization requiring conscription occurred when Congress responded to the expanding wars in Europe and Asia by passing the Selective Training and Service Act of 1940. This act set the basic terms of exemption from the system of compulsory military service that operated during World War II, the Korean War, and the Vietnam War, and during the intervening periods of time. The Selective Service Act of 1940 contained four significant changes from the conscientious objector exemptions in prior draft laws:

1. The act extended eligibility for conscientious objector status to persons whose objections were based on "religious training and belief" instead of limiting eligibility to pacifist sects only. With this provision, Congress eliminated the requirement that the conscientious objector be a member of an organized church.
2. The law permitted an applicant to appeal a denial of his claim by the local board.
3. The act authorized alternative civilian service for conscientious objectors so that they never would be inducted into the military.
4. This alternative service was not subject to military control or supervision.

The Selective Service System created by the 1940 Act processed 34,506,923 registrants, of whom approximately 72,000 received, or were eligible for, conscientious objector status.

Under the draft law then in force, conscientious objectors were divided into two classes. One class was composed of those who were found "to be conscientiously opposed" to all military service, no matter if it was combat or noncombat. These individuals were required to "perform alternative civilian service," that is, to serve in civilian work that contributed to the national welfare, such as the Red Cross, but were exempt from military service. The other class was composed of individuals who opposed only combat service. These conscientious objectors were drafted into the armed services for noncombat duty, such as in the medical corps.

During World War II, the 12,000 conscientious objectors who refused to accept noncombat military service were placed in so-called civilian public service camps, where the courts refused to extend the protections of the First and Fifth Amendments. They did not receive pay. Some 5,500 other conscientious objectors were imprisoned, including Jehovah's Witnesses, who claimed exemptions as ministers.

President Truman requested, and Congress approved, the nation's first true peacetime draft in 1948. Responding to a federal court of appeals decision interpreting "religious training and belief" very broadly, the Selective Service Act of 1948 retained the conscientious objector exemption from the 1940 act with the addition of a definition of the requirement that a registrant's conscientious objections derive from "religious training and belief," which added the following: "Religious training and belief in this connection means an individual's belief in a relationship to a Supreme Being involving duties superior to those arising from any human relation, but does not include essentially political, sociological, or philosophical views or a merely personal moral code." What Congress had attempted to do was relatively clear. It wanted to excuse only persons opposed to participation in all wars, not those opposed to a particular war, and it wanted to excuse only those whose opposition derived from religious belief in a rather traditional sense. Subsequent crucial U.S. Supreme Court cases sought to clarify these distinctions.

Although the 1948 Act was amended with the Universal Military Training and Service Act of 1951, that amendment did not change the conscientious objector exemption. Accordingly, the 1948 Act's exemption remained in effect into the era of the United States involvement in the Vietnam War.

By the mid-1960s the nation was deeply involved in military operations in Vietnam, although technically it was at peace. Opposition to the de facto war and the draft grew, however, as manifested by more frequent demonstrations and litigation. Judicial recognition of the Selective Service System's problems also became more frequent and some of these dealt with the issue of the exemption for conscientious objection.

The claim of exemption, under § 6(j) of the Selective Service Act of 1940, required only theistic religious beliefs and training. It would, however, not grant an exemption for a mere "personal moral code." The Court addressed this language in *United States v. Seeger* (U.S. 1965), a case that consolidated the appeals of three men who were denied exemption under § 6(j) on the grounds that their claims were not based upon "belief in a relation to a Supreme Being." Each had expressed skepticism about the existence of a traditional God. Nonetheless, each had described his beliefs in religious terms. Seeger had a "belief in and devotion to goodness and virtue for their own sakes, and a religious faith in a purely ethical creed." The second individual had said he believed in "Goodness," which was the "Ultimate Cause for the fact of the Being in the Universe." The third young man had spoken of "the consciousness of some power manifest in nature, which helps man in the ordering of his life in harmony with its demands."

As defendants in criminal draft evasion proceedings, the three contended that the statutory definition of religious training and belief as an individual's belief in relation to a Supreme Being was unconstitutional. They argued that the statutory definition violated both the Establishment and Free Exercise Clauses of the First Amendment because (1) it did not exempt nonreligious conscientious objectors, and (2) it discriminated between different forms of religious expression.

The Supreme Court, however, refused to take up the constitutional challenge. Instead, it narrowed the question before it to one of statutory interpretation. The issue became one of whether § 6(j) interprets the term "Supreme Being" to mean the orthodox God or the broader concept of a power or being, or a faith "to which all else is subordinate or upon which all else is ultimately dependent?."

Ignoring the legislative history of the 1948 amendment to the draft law, the Court ruled that an applicant who had a "religious faith in a purely ethical creed" was entitled to the exemption because his belief occupied a place in his life parallel to that of a belief in God for the more orthodox. In other words, a conscientious objector claimant need not declare a belief in a Supreme Being as long as the claimant had beliefs that served in the place of an orthodox belief in God. The Court broadly defined the term "Supreme Being" to mean something to which everything else is subordinate. Through a strained interpretation of the statute, the Court avoided a clear decision of whether Congress could limit the exemption to traditional religious believers.

Congress amended the Selective Service Act in 1967 to abolish the requirement that the objector believe in a relationship with a Supreme Being, but retained the exclusion of "essentially political, sociological, or philosophical views or a merely personal code." The 1948 Act, as amended, continues to be the draft law on which the United States' current selective service system is based, but authority to draft registrants under this law expired on 1 July 1973.

In *Welsh v. United States* (U.S. 1970) the Supreme Court was again asked to hold § 6(j) unconstitutional on the grounds that conscientious objector status cannot constitutionally be based upon a religious standard, not matter how liberal that standard is. On his application for exemption,

Elliott Welsh denied that his beliefs were religious and said that he did not know whether he believed in a Supreme Being. He was denied conscientious objector status because the government "could find no religious basis for the registrant's beliefs, opinions, and convictions." The government attempted to distinguish *Welsh* from *Seeger* on two grounds. First, Welsh more insistently denied that his views were religious. The Supreme Court, however, refused to place such "undue emphasis on the registrant's interpretation of his own beliefs." Although a registrant's characterization of his beliefs as religious should carry great weight, his characterization of his beliefs as nonreligious should not because "very few registrants are fully aware of the broad scope of the word *religious* as used in section 6(j)." Second, the government maintained that Welsh's objection stemmed from "essentially political, sociological, or philosophical views or a merely personal moral code." In attempting to devise a new test to apply § 6(f), the Court required an exemption for a claimant regardless of whether his objections rested on religious training or belief, as long as the claimant genuinely believed in pacifism. In a plurality opinion written by Justice Hugo L. Black, in which Justices William O. Douglas, Thurgood Marshall, and William J. Brennan, Jr., joined, the Court reversed Welsh's conviction because it was inconsistent with *Seeger*. Justice Harry A. Blackmun did not participate in the consideration of the case. Justice John M. Harlan concurred in the result reached by the plurality but agreed with the dissenters on the issue of statutory construction. Justice Byron R. White wrote the dissenting opinion, in which Chief Justice Warren E. Burger and Justice Potter Steward joined. Like Justice Harlan, the dissenters disapproved of the literal construction of the statute by the plurality. Unlike Harlan, however, they did not believe that the statute presented a First Amendment problem, and they voted to affirm Welsh's conviction.

The four justices who subscribed to the plurality opinion held that someone who presented no claim to being religious at all qualified because his ethical beliefs occupied a place in his life parallel to that of religious beliefs for others. Four other justices acknowledged that Congress had explicitly meant to exclude such applicants. Justice John Marshall Harlan urged that attempting to distinguish religious objectors from equally sincere nonreligious ones constituted a forbidden establishment of religion. The three other justices thought that Congress could favor religious objectors in order to promote the free exercise of religion. Because the plurality's view of the statute was so implausible, most observers believe that its members probably agreed with Justice Harlan on the ultimate constitutional issue, but this particular controversy between the "no establishment" and the "free exercise" concepts has not yet been decisively resolved.

Ultimately, the Court found Welsh "clearly entitled" to conscientious objector status under its new test for the applicability of § 6(j): "This section exempts from military service all those whose consciences, spurred by deeply held moral, ethical, or religious beliefs, would give not rest or peace if they allowed themselves to become a part of an instrument of war."

Gillette v. United States (U.S. 1971) again raised the issue of selective conscientious objection. Both defendants advanced a religion-based conscientious objection to a particular war, the Vietnam War, but not to "participation in war in any form" as required by § 6(j).

The defendants maintained that the "war in any form" limitation impermissibly discriminated among types of religious belief and affiliation, and that their religious beliefs, which distinguished between just and unjust wars, were as worthy of exemption under § 6(j) and the Establishment Clause as any other religious beliefs.

The Supreme Court held that § 6(j) was neutral on its face, that it "does not single out any religious organization or religious creed for special treatment." The Court also required defendants who claimed that § 6(j) "works to a de facto discrimination among religions," to prove "the absence of a neutral, secular basis for the lines government has drawn."

The Supreme Court found neutral secular reasons for limiting the conscientious objector exemption to those who opposed war in any form. The Court's decision on both religious and nonreligious objectors to the Vietnam War upheld Congress's decision not to exempt those opposed to participation in particular wars. Against the claim that the distinction between "general" and "selective" objectors was impermissible, the Court responded that the distinction was supported by the public interest in a fairly administered system, given the difficulty officials would have in dealing consistently with the variety of objections to particular wars. The Court also rejected the claim that the selective objector's entitlement to free exercise of religion created a constitutionally based right to avoid military service.

The current law remains that a conscientious objector must prove that he opposes any and all wars, and not just a particular war, in order to avoid conscription into the military service. The registrant does not have the right, in other words, to choose between "just" and "unjust" wars. [*United States v. Perdue* (9th Cir. 1970)] Under the Military Selective Service Act (50 U.S.C.A. App. §§ 451 et seq.) a registrant must prove only a "conscientious scruple" against war in all forms to obtain conscientious objector status. The objection must be based on deeply held moral, ethical, and religious convictions. Although this limits the exemption to those persons who object to war for essentially religious reasons, it does not restrict the exemption only to those who participate in organized religion. The test of a religious belief is not measured by traditional religious concepts but rather upon whether the belief is sincere and has an effect on the life of the nonconforming believer that is comparable with or parallel to traditional religious beliefs held by persons who believe in God. The objective truth of the belief is not the standard used to measure the sincerity of the individual claiming conscientious objector status. The test is completely subjective, determined by what the individual actually believes. A military board's skepticism as to the sincerity of an objector's belief is not enough to deny an exemption, although some objective evidence that the belief is sincere may be required.

Although the United States is currently at peace and there is no draft, conscientious objection is not a moot issue. Even in today's all-volunteer armed forces, the issue of conscientious objection can and does arise. Currently, it arises in the case of in-service conscientious objectors. The courts have ruled that even if a person enlists in the military service, that person is not automatically denied the right to later claim conscientious objection. [*United States v. Lauing* (7th Cir. 1955)] United States Department of Defense regulations have provided for those in the Armed Forces to request conscientious objector status since 1951 when it promulgated a directive authorizing reassignments to noncombat duties for soldiers conscientiously opposed to further combat service. In 1962 the Department of Defense issued a superseding directive providing a mechanism for active-duty soldiers possessing religiously based conscientious objections to continued service to either seek transfers to noncombat service or a discharge from the military. The current version of this procedure is a Department of Defense directive codified in the Code of Federal Regulations with implementing regulations in each of the services. Thus, the law creating the in-service conscientious objector program is a product of executive branch rule making, rather than an act of Congress.

Today, a person who seeks a discharge from the armed services based on conscientious objection must satisfy certain tests established by the federal courts. He or she must oppose all forms of war and object to any type of service in the armed forces. Total pacifism, however, is not required. Willingness to use force in self-defense to protect oneself and one's family will not refute a claim of opposition to all war.

The military's current program authorizing applications for reassignments or discharge on the basis of conscientious objections to military service continues the practice of accommodating religious conscientious objections. This program, while separate from the longer history of draft-based conscientious objector programs, draws its basic policy and fundamental standards from that history.

CONTRACEPTION   Commonly called birth control, contraception is anything done to prevent sexual intercourse from resulting in the conception of a child. Both Catholic and Protestant teaching originally rejected contraception as an article of faith. Both justified their opposition based on a literal interpretation of limited but significant biblical sources. The first was that God commanded Adam and Eve in the initial creation narrative to "Be fruitful and multiply and fill the earth." [Genesis 1:28] The second, was when Onan "spilled the semen on the ground," that is, practiced coitus interruptus, and frustrated Levitical law. The judgment of a displeased God was severe and swift: God "slew him." [Genesis 38:8–10] Catholic teaching, following St. Augustine, concluded that Onan's death was due to the sin of contraception. The Eastern Orthodox Church allows married couples to make their own decisions on contraceptive use. Jews, including Orthodox, Conservative, and Reform groups, leave the decision up to individual choice. Most Moslem traditions permit the use of birth control when health reasons are an issue or when the well-being of the family is concerned.

In the nineteenth century, temperance unions and antivice societies led efforts to prohibit birth control in the United States. Anthony Comstock, the secretary of the Society for the Suppression of Vice, advocated a law passed by Congress in 1873. It was entitled the Act for the Suppression of Trade in, and Circulation of Obscene Literature and Articles of Immoral Use, but was known popularly as the Comstock Act. The Comstock Act prohibited the use of the mail system to transmit obscene materials or articles addressing or for use in the prevention of conception, including information on contraceptive methods or devices as well as the birth control devices themselves.

Soon after the federal government passed the Comstock Act, over half the states passed similar laws. All but two of the rest of the states already had laws banning the sale, distribution, or advertising of contraceptives. Connecticut had a law that prohibited even the use of contraceptives—it was passed with little or no consideration of its enforceability.

Despite popular opposition, birth control had its advocates, including Margaret Sanger. In 1916 Sanger opened America's first birth control clinic, in New York City. For doing so, she and her sister Ethel Byrne, who worked with her, were prosecuted under the state's version of the Comstock law in the cases of *People v. Byrne* (N.Y. 1917) and *People v. Sanger* (N.Y. 1917). Both were convicted and sentenced to 30 days in a workhouse.

After serving her sentence, Sanger continued to attack the Comstock Act. She established the National Committee for Federal Legislation for Birth Control, based in Washington, D.C., which sought to achieve a right of reproductive autonomy. The organization proposed the Doctor's Bill, which would have dramatically changed the government's policy toward birth control, by citing the numerous instances in which women had died owing to illegal abortions and unwanted pregnancies. The bill was defeated, due, in part, to opposition from the Catholic Church and other religious groups.

When the issue of Sanger's sending birth control devices through the mail to a doctor was litigated in *United States v. One Package* (S.D.N.Y. 1936), the court ruled that the Comstock Act was not concerned with preventing the distribution of items that might save the life or promote the well-being of a doctor's patients. Sanger had sought to challenge the Comstock Act by breaking it and sending contraceptives in the mail. Her efforts were victorious and the exception was made. The doctor to whom Sanger had sent the device was granted its possession.

Sanger furthered her role in reforming attitudes toward birth control by founding the Planned Parenthood Federation of America in 1942. Planned Parenthood merged previously existing birth control federations and promoted a range of birth control options. In the 1950s Sanger went on to support Dr. Gregory Pincus, whose research eventually produced the revolutionary birth control pill.

By the 1960s, partly as a result of Sanger's efforts, popular and legal attitudes toward birth control began to change. The case of *Griswold v. Connecticut* (U.S. 1965) loosened the restrictions of the Comstock Act. When the Planned Parenthood League of Connecticut opened in 1961 its executive director, Estelle Griswold, faced charges of violating Connecticut's ban on the use of contraceptives. At issue were fundamental principles of individual freedom and rights to privacy within the home.

The Supreme Court, on a seven–to-two vote, overturned Griswold's conviction with a ground-breaking opinion that established a constitutional right to marital privacy. The Court threw out the underlying Connecticut statute, which prohibited both using contraception and assisting or counseling others in its use. The majority opinion, authored by Justice William O. Douglas, looked briefly at a series of prior cases in which the Court had found rights not specifically enumerated in the Constitution—for example, the right of association, which the Court had said is protected by the First Amendment, even though that phrase is not used there. [For example, *NAACP v. Alabama* (U.S. 1959)] Douglas concluded that various guarantees contained in the First, Third, Fourth, Fifth, Ninth, and Fourteenth Amendments, taken together, create "zones of privacy," which include a right of marital privacy. The Connecticut statute that allowed police officers to search a marital bedroom for evidence of contraception was held unconstitutional. The government henceforth had no right to make such intrusions into the marital relationship.

The other branches of the government followed the Supreme Court's lead. President Lyndon B. Johnson endorsed public funding for family planning services in 1966, and the federal government began to subsidize birth control services for low-income families. In 1970 President Richard M. Nixon signed the Family Planning Services and Population Research

Act. This act supported activities related to population research and family planning.

Increasingly, the Comstock Act came to be seen as part of a former era, until in 1971 the essential components of it were repealed. This repeal, however, was not necessarily followed by all the states. In the 1972 case of *Eisenstadt v. Baird* (U.S. 1972), the Supreme Court struck down a Massachusetts law that prohibited the distribution of contraceptives except to married couples. The Court held that the Massachusetts law denied single persons equal protection, in violation of the Fourteenth Amendment.

In the 1977 case of *Carey v. Population Services International* (1977), the Supreme Court continued to expand constitutional protections in the area of birth control. The Court imposed a strict standard of review for a New York law that prohibited anyone but physicians from distributing contraceptives to minors under 16 years of age. The law had also prohibited anyone but licensed pharmacists from distributing contraceptives to adults. *Carey* allowed makers of contraceptives more freedom to distribute and sell them to teenagers.

Although these early decisions of the Supreme Court opened up the sale and distribution of birth control to the general public, they did not address the issue of school distribution of condoms to high school students. In an effort to decrease the spread of AIDS among New York City's teenagers, the New York Board of Education in February 1991 directed high schools to make condoms available to students who requested them. AIDS-awareness classes were also required. Some of the students' parents objected. They claimed that the availability of condoms violated the New York Public Health Law. Condom distribution, the parents said, constituted a health service to minor children without parental consent. Parents also argued that condom distribution violated their free exercise of religion.

In December 1993 New York's Supreme Court, Appellate Division, issued a ruling in favor of the parents, prohibiting distribution of condoms to unemancipated students without prior consent. The court held that the condom distribution program lacked statutory or common law authority, and that it violated the parents' due process rights under the Fourteenth Amendment and the New York Constitution. [*Alfonso v. Fernandez* (N.Y. App. Div. 1993)]

In bringing suit, the parents in *Alfonso* complained that the "condom availability" component of the HIV/AIDS program burdened their free exercise of religion, as forbidden by the United States and New York Constitutions. The parents argued that the availability of condoms "may tempt their children to stray from their religious beliefs." The court, however, held that the availability of condoms to students in public schools does not violate parents' rights to the free exercise of religion because a merely objectionable program does not prohibit parents and/or their children from practicing their religion, "nor does it directly or indirectly coerce them to engage in conducts which are contrary to their religious beliefs." The court found that parents do not have a constitutional right to change public school programs to fit their religious beliefs. Because the students would not face any punishment if they chose not to participate in the condom distribution program, the parents could not successfully claim that their right to practice their religion or their children's right to do the same was violated under the Free Exercise Clause. The court, however, noted that children were not just being exposed to contrary ideas or disagreeable opinions. In dicta, the court suggested that if this were the situation, a due process claim would fail right alongside the free exercise of religion allegation. The court, however, thought that the distribution of condoms engendered more than just an environment that some parents found offensive. The physical availability of condoms went beyond the constitutional limit. Unlike literature or conversation, the school provided students with the means "to engage in sexual activity at a lower risk of pregnancy and contracting sexually transmitted diseases."

In a similar case, in *Curtis v. School Committee of Falmouth* (Mass. 1995), the Massachusetts Supreme Judicial Court granted summary judgment in favor of the school committee when parents alleged that a program of condom availability established in junior and senior high school violated their rights to familial privacy, parental liberty, and free exercise of religion. The court held that the program, which made condoms available to students without parental consent or a parental opt-out provision, did not violate either the fundamental liberty interest of parents to be free from unnecessary governmental intrusion in rearing their children, or the free exercise of religion under the First Amendment. The plaintiff, relying on *Alfonso*, argued that the condom program was coercive. Although participation was voluntary, the program had been implemented in the compulsory setting of the public schools. The Massachusetts court disagreed with the reasoning of the *Alfonso* court and stated that *Alfonso* was erroneously decided. Citing the dissent from *Alfonso*, the *Curtis* court held that no coercive burden on parental liberty existed because no classroom participation was required of students. Students were not required to seek out and accept the condoms, read the literature accompanying them, or participate in counseling regarding their use. The program did not qualify as state action of a coercive or compulsory nature, and did not constitute a viable claim under the Fourteenth Amendment.

Similar cases have been brought throughout the United States. The school boards of San Francisco, Seattle, and Los Angeles all disagreed with the New York court, and authorized the distribution of condoms to students. As a general rule, however, court decisions established that, although parents have no control over the public school curriculum, they may reserve the right to withdraw their children from classes on birth control and AIDS prevention.

🏛 **CRIMINAL CONDUCT**   In general, the Free Exercise Clause of the Constitution does not require exemptions from criminal laws or other governmental regulations for people whose religious beliefs prevent them from conforming their behavior to the requirements of the law. In other words, a law that regulates the conduct of all persons equally may also be applied to people who maintain that their religious beliefs prevent them from complying. The Free Exercise Clause cannot be used to challenge a law of general applicability, unless it can be shown that the law was motivated by a desire to interfere with religion. [*Employment Division v. Smith* (U.S. 1990)]

Although states may recognize religious practice exemptions from drug laws of general applicability, such exemptions are not required by the Constitution. Thus a state could constitutionally deny unemployment compensation benefits to Native Americans who were dismissed from drug counseling positions because of their sacramental use of the drug peyote in the Native American Church. Use of peyote was illegal under the state of Oregon's criminal laws. [*Employment Division v. Smith* (U.S. 1990)] Despite this, however, the U.S. Supreme Court has upheld the reversal of convictions of members of the Amish faith for violating a state's compulsory school attendance law requiring children to go to school until the age of 16. [*Wisconsin v. Yoder* (U.S. 1972)]

🏛 **CULT**   The term *cult* is currently used to designate a particularly unpopular and feared new religious group, often claiming a personal relationship between its leader and the divinity. Among the most prominent of these groups in recent times have been the Unification Church, the Worldwide Church of God, Inc, the Church of Scientology, and the International Society for Krishna Consciousness.

Cults, which have experienced varying degrees of discrimination and persecution by law enforcement officials, have consistently claimed that the Constitution does not sanction legal distinctions between them on the one hand and long-established and respected faiths on the other. They also argue that most of the now well-established and fully respected faiths, including the Baptists, Roman Catholics, Jews, Mormons, Christian Scientists, and Jehovah's Witnesses had been branded as cults and/or subjected to governmental discrimination in the early days of their existence.

Lower federal court and state court religious exemption cases almost always have involved members of small and nontraditional religions. Reported cases also support the argument that small and unfamiliar religions consistently receive less favorable treatment from elected officials than popular and well-known religions. Indeed, cases involving explicit discrimination against nontraditional religions have continued to surface. In the *Church of the Lukumi Babalu Aye, Inc. v. City of Hialeah* (U.S. 1993), for example, the U.S. Supreme Court invalidated a series of Hialeah, Florida, ordinances that prohibited ritual animal sacrifices, which were an essential part of a certain nontraditional religion's manner of worship.

The claim to equal treatment by a nontraditional religious group, the Unification Church, was upheld in *Larson v. Valente* (U.S. 1982) in which the U.S. Supreme Court held unconstitutional a Minnesota statute that imposed special registration and reporting requirements upon religions that received more than half of their income from nonmembers—a provision the court found to have been aimed at unpopular cults. This provision, the Court said, constituted precisely the sort of denominational preference and discrimination forbidden by the Establishment Clause in the absence of a compelling interest not otherwise amenable to protection. Moreover, the statute also violated the Establishment Clause by authorizing excessive governmental entanglement with and politicizing of religion.

In discussing nontraditional religion, it is worth recalling that the U.S. Constitution protects the liberty of conscience in order to protect the individual from coercion and discriminatory treatment by church or state officials and guarantees unencumbered, voluntary choices of faith. Free exercise of religion protects the individual's ability to discharge the duties of conscience through religious worship, speech, publication, assembly, and other actions without necessary reference to a prescribed creed or code of conduct. American pluralism protects multiple forms and forums of religious belief and action, in place of a uniformly mandated religious doctrine.

D

DAVIS V. BEASON (U.S. 1890)   This case involved an Idaho territorial statute directed at the practice of polygamy. The law required voters to foreswear membership in any organization that "teaches, advocates, counsels or encourages" its members to undertake polygamous relationships. Davis was convicted of swearing falsely.

Justice Stephen J. Field, speaking for the U.S. Supreme Court, saw the case as identical to *Reynolds v. United States* (U.S. 1879). The Free Exercise Clause of the First Amendment protects religious beliefs, not acts that prejudice the health, safety, or good order of society as defined by the legislature governing under its police power. Field concluded that if something is a crime, then to teach, advise, or counsel it cannot be protected by evoking religious tenets.

The decision became one of the principal underpinnings of what later came to be called the secular regulation approach to the Free Exercise Clause, whereby no religious exemptions are required from otherwise valid secular regulations.

DEFENSE OF MARRIAGE ACT (DOMA)   Three homosexual couples in Hawaii who sought to be legally married triggered a legal and political controversy in 1993, which eventually led Congress to enact a bill restricting same-sex marriages. The three couples challenged Hawaii's refusal to provide marriage licenses to same-sex couples under § 572–1 of the Hawaii Revised Statutes, which restricts marital relations to a male and a female. The Hawaii Supreme Court ruled that because the Hawaii constitution forbids discrimination on the basis of sex, Hawaii could justify § 572–1 only by showing a compelling state interest for barring same-sex marriages that was narrowly drawn to achieve those ends. On remand to the Circuit Court of Hawaii, Judge Kevin Chang ruled decisively in favor of the plaintiffs on 3 December 1996. [*Baehr v. Lewin* (Haw. 1993)]

Although the *Baehr* ruling covered only one state, its implications were national. Under the Full Faith and Credit Clause of the U.S. Constitution (Article IV, Section 1), states are obliged to honor the legal proceedings of other states, including marriages.

Some observers argued that the states could refuse to acknowledge gay marriages sanctioned outside their borders. The prevailing opinion, however, was that a marriage deemed valid in Hawaii would have to have been recognized as valid in the 49 other states.

The same clause of the U.S. Constitution also allowed Congress to regulate aspects of the states' reciprocal legal arrangements, although it was not clear how far that power went. With that in mind, two Republicans with close ties to social conservatives—Representative Bob Barr of Georgia and Senator Don Nickles of Oklahoma introduced similar bills in May 1996 to allow states to refuse recognition of same-sex marriages performed legally in other states. The law that resulted from these bills is known as the Defense of Marriage Act (DOMA).

Supporters of DOMA said the statute was needed to combat what they described as a radical effort to broaden the traditional concept of marriage. Representative Charles Canady (R-Fla) said, "What is at stake in this controversy? Nothing less than our collective moral understanding . . . of the essential nature of the family."

Proponents also contended that legalizing gay marriages would send children a message that homosexuality was appropriate, drawing them away from traditional heterosexual relationships. One supporter, Republican Bob Inglis of South Carolina, even suggested that loosening the definition of marriage might ultimately lead to the legalization of polygamy.

Majority Leader Senator Trent Lott (R-Miss) defended the bill and its proponents, asserting, "This is not prejudiced legislation. . . . It is a preemptive measure to make sure that a handful of judges in a single state cannot impose a radical social agenda upon the entire nation."

President Clinton signed the Defense of Marriage Act into law on 21 September 1996. Section 2, entitled "Powers Reserved to the States," on the issue of same-sex marriages states:

No State, territory, or possession of the United States, or Indian tribe, shall be required to give effect to any public act, record, or judicial proceeding of any other State, territory, possession, or tribe respecting a relationship between persons of the same sex that is treated as marriage under the laws of such other State, territory, possession, or tribe, or a right or claim arising from such relationship.

Section 3 of DOMA, entitled "Definition of Marriage," states that:

In determining the meaning of any Act of Congress, or of any ruling, regulation, or interpretation of the various administrative bu-
reaus and agencies of the United States, the word "marriage" means
only a legal union between one man and one woman as husband
and wife, and the word "spouse" refers only to a person of the opposite sex who is a "husband or a wife."

While the passage of DOMA was a major victory for social conservatives, a key Republican constituency, opponents of the law question its
constitutionality, focusing on possible effects of the legislation. For example, does it violate the Equal Protection Clause of the Constitution by excluding homosexuals from a benefit—marriage—bestowed by the state?
Does it transgress the constitutional requirements of the process? Does it
grant states a power they did not already possess—namely, the power to
ignore extraterritorial marriages? Article IV, Section 1 of the Constitution
requires each state to give "full faith and credit" to the public acts, records,
and judicial proceedings of every other state. Thus, a marriage legally contracted in one state must usually be recognized in all other states.

More pertinent to the issue of religion and the law, many critics of
DOMA have cast the constitutionality question in terms of the Act's intent. If the law has a "religious" intent it may well violate the Establishment Clause of the Constitution. As currently interpreted, the Establishment Clause forbids the government to give preference to any particular
religion, or to religion in general. According to the text of the Act,
DOMA's purposes are to "define and protect the institution of marriage:
where marriage is intended to exclude same-sex partners." Thus, to be
constitutionally valid under the Establishment Clause, the notion that
heterosexual marriages require "protection" from gay and lesbian persons must spring from a secular and not a religious source. Critics of
DOMA argue that the Act crosses this forbidden line between the secular
and the religious.

DOMA's opponents criticized the statute as "plainly religious" in both
scope and purpose in the minds of its sponsors. In the House of Representatives supporters of DOMA frequently made references to religious
teachings regarding marriages, even going so far as to read from the
Bible. Representatives argued that traditional heterosexual marriage has
been preferred by every religious tradition in recorded history, with some
calling marriage a "covenant established by God." Similar appeals to religious teachings as the source of the marriage tradition warranting
DOMA protections were made in the Senate, with frequent references to
the "holy estate of matrimony" and the "sanctity of marriage." Democratic Senator Bill Bradley (D-NJ) argued that "marriage is, first of all, a
predominantly religious institution."

DOMA's critics charge that the law was clearly a government "entanglement" with religion. Representative Jesse L. Jackson (D-Ill) warned that "religious groups may not govern who receives a civil marriage license . . . [W]hen I came to Congress, I placed my hand on the Bible and swore to uphold the Constitution, now I am being asked to place my hand on the Constitution and uphold the Bible." Representative Barney Frank (D-Mass), who organized and led opponents against DOMA, objected to the characterization of marriage as a sacrament. "We have no power to give anyone any sacraments. We are not in the business of dispensing sacraments, and I hope we never get there." Senator Charles Robb, a Democrat from Virginia, reminded his peers that "at its core marriage is a legal institution officially sanctioned by society through its government."

Opponents of DOMA in both the House and the Senate criticized its "political motivation" as designed to embarrass those who consistently supported the rights of gay and lesbian citizens. Opponents particularly criticized the bill as an attempt to embarrass President Bill Clinton shortly before the 1996 November general election. The president was faced with the dilemma of vetoing it in accordance with his long-standing belief in protecting the civil liberties of gay citizens, but by so doing alienating a large constituency who believed homosexuality to be morally wrong. Or, he could sign the bill and thereby repel another solid constituency. Thus, Clinton could not veto DOMA without endangering his chances for reelection. Clinton sought the path of minimal cost and in the middle of the night signed DOMA into law.

One unresolved issue is the constitutionality of DOMA. Generally, to have standing to bring a lawsuit challenging the constitutionality of a law, one must have suffered personal harm. Because as yet no one can marry a same-sex partner in any state, the provisions of DOMA do not impact a single individual. Only after at least one state legalizes gay unions, and after members of those unions are denied federal benefits or recognition in other states, could one imagine a first viable challenge to DOMA.

If an Establishment Clause claim against DOMA were brought, a court would apply the standards established in *Lemon v. Kurtzman* (U.S. 1971) and *Edwards v. Aguillard* (U.S. 1987). Under those tests DOMA would have to have a primary and sincere secular purpose to be valid. *Aguillard* indicated six places to look to ascertain that purpose, including the text of the statute, its legislative history, and the historical and social context out of which it arose.

DOMA opponents argue that the statute has no true secular purpose. Instead, they believe that DOMA symbolizes legislative support for fundamentalist Christianity, referring to the legislative history, which records the religious motivations of the bill's sponsors and supporters. The definition of "marriage" that DOMA seeks to defend comes from the fundamentalist Christian tradition. DOMA supporters clearly envision marriage as a religious practice, and often go so far as to deny any credible role of government in its regulation at all. As such, DOMA's goal to protect marriage was criticized as a transparent effort to foster one particular religious perspective on families. Moreover, while § 2 of DOMA grants no new powers and thus functions solely as a religious symbol, the operation of § 3 of DOMA is flatly underinclusive relative to its alleged secular goals.

Finally, DOMA's critics assert that the antigay animosity, of which DOMA is an undeniable manifestation, and religious fundamentalism are so tightly intertwined that the one implicates the others. Critic's cite DOMA for failing the *Aguillard* test, which determines whether stated secular purposes are valid or not, and assert that the Act is an "unconstitutional establishment of fundamentalist Christianity."

DEPROGRAMMING CASES   Deprogramming is the name given to a practice whereby putatively "brainwashed" adherents of new religious movements (or cults) were physically abducted, forcibly constrained, and subjected to counterindoctrination. Two involuntary methods were employed: (1) simple abductions without prior legal authorization (but legally defended after the fact through the defense of necessity); and (2) authorized actions under state law, usually in the form of temporary guardianship or conservatorship orders granted by courts (often in ex parte hearings) to relatives of adherents. The deprogramming controversy emerged in the 1970s.

Deprogramming under the aegis of guardianship or conservatorship orders rapidly disappeared after cases such as *Katz v. Superior Court* (Cal. 1977). In that case a California superior court judge initially awarded five sets of parents 30-day custody over their adult children, who were affiliated with the Unification Church, for purposes of conducting deprogramming. An appeal by the five Unificationists resulted in a ruling by an appellate court forbidding the parents from engaging in deprogramming activity prior to a review of the constitutionality of the conservatorship laws. A few weeks later a court order was issued dismissing the temporary conservatorships and releasing the five individuals from custody. The court ruled that "in the absence of such actions as render the adult believer gravely disabled . . . the process of this state cannot be used to deprive the believer of his freedom of action and to subject him to involuntary treatment." The court suggested that when it was asked to determine whether a change of religious attitude "was induced by faith or by coercive persuasion, [was] it not investigating and questioning the validity of that faith?"

Although a binding precedent only in California, this case appears to have discouraged the use of conventional guardianship and conservatorship statutes to legalize the involuntary deprogramming of devotees who could not be found "gravely disabled."

Coercive deprogramming has been legally costly for some deprogrammers. One case involving Rick Ross, as the chief defendant, along with the well-known Cult Awareness Network (CAN). Ross is perhaps the best known contemporary deprogrammer in the United States. A member of an evangelical Protestant group who was the target of a deprogramming sued Ross and CAN, which allegedly conspired with Ross in the deprogramming. A jury found the defendants liable and awarded over $5 million to the plaintiff. After the verdict, CAN declared bankruptcy and ceased operations. [*Scott v. Ross* (W.D. Wash. 1995)]

The anticult movement has retreated from espousing coercive deprogramming. Professional therapists, who became an increasingly powerful component of the movement, were unwilling to accept abducted individuals as clients and deprogrammers discovered that voluntary forms of deprogramming were as effective as coercion in many cases. Still, coercive deprogramming persists, and it is not easy for deprogrammees to obtain remedies in civil or criminal courts. As juries tend to sympathize with troubled families who have "lost" a member to a "cult" and there is reluctance to interfere in "family matters," the prospects of prosecutions and civil actions against deprogrammers and relatives who have employed them remain indeterminate.

DISCRIMINATION   *See* RELIGIOUS DISCRIMINATION

DISESTABLISHMENT   The severance of the connection between a particular religion and the state, removing its privileged legal status and reducing it to the level of a voluntary association is termed *disestablishment*.

Church-state understandings in the United States had their origins in the colonial period between 1607 and 1776. The law of this period reflected growing freedom arising from the colonists' adjustment to New World opportunities. The colonists had always to contend with the Church of England and English religious policy. Great diversity came out of the experience in the three major regions, the southern, middle, and New England colonies, which were to some extent distinct cultural groups, and this impacted their policy on establishment of religion. For example, the New England colonies generally supported a Congregational Church, while middle Atlantic and southern colonies had Episcopal establishments.

By the time of the American Revolution, physical persecution of religious dissenters had ended, and a measure of toleration existed. Yet 10 of the original 13 colonies (the exceptions were Rhode Island, Pennsylvania, and Delaware) continued to prefer and support one religion over all others. That church by law enjoyed the status as an established church. The American War for Independence was the occasion, if not the cause, of disestablishment in the 13 colonies (now states), and it is one of most interesting questions of the era whether causal relationship is more appropriately reversed—that is, to what extent the conflict was one between American dissenters and Anglican establishmentarians in England. There is much historical evidence that by disestablishment in the South, the patriot leadership hoped to enlist dissenters in the war efforts. The dissenters, in turn, recognized wartime as a perfect opportunity to gain equality from the tidewater gentries. Disestablishment was, in any event, a multifaceted reality, but not among its realities was hostility to state support of religion. The erosion of the preferential position of the established church lasted from the Revolution to the mid-nineteenth century, when for the first time in Western history, church and state were completely separated.

The states granted religious freedom of their own volition, since the federal government was without jurisdiction over a state's internal affairs (and this was the period before the First Amendment was incorporated and applied to the states. [*Permoli v. New Orleans* (U.S. 1845)] The disestablishment of state churches was the result of several factors: (1) The argument voiced by establishment proponents that religion and ultimately the state would die out without the continued support of the government was dramatically proven false by the growth of religion in states without established churches such as Rhode Island and Pennsylvania; (2) with the ease resulting from their wealth and legally secured position, the established churches had become stagnant, obtained few converts, and lacked fervent congregations, that would energetically oppose disestablishment; (3) as immigration to the New World increased and the dissenting churches gained more converts, the established groups become the political minority; and (4) the Bill of Rights, even though legally inapplicable to the states, added impetus to the disestablishment process by emphasizing individual liberties.

There has never been a federally established church. In the Articles of Confederation, there is only one reference to religion. Each state is guaranteed the assistance of its sister states if attacked "on account of religion." The Articles only maintained the status quo.

When the Constitutional Convention met in Philadelphia in 1787, the practical needs of the situation as much as the political and philosophical theories of the day demanded that only few, if any, references be made to religion. By 1789 the states were well on their way to religious freedom. To interfere with this development by establishing a federal church would have jeopardized the new union. Accordingly, Article VI of the new document proscribed a religious test of office.

In the state conventions called to ratify the Constitution, a desire for even stronger guarantees of religious liberty was articulated by the delegates. Whether a state still retained its own establishment or not, its delegates demanded that the federal government, if only to preclude encroachment on the privileges of the state establishment, should not establish a federal religion, but rather was required to remain impartial in that matter and to attend to its civil business.

Responding to this public sentiment, the First Congress drafted a Bill of Rights, ratified by the states in 1791, which in part declared that "Congress shall make no law respecting an establishment of religion, or prohibiting the free exercise thereof." Both Article VI and the religious guarantees of the First Amendment applied only to the federal government. [*Barron v. Mayor of Baltimore* (U.S. 1833)] In 1940 the U.S. Supreme Court extended the protection of the Fourteenth Amendment to guarantee religious freedom against state action. *Cantwell v. Connecticut* (U.S. 1940). This process is called incorporation.

DIVISIVENESS DOCTRINE   One of the Supreme Court's abiding concerns in adjudicating claims under the religion clauses of the First Amendment has been to avoid what it calls "political divisiveness," which can arise when one religion is seen as receiving favored treatment from the state. Without a complete separation of religion and government, political factions are "bound to divide along religious lines, one of the principal evils against which the First Amendment was intended to protect," said the Supreme Court in *Everson v. Board of Education* (U.S. 1947). Therefore courts enforcing the constitutional command of nonestablishment should defuse explosive issues by settling them judicially, before sectarian tensions arise.

Justice Robert H. Jackson opined in *Everson* that the First Amendment "above all" was to "keep bitter religious controversy out of public life by denying access to public influence." The end of such strife, Justice John Rutledge wrote in the same case, will either be domination by the strongest sect or constant turmoil and dissension engulfing the entire society. Justice Hugo Black, author of the majority opinion in *Everson*, wrote in 1968 that the Establishment Clause "was written on the assumption that state aid to religion . . . generates discord, disharmony, hatred, and strife among our people." Justice Rutledge continued in *Everson* that "public money devoted to payment of religious costs . . . brings the quest for more. It brings to the struggle of sect against sect for the largest share or for any." Justice John M. Harlan, II, observed in 1970 that "political fragmentation on sectarian lines must be guarded against" and expressly deputized "voluntarism" and "neutrality" as humble servants of this paramount concern. The seminal *Lemon v. Kurtzman* (U.S. 1971) opinion fully explained:

> Ordinarily political debate and division, however vigorous or even partisan, are normal and healthy manifestations of our democratic system of government, but political division along religious lines was one of the principal evils against which the First Amendment was intended to protect. The potential divisiveness of such conflict is a threat to the normal political process. . . . The history of many countries attests to the hazards of religions intruding into the political arena or of political power intruding into the legitimate and free exercise of religious belief.

The Supreme Court has held that the potential for political divisiveness alone can not serve to invalidate otherwise permissible conduct. [*Lynch v. Donnelly* (U.S. 1984); *Mueller v. Allen* (U.S. 1983)] Justice O'Connor wrote in her concurring opinion in *Lynch* that, although several "Supreme Court cases have discussed political divisiveness under the entanglement prong of the *Lemon* test, the Supreme Court has never relied on divisiveness as an independent ground for holding a government practice unconstitutional. Guessing the potential for political divisiveness inherent in a government practice is simply too speculative an enterprise, in part because the existence of the litigation itself may affect the political response to the government practice. Political divisiveness is admittedly an evil addressed by the Establishment Clause. Its existence may be evidence that institutional entanglement is excessive or that a government practice is perceived as an endorsement of religion. The constitutional inquiry, however, should focus ultimately on the character of the government activity that might cause such divisiveness, not on the divisiveness itself."

Divisiveness, of course, can attend any state action respecting religions, and neither its existence nor its potential necessarily invalidates the state's attempts to accommodate religion in all cases. [*Lee v. Weisman* (U.S. 1992)]

The political divisiveness doctrine has been criticized because it has armed opponents of religious interests with a potent weapon: their mere opposition becomes a basis for a finding of unconstitutionality. Of course, the political victories of either side in such controversies could be divisive; but the doctrine did not—and could not—work both ways. In effect, critics say, the doctrine results in blaming the religious side of any controversy for the controversy.

DIVORCE   Divorce is the dissolution of a marriage, other than by death, normally permitting each party to remarry. The religious authority of a country or the convictions of the parties may forbid divorce, but its possibility is increasingly being recognized in the Western world. The degree and kind of formalities required also varies, down to the case of divorce at will or by consent.

In the United States, each state and the District of Columbia has the power to regulate domestic relations within its borders. Divorce laws in most states have nonetheless evolved to recognize the difference between regulating the actual decision to divorce and regulating the practical ramifications of such a decision, such as property distribution, support obligations, and child custody. Most courts ignore marital fault in determining whether to grant a divorce, but many still consider fault in setting future obligations between the parties. To determine the exact nature of the rights and duties related to a divorce one must consult the relevant statutes for the state in which the divorce is filed.

Many major religions have extensive regulations and structures governing divorce. In the Christian tradition, the Roman Catholic Church provides the most thorough regulations on divorce. Well over one hundred canons, as Catholic regulations are called, address issues of marriage and ecclesiastical marriage courts. For Catholics marriage is a sacrament, something that imparts grace to the couple and glorifies God. The essential properties of marriage are unity and indissolubility, thus leaving no option for "divorce" in the modern sense of that term.

The absence of a divorce provision in canon law does not render unhappy Catholic couples devoid of any solution. There are three alternatives for Catholic couples who cannot fulfill their "duty and right" to maintain conjugal cohabitation:

1. The couple may separate. Several situations may justify a separation, including adultery, endangerment of the physical person or the spirit of a spouse or child, and rendering common life together too difficult. In cases of separation, the couple remains married in the eyes of the Church.
2. The couple may seek to have the marriage bond dissolved. Marital dissolution through the authority of the Church alone may

occur (a) if the marriage was never consummated by sexual intercourse, (b) in instances of the Pauline Privilege, or (c) through decree of the pope in favor of the faith, in a marriage between a baptized and a nonbaptized person.

3. The parties may seek an annulment from the ecclesiastical authorities. An annulment has the effect of declaring that there never was a valid, recognizable marriage according to the Church. Parties may choose to remarry after receiving an annulment (though "remarriage" is an odd term, because an annulment declares that there never was a valid marriage). Annulment may be sought on a number of grounds, including the presence of a diriment impediment, a defect of consent, or a lack of canonical form. All of these grounds for annulment are present (or not present) before the marriage ceremony. That is, there are more numerous procedures for entering valid marriages in the Catholic Church, which serve to counterbalance the increased difficulties of exiting a marriage.

Because the civil courts in the United States govern divorce law, Catholic couples may marry and divorce with impunity according to the civil law. They must, however, follow the prescriptions and proscriptions of the canon law if they desire to be in full communion with the Church. Thus, many Catholic couples wanting to end their marriages seek a civil divorce, but approach the ecclesiastical tribunals seeking an annulment. The judges and other tribunal personnel must follow careful guidelines set forth in several canons. While their decision regarding the validity of the marriage is binding as it pertains to marriage within the Catholic Church, their decision is not binding on the civil courts—in the spirit of the canon laws' claim that proper jurisdiction of marriage cases lies with ecclesiastical judges, and not civil judges. Thus, while the Roman Catholic Church has established and developed an elaborate system for marriage questions, it is barred from using that system to the fullest effect by the prevailing legal structures and lack of jurisdictional pluralism.

Judaism's long history and continuing vitality provides a helpful lens through which to view the interrelationship of the religious authorities and the civil authorities. When a Jewish couple gets married, the bride and groom sign a *ketubah*, or "writing." This signifies the validity of the marriage contract within the Jewish community. After marriage, the ketubah becomes the sole property of the wife. Its exclusiveness to the wife is for historical reasons: it is to discourage the husband from exercising what was his unilateral and unconditional power to divorce his wife. A procedure called a *get* was created to lessen the potential capriciousness of husbands who wanted to divorce. A get is a formal written document signifying and stating the husband's desire to divorce. The get process must conform to certain formal and technical rules; the standardization of this process was supposed to provide protection to the woman by making it harder for a husband to divorce his wife.

Even with the institution of the get, Jewish women are somewhat at the whim of their husbands, for the husband may be divorced only according to "his free will." This prerogative of the husband sometimes evolves into a situation in which a recalcitrant husband refuses to issue a get to his wife. Without a get, a Jewish woman cannot remarry according to Jewish law, and she becomes an *agunah*, or "chained woman."

Traditionally, rabbis have exerted various social pressures on recalcitrant husbands to encourage them to issue a get. These methods ranged from public declarations in the synagogue to social excommunication and banishment from the community. These pressures met moderate success when Jewish communities were fairly independent entities with virtually complete control over their internal affairs. However, in an age of increasing technology, mobility, and less isolation for most Jewish communities, these methods rarely effect the desired result. The problem is especially acute among the Orthodox community, which has not accepted some of the solutions read into Jewish law by Conservative communities. Only recently have Orthodox communities begun to discuss and attempt to deal with this insidious problem. In one effort to address the problem of recalcitrant husbands, the Orthodox rabbinate turned to the secular government for assistance. In 1983 New York passed a law permitting courts to withhold a civil divorce until all barriers, specifically including "any religious or conscientious restraint or inhibition . . . imposed on a party to a marriage, under the principles held by the clergyman or minister who has solemnized the marriage, by reason of the other party's commission or withholding of any voluntary act," are cleared— thus encompassing the agunah problem. The New York legislature expanded the law in 1992 to permit civil judges to consider a husband's refusal to issue a get when deciding distribution of marital assets.

The New York statutes have not solved the dilemma, however, and their constitutionality is often debated. Moreover, many Orthodox feminists disdain the efforts to rely on secular authorities. These women, many of whom have been deeply involved in the struggle on behalf of agunot, regard reliance on secular authorities as a concession that Jewish law is incapable of ensuring justice for Jewish women.

One promising solution from internal Jewish law is the use of a premarital agreement in which the husband commits to maintain and support his wife until the marriage is properly terminated. Both spouses then agree to let the rabbinical court adjudicate any attempts to dissolve the marriage. There is judicial precedent for legal recognition of such agreements: secular courts, in honoring the prenuptial agreement of the parties, affirm the authority of the Beth Din (the Jewish Court) to exercise oversight and regulation in these cases. In one well-known example, *Avitzur v. Avitzur* (NY 1983), a Conservative Jewish couple had signed a modified ketubah that required the appearance before the Beth Din at the request of either spouse (which would effectively force the husband to give his wife a get). A divided New York Court of Appeals ruled the ketubah was a valid prenuptial agreement and not violative of public policy under the First Amendment.

Although much more common in Conservative Judaism, Orthodox Judaism has also began advocating prenuptial agreements to prevent future agunah cases. The Rabbinical Council of America (the organization of Orthodox rabbis) has adopted and promulgated a standardized prenuptial agreement, which is regarded as the single most important step that Jewish couples can take before they get married. The purpose of drafting the agreement was to eliminate most future cases of agunah with the use of the prenuptial agreements. These prenuptial agreements provide a method whereby parties agree to internal religious resolution of marital disputes, but the agreement itself is enforceable by the external authorities.

The prenuptial option prevents the secular courts from becoming enforcers of religious doctrine, for it allows couples voluntarily choose their forum for dispute resolution. The civil court simply enforces the wishes of the parties to be governed by Jewish law in a Jewish court. The free exercise rights of the individuals are respected by allowing them to remain true to their religious convictions and by allowing for dispute resolution in a religious forum. The free exercise rights of the group are respected, as the Beth Din is empowered to resolve the disputes of its adherents. Establishment Clause problems are avoided, because the government is not forcing any person into a choice of law or forum that he or she did not voluntarily choose, and the government is not advocating one law or forum over the other.

In the Islamic tradition, marriage is basically seen as a contract, absent the Christian notions of sacrament. But it is unique in that it is an "adhesion contract," with terms dictated by the legislature (and not subject to any contrary agreement by the parties), and that it mostly regulated by religious jurisdiction (to preserve its sanctity), even though it is civil in nature. The marriage must be contracted in the presence of witnesses, the parties must not violate degrees of affinity, kindred, or fosterage, the proper form must be followed, and there must be no religious difference between the parties.

Once marriages are validly contracted, they may be dissolved during the lifetime of the parties in one of three ways:

1. The most common method of divorce is by the husband exercising the right of *talaq*, or "repudiation." The *Shari'ah*, the law of God, defines this as "the dissolution of a valid marriage contract forthwith or at a later date by the husband, his agent, or his wife duly authorized by him to do so, using the word *talaq*, a derivative or a synonym thereof. This method of repudiation by uttering *talaq* is an exclusive right of the husband. Variations of the talaq are revocable for a certain time period, while others are irrevocable. While the talaq is exclusive to the husband, traditional law does allow the husband to delegate his power to his wife under certain circumstances.
2. Divorce may also be effected by mutual agreement, known as *khul'* or *mubara'a*. This kind of mutual agreement rises to legal status though a form of offer and acceptance, usually through the wife paying the husband the amount of her dower.
3. Islamic law also provides for judicial dissolution of marriage under certain circumstances. These causes, which vary according to different schools of jurisprudence, include injury or discord, a defect on the part of the husband (ranging from any physical defect to impotence only), failure of the husband to pay maintenance, and prolonged absence or imprisonment of the husband.

Islamic law is codified in many countries, particularly in the Middle East. However, like Catholic canon law, Islamic law on marriage and divorce is not recognized as valid civil law in the United States. Thus, Moslems wishing to adhere to the Shari'ah in the United States must attempt to reconcile those wishes with the competing and often contradictory demands of the civil law on marriage and divorce.

DOREMUS V. BOARD OF EDUCATION **(U.S. 1952)**   A New Jersey statute provided for the reading of five verses of the Bible at the opening of each public school day. This was challenged as an impermissible establishment of religion by a taxpayer of the town of Hawthorne who had a child in its school system. The case reached the Supreme Court.

Justice Robert H. Jackson, writing for the Court, rejected the standing of the plaintiff to raise the constitutional question. The child had been graduated from school, so the claim of the parent was moot. Furthermore, because there was no proof that public money was spent on the religious practice, the plaintiff's taxpayer status gave him no stake in the litigation.

Justice William O. Douglas, along with Justices Stanley F. Reed, and Harold Burton, dissented. Taxpayers, Douglas argued, had a general interest in the management of the community's public schools. The effect of the Court's decision in this case was to defer for a decade a decision on the constitutionality of religious exercises in public schools.

DRAFT   See CONSCIENTIOUS OBJECTOR

DRUGS
The freedom of religion guarantee in the First Amendment to the U.S. Constitution is not an absolute defense to a drug charge. [*Peyote Way Church of God, Inc. v. Smith* (N.D. Tex. 1983); *United States v. Greene* (6th Cir. 1989)] Several cases have ruled in effect that the constitutional guarantee of freedom of religious practice is not a valid defense to a violation of criminal laws prohibiting or restricting possession of a particular controlled substance, even if the defendant possessed or utilized the drug in the practice of his or her bona fide religious beliefs. The general theory of this group of cases appears to be that the police power should and does predominate over one's right to freely practice his or her religious beliefs, where such religious practice involves conduct made criminal by law. [*Leary v. United States* (5th Cir. 1967) *rev'd on other grounds* (U.S. 1969)] The Fifth Circuit Court of Appeals, however, rejected the defendant's claim that he had a right to use marijuana that was protected by the First Amendment. The defendant claimed that his conviction for marijuana violations should be reversed because use of marijuana was called for by his Hindu faith. In assessing Leary's claim, the court noted that marijuana was not central to Hinduism in the way that peyote is in certain Native American sects.

In several cases, such as *Leary*, in which a defendant asserted a constitutional freedom of religion and religious practice as a defense to a psychedelic drug offense, courts have considered that there was a failure to show that the drug-related conduct was engaged in for a bona fide religious purpose. However, under certain very restricted conditions, a person's constitutional freedom to practice his or her religion can be a valid defense against a criminal prosecution for illegal drug use or possession.

In one case a court dismissed an indictment against a defendant for unlawfully importing peyote through the U.S. mail and possessing peyote with an intent to distribute. The defendant was not Native American. However, he was an active member of the Native American Church and used peyote in bona fide religious ceremonies of that Church. In rejecting the prosecution's case, the court held that the freedom to exercise one's religion by using peyote applied to all members of the Church regardless of race and the fact that the defendant was not a Native American did not mean he could not be a member of the Church. [*United States v. Boyll* (D.N.M. 1991)]

Prior to the emergence of the balancing test in *Sherbert v. Verner* (U.S. 1963) it was assumed that laws prohibiting the use of certain drugs could be applied to those who wished to use these drugs as a part of their religion. As the state has a clear secular interest in the regulation or prohibition of such drugs, the courts saw no free exercise interest requiring an exemption for any religious use. Following the development of the *Sherbert* balancing test, a new approach to cases emerged. First, the plaintiff must prove that the inability to use the drug seriously burdens the practice of his or her religion. Second, the state's interest in the regulation of the drug and the impact of an exemption for religious use must be assessed. If it is clear that the drug is dangerous, the state's interest would be of a magnitude that should not permit even religious use of it. If for no other reason, the danger of accidental distribution of a dangerous drug to persons outside of the religious sect claiming the exemption should constitute a compelling interest. However, it is possible that some proscribed drugs are not so dangerous that a narrow exemption for religious use would impair the state's interest in safety or health.

DUE PROCESS CLAUSE   The Fifth and Fourteenth Amendments to the U.S. Constitution contain provisions denying the federal and state governments respectively any right to deprive a person of "life, liberty, or property, without due process of law." The original purpose of these provisions was to ensure that a fair legal procedure was conducted before life, liberty, or property could be taken away from a citizen or be subjected to government interference. These provisions have resulted in much litigation and have been invoked in circumstances not envisioned when they were adopted.

The Fourteenth Amendment has been given wide interpretation in connection with civil liberties, in particular in making applicable to the states the guarantees of liberty in the Bill of Rights.

The U.S. Supreme Court, for example, in *Everson v. Board of Education* (U.S. 1947) held that the Establishment Clause applied to the states through the Due Process Clause of the Fourteenth Amendment.

E

ECCLESIASTICAL CORPORATION   Corporate bodies created for the promotion of religion and the securing of the rights of a particular religious group or sect are ecclesiastical corporations. The members of an ecclesiastical corporation are entirely "spiritual persons," a term referring to the clergy and religious orders that originated in English common law. They include corporations sole (for example, bishops, parsons, and vicars) and corporations aggregate (for example, deans and chapters). At common law, a corporation is considered an "artificial" person, who is endowed with the legal capacity of perpetual succession, consisting either of a single individual (called a "corporation sole") or a collection of individuals (called a "corporation aggregate").

Religious corporations incorporated under the laws of a U.S. state, however, are not "ecclesiastical corporations" in the sense of the English law. [*Robertson v. Bullions* (N.Y. 1854)]

William Blackstone defined ecclesiastical corporations as "where the members who compose it are entirely spiritual persons, such as bishops, certain deans, and prebendaries; all archdeans, parsons, and vicars, which are sole corporations; deans and chapters at present, and formerly priors and convents, abbots and monks, and the like bodies aggregate." Blackstone describes corporations known as "eleemosynary corporations" as neither strictly speaking lay nor ecclesiastical, "even though composed of ecclesiastical persons, and although they in some things partake of the nature, privileges and restrictions of ecclesiastical bodies." [1 Blackstone 470] Eleemosynary corporations are now defined as corporations with charitable functions and powers.

It is not the profession of piety by the individuals that renders the corporation of which they are the members "ecclesiastical." The corporation must be spiritual in a legal, and not in a popular or scriptural sense. Lay corporations may be for the advancement of religion, and the members may all be clergymen even, but that does not make the corporation ecclesiastical. [*Robertson v. Bullions* (N.Y. 1854)]

Ecclesiastical corporations were a category of corporation disfavored in the United States after the American Revolution and the disestablishment of the Anglican Church (the modern Episcopalian church). In the eighteenth century, Virginia's antipathy to the Anglican faith resulted in a wholesale confiscation of church funds and prompted a prohibition against ecclesiastical corporations that continues to this day in Virginia and West Virginia.

A special feature enjoyed by both eleemosynary and ecclesiastical corporations was visitatorial power, which was an enforcement mechanism and could compel the original purpose of the charity to be "faithfully fulfilled." The theory of the visitatorial power was that the private, charitable corporations founded and endowed by private persons were subject to the private government and rules of the founders. As in all charitable corporations, the individuals who originally donated funds and revenues, as well as their heirs, had the right to visit, inquire into, and correct all irregularities and abuses that arose in the course of the administration of the funds donated.

Under English common law, the ecclesiastical corporation sole dates back to the mid-fifteenth century. The corporation sole developed as a product of early property law principles that did not permit the devise of real property to a church in fee simple absolute. A conveyance to the religious leader (usually a parson or minister) personally thus ran the risk that the property might descend to the leader's heirs to be subject to personal debts or encumbrances. By making the person and his successors a corporation, the church accomplished the goal of preserving the property of the parsonage for the benefit of the church; because the present officeholder, his predecessor and his successor were deemed by law to be one and the same person, any property given to one was considered the property of the successor. As it developed in the New England colonies, the corporation sole functioned as a municipal corporation, and alienation of property required the consent of the parish.

ECCLESIASTICAL COURT   Courts or tribunals established by churches to adjudicate disputes between clerical authorities and disputes involving spiritual matters affecting either clerics or laity are ecclesiastical courts. Such courts exist in Christian denominations (for example, the Catholic tribunal), among Jews (the Bet Din), Muslims (the Sharia'ah), and other religious faiths.

In earlier times ecclesiastical courts were much more powerful than they are today. In Europe during the Middle Ages the courts of the Roman Catholic Church had wide jurisdiction, extending to many temporal matters, and often rivaled the secular courts in power. The range of spiritual matters under their jurisdiction often extended into the secular area. The cases they adjudicated included those involving marriage, divorce, legitimacy, wills, heresy, and all cases in which clerics were accused of either religious or secular crimes. Some ecclesiastical courts gained a harsh reputation. The Inquisition, which began in 1231 (particularly severe was the Spanish Inquisition of 1478–1808, 1814–1820, and 1823–1834), was one of the most brutal of the ecclesiastical courts and sentenced many people accused of heresy to be burned at the stake. As societies have become more secular, the jurisdiction of ecclesiastical courts has become strictly limited to religious issues, the governance of church property, and matters of ecclesiastical discipline. By the sixteenth century in Continental Europe, ecclesiastical courts largely ceased to have any secular functions. In England today, the ecclesiastical courts exercise jurisdiction in civil cases concerning church buildings and in criminal cases in which clergy members are accused of ecclesiastical crimes.

ECCLESIASTICAL DISPUTES   Where there is a dispute between factions of a religious organization, one or more of the parties may seek resolution of the dispute by a state court. The government cannot declare which party is correct in matters of religion, because that would violate the principles of both the Establishment and the Free Exercise Clauses of the Constitution. A judicial declaration on such matters would simultaneously establish certain religious views as correct for the organization, while inhibiting the free exercise of the opposing belief. Yet when the opposing groups both claim the same church property, the state is required to make some judgment as to who is entitled to its possession. This must be done under carefully circumscribed rules that avoid deciding matters of religious belief.

When the disputed property is subject to some express condition in a deed, a court may rule on the occurrence of the condition, if that does not involve a ruling on religious matters. Thus, if a building is deeded to a church for so long as it is used as a place of religious worship, the court could order the return of the property if it were used in any other manner. But if the condition is that the church can keep the property so long as it is true to its doctrine, that condition could not be enforced. Any ruling requiring the return of the church property in such a case would involve a government ruling on religious beliefs, which is forbidden by the Constitution.

Most ecclesiastical disputes involving property center around property that is not subject to such a specific condition. In these situations two or more groups present themselves to a court and claim the right to possess and control church property. The permissible basis for court rulings in these situations varies with the organization of the church involved in the dispute. When the church is an independent congregation that is not subject to a general or higher church authority, the will of a majority of the members must control the decision. As this is a self-governing unit, the only secular basis for a ruling between competing groups is based on the preferences of a majority of the members. A separate secular way to determine ownership might pertain if the deed to the property at issue or the incorporation documents of the church group specified some other form of resolving disputes that did not require the court to review religious doctrine. As it is highly unlikely that such a neutral, secular rule or dispute resolution could be found, it is only safe to assume that the majority rule principle must prevail in these cases.

Another controversial issue involves ecclesiastical discipline. Generally, secular courts have no ecclesiastical jurisdiction and cannot review church disciplinary actions for the purpose of reinstating expelled church members. [*Fowler v. Bailey* (Okl. 1992)]

ECCLESIASTICAL LAW   An ecclesiastical law is a law that has been enacted by a competent ecclesiastical authority. In a general sense, all laws relating to a church, whether imposed by secular authorities, by divine law, by the law of nature and reason, or by the rules of independent societies can be seen as ecclesiastical law. In a narrower sense ecclesiastical law embodies those rules established by the church itself for the spiritual welfare of the faithful and the orderly conduct of church affairs. Ecclesiastical laws include disciplinary laws, liturgical laws, procedural laws, and penal laws.

In the context of English law ecclesiastical law means the law of the Church of England as administered by the ecclesiastical courts, the constitution of the Church, its property, clergy, benefices, and services. It is derived largely from the canon and civil law. In England prior to the Reformation, which began in that country in 1534, ecclesiastical courts administered the general canon law of the Western Christian Church. At the Reformation, this became English ecclesiastical law. In England the Church of England is established by law and its law is a part of the law of the land. The Church in Wales was disestablished in 1920. The Church of Ireland was separated from the Church of England and disestablished in 1871. Other churches in England, although recognized by law, are fundamentally voluntary associations and their codes of law are binding on their members only by virtue of voluntary submission. As now restricted, ecclesiastical law applies mainly to the affairs, and the doctrine, discipline, and worship, of the established church.

In the United States, all churches are tolerated but none are established churches.

🏛 **EDUCATION**   See GOVERNMENT AID TO RELIGIOUS ORGANIZATIONS; PRIVATE EDUCATION; PUBLIC SCHOOL CURRICULUM

🏛 *EDWARDS V. AGUILLARD* **(U.S. 1987)**   Louisiana's Balanced Treatment Act compelled the public schools to teach Bible-inspired creationism whenever Darwinian evolutionary theory was introduced into the classroom. Although welcome to ignore both "theories," the law required that any public school teacher who taught evolution must also give equal time to teaching "creation science."

In *Aguillard* the U.S. Supreme Court struck down the Balanced Treatment Act, finding that it furthered a primarily religious, and therefore, unconstitutional, purpose. The Supreme Court agreed with and cited the court of appeals finding that the legislature's "actual intent was 'to discredit evolution by counterbalancing its teaching at every turn with the teaching of creationism, a religious belief.'"

In reaching this result, the Court first had to evaluate and ultimately dismiss a purported secular legislative purpose advanced to justify the Act. Although the first prong of the test originally set forth in *Lemon v. Kurtzman* (U.S. 1971) required that the legislative purpose be secular and not religious, the *Aguillard* Court also explicitly required that the "statement of such purpose be sincere and not a sham." In other words, while the *Lemon* test directs courts to ask the crucial question—what is the purpose of the law?—*Aguillard* provides the courts with the kinds of information that they can consult to arrive at a proper answer. The Supreme Court identified six areas of permissible inquiry to facilitate the evaluation of a law's purpose. These are:

1. Whether the legislative history of the law contains overt religious justification for it, especially from the sponsor

2. Whether the law functions solely symbolically by failing to grant any new authority

3. The extent to which the law's operation is underinclusive relative to its stated purpose

4. The history behind the topic and its prior ties to religion

5. The social and political context from which the law emerged, and

6. Whether the explicit text of the law expresses a religious purpose.

The Balanced Treatment Act presented problems on all six inquiries except the last. Although advocates of the Act offered the secular reason of advancing academic freedom, the sponsor, Senator Bill Keith, intended to narrow the science curriculum. "My preference would be that neither [creationism nor evolution] be taught." The Court found this attitude inconsistent with the purported goal of advancing academic freedom. The Court found that the legislative history revealed no identified secular purpose and that the primary purpose of the Act was to promote a particular religious belief. (In his dissent, Justice Antonin Scalia argued that the Louisiana statute had as its secular purpose the protection of academic freedom.)

The majority of the justices further rebutted the sincerity of the purported purpose of advancing academic freedom because "[the] Act [did] not grant teachers a flexibility that they did not already possess. . . . The Act provides Louisiana school teachers with no new authority. Thus the stated purpose is not furthered by it." This failure to grant new authority to the teachers led the Court to conclude that "[t]he Act violates the Establishment clause of the First Amendment because it seeks to employ the symbolic and financial support of government to achieve a religious purpose."

The *Aguillard* Court also argued that the purported purpose of the Act, that of protecting academic freedom, was inconsistent with its effect, which was promoting a religious belief, and thus made the sincerity of the "academic freedom" purpose suspect. The Court noted that if by such freedom the state meant to encourage the fair "teaching [of] all of the evidence," the Act displayed a "discriminatory preference of the teaching of creation science and against the teaching of evolution," which contradicted the claims of promoting fairness.

The *Aguillard* Court also noted a historical "link between the teachings of certain religious denominations and the teaching of evolution," which was reviewed in *Epperson v. Arkansas* (1968). This history supported the Court's conclusion that "the term 'creation science,' as contemplated by the legislature that adopted this Act, embodies the religious belief that a supernatural creator was responsible for the creation of humankind." Finding that the antagonistic link between creation science and evolution is not only historic, but "contemporaneous," the Court also examined present-day influences. In this process the Court found that the legislators' religious views influenced the passage of the Act: "The state senator [Senator Bill Keith] repeatedly stated the scientific evidence supporting his religious views should be included in the public school curriculum to redress the fact that the theory of evolution incidentally coincided with what he characterized as religious beliefs antithetical to his own." Thus, "because the primary purpose of the Creationism Act is to endorse a particular religious doctrine, the Act furthers religion in violation of the Establishment Clause."

Given that the Balanced Treatment Act violated five of the six inquiries set forth as a test of the law's secular purpose, the Court judged the Act's stated purpose of promoting academic freedom or basic educational fairness to be a subterfuge intended to hide the fundamentally religious nature of the law.

In their dissenting opinion, Chief Justice William H. Rehnquist and Justice Antonin Scalia criticized the majority for presuming the law unconstitutional because "it was supported strongly by organized religion or by adherents of particular faiths." "Political activism by the religiously motivated is part of our heritage," Scalia wrote. "Today's religious activism may give us [this law] . . . but yesterday's resulted in the abolition of slavery, and tomorrow's may bring relief for famine victims." Scalia also pointed out the contradiction of ruling that secular humanism is protected as a "religion" in some court cases, and then depicted as a neutral nonreligion in this case.

EMPLOYMENT DIVISION V. SMITH (U.S. 1990)   In this case the U.S. Supreme Court held that Oregon's prohibition of peyote in religious ceremonies did not violate the Free Exercise Clause of the First Amendment.

Two drug and alcohol abuse rehabilitation counselors, both of whom were members of the Native American Church, were terminated from their jobs with a private corporation because they ingested peyote, a hallucinogenic drug, for sacramental purposes at a church ceremony. Use of the drug was prohibited by state law. The counselors applied to the Employment Division of Oregon's Department of Human Resources for unemployment compensation, but their claim was rejected because they had been fired for violating the state's drug laws. The former drug counselors appealed, claiming that the Free Exercise Clause of the First Amendment protected their use of peyote in connection with a religious ceremony.

The U.S. Supreme Court ruled that (1) the Free Exercise Clause did not require an exemption from criminal laws banning the use of peyote, and (2) unemployment compensation could be denied to persons whose discharge had been based on their violation of a valid criminal statute.

Justice Scalia wrote the majority opinion, which held that the Free Exercise Clause did not require the government to justify its refusal to exempt religiously motivated drug use from the general prohibition of drug use. The majority believed that the judiciary was not authorized by the Free Exercise Clause to balance the societal interest in the drug proscription against the degree to which compliance with the law burdened the sincerely held religious beliefs of the individuals in the case.

ENDORSEMENT TEST   The endorsement test is used to determine whether state participation in a religious activity violates the First Amendment's ban against government establishment of religion. The test asks whether the state activity involved constitutes either an endorsement or disapproval of religion. [*Chaudhuri v. Tennessee* (M.D. Tenn. 1995)]

The endorsement test was best articulated by Justice Sandra Day O'Connor in her concurrence in *Allegheny County v. ACLU* (U.S. 1989). This case reviewed the constitutionality of a holiday display on public property that included both a menorah and a Christmas tree. The city had placed a sign at the foot of the tree that read: "During this holiday season, the City of Pittsburgh salutes liberty. Yet these festive lights remind us that we are keepers of the flame of liberty and our legacy of freedom." Justice O'Connor found that the display "did not endorse Judaism or religion in general, but rather conveyed a message of pluralism and freedom of belief."

ENGEL V. VITALE (U.S. 1962)   For years many public school districts mandated that the school day begin with some sort of prayer. The first case to come before the Supreme Court challenging that practice was *Engel v. Vitale*. A group of 10 parents sued the Board of Education of Union Free School District No. 9 in Hyde Park, New York, for requiring students to recite the following prayer aloud every day in the classroom: "Almighty God, we acknowledge our dependence on Thee, and we beg Thy blessings upon us, our parents, our teachers, and our Country." The prayer was composed by the New York State Board of Regents, which was a state agency having broad supervisory powers over the state's public schools.

The plaintiffs felt that the prayer was contrary to their families' religious practices and maintained that its mandatory use in the public schools violated the federal Constitution. Specifically, they felt that the prayer violated the clause in the First Amendment that states "Congress shall make no law respecting the establishment of religion." This clause, called the Establishment Clause, was made applicable to the states by the Fourteenth Amendment to the Constitution.

The lower courts that heard the case upheld the power of New York to allow the prayer to be said each day as long as no student was forced to participate. The case was appealed to the Supreme Court.

The Supreme Court reversed the lower courts and ruled that the use of a government-composed, nondenominational voluntary prayer in the public schools violates the Establishment Clause. The Court's five-to-two decision was delivered by Justice Hugo Black:

> The religious nature of prayer was recognized by Jefferson, and has been concurred in by theological writers, the United States Supreme court, and State courts and administrative officials, including New York's Commissioner of Education. A committee of the New York legislature has agreed.
>
> The petitioners contend . . . that the state laws requiring or permitting use of the Regents' prayer must be struck down as a violation of the Establishment Clause. . . . We agree with this contention since we think that, in this country, it is no part of the business of government to compose official prayers for any group of the American people to recite as a part of a religious program carried on by government.
>
> The New York laws officially prescribing the Regent's prayer are inconsistent both with the purposes of the Establishment Clause and with the Establishment Clause itself.

In his dissenting opinion, Justice Potter Stewart wrote:

> I think the Court has misapplied a great constitutional principle. I cannot see how an "official religion" is established by letting those who want to say a prayer say it.
>
> On the contrary, I think that to deny the wish of these school children to join in reciting this prayer is to deny them the opportunity of sharing in the spiritual heritage of our Nation.

The principles outlined in *Engel v. Vitale* were extended to a voluntary moment of silence in the 1985 case of *Wallace v. Jaffe* (U.S. 1985).

ENLIGHTENMENT   The philosophical movement known as the Enlightenment originated in the rational approach to society, religion, and science of John Locke and Isaac Newton. Spreading in the late seventeenth and eighteenth centuries over most of Europe, it influenced many thinkers, notably Voltaire, Montesquieu, Helvetius, Beccaria, and Rousseau, who all held the belief that man was a rational being who could work out his salvation without the intercession of the church. With this anticlerical and rationalist attitude these and other thinkers greatly influenced thought throughout Europe in the direction of reforms.

The Enlightenment thinkers championed the French Revolution, religious toleration, and a more rational approach to justice and law. Accordingly, man-made law had to be examined in the light of reason and nature. Law was not made by edicts, according to the Enlightenment, but was discoverable by right reason. The means of reforming the law and restating it in accordance with reason was the codification. This rationalism was the impetus behind the Prussian, Austrian, and French legal codes, which appeared in the late eighteenth and nineteenth centuries and replaced earlier codes and bodies of customary law.

ENTANGLEMENT   *See* EXCESSIVE ENTANGLEMENT

EPPERSON V. ARKANSAS **(U.S. 1968)**   This case represents an early effort to articulate which laws violate the Establishment Clause of the U.S. Constitution. In *Epperson,* the U.S. Supreme Court struck down an Arkansas statute that outlawed the teaching of evolution. The statute made it unlawful for a teacher in any state-supported school or university to teach "that mankind ascended or descended from a lower order of animals."

Susan Epperson, an Arkansas public school teacher, and H. H. Blanchard, a father of two Little Rock students, brought a lawsuit challenging the constitutionality of the law on the grounds that it was an abridgment of free speech violating the First and Fourteenth Amendments. The plaintiffs lost their case in the Arkansas Supreme Court, which found that the law was "a valid exercise of the state's power to specify the curriculum of the public schools." The plaintiffs appealed this ruling to the U.S. Supreme Court.

The U.S. Supreme Court held that the statute violated the Fourteenth Amendment, which incorporates the First Amendment's prohibition of state laws respecting an establishment of religion. The majority found that the sole reason for the Arkansas law was that a particular religious group considered the evolution theory to conflict with the account of the origin of man set forth in the Book of Genesis. A state's right to prescribe the public school curriculum does not include the right to prohibit teaching a scientific theory or doctrine for reasons that are contrary to the principles of the First Amendment. The statute, the court concluded, conflicted with the First Amendment, which mandates governmental neutrality between religion and religion, and between religion and non-religion.

After finding that the Arkansas statute was not a manifestation of religious neutrality, the court concluded that "fundamentalist sectarian conviction was and is the law's reason for existence." The Court then established two precedents: First, the Court held that any law wholly without a secular purpose is a law presumptively motivated by religion, and therefore forbidden by the First Amendment.

Second, the Court looked for the law's motive beyond explicit claims and into the unspoken social and political contexts that influenced the legislative process. Thus, although the Arkansas statute did not explicitly claim that its purpose was to further fundamentalist Christianity, its text was modeled on a Tennessee statute that did include such language. The Court compared one statute to the other, and concluded that "the motivation for the [Arkansas] law was the same" as the Tennessee law. Thus, even if the overt language of a law is inoffensive, *Epperson* instructs that knowledge of the specific social, intellectual, and philosophical pedigree of a statute may find a violation of the Constitution.

The ruling was unanimous, although Justices Black, Harlan, and Stewart disagreed with the majority's reasoning and held instead that the law should have been struck down because it was unconstitutionally vague. Justice Black argued that the Court's opinion, written by Justice Fortas, could lead to further restrictions on state control of the school curriculum.

The influence of the *Epperson* case was particularly important in 1971 when the Court created an actual test to determine violations of the Establishment Clause in *Lemon v. Kurtzman* (U.S. 1971).

ESTABLISHED CHURCH   A church that is recognized by law and supported by the secular government as the official church of a nation is an established church. Establishment implies that there is some definite and distinctive relation between the civil authority of the state and a religious faith and that this relation is not shared by any other religious faith in the country. Establishment does not imply any particular form of relationship between church and state. It merely means that some kind of relationship exists. It usually implies some form of financial support. An established church enjoys a privileged position, but in return, it has obligations toward the state.

In Great Britain, two established churches are found, one in England, the other in Scotland. In England, the established church is the Church of England or Anglican Church. The establishment of the Church of England does not date from any particular year, as church and state have always cooperated closely in England and developed along side each other. Certain events, however, helped to solidify the relationship. The first was King Henry VIII's repudiation of the authority of the pope in England. By the Act of Supremacy (1534) the king became "the only supreme head on earth of the Church of England." Under Queen Elizabeth I (1533–1603) the established church assumed a more protestant character, which it still retains today. Nevertheless many of its teachings and forms have been inherited directly from the medieval church, and so its claim that it is both reformed and catholic has some measure of justification. The Presbyterian Church is the established church of Scotland, the Lutheran Church for much of Scandinavia, Judaism for Israel, and Islam for much of the Middle East. In pluralistic societies such establishment is becoming rarer.

The United States has no established church. All religious organizations, including Christian churches, are considered voluntary organizations under American law. The Establishment Clause of the First Amendment to the U.S. Constitution prohibits a state or the federal government from establishing a church, or passing laws that aid one—or all—religions, or from giving preference to one religion, or forcing belief or disbelief in any religion. [*Everson v. Board of Education* (U.S. 1947)]

ESTABLISHMENT CLAUSE   The provision of the First Amendment to the U.S. Constitution that prohibits the government from establishing a religion is known as the Establishment Clause. Specifically, the Clause reads: "Congress shall make no law respecting an establishment of religion."

The basic purpose of the Establishment Clause is, in the words of Thomas Jefferson, to erect a "wall of separation between church and state." The image of a wall, however, does not help very much in determining what types of state actions violate the Clause. Modern Supreme Court caselaw has interpreted the Establishment Clause.

In 1898 the prominent legal scholar Thomas Cooley, in his *Commentaries on the Constitution,* defined the Establishment Clause as follows: "By establishment of religion is meant the setting up or recognition of a state church, or at least the conferring upon one church of special favors and advantages which are denied to others. It was never intended by the Constitution that the government should be prohibited from recognizing religion . . . where it might be done without drawing any invidious distinctions between different religious beliefs, organizations, or sects."

The first time that the U.S. Supreme Court was called on to rule on the Establishment Clause was in 1899, when it considered the case of *Bradfield v. Roberts* (U.S. 1899), in which a challenge was made to a federal construction grant to a Roman Catholic hospital. The case was handled as a matter of corporation law. So long as the hospital fulfilled its contract (that is, to treat illness), the Court held that its operation by a religious order was of no consequence. The aid given had only indirectly benefitted the church.

In *Quick Bear v. Leupp* (U.S. 1908) the Supreme Court decided that federal money in trust funds belonging to Native Americans could be used to pay to educate Native American children in Catholic schools because it was the Indians' money, not the government's.

The case of *Pierce v. Society of Sisters* (U.S. 1925) challenged an Oregon law requiring that all able-bodied children of school age attend public school, thus potentially threatening the existence of parochial and other private schools. The Court held that the law was unconstitutional, but the decision was made on the basis of the Fourteenth Amendment, not the First, because it involved an action of state government. *Pierce* was decided before the religion clauses of the First Amendment were "incorporated" into the Fourteenth Amendment, or made applicable to the states. Incorporation was announced in the case of *Cantwell v. Connecticut* (U.S. 1940). The modern basis for the *Pierce* holding is sharply debated. The Supreme Court in *Board of Education v. Allen* (U.S. 1968), treated *Pierce* as a decision based on the free exercise of religion.

A later case that seemed to raise Establishment Clause issues was *Cochran v. Louisiana Board of Education* (U.S. 1930). The issue was whether Louisiana could use state funds to provide textbooks for students attending parochial schools. Holding that the program was constitutional, the Supreme Court again based its argument upon the Fourteenth Amendment, rather the First, because the First Amendment provisions had not yet been "incorporated" into the Fourteenth Amendment, and were, hence, not applicable to the states.

Most of the Supreme Court's Establishment Clause rulings have been issued since the Court declared the Clause applicable to the states in *Everson v. Board of Education* (U.S. 1947). There are at least three reasons why no litigation explicitly based on Establishment Clause grounds was decided by the Supreme Court prior to 1947. First, persons who wanted to challenge the use of tax monies in support of religious institutions or practices encountered extreme difficulty in obtaining standing to sue. Second, many states had statutory or constitutional provisions that were more specific than those of the federal Constitution in prohibiting the use of governmental funds for particular religious activities. These prohibitions tended to minimize state involvement in religious matters. Third, the Establishment Clause of the First Amendment had not been applied to the states prior to that time. Indeed, it is commonly understood that the case of *Everson v. Board of Education* (U.S. 1947) was the first in which the Establishment Clause was incorporated into the Fourteenth Amendment. The case setting the precedent for the incorporation of provisions of the Bill of Rights, *Gitlow v. New York* (U.S. 1925), had been decided in 1925. In the 1940 case *Cantwell v. Connecticut* (U.S. 1940), the Supreme Court made the following observation:

The First Amendment declares that Congress shall make no law respecting an establishment of religion or prohibiting the free exercise thereof. The Fourteenth Amendment has rendered the legislatures of the states as incompetent as Congress to enact such laws.

In spite of this broad language, *Cantwell* was decided solely on a free exercise question. As a result the Establishment Clause was not specifically applied to the states until *Everson*.

In modern times the Establishment Clause has not been read as a mere prohibition against a government-sponsored church [but see *Wallace v. Jaffree* (U.S. 1985)(Rehnquist, J., dissenting)] or as simply a demand of equal treatment of religions (that is, an antidiscrimination guarantee), but as a broader prohibition against laws "which aid one religion, aid all religions, or prefer one religion over another." [*Everson v. Board of Education* (1947)] Congress, in other words, may not pass laws that aid one or all religions, or that give preference to one religion, or force belief or disbelief in any religion.

The issue in *Everson v. Board of Education* (U.S. 1947) was whether state tax money could be used to reimburse parents for the cost of transporting children by bus to parochial schools. A New Jersey taxpayer sued in a state court, claiming that such a use of state money was a violation of the Establishment Clause made applicable to the states by the Fourteenth Amendment. The plaintiff based his argument on the broad language in *Cantwell*. The Supreme Court agreed to hear the case because it raised a compelling federal question. The Court, in *Everson*, declared that neither any state nor the federal government could use tax money to support even the most general and impartial religious activity.

In writing the opinion of the Court, Justice Hugo Black included a paragraph defining the limits of the Establishment Clause that has served as the baseline for subsequent Establishment Clause litigation:

The "establishment of religion" clause of the First Amendment means at least this: Neither a state nor the federal Government can set up a church. Neither can it pass laws which aid one religion, aid all religions, or prefer one religion over another. Neither can force nor influence a person to go to or remain away from church against his will or force him to profess a belief or disbelief in religion. No person can be punished for entertaining or professing religious beliefs or disbeliefs, for church attendance or non-attendance. No tax, in any amount, large or small, can be levied to support any religious activities or institutions, whatever they may be called, or whatever form they may adopt to teach or practice religion. Neither a state nor the Federal Government can, openly or secretly, participate in the affairs of any religious organizations or groups and vice versa. In the words of Jefferson, the clause against establishment of religion by law was intended to erect a "wall of separation between church and state."

In the light of this separationist language, many were surprised when Justice Black and four colleagues found that reimbursements for transportation were not a violation of the Establishment Clause.

In the passage quoted above, as elsewhere in the majority opinion, Justice Black simply assumed that the precedent of incorporation of the Establishment Clause into the Fourteenth Amendment was well established. He did not argue in support of the concept. For him the Establishment Clause should be applied to the states. The court has followed that precedent in all subsequent Establishment Clause cases.

In modern times the Supreme Court interpreted the intent of the Framers as follows: "[F]or the men who wrote the Religion Clauses of the First Amendment the 'establishment' of a religion connoted sponsorship, financial support, and active involvement of the sovereign in religious activity." [*Walz v. Tax Commission* (U.S. 1970)] However, the Court's reading of the Clause has never resulted in the barring of all assistance that aids, however incidentally, a religious institution. Outside this area, the decisions generally have more rigorously prohibited what may be deemed governmental promotion of religious doctrine.

In 1971 the Supreme Court enunciated the test it still uses to determine whether a law violates the Establishment Clause of the Constitution in *Lemon v. Kurtzman* (1971). The Court requires that each part of a three-part test be satisfied in order to withstand an Establishment Clause challenge: (1) the law must have a secular legislative purpose; (2) the principal or primary effect of the law must neither advance nor inhibit religion; and (3) the law must not foster "an excessive government entanglement with religion." The *Lemon* test was very important because it provided a frame of reference for judging whether laws violated the Establishment Clause. In subsequent cases, the Court would disagree on whether the *Lemon* test was a strict standard or simply a loose guideline. The real issue became whether the Court would allow government accommodation of religion or insist on strict separation of the two spheres of government and religion.

The *Lemon* test has been severely criticized as too strict. Further, the Court has departed from the test in upholding prayers opening legislative sessions, emphasizing instead the historical acceptance of the challenged practice, which makes it a "part of the fabric of our society." [*Marsh v. Chambers* (U.S. 1983); *Walz v. Tax Commission* (U.S. 1970) (emphasizing historic practices in upholding state tax exemptions for property and income of religious institutions)] *Larson v. Valente* (U.S. 1982) also avoided the *Lemon* test in invalidating a state law imposing disclosure requirements only on religious organizations soliciting more than 50 percent of their funds from nonmembers on the grounds that it discriminated against nontraditional religions in violation of the Establishment Clause. *Larson* used the strict scrutiny test for laws discriminating against some religions in favor of others. Strict scrutiny is the standard of review that federal courts use in equal protection cases involving the constitutionality of government classifications that infringe on fundamental constitutional rights. To meet this scrutiny, a challenged governmental action must be "closely related to a compelling governmental interest" or it will not be valid. This strict scrutiny is the toughest of the three levels of investigation used by federal courts when deciding whether actions by the government are permissible. The other levels are "ordinary" (or rational basis) scrutiny and "intermediate" scrutiny.

Whether the three-pronged *Lemon* test will survive is not clear. There are new tends that have become apparent. Increasingly, the Supreme Court is asking whether the law at issue constitutes an endorsement of religion or a particular religious belief. Justice O'Connor has indicated that she believes that this is a more useful test than the *Lemon* test. [*Lynch v. Donnelly* (U.S. 1984)] Justice Kennedy, on the other hand, believes that endorsement is too imprecise a concept and that the appropriate inquiry is whether the state is proselytizing so that the government action is coercive. [*Board of Education v. Mergens* (U.S. 1990)(Kennedy J., concurring)] The *Lemon* test has not yet been repudiated, but *Lee v. Weisman* (U.S. 1992), which did not apply *Lemon* at all, suggests that the issue remains open.

ETERNAL LAW   Eternal law is a concept developed first by Stoic philosophy, which emphasizes that true happiness and true freedom comes from setting aside passion, unjust thoughts, and indulgences, and by performing one's duty with the right disposition. It is distinct from natural law (ius naturale) and human law (ius humanum). It is the law of reason of the cosmos that rules the universe. Human reason, an imitation of cosmic reason, rules the lives of natural men, so that natural law partakes of eternal law. The concept was adopted and elaborated by Cicero (106–43 B.C.), a Roman orator, politician, and philosopher, and later by St. Augustine (A.D. 354–430), one of the fathers of the Catholic Church and bishop of Hippo, who identified eternal law with the reason or will of God. St. Thomas Aquinas (1225–1274) saw divine law as the part of eternal law that God made known through divine revelation, not to be grasped by human beings but given to man as an eternal truth. Natural law was the part of eternal law that man could apprehend with his unaided reason but could neither create nor change by reason or will, and within the limits that natural law prescribed human or positive law was created by human reason for the common good. Later still Francisco Suarez (1548–1617), a Spanish Jesuit philosopher, maintained that law had rational foundations.

According to its proponents, eternal law influences the law of contemporary society because such law deals with human conduct and its principles are inspired or revealed by God. These principles exist whether or not governments choose to recognize or enforce them and governments must incorporate these principles into their legal systems for justice to be achieved.

Everson v. Board of Education (U.S. 1947)

By a five-to-four vote, the Supreme Court in this case upheld a government program for reimbursing parents for funds spent in transporting parochial students to school in public buses. The law was "a general program to assist parents by transporting their children, regardless of their religion, safely and expeditiously to and from accredited schools." A majority of the justices upheld the program even though they took the position that no aid could be given to a religion in accordance with the ban set forth in the Establishment Clause of the First Amendment to the Constitution. The majority was of the view that the provision of free bus transportation to all school children on an equal basis constituted only a general service to benefit and safeguard children, rather than an aid to religion. The opinion noted that basic governmental services, such as fire and police protection, could be extended to religious institutions along with the rest of the public without aiding religion. As the majority saw the general provision of free transportation to be akin to such a service, the program was approved. The public welfare benefit was available to all students and any aid to religion was only incidental. In short, the law had a secular purpose and a secular primary effect.

Despite strong opposition in some quarters, *Everson* remains the law of the land and the Supreme Court has shown no inclination to reverse its position on basic bus fare reimbursement programs. Similarly, state-approved secular textbooks may be lent to private school students, including parochial school students. [*Board of Education v. Allen* (U.S. 1968)] A law that imposes a general obligation on the state to provide a sign language interpreter for a deaf student can be applied to a student at a

Catholic high school. The Establishment Clause is not violated just because a sectarian institution receives an "attenuated financial benefit" from a government program that neutrally distributes benefits. [*Zobrest v. Catalina Foothills School District* (U.S. 1993)] On the other hand, the loan of instructional materials (for example, maps, magazines, and tape recorders) and providing public transportation for field trips to parochial school students have been struck down. [*Wolman v. Walter* (U.S. 1977)] The *Wolman* Court concluded: "In view of the impossibility of separating the secular education function from the sectarian," the state aid presented too great a danger of advancing the religious teaching mission of the parochial schools. The court based its decision on *Meek v. Pittenger* (U.S. 1975), which held that state loans of nontextbook instructional materials and equipment to private schools was unconstitutional.

EXCESSIVE ENTANGLEMENT   Excessive entanglement between the state and religion is perhaps most simply defined as an impermissible merging or intermeddling of the proper spheres of religion and government.

The idea of "excessive entanglement" as a standard to determine the constitutionality of laws under the requirements of the First Amendment first arose in *Lemon v. Kurtzman* (U.S. 1971). In that case Justice William O. Douglas wrote that "[t]he Constitution decrees that religion must be a private matter for the individual, the family, and the institutions of private choice, and that while some involvement and entanglement may be inevitable, lines must be drawn."

Any program under which the government grants aid to a religiously affiliated institution of any type must be tested under the Establishment Clause by using the three-part test set forth in *Lemon*. To pass constitutional muster the program must have (1) a secular purpose, (2) a primary effect that neither advances nor inhibits religion, and (3) no "excessive entanglement" between the government and religious authority.

Factors considered by a court when testing for "excessive entanglement" of the government with religion in any program include: (1) the character of the institution aided, (2) the type of aid given, and (3) the resulting administrative relationships. [*Black v. Snyder* (Minn. App. Ct. 1991)] Additionally, the potential of the aid program for causing political divisions along religious lines is an important factor in determining its validity.

Government financial grants are found to foster "excessive entanglement" with religion if they necessitate government oversight of a religious institution's affairs in order to ensure that the government aid flowing to the institution is utilized for secular purposes and not for the advancement of religion. [*State v. Pendleton* (N.C. App. Ct. 1993; N.C. 1994); *Bowen v. Kendrick* (U.S. 1988); *Wallace v. Jaffree* (U.S. 1985)] A law fosters "excessive entanglement" between church and state when it necessitates sustained and detailed administrative relationships between church and state.

Whether excessive entanglement exists in a certain program involves determination of the degree of independent secular function in the institution to be aided. If the institution is pervasively religious, it will be practically impossible to aid the institution without either having the impermissible effect of adding religion or else having to establish so many procedural safeguards that an excessive entanglement results. However, if the institution has a clearly independent secular function, the state should be able to design a program that aids only the secular activities. This type of institution can then be aided with a minimum of administrative entanglement, as the lesser potential for aiding the religious function requires fewer safeguards.

During the last century, the U.S. Supreme Court upheld grants to church-affiliated hospitals in *Bradfield v. Roberts* (U.S. 1899), recently cited with approval by the Court in *Roemer v. Board of Public Works* (U.S. 1976). As religious hospitals seem to have an independent secular function, the analysis should be the same as that for religious colleges—the state need only avoid aiding pervasively religious institutions or clearly religious activities. So long as the hospital aided is not so "pervasively sectarian" as to subsume its role as a hospital in its religious mission, its secular medical function may receive state aid.

The government may not delegate governmental power to religious organizations because such action would involve excessive governmental entanglement. [*Larkin v. Grendel's Den, Inc.* (U.S. 1982) (statute impermissibly gave church-affiliated schools power to veto liquor licenses for nearby businesses)]

F

FAITH HEALING Praying for the miraculous healing of the sick has been reported sporadically throughout the history of Christianity, but the modern-day faith-healing movement finds its origins in the "Faith Cure" movement that was a part of the larger Holiness movement of the late nineteenth century. The most influential Holiness faith healer was Episcopalian Charles Cullis, who wrote *Faith Cures* (1879), emphasizing the "prayer of faith" [James 5:14–15] especially as the key to healing. Cullis persuaded many others who would become major faith healers.

Traditionally, American courts have held that the government's interest in the general health of the populace overrides individual religious objections to medical and health regulations.

Faith healing has given rise to legal liability in two distinct situations: (1) when a parent refuses all forms of conventional medical treatment for his or her child, and instead adheres strictly to faith healing for a cure, and (2) when an adult patient refuses all forms of conventional medical treatment for himself or herself, relying strictly on faith healing to cure illnesses. Faith healing derives from the healing miracles, in which disease is cured by faith and prayer. Faith healers profess to cure disease utilizing faith and prayer and some denounce the use of conventional medicine.

American courts have upheld the right of the state to protect the health and safety of minor children over the religiously based objections of the child or his or her parents. Thus, courts have appointed guardians to consent to necessary medical treatment (such as blood transfusions) for children, even though the treatment violates the child's or parent's religion. [*In re Sampson* (N.Y. 1972)]

Similarly, appropriate action may be taken against parents for the neglect of the health or safety of their children regardless of whether the parent acted on the basis of religious principles. [*Perricone v. New Jersey* (N.J. 1962, *cert. denied* U.S. 1962)]

In 1997 Congress amended the Child Abuse Prevention and Treatment Act in order to protect parents from any federal requirement to provide their children with medical intervention that would be against the parents' religious beliefs. The statute also provides that it may not be interpreted to require a state to find, or prohibit a state from finding, abuse or neglect when a parent relies on "spiritual means" rather than medical treatment to provide for the health needs of the child.

Faith-healing practitioners have been criticized on several grounds, including for perceived healings that do not last, for healings that are never verified by medical professionals, for blaming the lack of healing on the inadequate faith of the patient, which produces intense feelings of guilt, and for excessively high numbers of healings claimed. Many critics contend that the healings are psychosomatic at most. Some healers have brought disrepute to the movement through fraudulent healings, lack of financial accountability, and highly publicized moral failures. The most controversial development in the faith-healing movement may be the so-called Faith Teachers, led by Kenneth Hagin, who emphasize a health and wealth gospel in which people with enough faith can claim (not just request) their healing from God.

The plaintiff in *Winters v. Miller* (2d Cir. 1971) sued for civil damages, alleging that her constitutional rights were violated. The plaintiff was a 59-year-old female Christian Scientist, who had been receiving welfare benefits. She was admitted involuntarily to the hospital for mental illness after she had refused to change hotel rooms, which were entirely subsidized by welfare, upon management's request. At the hospital she repeatedly expressed to the medical staff her adherence to faith healing and refused all medical treatment, even the taking of her blood pressure. Despite her objection to medical treatment on religious grounds, the hospital staff regularly gave her medication, mostly tranquilizers, for the approximately month and a half that she remained in the hospital.

The Second Circuit Court of Appeals addressed whether the state constitutionally could compel the plaintiff to submit to conventional medical treatment, such as taking medications, in violation of her religious belief in faith healing as her only means of medical treatment. Relying on U.S. Supreme Court precedent, the court stated that "freedom of speech and of the press, of assembly, and of worship may not be infringed on such slender grounds [as the rational basis inquiry]. They are susceptible of restriction only to prevent grave and immediate danger to interests which the state may lawfully protect." The court dismissed the state's argument that its interest in caring for people suffering from mental illness, and in protecting the mental health of the state, outweighed the appellant's freedom of religion. In so doing, the court stated that by "forcing the unwanted medication on Miss Winters, the state was in [no] way protecting the interest of society or even a third party."

A similar case regarding a violation of a plaintiff's constitutional right to religious freedom to reject life-saving medical treatment arose in Ohio in *In re Milton* (Ohio 1987). A 53-year-old woman believed in faith healing as her sole means of medical treatment. The plaintiff's competency was questioned because she had delusions that she was married to a locally well-known faith healer, who, she believed, would cure her. However, the plaintiff was never legally declared to be incompetent due, in large part, to at least one doctor who testified that her belief in faith healing was long-standing and genuine. The Ohio Supreme Court held that a competent adult ultimately could decide medical treatment decisions. More importantly, the court held that the state's interest in enforcing its police powers does not outweigh a competent adult's decision to adhere to faith healing, despite the availability of a recognized medical remedy.

In *People v. Vogel Saney* (N.Y. App. Ct.), a spiritual healer associated with a body called the Spiritualist Church engaged in silent prayer while prescribing herbal remedies. He claimed that this was a religious practice, and hence, was protected by the Free Exercise Clause of the First Amendment so that he was exempt from state licensing requirements for doctors. The court did not agree and classified the faith healer as a medical doctor, requiring him to abide by the state's licensing laws for medical professionals. Noncompliance with the state licensing laws constituted the unlicensed practice of medicine. The court distinguished between faith healers and medical doctors thus: faith healers utilize religious beliefs and prayer to cure illnesses, while doctors use learned skills, training, and instruments. Consequently, as long as the faith healer relied solely on the practice of religion, faith, and prayer to heal the patient, the faith healer fell within the statutory exemption contained in the medical licensing statute for such practices. However, if the faith healer relied on any physical means or substances—such as herbal remedies—the exemption was not available.

The caselaw demonstrates that an individual's right to freedom of religion is of paramount importance, and will be considered secondary only if a legitimate state interest exists. The U.S. Supreme Court applies a balancing test to determine whether the state's interest outweighs the individual's right to freedom of religion. The standard to be applied is whether the restriction on religious freedom "prevents grave and immediate danger to interests which the state may lawfully protect." The lawful state interests that have qualified to tip the balance in favor of restricting religious freedom are protection of society or a third person.

FAMILY LAW   Family plays a crucial role and is a regarded as a positive good in most of the world's religions. Family relations have an uncertain, even ambivalent constitutional status in Supreme Court decisions. If the U.S. Constitution protects the family against external interference, it also permits the establishment of public moral standards and to protect and regulate social relationships among adults and to protect children from apparently harmful parental conduct.

In *Meyer v. Nebraska* (U.S. 1929) the Supreme Court held that the "liberty" guaranteed under the Fourteenth Amendment to the Constitution includes the right to "marry, establish a home and bring up children."

Emphasizing the religious basis for the parents' claims, the Supreme Court in *Wisconsin v. Yoder* (U.S. 1972) held that school officials could not require Amish children to attend secondary schools in the face of their parents' objections that this imposition was harmful to the children and inconsistent with the parents' views on proper child-rearing practices. Justice William O. Douglas's dissent in the case focused on the narrowness of the Court's framework, which encompassed only the interests of the parents and the state. He argued that the children should first have been heard as to their desire for a high school education and emancipation from the Amish religion and community. In addition, he questioned whether only formal religious communities can seek an exemption from compulsory high school for their adherents.

Some commentators argue that the Supreme Court is not prepared to find constitutional protection for family status as such but only for those families whose conduct meets with the justices' particular approval. This principle could explain the Court's deference to Amish parents, who generally succeed in imposing rigid behavioral controls on their children—as the Court repeatedly stressed in *Yoder*—or its deference to parents' wishes to confine their socially disruptive children in psychiatric institutions. A judicial preference for such behavior controls might also explain the Court's refusal to defer to parents' objections to school corporal punishment or to parents' resistance to abortions when they failed effectively to convince their unmarried minor daughters to abstain from sexual relations.

The Court has not been unanimous in these cases, and no justice has explicitly defended this particular child-rearing principle as a constitutional norm. Yet the Court does suggest that current constitutional doctrine gives no special status to family relations as such, either between parents and children or among adults. The occasional rhetorical flourishes in Supreme Court opinions on the "constitutional sanctity" of the family does not yet reflect any consistent constitutional principle.

By the 1990s the Supreme Court had issued extensive rulings on family life. These cases involved issues ranging from religion to gender equity. They generated intense debate and controversy. Despite their inconsistencies and contradictions, the Court's rulings had redefined the legal and constitutional basis of the American family. Significantly, the Court had become a major source of national family policies. Its decisions helped structure American family life on everything from birth to death.

FEDERALISM   Federalism may be loosely defined as contractual noncentralization, or the structured dispersion of power among many centers whose legitimate authority is constitutionally guaranteed. Federal democracy is an original American contribution to democratic thought and republican government. Its conception represents a synthesis of the Puritan idea of the covenant relationship as the foundation of all proper human society and the constitutional ideas of the English natural rights school of the seventeenth and early eighteenth centuries.

Federal democracy is a composite democracy that includes a strong religious component. The religious expression of federalism was brought to the United States through the theology of the Puritans, who viewed the world as organized through the covenants that God made with mankind, binding God and man into a lasting union and partnership to work for the redemption of the world, but in such a way that both parties were free—as partners must be—to preserve their respective integrities. Implicit in the Puritan view is the understanding that God relinquished some of his omnipotence to enable people to be free to contract with him.

Under federalism, all social and political relationships are derived from that original covenant. This theological perspective found its counterpart in congregationalism as the basis of church polity. Thus, communities of believers were required to organize themselves by covenant into congregations, just as communities of citizens were required to organize themselves by covenant into towns. The entire structure of religious and political organization in early New England reflected this application of a theological principle to social and political life.

One characteristic of modern federalism in the United States is the essence of federal norms, whether legal, administrative, or judicial, that bear directly upon the federation's citizens, without any need of intervention of the member states. The architects of the American system recognized that a successful federal system, something more than a loose confederation of states, required that both the national and the state governments be given substantial autonomy. They also recognized that each had to have some way to influence the other from within as well as through direct negotiation. The federal government has the power to deal directly with the public, that is to say, with the citizenry of the states. The states, in turn, have a major role in determining the composition of the federal government and the selection of those who make it function.

By the 1980s the United States Supreme Court had become an active interpreter of the constitutional provisions on free exercise and no establishment of religion. It was not always thus. The Court had few occasions in the nineteenth and early twentieth centuries to render opinions in these areas. The text of the First Amendment, which includes the religion clauses, limits only the federal government, not the states. Because the jurisdiction of the federal judiciary does not normally extend to claims made under state constitutional provisions, the long silence of the federal courts on issues of religious liberty is understandable.

It was not until the United States Supreme Court "incorporated" the free exercise and no establishment principles as substantive parts of the Fourteenth Amendment's Due Process Clause (an amendment that does apply to the states) that the federal judiciary gained jurisdiction over claims of state violations of religious liberty. This incorporation did not occur until the Free Exercise Clause was incorporated by the Court's decision in *Cantwell v. Connecticut* (U.S. 1940) and the Establishment Clause was incorporated in *Everson v. Board of Education* (U.S. 1947).

By the mid-1960s, as the nation committed itself to the recognition and implementation of civil rights, the values of federalism were in eclipse. The U.S. Supreme Court had incorporated virtually all of the Bill of Rights into the Fourteenth Amendment for application to the states, and it aggressively enlarged its interpretation of the scope of those rights. The Court's expansion of the First Amendment guarantees of religious liberty resulted in the invalidation of numerous state regulations that had heretofore been deemed perfectly acceptable reflections of local culture.

Thus, for almost 150 years, judicial interpretation of the rights of religious liberty was largely a matter for the separate state judiciaries under their own constitutional provisions. The result of incorporation into the Fourteenth Amendment of the federal Bill of Rights has been not only to open the federal courts to state claimants but also to bind state courts to the authoritative decisions of the U.S. Supreme Court on issues of religious liberty. These decisions establish the minimum or base standard of no establishment and free exercise. State courts are then free under their own constitutional provisions to expand or enlarge on the federally defined base. In requiring a higher standard than is demanded under the federal Constitution, however, a state may not transgress other federally protected constitutional rights. [*Widmar v. Vincent* (U.S. 1981)]

President Ronald Reagan announced his own brand of "new federalism" on taking office in 1981. Both in his rhetoric and administrative actions, he sought to turn the clock back dramatically on many features of modern federalism. Generally speaking, Reagan's policies were based on an orthodox, small-government, anticentrist ideology, seldom stressed since the New Deal era of the 1930s and 1940s. Reagan's new federalism included support to constitutional amendments designed to permit school prayer in public schools and to permit the states to prohibit abortion.

During the Reagan years, federalism again emerged at the center of political debate in America and once again the values of federalism were being invoked for purposes that transcended the mere reordering of federal-state relationships. The classic concerns of federalism in theory—diffusion of power, diversity, liberty, and efficiency—remained in the forefront of public attention. How to reconcile the ideals expressed in the original understanding of federalism with the social and economic realities of the late twentieth century remains a profoundly important issue.

FETAL RIGHTS
The rights of any unborn human fetus, which is generally a developing human being from roughly eight weeks after conception to birth. Like other categories of rights, fetal rights embrace a complex variety of topics and issues involving many legal areas, including criminal, employment, health care, and family law.

Historically, under both English common law and U.S. law, the fetus has not been recognized as a person with full rights. The common law, although considering postquickening abortions a crime, regarded them as a lesser offense than the killing of a born child. Instead, legal rights have centered on the mother, with the fetus treated as a part of her. Nevertheless, U.S. law has in certain instances granted the fetus limited rights, particularly as medical science has made it increasingly possible to directly monitor, diagnose, and treat the fetus as a patient.

The term *fetal rights* came into wide usage following the landmark abortion case *Roe v. Wade* (U.S. 1973). In that case, the Supreme Court ruled that a woman has a constitutionally guaranteed unqualified right to an abortion in the first trimester of her pregnancy. She also has a right to terminate a pregnancy in the second trimester, although the state may regulate abortion procedures as long as the regulations are reasonably related to the promotion of the mother's health. In its holding, the Court ruled that a fetus is not a person under the terms of the Fourteenth Amendment of the U.S. Constitution. The Court, however, also maintained that the state has an interest in protecting the life of a fetus after viability—that is, after the point at which the fetus is capable of living outside the womb. As a result, states were permitted to outlaw abortion in the third trimester of pregnancy, except when the procedure is necessary to preserve the life of the mother.

Roe was bitterly criticized by those who were morally or religiously opposed to abortion, and in the years following that case, abortion became one of the most contentious issues in the United States. Abortion opponents became a powerful political lobby and their efforts to promote the rights of unborn humans significantly influenced the law. The prolife (antiabortion) movement has actively lobbied for legislation on both the state and federal level, resulting in laws requiring parental notification of an adolescent's decision to have an abortion, prohibiting research using aborted fetal tissue, cutting off federal funding for abortion research, and banning partial-birth abortions. They also supported a "human life" amendment to the U.S. Constitution that would restrict the right to an abortion.

FIRST AMENDMENT (U.S. CONSTITUTION)   The

First Amendment to the U.S. Constitution has two distinct clauses affecting religion, each representing a fundamental principle and both together designed to protect religious liberty. One is the Establishment Clause, which prohibits any law "respecting an establishment of religion." The other is the Free Exercise Clause, which bans laws "prohibiting the free exercise of religion." The First Amendment's religion clauses have generated much litigation, and balancing the sometimes contradictory provisions of the two clauses has generated many complex legal rules.

The two religion clauses are designed to protect the same basic value: the freedom of every individual to worship (or not to worship) as he or she wishes without governmental interference. The two clauses have been summarized as requiring "that government neither engage in nor compel religious practices, that it effect no favoritism among sects or between religion and nonreligion, and that it operate to the detriment of no religious belief." [*Abington School District v. Schempp* (U.S. 1963)] Some authorities believe the Free Exercise Clause was especially intended to protect the religious freedom of minority religious groups.

So long as one is dealing with beliefs and expressions, which are separable from conduct harmful to other individuals or the community, the essential unity of the philosophical core of the First Amendment makes it unnecessary to distinguish for legal purposes among religious belief, political ideologies, and other equally sincere convictions. In upholding the First Amendment privilege of Jehovah's Witnesses to refuse to join other school children in a daily salute to the U.S. flag, the Supreme Court pointedly refrained from specifying whether the privilege arose under the Free Exercise Clause or the guarantee of freedom of speech: "[C]ompelling the flag salute and pledge, . . . invades the sphere of intellect and spirit which it is the purpose for the First Amendment to reserve from all official control." [*Minersville School District v. Gobitis* (U.S. 1940); *West Virginia State Board of Education v. Barnette* (1943)] Test oaths, like particular beliefs, cannot be required for holding public office or receiving public grants.

In upholding the conviction of a Mormon for polygamy in *Reynolds v. United States* (U.S. 1879), despite a plea from the defendant that the Free Exercise Clause protected him in his religious duty, the U.S. Supreme Court sought to distinguish between the realm of ideas and the world of material action in fashioning a constitutional principle: "Congress was deprived of all legislative power over mere opinion, but was left free to reach actions which were in violation of social duties or subversive of good order."

In the beginning, religion and established churches were dominant in American life. Nearly all Americans were Christians, with Protestantism being predominant. In South Carolina the Constitution of 1778 declared the "Protestant religion to be the established religion of this State." Church and state were intertwined in Massachusetts. Even where there was no official connection, both the laws and practices of government bore evidence of benevolent cooperation with the prevailing creeds: Sunday closing laws were universal, religious oaths were often required of state officials, and legislative sessions began with prayer. Even today the crier in the U.S. Supreme Court still begins each session by invoking divine blessing, the country's coinage states "In God We Trust," and church property remains exempt from taxation. As public education spread, prayers and Bible reading began each school day in many areas.

The basis for extending the First Amendment to the states was established by the adoption of the Fourteenth Amendment in 1868, which provides in part "[N]or shall any State deprive any person of life, liberty, or property without due process of law."

The effects of the Fourteenth Amendment on First Amendment rights generally, and upon religious liberty in particular, were slow to develop. As late as 1922 the Supreme Court declared in *Prudential Insurance Co. v. Cheek* (U.S. 1922) that "neither the Fourteenth Amendment nor any other provision of the U.S. Constitution imposes upon the States any restrictions about 'freedom of speech.'" But within another decade the First Amendment's guarantee of freedom of expression had been incorporated into the Fourteenth Amendment by judicial interpretation. Incorporation of the other clauses, including the prohibition against any law "respecting an establishment of religion," followed somewhat later. [*Cantwell v. Connecticut* (U.S. 1940); *Everson v. Board of Education* (U.S. 1987)] Today, the First Amendment restricts both state and federal governments to the same extent and in the same fashion.

Prior to incorporation of the religion clauses into the Fourteenth Amendment, the U.S. Supreme Court and lower federal courts had the power to review alleged Establishment or Free Exercise Clause violations by Congress under Article III, which states that the "judicial power [of the United States] shall extend to all cases, in law and equity, arising out of this Constitution." No authority existed, however, for federal courts to review religious liberty claims arising under state law. The paucity of federal cases interpreting the religion clauses between the late eighteenth and the early twentieth centuries is thus attributable to at least two factors: the small number of religion-based claims initiated against the federal government and the limitations of federal review of state actions involving religion.

The traditional links between church and state were challenged after incorporation of the First Amendment into the Fourteenth Amendment, not only by atheists or agnostics, but also by religious minorities whose members were distinguished by official involvement in religious practices, who were fearful that their isolation would hamper full assimilation into all aspects of American life or stimulate invidious discrimination against them. The Supreme Court was then forced to choose among the competing strains of religious and political philosophy whose adherents heretofore had agreed only that the federal government, but not the states, should be barred from "an establishment of religion." The majority's inclination during the years 1945 to 1980 toward a strongly secular, separationist view of the wall of separation between church and state led to two important lines of decisions.

At issue for contemporary courts has been where to draw the line for government-provided services that benefit religious organizations. Some aid obviously must be permitted, such as police and fire protection for church property. Less clear and more controversial are government financial subsidies to parochial schools, or to parents who send their children to such schools. One line of important court decisions prohibits both state and federal governments from giving direct financial aid to sectarian primary and secondary schools, even though the same or greater aid is given to the public schools maintained by the government. These decisions leave somewhat greater latitude for aid to parents of parochial students, and also for government grants destined to promote higher education, including programs offered by religious institutions.

The second important line of decisions required discontinuance of the widespread and traditional practice of starting each day in the public schools with some form of religious exercise, such as saying an ecumenical prayer or reading from the Bible. The latter decisions provoked such controversy that in the 1980s, more than two decades after the decisions were rendered, fundamentalist groups were actively pressing for legislation to abolish the Supreme Court's jurisdiction to enforce the Establishment Clause in cases involving school prayer, thus leaving interpretation of the Clause to individual state courts.

Even though the line between the realm of the spirit and the world of material conduct subject to government regulation is fundamental to the jurisprudence of the First Amendment, the simple line between belief and conduct drawn in the polygamy cases was too inflexible to survive as a complete constitutional formula. Religious duties too often conflict with the commands of civil authority. Conversely, the public has compelling interests in the world of conduct that sometimes cannot be secured without interference with the expression of ideas.

Two cases suggest the one limiting constitutional protection for religious disobedience to the commands of the state. In *Wisconsin v. Yoder* (U.S. 1972) the Supreme Court held that the Free Exercise Clause secured Amish parents the privilege of keeping 14- and 15-year-old children out of high school, contrary to a state law requiring school attendance until age 16. The decision allowed the Amish to pursue their religious conviction that salvation requires simple life in a church community apart from the world and worldly influences. The Court saw its judicial duty to be striking a proper balance between the importance of the interests served by the state law against the importance to believers of adherence to the religious practice in question. The balance swung the opposite way in *Negre v. Larsen* (U.S. 1971). In that case the Court held that a faithful Roman Catholic's belief that the "unjust" nature of the war in Vietnam required him to refuse to participate did not excuse his refusal to be inducted into the armed forces.

Where religious objectors seek exemption from laws of general application, both federal and state governments must walk a narrow line. On the one hand the Free Exercise Clause may require exemption. On the other hand excepting religious groups from laws of general application may constitute an unconstitutional "establishment" of religion. Here again the decision calls for ad hoc balancing of the individual and public interests affected by the particular legislative act.

Beginning in the 1960s the Supreme Court applied the First Amendment's limitations rigorously. To test compliance with the Establishment Clause, the Court required government actions to pass a three-part examination. To determine if a government action interfered with the Free Exercise Clause, the Court subjected it to strict judicial scrutiny; that is, to be constitutional the government interest advanced by an action had to be "compelling" and not attainable by any alternative means less disruptive to the religious interests affected by it.

The three-part review of laws for constitutionality in light of the Establishment Clause was set forth in *Lemon v. Kurtzman* (U.S., 1971). To pass constitutional muster under this test, a law must first have a secular purpose. In other words, there must be a valid nonreligious reason for the law. Second, the law's primary effect must neither advance nor inhibit religion. Finally, the statute must not foster "an excessive government entanglement with religion." Any rule that forces government at any level to become intertwined with religious institutions or principles is prohibited.

Several statutes and government actions have been found unconstitutional when subjected to the *Lemon* test. For example, government could not provide financial support to educational programs in parochial schools as this would "entangle" government with the religious institution. [*Committee for Public Education & Religious Liberty v. Nyquist* (U.S. 1973); *Meek v. Pittenger* (U.S. 1975)] A mandated moment of silence to allow for meditation or prayer in public schools was struck down because it lacked any "secular purpose." [*Wallace v. Jaffree* (U.S. 1985)] And prohibiting the teaching of evolution unless "creation science" was also taught violated the Constitution because the "primary effect" of the law was the advancement of a particular religious belief. [*Edwards v. Aguillard* (U.S. 1987)]

The "strict scrutiny" test of any law that might infringe on the free exercise of one's religion was set forth in *Sherbert v. Verner* (U.S. 1963). If a law or regulation substantially infringed on a religious practice, the government had to show a "compelling government interest" for the provision and even then had to show that the law was the least restrictive method to achieve that significant interest. Under this test, the Supreme Court upheld the right of a Jehovah's Witness to quit his job in a defense factory and still get unemployment insurance because of an "honest conviction" that his religion barred him from doing any war-related work. It declared invalid a state prohibition of unemployment compensation for anyone who would not work on the Sabbath. [*Sherbert v. Verner* (U.S. 1963)] It also invalidated a law that required Amish parents to send their children to high school. [*Wisconsin v. Yoder* (U.S. 1972)]

The First Amendment is typically understood to protect from government abridgment a broad realm of what might be called "symbolic activity," which includes religious expression.

Because religious expression, like every other type of expression protected by the First Amendment, is intertwined with many other activities that the government is clearly empowered to regulate—for instance, education and economic activities—the courts have experienced considerable difficulty in distinguishing impermissible infringement on First Amendment freedoms from legitimate exercises of governmental authority. The Supreme Court has fashioned many diverse and detailed rules with which to make the determination. The determination must be content neutral, that is, without regard to the content of the expression under consideration. So much of this doctrine now exists and it is so overlapping that ample room remains for disagreement among the justices, the advocates, and the commentators about how to characterize and hence decide particular First Amendment cases. The result is that by the 1980s the First Amendment—especially in the area of religion—has followed the Fourth Amendment in a proliferation of fragmentary, ephemeral, and highly bureaucratized doctrines.

Politicization, the problem of distinguishing content-neutral from content-based regulation, and the tendency to produce more complex context-specific doctrine has been evident in the Supreme Court's treatment of religion cases. In *Allegheny County v. ACLU* (U.S. 1989), for instance, the Court fragmented over the constitutionality of two religious displays on public property during the December holiday season. One display was of a Christian nativity scene; the other display exhibited a Christmas tree and a Hanukkah menorah. On the basis of some exceedingly fine distinctions, the various opinions established that the menorah exhibition was constitutional, while the nativity scene was not.

The importance of the distinction between content on the one hand, and form and effect on the other was especially evident in the judicial disagreement over the constitutionality of the nativity scene display. Writing at times for the Court, for a plurality, and for himself, Justice Harry A. Blackmun concluded that the display of a nativity scene on public property during the Christmas season violated the Establishment Clause because it endorsed a patently Christian message. Focusing on the message conveyed by the display, Justice Blackmun noted that the nativity scene was accompanied by the words: "Glory to God in the Highest" and that unlike the display in the case of *Lynch v. Donnelly* (U.S. 1984), there was nothing in its context to detract from the scene's religious message. Accordingly, Justice Blackmun concluded that the government was endorsing a religious message in violation of the Establishment Clause. One group of dissenting and concurring justices, Anthony M. Kennedy, Byron White, and Antonin Scalia, rejected Blackmun's reasoning and result. Turning away from an inquiry into the meaning of the government display of a nativity scene, this group of justices focused attention on the effects of the scene: they noted that there was no evidence of coerced participation in religion or religious ceremonies or of significant expenditures of tax money. On the whole, then, the judicial disagreement here also organized itself around the determination of whether it is the conceptual meaning of the government action that matters or its forms and effect.

FLAG SALUTE CEREMONY   The flag salute ceremony developed in the latter half of the nineteenth century. In the original ceremony the participants faced the flag and pledged "allegiance to my flag and the republic for which it stands, one nation indivisible, with liberty and justice for all." While repeating the words "to my flag" the right hand was extended palm up toward the flag. Over the years the ceremony evolved slightly, with minor changes of wording and with the extended arm salute dropped in 1942 because of its similarity to the Nazi salute. At this point in its evolution, however the salute had official standing: Congress had prescribed the form of words and substituted the right hand over the heart for the extended arm.

Beginning in 1898 with New York, some states began requiring the ceremony as part of the opening exercise of the school day. The early state flag salute laws did not make the ceremony compulsory for individual students, but many local school boards insisted on participation. Many patriotic and fraternal organizations supported the flag salute; opposition came from civil libertarians and some small religious groups. The principal opponents of the compulsory school flag salute were the Jehovah's Witnesses, a tightly knit evangelical sect whose religious beliefs commanded them not to salute the flag as a "graven image."

In the two cases known as the flag salute cases, *Minersville School District v. Gobitis* (U.S. 1940) and *West Virginia Board of Education v. Barnette* (U.S. 1943), the U.S. Supreme Court held that students could not be compelled to salute the flag against their beliefs, based on the right of free speech. The Court found that the requirement invaded the sphere of free intellect and belief that was at the core of these First Amendment principles. Although the Jehovah's Witnesses brought these cases because of their religious objections to the honoring of "idols," the infringement of religious beliefs was not crucial to the decisions. Anyone opposed to saluting the flag had to be excused from the requirement without regard to whether their refusal was based on religious or nonreligious grounds.

FOREIGN POLICY The United States State Department has asserted that an important part of American foreign policy is to promote greater freedom of religion and to encourage reconciliation among religious groups. The United States adopted this stand because it is consistent with American values and the belief that nations are stronger and the lives of their people richer, when citizens have the freedom to choose, proclaim, and exercise their religious identity.

The United States has also learned that the denial of religious freedom or threats to it can cause, fear, flight, fighting, and even all-out war. Thus the United States has developed a focus in our policy on regions where religious divisions have combined with other factors to engender violence or endanger peace. Promoting religious freedom is an American foreign policy priority.

To this end United States diplomats are instructed to provide frequent and thorough reports on the status of religious freedom in the countries to which they are assigned. The United States has intensified the spotlight on religious freedom in the reports that the State Department issues annually on human rights practices around the world.

The United States is also modifying its procedures for reviewing requests for political asylum to ensure that those fleeing religious persecution are treated fairly.

In addition, the United States promotes religious freedom through foreign broadcasting, by sponsoring programs and exchanges that foster understanding, and through work in international organizations such as the United Nations Human Rights Commission and the Organization for Security and Cooperation in Europe.

The United States often raises issues related to religious freedom with foreign governments and their representatives. That was the case, for example, in 1997 when Secretary of State Madeleine Albright discussed restrictions on religious activity in Vietnam, and when President Clinton raised with President Yeltsin serious concerns about Russia's new law on religion. The law classified five religions as "traditional" to Russia: Russian Orthodoxy, Buddhism, Islam, Hinduism, and Christianity. The law would have restricted groups such as Roman Catholics, Pentecostalists, Seventh-Day Adventists, Baptists, and Mormons. Restricted groups would not be able to operate schools, distribute religious literature, or invite foreign preachers. Other groups that refused to register would be subject to even heavier restriction. During the United States-China summit meeting in 1997, the United States stressed to President Jian Zemin the importance of respecting the religious heritage of the people of Tibet and of ensuring that China's growing Christian community is allowed to worship freely.

The United States reinforced its commitment to religious tolerance in 1996 when Secretary of State Warren Christopher established an Advisory Committee on Religious Freedom Abroad. The Committee includes distinguished scholars, activists, and religious leaders representing the major American spiritual traditions. Its purpose is to help direct attention to the problem of religious persecution abroad and to provide advice on how to achieve reconciliation in areas affected by religious enmity.

FRAZEE V. ILLINOIS DEPARTMENT OF EMPLOYMENT SECURITY (U.S. 1989)

This case expanded the protection of the Free Exercise Clause of the First Amendment by allowing a Christian to refuse to work on the Sabbath without being denied unemployment benefits. The Supreme Court had already held that such benefits could not be denied to persons whose religious beliefs obligated them to refuse work on the Sabbath, but in these earlier cases [for example, *Sherbert v. Verner* (U.S. 1963)] the claimant had belonged to a religious sect or particular church. Frazee was not a member of either and did not rely on a specific religious tenet. He did assert, however, that he could not work on Sunday due to his beliefs "as a Christian," but he was not a member of an organized church, sect, or denomination. The Illinois courts therefore upheld the denial to him of unemployment compensation.

Unanimously, the Supreme Court reversed the Illinois courts and sustained Frazee's right to free exercise of his religious beliefs. Frazee had asserted that he was a Christian, and no authority had challenged his sincerity. As a Christian, Frazee felt that working on Sunday was wrong. The Court held that a professing Christian, even if not a churchgoer or member of a particular sect, was protected by the Free Exercise Clause from having to choose between his or her religious belief and unemployment compensation. Denial of compensation violated the clause.

FREE EXERCISE CLAUSE This Clause, contained in the First Amendment to the U.S. Constitution, forbids the government from making any law "prohibiting the free exercise" of religion. The Free Exercise Clause, like the Establishment Clause, applies not only to the federal government but also the states through the Fourteenth Amendment. This constitutional provision "withdraws from legislative power, state and federal, the exertion of any restraint on the free exercise of religion. Its purpose is to secure religious liberty in the individual by prohibiting any invasions there by civil authority." [*Abington School District v. Schempp* (U.S. 1963)] The Free Exercise Clause bars "governmental regulation of religious beliefs as such," and prohibits secular government programs "to impede the observance of one or all religions" or "to discriminate invidiously between religions . . . even though the burden may be characterized as being only indirect." [*Braunfeld v. Brown* (U.S. 1961)] "A regulation neutral on its face may, in its application, nonetheless offend the constitutional requirement for governmental neutrality if it unduly burdens the free exercise of religion." [*Wisconsin v. Yoder* (U.S. 1971)]

Freedom of conscience is the basis of the Free Exercise Clause, and government may not penalize or discriminate against an individual or a group of individuals because of their religious views, nor may it compel persons to affirm any particular beliefs. [*Sherbet v. Verner* (U.S. 1963)] Yet the Free Exercise Clause does not prevent government from either requiring the doing of some act or forbidding the doing of some act merely because religious beliefs underlie the conduct in question. [*See Reynolds v. United States* (U.S. 1879)(case challenging Mormon practice of polygamy, which established principle that under guarantee of religious liberty, government may not punish religious beliefs but may punish religiously motivated practices that injure public interest); *Jacobson v. Massachusetts* (U.S. 1905)(Court rejected plaintiff's religious objections to town vaccination ordinance); *United States v. Lee* (U.S. 1979)(holding that Amish employers had to pay social security and unemployment taxes, regardless of their religious objections to them; compelling government interest is served by federal revenue system, so no member of any religious sect can claim exemption from taxation); *Employment Division v. Smith* (U.S. 1990)(state's interest in ensuring integrity of unemployment insurance fund sufficiently important to justify refusal to pay benefits to claimants who were fired for use of peyote, despite fact that use was for religious purposes)]

The Free Exercise Clause flatly prohibits the outlawing of any religious belief. The difficult issues arise not in connection with pure beliefs, but in connection with conduct that is related to beliefs. Normally, free exercise problems arise when the government, acting in pursuit of a nonreligious objective, either (1) forbids or burdens conduct that happens to be dictated by someone's religious beliefs or (2) compels or encourages conduct that is forbidden by someone's religious beliefs. However, not all statutes that forbid conduct required by religious beliefs or that compel conduct forbidden by religious beliefs are automatically violative of the Free Exercise Clause. The Court has not developed a clear test for determining when such a violation exists (in contrast to the three-prong standard in Establishment Clause cases).

Just as the body of Establishment Clause caselaw is of recent vintage, so is the body of Free Exercise Clause caselaw. The early state constitutions made extensive provisions for the protection of freedom of worship and conscience. One must presume that these provisions adequately served the needs of the major Protestant denominations of pre–Civil War America. The removal in the early nineteenth century of some implicit political disabilities against Roman Catholics and Jews ensured that all the major religious denominations were not only free to worship but free to enjoy equal civil rights. Although anti-Semitism and anti-Roman Catholicism were problems throughout the nineteenth century, religious bigotry did not prevent Jews and Roman Catholics from practicing their religion. They built their churches and temples, flourished, and became a part of the dominant culture. In short, throughout the greater part of the nineteenth century the free exercise of religion was simply not a problem for those religious groups within the Judeo-Christian mainstream. Even nonconformity of religious beliefs posed no problem: what became a problem was nonconformity to the laws motivated by religious belief. The major example of this kind of behavior was the Mormon practice of polygamy.

There is a natural antagonism between a command not to establish religion and a command not to inhibit its practice. The general guide here is the concept of neutrality. The opposing values require that the government act to achieve only secular goals and that it achieve them in a religiously neutral manner.

FREE EXERCISE OF RELIGION   *See* FREE EXERCISE CLAUSE

FREEDOM FROM RELIGIOUS PERSECUTION ACT

In early 1998 Congressman Frank R. Wolf (R-Va) offered a bill to help people who suffer because of their religious beliefs. As of early 1999 President Clinton opposes the bill because it would take power away from him to negotiate with countries that participate in widespread and ongoing religious persecution.

The bill (HR 2431) would establish the Office of Religious Persecution Monitoring in the State Department. It would be headed by a director who would report directly to the secretary of state and the president and would be subject to Senate confirmation. The new office would provide a permanent mechanism for investigating religious persecution and would help ensure that this issue would receive the highest level of attention at the U.S. State Department.

Under the proposed law, the director of the office would be required to identify and report to Congress each year on which countries, if any, are engaged in "widespread and ongoing" acts of religious persecution, which includes "abduction, enslavement, killing, imprisonment, forced mass relocation, rape, crucifixion or other forms of torture, and the imposition of systematic fines or penalties that have a confiscatory purpose or effect."

The bill defined two categories of persecution: Category 1 persecution occurs when the government of a state or locality is directly involved; and Category 2 persecution occurs when the government, though not directly involved, fails to take serious and sustained efforts to eliminate the persecution when it has the ability to do so.

If a country were found to be engaged in either category of persecution, the proposed law would:

1. Terminate nonhumanitarian U.S. aid and related support to the country as well as require the United States to oppose any loans to the country from taxpayer-supported international agencies
2. Prohibit the export of an "persecution facilitating product" (including torture, surveillance, and crime control goods) to countries whose governments engage in religious persecution or do nothing to stop it, and ban trade with governmental entities that directly conduct persecution activities (such as prisons and labor camps), and
3. Ban visas to known persecutors.

The religious organizations supporting the bill included the Christian Coalition, B'nai B'rith, and the Southern Baptist Coalition. Groups opposing the measure included the National Council of Churches, Human Rights Watch, and the U.S. Chamber of Commerce.

FREEDOM OF RELIGION   As the nation's tolerance for religious diversity has broadened, so has the U.S. Supreme Court's definition of beliefs it considers religious, and therefore entitled to First Amendment protection. Originally, the Court considered religion only in the traditional Judeo-Christian sense, which demanded belief in a divine being. "The term 'religion' has reference to one's views of his relations to his Creator, and the obligations they impose of reverence for his being and character, and of obedience to his will." [*Davis v. Beason* (U.S. 1890)]

Freedom of religion refers to the liberty of individuals to believe and to practice or exercise their religious beliefs. Important aspects of the freedom of religion include the freedom of meeting, in private or in public, to worship, teach the aims of the religious group, teach children, win adherents, and more. The First Amendment to the U.S. Constitution provides protection for both the freedom to believe and the freedom to act. The first of these is absolute, but the second remains subject to regulation for the protection of society. Freedom of religion means not only that civil authorities may not intervene in the affairs of a church; it also prevents a church from exercising its authority through mechanisms of the state.

The freedom of religion guarantee of the First Amendment encompasses two clauses. One clause prohibits the government from interfering with the free exercise of religion. The other clause prevents the government from acting to "establish" a religion or religion in general. Both guarantees have been made applicable to the states through the Due Process Clause of the Fourteenth Amendment. [*Cantwell v. Connecticut* (U.S. 1940)(free exercise) and *Everson v. Board of Education* (U.S. 1947)(no establishment)]

FUNDAMENTAL RIGHT, RELIGIOUS FREEDOM AS A   Because individual liberty lies at the core of the American constitutional system, more rights are protected under law in the United States than in other societies. Under such conditions, not all rights will be considered equal, but a hierarchy of valued liberties will emerge. The freedoms that Americans deem the most important are called fundamental rights.

Although inherent in the Anglo-Saxon heritage of due process of law, the concept of fundamental rights can be difficult to delineate. Yet it constitutes one of those basic features of democracy that are the test of its presence. As defined by Justice Felix Frankfurter, dissenting in *Solesbee v. Balkcom* (U.S. 1950), it embraces a "system of rights based on moral principles so deeply embedded in the traditions and feelings of our people as to be deemed fundamental to a civilized society." The justice whom Frankfurter succeeded on the high bench, Benjamin Cardozo, had spoken in *Snyder v. Massachusetts* (U.S. 1934) of "principles of justice so rooted in the traditions and conscience of our peoples as to be deemed fundamental." Three years later, in *Palko v. Connecticut* (U.S. 1937), Cardozo articulated fundamental rights as "implicit in the concept of ordered liberty."

Because these rights are fundamental, they have been given special protection by the judiciary, which has thus viewed them as preferred freedoms that command particularly strict scrutiny of their infringement by legislative or executive action. In other words, to pass judicial muster, laws or ordinances affecting fundamental rights must demonstrate a more or less "compelling need," whereas those affecting lesser rights need only be clothed with a rational basis justifying the legislative or executive action at issue. As such, fundamental rights should prevail in conflict with governmental authority over other, less valued, liberties.

In the twentieth century personal liberties have taken on fundamental status. Through the process of selective incorporation, the U.S. Supreme Court has determined that with only a few exceptions, all of the rights in the U.S. Constitution and its amendments meet the definition of fundamental liberties, and thus, are constitutionally protected from encroachment by state and local governments as well as federal authorities. Some fundamental rights remain preferred. To what extent that arrangement will stand the test of time and experience will depend largely on the courts. In recent years, the right to privacy and protection against various forms of discrimination have been seen as fundamental.

FUNDAMENTALISM   *See* RELIGIOUS FUNDAMENTALISM

G

***GILLETTE V. UNITED STATES* (U.S. 1971)**   In this case the Supreme Court addressed the compatibility of the exemption from military service for conscientious objectors with the religion clauses of the First Amendment to the U.S. Constitution. Under the conscientious objector provision of the Selective Service Act (50 U.S.C. §§ 451–471a), the current statutory exemption is clearly granted only to those who oppose participation in any war and denied to those who object only to some wars. This interpretation was challenged in this case by two plaintiffs whose formal religion or religious philosophy required them to refrain only from participation in "unjust" wars. A majority of Supreme Court justices found that the narrow definition of the statute was compatible with both religious clauses. The Court held that the granting of conscientious objector exemptions only to those whose beliefs opposed all war did not violate the Establishment Clause. The majority found that the transition was based on secular reasons relating to the persons involved rather than adherence to accepted beliefs.

The claimants in *Gillette* also argued that failure to grant an exemption to those who opposed only unjust wars on a religious basis violated the Free Exercise Clause. The majority opinion found that the burden on these persons was justified by substantial government interests in defense and the power to raise armies. It was clear that the Court reached this result by granting great deference to these governmental interests and without any real weighing of the individual interests involved. With these important national interests at issue, the Court simply refused to review the legislative determination of who should serve in the armed forces, as the justices did not view the law as a penalty against any belief or religion.

Finally, the treatment of those who had done alternative service as conscientious objectors did raise one further issue. The person who was granted this exemption but required to perform alternative service did not receive the same benefits as those who served in normal military operations.

GOLDMAN V. WEINBERGER (U.S. 1986)

S. Simcha Goldman, an Orthodox Jew and ordained rabbi, was forbidden to wear a yarmulke while on duty as an air force officer. The prohibition was based on an air force regulation enjoining the wearing of headgear indoors "except by armed security police." Goldman sued, claiming that the prohibition violated his First Amendment right to the free exercise of religion. The Supreme Court found against Goldman on a five-to-four vote.

Writing for the majority, Justice William H. Rehnquist declined to require a government showing of either a compelling state interest or a rational basis to justify the yarmulke prohibition. Rehnquist argued simply that the military must be accorded wide-ranging deference by the courts in order to carry out its mission. Hence he refused to second-guess the air force's "professional judgment" about how to maintain a uniform dress code. Justice Rehnquist used similar reasoning a year later to uphold the power of prison authorities to restrict the free exercise rights of prisoners in *O'Lone v. Estate of Shabbazz* (U.S. 1987).

Justices William J. Brennan, Harry A. Blackmun, and Sandra Day O'Connor each filed separate dissents. All three believed that the Court should have attempted to weigh Goldman's free exercise rights against the government interest at stake. They further agreed that the government interest should give way in this case because the military had made no attempt to show a reasonable basis for the regulation as applied to Goldman. They noted, in particular, that Goldman had been allowed to wear his yarmulke by the air force for almost four years before the practice was challenged.

GOVERNMENT AID TO RELIGIOUS INSTITUTIONS

The Establishment Clause of the First Amendment to the U.S. Constitution states: "Congress shall make no law respecting an establishment of religion." This prohibition today applies to both the federal and state governments. It forbids government sponsorship of religion and requires that the government neither aid nor formally establish a religion. Although at its inception the clause might not have been intended to prohibit governmental aid to all religions, the accepted view today is that it also prohibits a preference for religion over nonreligion.

In some circumstances, however, it is impossible for the government to avoid aiding religion in some manner without actively opposing religion—something that it is forbidden to do by the Free Exercise Clause of the First Amendment. For example, providing police or fire protection to churches clearly aids the practice of religion, but the withholding of such services would single out religious activities for a special burden. Thus it is clear that some test is required to determine when incidental aid is permissible and when it is prohibited.

The constitutionality of government aid to religious institutions in the form of financial subsidies is most often challenged under the Establishment Clause. When the purpose of the subsidy is to finance obviously religious activities, such as the erection or repairing of a church building, the subsidy is generally recognized to be unconstitutional. Largely, the purpose of the Establishment Clause was to forbid such grants, as is indicated in the Supreme Court's opinion and Justice Wiley Rutledge's dissenting opinion in *Everson v. Board of Education* (U.S. 1947). Using the writings of Madison and Jefferson, Justice Rutledge argued that the New Jersey program could not be justified as a public safety expenditure. He added that publicly supported transportation of parochial school children benefits not only their secular education, but also their religious education: "Two great drives are constantly in motion to abridge, in the name of education, the complete division of religion and civil authority which our forefathers made. One is to introduce religious education and observances into the public schools. The other, to obtain public funds for the aid and support of various private religious schools. . . . In my opinion, both avenues were closed by the Constitution. Neither should be opened by this Court."

On the other hand, when government-provided funds are used for what would generally be considered secular activities, such as maintaining hospitals, the constitutional validity of such programs is fairly unanimously assumed.

Most forms of public aid for parochial schools, even to support secular courses, have been held to violate the Establishment Clause, particularly when the aid has been provided directly to the schools themselves rather than to the parents of the students who attend them. Because the U.S. Supreme Court has found that these schools are permeated by religious teaching, any significant aid to them will probably have the effect of aiding religion. The only way to avoid such an effect would be the imposition of so many procedural checks that the program would result in an "excessive entanglement" of government with religious entities. (But see the separate opinion of Justices Anthony Kennedy and Antonin Scalia in *Bowen v. Kendrick* [U.S. 1988], which reasons that government assistance to parochial schools would not violate the Constitution so long as it does not exceed the value of the secular educational services the schools render. In such case there is no use of tax-raised funds to aid religion and thus no threat of danger to religious liberty.)

Additionally, government programs that aid parochial schools have a history of causing serious political divisions. For these reasons the Court has been quite strict in applying the purpose-effect-entanglement test to these programs. Known as the *Lemon* test [from *Lemon v. Kurtzman* (U.S. 1971)], this requires government action to meet three criteria in order to be constitutional under the Establishment Clause. The action must: (1) have a secular legislative purpose; (2) have a primary effect that neither advances nor inhibits religion; and (3) must not result in excessive entanglement of government with religion. Because the First Amendment principles that govern this area are the product of a series of Supreme Court decisions on very specific types of aid to religiously affiliated schools, a review of those decisions is necessary to understand the current state of the law.

In *Everson v. Board of Education* (U.S. 1947) the Supreme Court upheld as a valid exercise of police power a state statute financing bus transportation to parochial schools. The decision rested on the conclusion that the purpose of the law was not to aid religion, but to finance the operations of the schools and help ensure the safety of children going to or returning from them.

The *Everson*, or "no-aid," interpretation of the Establishment Clause as applied to governmental financing of religious schools next reached the U.S. Supreme Court in the case of *Board of Education v. Allen* (U.S. 1968). In that case the Court upheld a New York statute providing for the loan to students attending nonpublic schools of secular textbooks authorized for use in public schools. The Court concluded that the statute did not impermissibly aid religious schools within the meaning of *Everson*, nor did it violate the Establishment Clause ban on laws lacking a secular purpose or having a primary effect that either advances or inhibits religion, as that Clause had been interpreted in *Abington School District v. Schempp* (U.S. 1963). In upholding the New York law, the Court recognized that the police power rationale of *Everson* was not readily applicable to textbook laws, but it adjudged that the processes of secular and religious training are not so intertwined that secular textbooks furnished to students by the public are in fact instrumental in the teaching of religion.

The *Allen* rationale could be used to justify state aid to religious schools considerably more extensively than mere financing of transportation or provision of secular textbooks. It could, for example, justify state financing of supplies other than textbooks, the costs of maintenance and repair of parochial school premises, or most important, the paying of salaries to instructors who teach the nonreligious subjects that constitute the major part of the parochial school curriculum.

This extension was intended by Justice Byron White, the author of the *Allen* opinion, who thereafter dissented in all the decisions prohibiting aid to church-related schools. The first of these decisions came in the companion cases of *Lemon v. Kurtzman* (U.S. 1971) and *Earley v. DiCenso* (U.S. 1973). In *Lemon*, the state of Pennsylvania purchased the services of religious schools in providing secular education to their students. In *Di-Censo*, Rhode Island paid 15 percent of the salaries of religious school teachers who taught only secular subjects. The statutes involved in *Lemon* and *DiCenso* violated the Establishment Clause, the Court held, because in order to ensure that the teachers did not inject religion into their secular classes or allow religious values to affect the content of secular instruction, it was necessary to subject the teachers to comprehensive, discriminating, and continuing state surveillance, which would constitute forbidden entanglement of church and state.

Despite *Lemon* and *DiCenso*, the Court has upheld the constitutionality of reimbursement for noninstructional health and welfare services supplied to parochial school students, such as meals, medical and dental care, and diagnostic services on speech, hearing, and psychological problems. In *Committee for Public Education and Religious Liberty v. Regan* (U.S. 1980) the Court allowed reimbursement for the expense of administering state-prepared and mandated objective examinations, and the decision in *Bowen v. Kendrick* (U.S. 1988) revealed the Rehnquist Court's inclination to interpret the term *secular activities* broadly. That case upheld the constitutionality of government funds granted to a variety of public and private agencies (including religious organizations) to provide counseling for the prevention of adolescent sexual relations and to promote adoption as an alternative to abortion. Whereas this program may be fairly characterized as having a "secular" purpose (even though it coincides with the approach of certain prominent religious groups), there appears to be a substantial danger that the program's primary effect will be to further religious precepts when religiously employed counselors deal with a subject so closely and inextricably tied to religious doctrine.

In the mid-1980s, probably the most important uncertainty regarding government assistance to parochial schools concerned school choice vouchers. Under a typical voucher program, vouchers are given to parents who may then turn them in to any public or private school in lieu of tuition. The voucher is redeemed by the school for government (taxpayer) funds. Although the decision in *Witters v. Washington Department of Services for the Blind* (U.S. 1986) involved only a special type of voucher and did not speak to the constitutionality of school vouchers generally, its rationale greatly sustains their validity. The case upheld a state program providing visually handicapped persons a voucher (although it was not called that) for use in vocational schools for the blind. Witters was studying religion at a Christian college "in order to equip himself for a career as a pastor, missionary, or youth director." The fact that Witters attended college was significant to the holding. The strict ban on government aid to schools involves primary or secondary schools where the fear of state-sponsored religious inculcation is of paramount concern. In general, the courts seem more relaxed when the institution involved in a voucher program is one of higher education. A majority of the Supreme Court, even before Justices Anthony Kennedy and Antonin Scalia had been appointed, agreed that "state programs that are wholly neutral in offering educational assistance to a class defined without reference to religion do not violate the [Establishment Clause], because any aid to religion results from the private choices of individual beneficiaries." The state's money, however, was plainly being spent for religious purposes. Criticizing the decision, separationists argue that if the government, whether through a voucher or a direct grant to parochial schools, is financing not only the value of secular education in those schools, but also all or part of the cost of religious education, the support is an expenditure of compulsorily raised tax funds for religious purposes and should be held to violate the Establishment Clause.

Direct government subsidies to religious schools, whether in the form of payments for services, such as student transportation, or redemption of vouchers are but one issue invoking Establishment Clause concerns. Religious institutions may also be "aided" by exempting them from laws of general application. For example, a tax exemption may be considered an indirect form of government aid. Historically, the federal government, every state, and the District of Columbia have exempted churches from paying property and income taxes. The Establishment Clause prohibits Congress from providing any direct support to religion, in addition to not designating a national church. [See Lemon v. Kurtzman (U.S. 1971)]

In Walz v. Tax Commission (U.S. 1970) the Court upheld the constitutionality of tax exemptions accorded to property used exclusively for worship or other religious purposes. Tax exemptions, the Court held, do not entail sponsorship of religion and involve even less entanglement than nonexemption, because they do not require the government to examine the affairs of the church and audit its books or records. The longevity of the exemption, dating as it does from the time the United States was founded, constitutes strong evidence of its constitutionality.

The Court in Walz did not hold that the Free Exercise Clause would be violated if exemption were disallowed (despite being urged to do so in the amicus curiae brief submitted by the National Council of Churches). Nor, on the other hand, did it decide to the contrary. Presently, therefore, it seems that governments, federal or state, have the constitutional option of granting or denying tax exemptions to religious organizations.

Tax relief—either exemptions for property used exclusively for worship or other religious purposes, or income tax deductions for parents who send their children to parochial schools—has been held not to violate the Establishment Clause as long as the benefits extend beyond religion-related recipients. For example, the Court had upheld property tax exemptions for educational and charitable institutions and tax deductions for school expenses to all parents of school children. In *Texas Monthly, Inc. v. Bullock* (U.S. 1989) the Court invalidated a state sales-tax exemption for books and magazines that "teach" or are "sacred" to a religious faith. Because the exemption was for religious purposes only and not the broad-based type of tax relief provided in the earlier cases, the Court held that this governmental aid violated the Establishment Clause.

In addition to Establishment Clause issues, government aid to religious institutions also raises concerns regarding the right to free exercise of religion contained in the First Amendment to the Constitution. In the early 1990s the Supreme Court dramatically reduced protection for religious liberty in a case involving the rights of Native Americans to use peyote, a hallucinogenic substance, for religious reasons. In *Employment Division v. Smith* (U.S. 1990), the Court held that the Free Exercise Clause of the First Amendment affords no religious exemption from a neutral law that regulates conduct, even though that law imposes a substantial burden on religious practice. *Smith* essentially adopted a per se neutrality rule that states that the Free Exercise Clause does not provide any relief when "a valid and neutral law of general applicability" burdens a religious practice. A facially neutral criminal law that serves some secular purpose, but inadvertently outlaws a religion's central practice will, thus, always satisfy the *Smith* rule.

Similarly, under the neutrality of treatment approach, the Court held in *Board of Education v. Mergens* (U.S. 1990) that the First Amendment's ban on laws respecting an establishment of religion permits student religious groups in secondary schools to meet for religious purposes (including prayer) on school premises during noninstructional time as long as other noncurriculum-related student groups are allowed to do so. The Equal Access Act, which was at issue in *Mergens,* was interpreted as a facially neutral law. This theme of neutral treatment of religious and secular groups has been prominent in issues involving government aid as well. The "formal neutrality" standard refers to a rule that deems acceptable all laws that do not explicitly mention religion or differentiate among religions or between religions and nonreligion. Thus, all "neutral" laws should be acceptable under the Constitution. In the aftermath of the *Smith* decision, formal neutrality plays a clear and decisive role in establishing the bounds of constitutionally protected religious freedom. In *Mergens* the doctrine of "equal access" is premised on free speech and free association protections embodied in the Free Exercise Clause of the First Amendment.

GOVERNMENT DISPLAYS OF RELIGIOUS SYMBOLS   *See* HOLIDAY DISPLAYS

GOVERNMENT NEUTRALITY   *See* NEUTRALITY STANDARD

GRAND RAPIDS SCHOOL DISTRICT V. BALL (U.S. 1985)

In this case, also known as the *Grand Rapids Shared-Time Case,* the U.S. Supreme Court invalidated a community education program financed by the public school system that held classes in space leased from private schools. Justice William Brennan, for the majority, concerned himself solely with the possibility that the state-paid teachers might advance religion by conforming their instruction to the environment of the private sectarian schools. Stressing the "pervasively sectarian" nature of almost all of the private schools involved, Brennan identified three factors as establishing that the programs had the primary effect of advancing religion.

"First, the teachers participating in the programs may become involved in intentionally or inadvertently inculcating particular religious tenets or beliefs." Even though many of the teachers in the shared-time program had never worked in religious schools and the courses were supplemental and secular in content, the religious atmosphere of the schools could influence the instructors to conform to the environment. The private school students would be receiving the instruction in the usual religious environment "thus reinforcing the indoctrinating effect."

"Second, the program may provide a crucial symbolic link between government and religion, thereby enlisting—at least in the eyes of impressionable youngsters—the powers of government to the support of the religious denomination operating the school." A core purpose of the Establishment Clause, said Justice William Brennan, is to avoid any message of governmental approval of religion. Young religious school students, moving from religious to secular classes in the same religious-school building, would be unlikely to be able to discern the "crucial difference" between the religious-school classes and the public-school classes. This would have the effect of promoting "the symbolic union of government and religion in one sectarian enterprise."

"Third, the programs may have the effect of directly promoting religion by impermissibly providing a subsidy to the primary religious mission of the institutions affected." A public subsidy was involved because the public school assumed responsibility for providing a substantial portion of the teaching of the private school students. Not only instructional material as in *Meek v. Pittenger* (U.S. 1975) and *Wolman v. Walter* (U.S. 1977) was involved, but "also the provision of instructional services by teachers in a parochial school building." The primary effect was the "direct and substantial advancement of the sectarian enterprise."

The decision in the *Grand Rapids Shared-Time Case* was criticized on the grounds that the evidence did not validate the Court's fears.

H

HARE KRISHNAS *See* HEFFRON V. INTERNATIONAL SOCIETY FOR KRISHNA CONSCIOUSNESS (U.S. 1981)

HATE CRIMES Certain aggravated types of assault may be distinguished from simple assault by statute. Several states have enacted civil or criminal statutes prohibiting offensive conduct (such as physical injury) toward another based on factors such as perceived race, color, religion, and the like. These provisions have been challenged on various grounds. In *State v. Plowman* (Ore. 1992), a state court upheld an ethnic intimidation statute against vagueness and a First Amendment challenge.

The U.S. Supreme Court has recognized that the right of free speech does not render immune utterances tending to incite an immediate breach of the peace or disorderly conduct or rioting, particularly where such utterances are made for the purpose of attacking racial and religious groups. Thus a state may constitutionally punish "fighting words"; that is, words that by their very utterance inflict injury or tend to incite an immediate breach of the peace. However, they must do so under carefully drafted statutes or ordinances that by their own terms, or as construed by the courts, are limited in their application only to "fighting words" and are not susceptible of application to protected expression.

Perversions of religion are viewed as responsible for many hate crimes. Followers of a racist version of Christianity were charged recently with the murder of an entire Arkansas family, including an 8-year-old girl, in pursuit of an "Aryan" republic that they were planning. They justified the murders on their interpretation of the Bible. Another white racist group was convicted of bombing and robbing banks in Washington, on the grounds that the Bible outlaws the charging of interest. Still others were convicted of robbing Midwestern banks to build a white "army."

Just as white supremacists interpret the Bible to justify their cause,

191

black separatists look to Christianity and other religions to support their views. In 1997 officials began investigating a group of alleged Black Hebrew Israelites, a black supremacist religion, in New Mexico. The group's headquarters was said to be decorated with a mural depicting sword-carrying African Americans standing heroically over bloodied white bodies. Police believe adherents of the same theology may have instigated attacks on police officers in Memphis during a Ku Klux Klan rally early in 1998. And prison officials in several states have noted a rise in black supremacist gang activity.

IIII HEALTH   *See* MEDICAL TREATMENT

IIII HEFFRON V. INTERNATIONAL SOCIETY FOR KRISHNA CONSCIOUSNESS (U.S. 1981)   In this case the U.S. Supreme Court upheld a Minnesota state fair regulation that restricted the distribution, sales, and solicitation activities of fair participants to a fixed-booth location. The International Society for Krishna Consciousness (ISKON) challenged the fixed-booth rule because it interfered with its adherents' practice of a religious ritual called sankirtan, which required them to proselytize, sell literature, solicit donations, and beg for alms. ISKON contended that the rule violated its First Amendment rights of freedom of speech and free exercise of religion.

Although the Supreme Court accepted that the regulation burdened the Krishna religion, it concluded that the regulation was a valid restriction on the time, place, and manner of exercising a First Amendment right and did not violate the Constitution. First, the Court noted that the rule was not based on the content or subject matter of participants' speech. The rule applied to all enterprises at the state fair, whether nonprofit, charitable, or commercial. It also allowed anyone to engage in face to face discussions on the fairgrounds. Second, the method of allocating rental space was nondiscriminatory and not open to arbitrary application. Third, the rule served a significant government interest because of the state's need to maintain the orderly movement among exhibitors of the large number of visitors attending the fair. Given the need to control the flow of crowds within a congested area, the regulation served to prevent disorder, a goal that could not be achieved if all groups at the fair were granted exemptions from the regulation.

The *Heffron* case stands for the principle that neutral regulations of the time, place, or manner of speech may be applied to the speech and activities of religious organizations. When *Heffron* was originally decided, if the regulatory statute at issue imposed a burden on the members of the religious organization, those individuals might have a right to an exemption from the statute under the Free Exercise Clause, unless the Court found that the government has an overriding interest in denying an exemption.

The U.S. Supreme Court, however, in *Employment Division v. Smith* (U.S. 1990), abolished the "compelling interest" standard for free exercise claims. In the *Smith* opinion, the Court basically imposed a "neutrality" standard for determining whether a law that impacted religious practices was constitutional. Religious liberty became protected by general rights applicable to all, rather than by specific exemptions granted to those who hold peculiar religious beliefs. The principle of equality before the law will be maintained.

▥ HERNANDEZ V. COMMISSIONER OF INTERNAL REVENUE (U.S. 1989)

In this case the Supreme Court upheld a refusal by the Internal Revenue Service to allow members of the Church of Scientology to deduct expenditures for training sessions as charitable contributions. The Court first questioned whether the refusal really imposed a substantial religious burden on the Church's members, because—unlike the Amish faith that prohibits the payment of Social Security taxes—nothing in the Scientology faith prohibited the payment of taxes. The only "burden" the Court could see from the refusal to allow the deduction was that Church members would have less money available to them to gain access to the training sessions. But even if this indirect burden was sufficiently substantial, the Court went on to note that the burden was "justified by the broad public interest in maintaining a sound tax system" that is free of myriad exceptions flowing from a wide variety of religious beliefs.

The IRS ruling in this case applied to all religious entities and involved no denominational preference. *Hernandez* held that the IRS ruling was constitutional under the *Lemon* test [based on *Lemon v. Kurtzman* (U.S. 1971)], which requires that legislation have a secular purpose, with a primary effect that neither advances nor inhibits religion, and does not entail "excessive entanglement" of the government with religion in order to enforce. The government action at issue in this case was neutral in design and purpose. Nor was there a significant danger of excessive entanglement, even though the IRS was required to examine Church practices and financing. The Court observed that "routine regulatory interaction which involves no inquiries into religious doctrine, no delegation of state power to a religious body, and no 'detailed monitoring and close administrative contact' between secular and religious bodies, does not of itself violate the nonentanglement command."

███ **HOLIDAY DISPLAYS**   Holiday displays set up on public
███ property during the Christmas season, often paid for and sponsored by government entities, used to be standard fare in cities and towns throughout the United States. Increasingly, however, religious and secular groups have challenged such practices on the grounds that they violate the constitutional doctrine of separation between church and state. Specifically, such displays come under attack for transgressing the Establishment Clause of the First Amendment, which forbids the government to make any law "respecting" the establishment of religion.

The Supreme Court has ruled on numerous challenges of this type, including *Allegheny County v. ACLU* (U.S. 1989). If any basic rule can be derived from the many opinions set forth by the justices in *Allegheny* it is that the three-part *Lemon* test for Establishment Clause cases is still valid for determining the constitutionality of holiday displays. That test, first developed in *Lemon v. Kurtzman* (U.S. 1971), provides that government action is constitutional under the First Amendment if it (1) has a secular purpose, (2) has a primary effect that neither advances nor inhibits religion, and (3) does not entail an "excessive entanglement" of government with religion in order to enforce.

Although holiday displays almost inevitably contain some religious symbols, they can still meet the requirement of having a "secular" purpose if it appears that the intent of the display is simply to acknowledge the history and traditions of holiday celebrations in the community and wider nation. In *Allegheny,* for example, a display on the grounds of the county courthouse that consisted of a Christmas tree and a menorah (a Hanukkah symbol) did not violate the Constitution because together the displayed items merely symbolized the different facets of the "same winter-holiday season, which has attained a secular status in our society."

Conversely, a display inside the county courthouse that consisted only of a Christian nativity scene accompanied by a banner reading "Gloria in Excelsis Deo" ("Glory to God in the Highest") was found to be unacceptable by the Supreme Court, because it appeared to be a government endorsement of a particular religious message. Unlike the outdoor display, this interior nativity scene was found to have the primary effect of advancing religion, perhaps because of its isolated, prominent placement in the government building with a sign containing a religious exhortation for the Christian faith.

As regards the third prong of the *Lemon* test, which forbids "excessive entanglement" of the government in religious activities, the Court found no undue "administrative entanglement" or "political divisiveness" endangered by the nativity scene. With respect to the former, it was significant that erection and maintenance of the display was done without any contact between the city and religious authorities. With respect to the latter, the Court noted that the only "political divisiveness" arguably caused was that manifested by the filing of the lawsuit itself, yet "a litigant cannot, by the very act of commencing a lawsuit . . . create the appearance of divisiveness and then exploit it as entanglement." [*Lynch v. Donnelly* (U.S. 1984)]

In addition to reaffirming the use of the *Lemon* test in holiday display cases, the *Allegheny* decision pointed up the ad hoc character of these determinations; that is to say, because each display is different, each must be evaluated on a case-by-case basis, virtually ensuring that these types of legal challenges will continue to flood the courts for some time to come.

Indeed, the issue of holiday displays remains controversial and caselaw arising from courts below the Supreme Court is equally without usefulness in presenting hard and fast rules. Holiday displays continue to require a fact-specific evaluation to determine whether the religious message is sufficiently mixed with the secular holiday observance to avoid the overall impression of governmental endorsement of religion. A subject as intensely personal as religion is likely to evoke strong reactions if religious displays are constructed with public funds or if they are placed in locations that give them some type of official status.

Displays that are sponsored by private groups, albeit on public property, seem more likely to be found constitutional than those sponsored by government entities.

Moreover, displays that are placed in traditional public forums, like parks and plazas, which are normally used for speeches, displays, or other expressions of opinion, are even less likely to run afoul of the Constitution. Indeed, the free speech provisions of the First Amendment probably protect the right of a private group to display a nativity scene or menorah in a public forum, even without holiday trappings, as the symbolic expression of the celebration of the holiday season.

If governments desire to participate more actively in celebrating the Christmas season, the traditional Christmas tree provides a constitutionally acceptable alternative to overtly religious-themed displays. Christmas trees have acquired a sufficiently secular meaning as a symbol of the holiday season so that their display does not endorse Christianity, regardless of who bears the cost or wherever the tree may be located.

Since the Supreme Court's decision in *Allegheny County,* there is evidence that local communities have indeed adopted policies that avoid the divisiveness that the Establishment Clause was intended to prevent. They have relied increasingly on private groups to sponsor religious holiday displays and have selected locations that are not adjacent to public buildings such as city halls and courthouses. This development has the salutary effect of compelling governments, private parties, and courts to consider the nature of the forum rather than the numbers of reindeer, the prominence of Santa Claus, or the relative sizes of a menorah and a Christmas tree.

The Sixth Circuit Court of Appeals recently found that a menorah display erected during Hanukkah in Grand Rapids, Michigan, did not violate the Establishment Clause of the First Amendment. The appeals court said that the facts before it were different from many other holiday display cases in two crucial ways: First, the display was erected by a private group, and second, it stood in a traditional public forum to which all citizens had equal access. [*Americans United for Separation of Church and State v. City of Grand Rapids* (6th Cir. 1992)]

In a similar case, the Ninth Circuit Court of Appeals ruled that a religious group could display a biblical tableau in a public park during Christmas without violating the Establishment Clause. [*Kreisner v. City of San Diego* (9th Cir. 1993)] The court characterized the issue as whether "placement of a private, overtly religious holiday display on public property represents government endorsement of religion."

Although the park where the display was set up was owned by the municipality, it was still "unquestionably a public forum," according to the court. "The mere fact that no other speaker [in the park] has chosen the medium of an unattended display cannot justify a rule of law that would force the city to forbid such displays based upon their religious content."

The fact that the park housed a half-dozen public museums did not transform the character of the park as a public forum. "Even if we assume [these buildings] are owned or operated by the city, they appear to have nothing to do with the seat of government. Rather, consistent with the nature of [the park] itself, they involve cultural and recreational activities unrelated to core governmental functions. . . . Although [the park] may be a well-known [city] landmark, it is not the equivalent of a City Hall or a city office building."

The court went on to explain its standard of review: "[I]n evaluating the effect of the city's grant of a permit to [the religious group], we apply the standard of a reasonable observer. . . . [S]uch an observer could not fairly interpret the city's tolerance of the . . . display as an endorsement of religion."

Judge Alex Kozinski concurred, noting that "the establishment clause prevents the government from treating religious speech more favorably than nonreligious speech. But both the establishment and free speech clauses prevent the government from treating religious speech less favorably."

Even holiday displays that are unabashedly government sponsored may yet be permissible, provided they do not appear to "endorse" religion. In *Elewski v. City of Syracuse* (2d Cir. 1997) the Second Circuit Court of Appeals held that a nativity scene erected by the city of Syracuse in a downtown public park did not violate the Establishment Clause of the First Amendment. In assessing the Syracuse crèche, the Second Circuit employed the now-familiar Establishment Clause "endorsement test" by asking: "Would a reasonable observer of the display in its particular context perceive a message of governmental endorsement or sponsorship of religion?" To answer the endorsement question, the court relied on the perceptions of a "reasonable observer" as defined by Justice Sandra Day O'Connor's concurrence in *Capitol Square Review and Advisory Board v. Pinette* (U.S. 1995). Critics of the test argue that Justice O'Connor's formulation imports to the reasonable observer the perceptions of a member of the religious majority or of an adherent of the religion on display, thereby rendering the endorsement test insufficiently sensitive to displays of majority religious symbols.

HOME SCHOOLING

The home schooling movement has grown rapidly in the last two decades of the twentieth century, yet it is by no means a new phenomenon in the United States. Before public schools became ubiquitous institutions in the nineteenth century, most children were educated at home, although a certain number attended church schools or private academies when their families could afford to send them. Indeed, many prominent figures in American history were trained at home. Home schooling has generated legal controversy, however, because it sometimes pits two important values in American society against each other. The first of these is the fundamental right of parents to direct the education of their children. [*State v. Melin* (N.D. 1988); *People v. DeJonge* (Mich. 1993)] The second is the state's interest in ensuring that its citizens have a good basic education. To this end compulsory attendance laws requiring children to attend school until a certain age have been routinely upheld as constitutional. [*Pierce v. Society of Sisters* (U.S. 1925)] States also have the right to set educational standards for both public and private schools (including home schools) and to require licensing and competency tests for teachers. Even parents who school their children at home concede the government's right to ensure that their children are being educated. The real issue is the nature and extent of the state's requirements.

State regulation of home schooling is especially controversial when the choice to school one's children at home is religiously motivated. In *Michigan v. Bennett* (Mich. 1993), the Michigan Supreme Court upheld a state law requiring parents who educate their children at home to provide them with licensed teachers. But in a case decided the same day, *People v. DeJonge* (Mich. 1993), the court held that this same law could not be applied to parents whose decision to teach their children at home was compelled by the family's religious beliefs.

The issue before the Michigan Supreme Court in *DeJonge* was whether the state teacher certification requirement violated the First Amendment guarantee of free exercise of religion. The court applied the U.S. Supreme Court's holding in *Employment Division v. Smith* (U.S. 1990), which ruled that states could impose laws that incidently limit religious conduct so long as they serve a valid state purpose and are not aimed at inhibiting religion.

The court in *DeJonge* found that Michigan had failed to prove that teacher certification was essential to meeting its interest in child welfare, because the court record showed that the children were "receiving a more than adequate education."

In *State v. Schmidt* (Ohio 1987), parents attempting to educate their children at home refused to seek approval of their home education program from the local school superintendent, as required. The Court refused to apply a balancing test, ruling that, without a submission of their proposal to the superintendent, there was "no way to balance the appellant's right to the free exercise of their religion . . . against the state's interests."

Many states' home schooling regulations during the 1970s and 1980s required that children be taught by certified teachers. [*State v. Melin* (N.D. 1988)] The growth of home schooling has had its political effect in the state legislatures. Currently, no state requires that home school teachers be certified. If the parent is the home school teacher, most states have no qualification requirements whatsoever.

HOMOSEXUALITY

Homosexual acts, particularly of males, were considered evil in biblical times, essentially because they wasted human seed, disgraced a fellow human being, or represented idolatrous pagan practices.

The gay rights movement has challenged the predominantly negative stance maintained by the Christian church since the first century. Religion is not merely correlated with opposition to homosexuality, but religion has largely cultivated and encouraged opposition to homosexuality. Indeed, homosexuality is actively opposed by many religious organizations in modern American society. Fundamentalist Christianity especially strongly condemns homosexuality. The conservative Christian Coalition organization regards homosexuality as a virulent threat to morality and family, supporting "ex-gay" ministries to save repentant homosexuals from their "sin." Some Roman Catholic leaders believe that homosexuality is a "basic human disorder."

On the other hand, more liberal churches, seeking "more light" in dialogue with gays and lesbians condemn homophobia as the sin to be repented, a violation of the commandment against bearing false witness (Exodus 20:16), and have debated issues such as the ordination of homosexuals and blessing the unions of gay and lesbian people. Liberal theologians argue that same-sex love has integrity and that homosexual orientation is a gift.

The religious condemnation of homosexuality found expression in many antisodomy and other laws uniformly passed by the states in the past century. Many of these are still on the books, and in 1986 the United States Supreme Court rejected a challenge to one such Georgia law that made consensual homosexual acts in the privacy of one's own home a crime. [*Bowers v. Hardwick* (U.S. 1986)]

The effort to lift the burden of criminal sanctions against same-sex intimacy has stimulated a lively debate about government regulation of sexual conduct, the way in which the courts identify "new rights" protected by the Constitution, and the proper role of majority concepts of morality in regulating the private, consensual conduct of minorities. Lesbians, gay men, and bisexuals have invoked the Constitution's guarantees of equal protection in the public debate. The U.S. Supreme Court has rejected the claim that the laws outlawing homosexual conduct are unconstitutional, but its decisions have generated extensive commentary on alternative theories for prescribing the limits of state regulation of private adult sexual conduct. The U.S. Supreme Court's unwillingness to protect homosexuals has led state courts to provide the necessary protection.

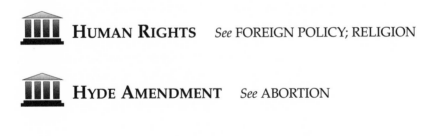

HUMAN RIGHTS   *See* FOREIGN POLICY; RELIGION

HYDE AMENDMENT   *See* ABORTION

I

"IN GOD WE TRUST"   Two federal statutes mandate that the phrase, "In God We Trust" be inscribed on all U.S. coins and currency. [31 U.S.C. §§ 5112 and 5114 (1999)] A third statute declares the phrase to be the national motto. [36 U.S.C. § 302 (1999)] Several lawsuits have been filed over the years alleging that these statutes violate the Free Establishment Clause of the First Amendment, but no court has yet held them to be unconstitutional.

J

JIMMY SWAGGERT MINISTRIES V. BOARD OF EQUALIZATION (U.S. 1990) This case involved the imposition of a state sales and use tax on religious merchandise sold by a religious organization. The Jimmy Swaggert Ministries had argued that merchandise with a religious content was exempt from taxation based on the First Amendment's proscription against government action that infringed on the right of the people freely to worship. The U.S. Supreme Court unanimously disagreed, holding that the application of a sales tax to the religious merchandise did not violate either the Free Exercise Clause or the proscription against excessive entanglement of the government with religion enunciated by the Supreme Court in *Lemon v. Kurtzman* (U.S. 1971).

Applying the *Lemon* test, the Supreme Court concluded that the taxes were neutral and nondiscriminatory regarding religion or religious belief. Nor was there an excessive entanglement of church and state. The religious materials were simply subject to the tax without any need for government inquiry into their contents or the motives of the parties involved in the sale.

In ruling that a religious organization and its members had no right to refuse to pay a state's general sales and use taxes on the sales and use of religious products and religious literature, Justice Sandra Day O'Connor wrote the Court's unanimous decision, which applied the same reasoning used in *Hernandez v. Commissioner of Internal Revenue* (U.S. 1989). California's general sales and use taxes did not employ religious criteria for determining who should pay them and they did not constitute a special tax on religious goods or activities. Because the taxes were neutrally and consistently applied to everyone selling goods in the state, they did not have to be justified by a compelling interest. The taxes did not violate the Establishment Clause because the general sales and use taxes had a nonreligious purpose, a primary nonreligious effect, and the collection of taxes from a religious person or organization does not constitute an excessive entanglement between government and religion.

The Supreme Court distinguished *Swaggert* from prior caselaw that had invalidated the application of general licensing fees to those who sold and distributed religious materials door to door. In both *Murdock v. Pennsylvania* (U.S. 1943) and *Follett v. McCormick* (U.S. 1944), the Supreme Court had objected to such licensing fees because they acted as a prior restraint on religion. In the same cases, however, the Court clearly stated that the First Amendment did not exempt religious groups from generally applicable taxes on income and property. The Court reaffirmed that principle in *Swaggert*, noting that the tax under attack was a general levy on revenues raised from the sale of certain products. The Court acknowledged that in some cases a generally applicable tax of this sort might effectively choke off an adherent's religious practices, but reserved for the future a determination on whether such a tax would violate the Free Exercise Clause.

JOHNSON V. ROBISON (U.S. 1974)   In this case the Supreme Court upheld the granting of educational benefits to veterans who served active duty in the military but denied them to conscientious objectors who performed alternative service. Such differential treatment, the court said, did not violate the First Amendment. The plaintiff had alleged that certain portions of the Veterans Readjustment of Benefits Act of 1966 violated his free exercise rights.

In finding that there was no violation of the Free Exercise Clause, the majority first noted that there was little, if any, real burden on religious practices that resulted from the policies governing these programs. Second, the government interest in the raising and supporting of armies was of a "kind and weight" sufficient to overcome the alleged burden on the free exercise rights of those who did not receive the educational benefits. Thus, the program survived scrutiny under a balancing test.

The majority of justices found both a secular distinction between the types of service and a minimal burden on the practice of religion resulting from the exclusion of conscientious objectors from the benefits at issue. The Court noted that there had been no legislative intent to interfere with the plaintiff's religion, and that including conscientious objectors in the benefits would not rationally promote the Act's objectives of enhancing military service and the readjustment to civilian life of military personnel who served on active duty. The justices had little trouble in ruling that the secular governmental interest was sufficient to overrule the conscientious objector's claim for further benefits. Relying on *Gillette v. United States* (U.S. 1971), the U.S. Supreme Court upheld the statute, once again recognizing that "the Government's substantial interest in raising and supporting armies, is of a kind and weight sufficient to sustain the challenged legislation against an attack based on the petitioner's free exercise rights." In other words, the governmental interest in raising and supporting armies is compelling.

JONES V. WOLF (U.S. 1979)   A schism developed in a local church that was a member of a hierarchical church and the majority of its members voted to withdraw from the general church. The proper authority of the general church determined that the minority that remained constituted the "true congregation" of the local church and awarded them authority over its property. The breakaway majority of the congregation filed a lawsuit contesting this ruling in a state court and an appeal reached the Supreme Court.

A divided Supreme Court, while formally adhering to neutral principles regarding church property in the event of a church schism, appeared to depart in substance from their application. In its ruling the Supreme Court first approved the approach of the state court, which applied neutral principles in examining the deeds to the church property, relevant state statutes, and provisions of the general church's constitution concerning ownership and control of church property. The state court determined that there was no language of trust in favor of the general church contained in any of these documents and that the property thus belonged to the local breakaway congregation. The Supreme Court then held that the First Amendment did not prevent the state court from applying a presumption of majority rule to award control of the property to the breakaway majority of the local congregation, provided that it permitted defeasance of the presumption upon proof that the identity of the local church was to be determined by some other means, as expressed perhaps in the general church charter.

The dissenting justices in the case argued that to permit a court to narrowly view only the church documents relating to property ownership allowed it to ignore the more important fact that the dispute was really over ecclesiastical matters and that the general church had decided which faction of the broken congregation was the "true" church.

Thus, it is unclear where the Court stood on this issue. *Jones* continues to state that it is improper to review an ecclesiastical dispute and that deference is required in those cases, but by approving a "neutral principles inquiry" that can filter out, in effect, the doctrinal issues underlying a church dispute the Court seems to have approved at least an indirect limitation of the authority of hierarchical churches.

The Supreme Court did indicate that the general church could always expressly provide in its charter or in deeds to its property the proper disposition of disputed property. But here the general church had decided which faction was the "true congregation"—a decision that would appear to constitute as definitive a rule as the Court required.

JUDICIAL DEFERENCE   The First Amendment, as it has been applied to state governments through the Fourteenth Amendment, requires judicial deference to religious organizations on religious matters, for example on matters relating to clergy. [*Kreshik v. St. Nicholas Cathedral* (U.S. 1960)]

Courts avoid constitutional questions through several different methods. They can, for example, construe a statute to reconcile it with the Constitution. Federal courts can also abstain from hearing a case until appropriate state agencies have had a chance to address it. A First Amendment doctrine that applies in many church autonomy issues is that of *judicial deference*, by which courts refuse civil jurisdiction and defer to church authorities whenever a dispute might otherwise embroil the court in an internal dispute. [*See Jones v. Wolf* (U.S. 1979)]

The Court also followed the principles of judicial deference in bowing to the judgment of military commanders on questions of military discipline. In one case, the Court did so on the issue of a military regulation prohibiting personnel from wearing religious apparel while on duty. The Supreme Court ruled that the Air Force did not have to make an exception to its rules requiring personnel to wear uniforms for members who wanted to wear religious garb as part of their practice of religion, even if the regulation did have the effect of substantially burdening religion. [*Goldman v. Weinberger* (U.S. 1986)]

JURY SERVICE   Those religiously opposed to jury duty cannot be compelled to serve. [*In re Jenison* (U.S. 1963)] Some of the issues involving religion and jury service include:

- Should those who refuse for religious reasons to sit as jurors be constitutionally excused?
- Should an attorney be permitted to strike a juror based on the attorney's perception that the juror's religious beliefs will make him or her partial?
- Is a lawyer permitted to ask prospective jury members questions about their religious faith in order to reach a decision regarding their impartiality?

- To what extent can jurors rely on their religious beliefs in reaching a verdict?
- Are such verdicts impeachable by the party against whom the jury finds?

The South Carolina Supreme Court held early in the nineteenth century that a religious group known as the Covenanters enjoyed no constitutional right to be exempt from jury service. [*State v. Willson* (S.C. 1823)] Generally speaking, the caselaw on this issue is meager. In fact, as of 1963, there were no reported cases involving an interpretation of a statute that contained an exemption for jury service due to religious objections. Shortly after deciding *Sherbert v. Verner* (U.S. 1963), which allowed individuals to make First Amendment claims against government policies that indirectly burdened their free exercise of religion and required the government to show that any such burdens were justified by a compelling state interest, the Supreme Court, basing its holding on *Sherbert*, vacated a judgment of the Minnesota Supreme Court holding Mrs. Owen Jenison in contempt of court for refusing on religious grounds to serve as a juror. [*In re Jenison* (U.S. 1963)] On remand, the Minnesota court held that a person whose religious beliefs prohibited jury service was constitutionally exempt from jury service. [*In re Jenison* (Minn. 1963)] The court, in relying on *Sherbert*, found that there was no immediate threat to the jury system and the state's interest in the efficient administration of justice did not outweigh Jenison's free exercise rights.

In *West Virginia v. Everly* (W. Va. 1966), a Jehovah's Witness was excused from jury duty because he believed that contributing to the mechanisms of a worldly government was inconsistent with his role as a representative of the Kingdom of God. On the other hand, another court dealt with the issue of conscientious objection to the juror's oath, at least tangentially, when the court excused jurors because the trial began on a holy day of their religion. In one such case, the trial judge's excusal of all Jewish venire men who requested excusal because the trial began on Yom Kippur (the Day of Atonement) was not a violation of the Constitution, nor did it invalidate a criminal trial jury. [*Grech v. Wainwright* (5th Cir. 1974)]

In an early religious liberty case, *United States v. Hillyard* (E.D. Wash. 1943), the court refused to hold in contempt a Jehovah's Witness who refused to serve as a juror. Relying on the views of Madison and Jefferson, the court concluded:

I feel constrained to resolve the very considerable doubt in my mind in favor of the defendant. While I cannot understand defendant's reasoning and cannot accept his conclusion, I must admit that his refusal to serve does not amount to a breaking out "into overt against peace and good order."

The Supreme Court has developed a new peremptory challenge jurisprudence holding unconstitutional challenges based on gender and race. [See *J.E.B. v. Alabama ex rel. T.B.* (U.S. 1994)(unconstitutional to use peremptory challenges to exclude men from jury in paternity suit); *Batson v. Kentucky* (U.S. 1986)(unconstitutional to use peremptory challenges to strike prospective jurors on basis of race in criminal case in which defendant and prospective jurors are of same race); *Powers v. Ohio* (U.S. 1991)(peremptory challenges based on race are unconstitutional when the defendant and prospective jurors are of different races); *Edmonson v. Leesville Concrete Co.* (U.S. 1991)(applying *Batson* to civil cases); *Georgia v. McCollum* (U.S. 1992)(finding criminal defendant to be "state actor" when exercising peremptory challenges, thus making defendant's peremptory challenges subject to judicial review)] So far the Supreme Court has not ruled on peremptory challenges based on a prospective juror's religious beliefs. However, in his dissent in *J.E.B. v. Alabama ex rel. T.B.* (U.S. 1994), Justice Scalia noted that the *Batson* principle "presumably would include religious belief." But in *State v. Davis* (Minn. 1994), which was decided before the Supreme Court decided *J.E.B.*, the Minnesota Supreme Court declined to extend *Batson* to peremptory challenges made for reasons of the prospective juror's religious faith.

Shortly after *J.E.B.* was decided, the Supreme Court denied certiorari in *State v. Davis* (Minn. 1994). Justice Clarence Thomas, joined by Justice Scalia, dissented: "[G]iven the Court's rationale in *J.E.B.*, no principled reason immediately appears for declining to apply *Batson* to any strike based on a classification that is accorded heightened scrutiny under the Equal Protection Clause." Most antidiscrimination statutes, including the Civil Rights Act of 1964, are written to prohibit discrimination on the basis of race, gender (or sex), and religion, among other forms of discrimination.

Justice Ginsberg wrote a short opinion concurring in the denial of the petition for writ of certiorari, complaining that the dissent's "portrayal of the opinion of the Minnesota Supreme Court is incomplete." The dissent, in her opinion, failed to note that the Minnesota Supreme Court concluded that religion is not as self-evident as race, and that inquiries during voir dire of a witness's religious beliefs are ordinarily impermissible.

Despite Justice Ginsberg's conclusion that such inquiries are impermissible, attorneys often question members of the venire about their religious beliefs. In Texas, prospective jury members are asked to state their religious faith on a form used by lawyers to help make peremptory challenges and challenges for cause. State courts confronting the issue of the propriety during voir dire of questions concerning the religion or religious beliefs of prospective jurors have both permitted and excluded such questions. As a general rule, a person otherwise competent is not disqualified as a juror because of his or her religious beliefs. Courts have reached different results, however, under the circumstances involved as to whether the religious belief, affiliation, or prejudice of a prospective juror is a proper subject of inquiry on voir dire or a proper ground of challenge for cause. Thus, it has been held that inquiry as to a prospective juror's religious beliefs or affiliation was properly allowed or improperly denied in cases involving prosecution for abortion [*Wasy v. State* (Ind. 1955); *State v. Barnett* (Or. 1968)], or a prosecution for polygamy [*United States v. Miles* (U.S. 1877)], or a prosecution relating to selective service laws [*U.S. v. Jones* (U.S. 1947)]. On the other hand, it has also been held that inquiry as to a prospective juror's religious belief was properly denied in prosecutions relating to abortion [*People v. Dailey* (Cal. App. Ct. 1958); *Adams v. State* (Md. 1952)] or relating to selective service laws [*United States v. Cullen* (7th Cir. 1971); *Hoapili v. United States* (9th Cir. 1968)] or other criminal cases [*People v. Velarde* (Colo. 1980); *Hamling v. United States* (U.S. 1974)]. As noted in *Davis*, although such inquiries are often prohibited, these questions may be allowed based on the discretionary judgement of the trial judge.

Although many lawyers have used religious affiliation and religious belief to guide their peremptory challenges, there is no present social scientific data linking religious affiliation or intensity of religious belief with particular patterns of juror behavior.

L

LARKIN V. GRENDEL'S DEN, INC. (U.S. 1982) In his solitary dissent, Justice William H. Rehnquist observed that "silly cases' like this one, as well as great or hard cases, make bad law. Chief Justice Warren E. Burger, for the majority, had aimed the Supreme Court's "heavy First Amendment artillery" (in Rehnquist's phrase) at a statute that banned the sale of alcoholic beverages within 500 feet of a school or church, if either objected to the presence of a neighboring tavern. Originally, Massachusetts had absolutely banned such taverns but found that the objective of the state police power, promoting neighborhood peace, could be fulfilled by the less drastic method of allowing schools and churches to take the initiative of registering objections. In this case a church objected to a tavern located 10 feet away. A federal district court refused to follow the decision of the Massachusetts Supreme Judicial Court upholding the statute, and the federal First Circuit Court of Appeals affirmed that decision.

The U.S. Supreme Court ruled that the statute could not be characterized as a simple exercise of legislative power, because it delegated governmental power to private, nongovernmental entities. Justice Burger held that vesting the church with the state's veto power breached the prohibition against an establishment of religion, because the church's involvement vitiated the secular purposes of the statute, advanced the cause of religion, and excessively entangled state and church. Justice Rehnquist argued in dissent that a sensible statute had not breached the wall of separation between church and state. He said that the statute did not subsidize any religious group or activity and did not encourage participation in religious activities. The Court itself conceded that the legislature could enact a flat ban on the sale of liquor within 500 feet of a church, the dissent said, and that ban would be more protective of churches and more restrictive of liquor sales than the statute at issue.

LARSON V. VALENTE (U.S. 1982)   A Minnesota statute required charitable organizations to register and make disclosure of their finances when they solicited contributions. Religious organizations were exempted if more than half their contributions came from members. Members of the Unification Church of the Reverend Sun Myung Moon sued in federal court to challenge the law's constitutionality. A federal district court struck down the law. The Eighth Circuit Court of Appeals upheld the lower court. The Supreme Court, by a five-to-four vote, held the law invalid.

Justice William J. Brennan, for the Court, argued that the law effectively granted denominational preferences, favoring well-established churches and disfavoring newer churches or churches that preferred public solicitation. He said that the law did "not operate even-handedly, nor was it intended to." This discrimination took the case out of the purpose-effects-entanglement test of *Lemon v. Kurtzman* (1971) for Establishment Clause challenges. Instead, Brennan invoked a searching form of strict scrutiny, which the state here failed to pass. The state's purported interests in preventing abuse in solicitation were not supported in the record. In any case, Brennan said, the Minnesota law failed *Lemon's* "entanglement" test by raising the politicizing of religion.

Justices William Rehnquist, Byron White, Sandra Day O'Connor, and Chief Justice Warren Burger dissented. The four dissenters thought that the plaintiffs lacked standing to challenge the law, because they argued that the Unification Church was not a religion. Justices White and Rehnquist also dissented on the merits of the case, arguing that the law did not constitute an intentional discrimination among religions. They wrote that the statute on its face "did not discriminate against some religious beliefs, as Justice Brennan indicated."

LEMON V. KURTZMAN (U.S. 1971)   This case involved one of the school aid statutes produced by state legislatures in the aftermath of the Supreme Court's *Board of Education v. Allen* (U.S. 1968) decision. *Lemon I* represents three cases joined for decision by the Court. Pennsylvania passed a law that authorized the superintendent of public instruction to reimburse nonpublic schools for teachers' salaries, textbooks, and instructional materials in secular subjects. The plaintiff, Alton Lemon, challenged the law because he believed that state support for parochial schools would siphon away much-needed funds for public schools and that African Americans and other ethnic minorities would suffer. The other cases consolidated with Lemon's appeal were *Earley v. DiCenso* and *Robinson v. DiCenso* (U.S. 1971), which challenged a Rhode Island statute that made available direct payments to teachers in nonpublic schools in amounts of up to 15 percent of their regular salaries.

The Court held that both statutes were unconstitutional under the religion clauses of the First Amendment, as the cumulative impact of the entire relationship arising under the statutes involved excessive entanglement between government and religion.

The entanglement in the Rhode Island program arose because of the religious activity and purpose of the church-affiliated schools, especially with respect to children of impressionable age in the primary grades, and the dangers that a teacher under religious control and discipline posed to the separation of religious from purely secular aspects of elementary education in such schools. These factors would require continuing state surveillance to ensure that the statutory restrictions were obeyed and the First Amendment otherwise respected. Furthermore, under the Rhode Island law, the government would be required to inspect school records to determine what part of its expenditures were attributable to secular education, as opposed to religious activity, in the event a nonpublic school's expenditures per pupil exceeded the comparable figures for public schools.

The excessive entanglement in the Pennsylvania program also arose from the restrictions and surveillance necessary to ensure that teachers would play a strictly nonideological role and the state supervision of nonpublic school accounting procedures required to establish the cost of secular, as distinguished from religious, education. In addition, the Pennsylvania statute had the further defect of providing continuing financial aid directly to the church-related schools. Historically, governmental control and surveillance measures tend to follow cash grant programs, and here the government's postaudit power to inspect the financial records of church-related schools created an intimate and continuing relationship between church and state.

Political division along religious lines is one evil the First Amendment attempts to avoid, and in these programs, where successive and probably permanent annual appropriations benefitting relatively few religious groups were involved, political fragmentation and divisiveness on religious lines were likely to be intensified.

Unlike the tax exemption for places of religious worship, upheld in *Walz v. Tax Commission* (U.S. 1970), which was based on a practice of 200 years, the programs involved in *Lemon* had self-perpetuating and self-expanding propensities that provided a warning signal against entanglement between government and religion.

Chief Justice Warren Burger delivered the opinion of the Court, in which Justices Hugo Black, William O. Douglas, John M. Harlan, Potter Stewart, Thurgood Marshall, and Harry Blackmun joined. Justice Douglas filed a concurring opinion, in which Justices Black and Marshall

joined as to the Rhode Island cases. Justice Brennan filed a separate concurring opinion, and would reserve judgment in the Pennsylvania case.
Justice White filed an opinion concurring in the judgment in the Pennsylvania case and dissenting in the Rhode Island case. Justice Marshall
took no part in the consideration or decision.

Lemon returned to the Court two years later (known then as Lemon II)
on the question of whether the Pennsylvania schools could retain the
monies paid out in the period between the implementation of the law and
the decision of the Supreme Court invalidating the statutes in Lemon I. In
a plurality opinion for himself and Justices Harry Blackmun, Lewis F.
Powell, and William H. Rehnquist, Chief Justice Burger held that they
could. An unconstitutional statute, he suggested, is not absolutely void,
but is a practical reality upon which people are entitled to rely until au-
thoritatively informed otherwise. Justice Byron R. White, concurred. Justice William O. Douglas, joined by Justices William J. Brennan and Potter
Stewart dissented. Douglas argued that there was "clear warning to those
who proposed such subsidies" that they were treading on unconstitutional ground. "No consideration of equity," Douglas suggested, should
allow them "to profit from their unconstitutional venture."

In Lemon I the Supreme Court announced a three-part test for determining whether a law is constitutional under the Establishment Clause of
the First Amendment. In most cases each part of the test must be satisfied
for a law to withstand an Establishment Clause challenge. The test requires that a law (1) have a secular legislative purpose, (2) the principal
or primary effect of which neither advances nor inhibits religion; and (3)
must not foster "an excessive government entanglement with religion."

The purpose prong of the Lemon test focuses on what the legislators
could reasonably be presumed to have been thinking when they enacted
the new law. The inquiries it authorizes include: Did they know, or could
they reasonably be presumed to have known, that a piece of legislation
had its origins as a religious mandate? Was this knowledge just one of
many influences on their decision to enact the law, or was it the sole or
primary factor?

The Lemon test has been severely criticized. Some commentators, for
example, have found that the Lemon test has been inconsistently applied,
is unprincipled, and is too easily manipulable. Other view it as containing dichotomies too sharp (for example: secular vs. religious, advance vs.
inhibit religious interest, and excessive vs. acceptable government entanglement) and thus too rigid to do justice to the complex nature of modern church-state relationships. Others find that the test undermines the
value of religious autonomy, especially in public settings, as in Lynch v.
Donnelly (U.S. 1984), a case in which the U.S. Supreme Court allowed a
nativity scene to be placed among less sectarian symbols of Christmas in

publicly funded holiday display. They view the test when weakly applied as violating the Establishment Clause principles by allowing majority religions to impose their beliefs on nonadherents. Further, the Supreme Court has departed from the test in upholding prayers that open legislative sessions, emphasizing instead the historical acceptance of the challenged practice that makes it "a part of the fabric of our society." [*Marsh v. Chambers* (U.S. 1983)] Similarly, *Walz v. Tax Commission* (U.S. 1970) emphasized historical practices in upholding state tax exemptions for the property and income of religious institutions. *Larson v. Valente* (U.S. 1982) also avoided *Lemon* in invalidating a state law imposing disclosure requirements only on religious organizations soliciting more than 50 percent of funds from nonmembers, because it discriminated against nontraditional religions in violation of the Establishment Clause. The *Larson* Court used the so-called strict scrutiny test for detecting laws that impermissibly discriminate against some religions in favor of others.

Whether the tripartite *Lemon* test will survive is not clear. A majority of the Supreme Court came to openly speculate about finding more workable constitutional formulas to replace it. New trends arose. Increasingly, the Court is asking whether the law at issue constitutes an endorsement of religion or a particular religious belief. Justice Sandra Day O'Connor has shown that she believes that this is a more useful test than *Lemon*. [*Lynch v. Donnelly* (U.S. 1984)] Justice Anthony Kennedy, on the other hand, believes that endorsement is too imprecise a concept and that the appropriate inquiry is whether the state is proselytizing so that the government action is coercive. [*Board of Education v. Mergens* (U.S. 1990)(concurring opinion)] Justice Antonin Scalia reasons that the purpose prong of *Lemon* is impermissible because a purpose inquiry is "almost always an impossible task." [*Edwards v. Aguillard* (U.S. 1987)(dissenting opinion)] If religious motivation by itself invalidates a piece of legislation, wrote Scalia, then there is much legislation that must be invalidated. Swayed by Scalia's arguments, some have called for the elimination of the purpose prong, stating that it "[p]resent[s] a test too difficult to appl . . . [because the] sources which reveal such intent can be 'contrived and sanitized, favorable media coverage orchestrated, and post-enactment [sic] recollections conveniently distorted.'"

Despite these misgivings, the *Lemon* test is still the official standard for courts adjudicating appeals involving the Constitution's Establishment Clause. However, there have been such notable exceptions as *Marsh v. Chambers* (U.S. 1983), in which the Court held that, because the Founding Fathers who wrote the First Amendment approved of legislative chaplains, Nebraska's chaplaincy practice did not violate the Establishment Clause.

In a recent case, *Jones v. Clear Creek Independent School District* (5th Cir. 1998), the Fifth Circuit Court of Appeals addressed the issue of whether a Texas high school's policy of permitting high school seniors to select student volunteers to deliver "nonsectarian and nonproselytizing" prayer during graduation was constitutional. Applying the three-part *Lemon* test, the court held that the policy did not violate the Establishment Clause of the First Amendment. The prayer was intended to promote the secular purpose of solemnization, and unlike the policy at issue in *Lee v. Weisman* (U.S. 1992), the resolution was designed to minimize state entanglement with religion and coerced participation in religious activity. Specifically, the court noted that the school delegated to the senior class the discretion to use invocation or benediction during graduation ceremonies, and that students, rather than clergy were permitted to deliver a nonsectarian and nonproselytizing prayer. Also, prayer was not mandatory, because the resolution merely allowed prayer based on a senior class vote.

LEVITT V. COMMITTEE FOR PUBLIC EDUCATION (U.S. 1973)

In this case, the Supreme Court rejected state reimbursement of parochial schools on a lump sum per project basis for the costs of administering tests when some of them were prepared by the private school teachers. The lump sum per student payment was to cover the cost of keeping certain records, preparation of various reports to the state, and the testing of students on required subjects. The Court said that the program aided religion and that there was no guarantee that the aid would be used to defray only secular costs and would not be used to advance religion. Given the nature of religious primary and secondary schools, the Court reasoned, these unrestricted lump sum grants might go to advance the sectarian activities as well as the secular functions of these schools. The fact that these services were required by the state could not furnish a way to avoid the prohibition against subsidizing religious activities.

LYNCH V. DONNELLY (U.S. 1984)

This was the first Supreme Court case since the *Sunday Closing Law Cases* (U.S. 1961) to deal with state-supported recognition of a religious holiday. It was also the first case to introduce the Establishment Clause "endorsement test" as an alternative to the *Lemon* test. Under the endorsement test, a state's action may neither have the purpose of endorsing religion, nor may it convey a message of support for religious practices. Under the *Lemon* test [from *Lemon v. Kurtzman* (U.S. 1971)], for a statute not to be in violation of the Establishment Clause, it must meet each of the following conditions: (1) it must have a secular legislative purpose; (2) its principle or primary effect must be one that neither advances nor inhibits religion; and (3) it must not foster an excessive entanglement between the government and religion.

The Supreme Court significantly lowered the wall of separation between church and state by sanctioning an official display of a sacred Christian symbol. It found instead a constitutional mandate for religious accommodation. The city of Pawtucket, Rhode Island, included a nativity scene (or crèche) in its annual Christmas exhibit in the center of the city's shopping district. The plaintiffs argued that Pawtucket's display violated the Constitution's prohibition of establishment of religion because it demonstrated official support for Christianity.

The federal district court held that the city's inclusion of the creche in the display violated the First Amendment's Establishment Clause made binding on the states through the Fourteenth Amendment, and permanently enjoined the city from including the crèche in the display. The First Circuit Court of Appeals affirmed.

Reversing the lower court decisions, the U.S. Supreme Court upheld on a five-to-four vote the legality of the municipality's erection of a crèche or nativity scene as a part of an annual Christmas display. For the majority, Chief Justice Burger said the display had the secular purpose of celebrating the Christmas holiday and of depicting the origins of the holiday. This secular purpose was shown by the fact that the exhibit proclaimed "Seasons Greetings" and included Santa Claus, his reindeer, a Christmas tree, and figures of carolers, a clown, an elephant, and a teddy bear. The Court noted frequent government recognition of religious holidays and events. The First Amendment, Burger argued, did not mandate complete separation, as shown by our national motto "In God We Trust," paid chaplains, presidential proclamations invoking God, the pledge of allegiance with its mention of "under God," and religious art in publicly supported museums. The Court also focused on the increasing secularization of Christmas. Further, the religious effects were no more egregious here than in many public aid programs approved by the Court. The chief justice concluded that any benefit to religion from the display was "indirect, remote, and incidental." The absence of any ongoing day-to-day interaction between church and state made any entanglement concerns minimal. Fear of political divisiveness alone could not serve to invalidate otherwise permissible municipal conduct.

Justice William Brennan, joined by Justices Marshall, Blackmun, and Stevens, dissented on the grounds that the city's display was an unconstitutional endorsement of a particular religious faith.

A spokesman for the National Council of Churches complained that the Court had put Christ "on the same level as Santa Claus and Rudolph the Red-Nosed Reindeer." Other critics teased that the Court had created a "two-reindeer" rule for testing the constitutionality of holiday displays and, more seriously, for demonstrating extreme insensitivity to non-Christians. Clearly, said detractors of the decision, the Court had a topsy-turvy understanding of what constitutes an establishment of religion, because in *Larkin v. Grendel's Den* (U.S. 1982) it saw a forbidden establishment in a state police power measure aimed at keeping boisterous patrons of a tavern from disturbing a church, yet here saw no establishment in a state-sponsored nativity scene.

Sandra Day O'Connor's concurring opinion championed the position that the holding in *Lemon v. Kurtzman* (U.S. 1971) is best viewed through the lens of an "endorsement analysis." She suggested that Establishment Clause jurisprudence would be clarified if the Court assessed whether the state action was an effort to "endorse" religion. The benefit of the "endorsement" test was that it focused attention on whether the government's action made adherence to religion "relevant in any way to a person's standing in the political community." Endorsement of religion by the government depended both on the subjective intent of the governmental speaker and the objective meaning of the statement in the community. In this case, she concluded, the City of Pawtucket had not "endorsed" a view favoring religion (or particular religious beliefs) over nonreligion, and thus the display was constitutional. "Endorsement," she wrote, "sends a message to nonadherents that they are outsiders, not full members of the political community." Based on this interpretation of *Lemon,* Justice O'Connor concluded that the purpose of the nativity scene was not to endorse Christianity but to celebrate a public holiday of secular significance, notwithstanding its religious aspect. As for the effect of the nativity scene, its "overall holiday setting negates any message of endorsement" of the religious aspect of the display. Justice O'Connor's "endorsement" test provided a more focused approach then the open-ended emphasis on "accommodation" in Chief Justice Burger's opinion and has been widely followed in subsequent cases even by justices who disagreed with her conclusion that the Pawtucket crèche was constitutional.

▅▅▅ *LYNG V. NORTHWEST INDIAN CEMETERY PROTEC-*
▅▅▅ *TIVE ASSOCIATION* **(U.S. 1988)**   Unlike some other religious groups' practices, Native American religious rituals have not fared well before the U.S. Supreme Court. This case involved a plan by the U.S. Forest Service to build a paved road and allow timber harvesting in an area held sacred by certain Native Americans. The case concerned the Chimney Rock section of the Six Rivers National Forest in northwestern California. The Native Americans used the area, now a part of a national forest, for at least 200 years to perform religious rituals. The area was considered sacred and an essential part of an ancient Native Ameri-

can religion in which land is more than a mere place of worship, but in a sense God itself. The Native Americans believed that their religious leaders received power from the land that would permit them to fill their religious roles.

The Supreme Court held five to three that the Forest Service action would not violate the Free Exercise Clause of the First Amendment. Writing for the majority, Justice Sandra Day O'Connor maintained that the Free Exercise Clause was not implicated here because the Native Americans would not be coerced by the government's action into violating their religious beliefs. She further wrote that "[g]overnment simply could not operate if it were required to satisfy every citizen's religious needs and desires." Hence, the government did not have to supply a compelling state interest to justify its action. The fact that the government activity would interfere with the Native American's religion was irrelevant because the "Free Exercise Clause is written in terms of what the government cannot do to the individual, not in terms of what the individual can extract from the government." Moreover, even if the Forest Service actions should "virtually destroy the Indians' ability to practice their religion, . . . the Constitution simply does not provide a principle that could justify upholding" their claims.

Writing for the dissenters, Justice William J. Brennan rejected the majority's narrow reading of the Free Exercise Clause and argued that because the beliefs and activities implicated by the government action were "central" to the religion of the American Indians, the government must supply a compelling state interest to justify its action. Justice Blackmun wrote that the majority's reasoning was "surreal," that government action that "will virtually destroy a religion is nevertheless deemed not to 'burden' that religion."

M

MADISON'S *MEMORIAL AND REMONSTRANCE AGAINST RELIGIOUS ASSESSMENTS* (1785) This writing is considered the best evidence of what James Madison, the framer of the First Amendment to the U.S. Constitution, intended by the phrase "an establishment of religion." In 1784 the Virginia General Assembly considered legislation to benefit "Teachers of the Christian Religion" by assessing a small tax on property owners. Each taxpayer could designate the Christian church of his or her choice as the recipient of his or her tax money; the bill allowed nonchurch members to earmark their taxes for the support of local schools, and it upheld the "liberal principle" that all Christian sects and denominations were equal under the law, none preferred to others. The bill did not speak of the "established religion" of the state as had a failed bill of 1779, and it purported to be based on only secular considerations—the promotion of the public peace and morality, rather than Christ's kingdom on earth.

Madison denounced the bill as an establishment of religion, no less dangerous to religious liberty than the proposal of 1779 and differing "only in degree" from the Inquisition. In an elaborate argument of 15 sections, Madison advocated a complete separation of church and state as the only guarantee of the equal right of every citizen to the free exercise of religion, including the freedom of those "whose minds have not yet yielded to the evidence that has convinced us." He regarded the right to support religion as an "unalienable" individual right to be exercised only on a voluntary basis. Religion, he contended, must be exempt from the power of society, the legislature, and the magistrate. Assaulting establishments including the one proposed by this bill, he wrote "it is proper to take alarm at the first experiment on our liberties" and in his eloquent defense of separation, Madison emphasized that separation benefitted not only personal freedom but also the free state and even religion itself. His *Remonstrance*, which circulated throughout Virginia in the summer of 1785, actually redirected public opinion, resulting in the election of legislators who opposed the bill, which had previously passed a second reading. The *Remonstrance* generated unified opposition to the bill from Baptists, Methodists, Presbyterians, and Enlightenment thinkers. Madison then introduced Thomas Jefferson's proposal that was enacted into law as the Virginia Statute of Religious Freedom.

Madison's *Memorial and Remonstrance* became one of the most influential documents in the history of law and religion, and was embraced by the U.S. Supreme Court as a key indicator of the meaning of the First Amendment. [*See, e.g., Everson v. Board of Education* (U.S. 1947); *Engel v. Vitale* (U.S. 1962)]

MARSH V. CHAMBERS (U.S. 1983)   In this case the U.S. Supreme Court upheld Nebraska's practice of opening each legislative day with a prayer spoken by a chaplain. The decision was based solely on the history of the practice, which it traced back to the appointment of chaplains by the first Congress. A six-to-three majority of the Court sustained the constitutionality of legislative chaplaincies as not violative of the principle of separation of church and state mandated by the First Amendment. Chief Justice Warren E. Burger, writing for the Court, abandoned the three-part test of *Lemon v. Kurtzman* (1971) previously used in cases involving the Establishment Clause and grounded his opinion wholly upon historical custom. Prayers by tax-supported legislative chaplains, traceable to the First Continental Congress and the very Congress that framed the Bill of Rights, have become "part of the fabric of our society."

Justice John Paul Stevens, dissenting, asserted that Nebraska's practice of having the same Presbyterian minister as the official chaplain for 16 years preferred one denomination to others. Justices William J. Brennan and Thurgood Marshall, also dissenting, attacked legislative chaplains generally as a form of religious worship sponsored by government to promote and advance religion and entangling the government with religion, contrary to the values implicit in the Establishment Clause—privacy in religious matters, government neutrality, freedom of conscience, autonomy of religious life, and withdrawal of religion from the political arena.

MARYLAND TOLERATION ACT (1649)   This landmark in the protection of liberty of conscience was the most liberal provision in colonial America at the time of its passage on 2 April 1649 by the Maryland Assembly under the title "An Act Concerning Religion." It was far more liberal than the English Parliament's Toleration

Act that came 40 years later. Until 1776 only the Rhode Island Charter of 1634 and Pennsylvania's "Great Law" of 1682 guaranteed fuller religious liberty.

Maryland's statute, framed by its Roman Catholic proprietor, Lord Baltimore (Cecil Calvert), was the first public act to use the phase "free exercise" of religion, later embodied in the First Amendment of the United States Constitution. More noteworthy, the law symbolized the extraordinary fact that for most of the seventeenth century in Maryland, Roman Catholics and various Protestant sects openly worshiped as they chose and lived in peace, although not in amity. The statute applied to all those who professed belief in Jesus Christ, except anti-Trinitarians, and guaranteed them immunity from being troubled in any way because of their religion. In other provisions more characteristic of the time, the law prescribed the death penalty for blasphemers against God, Christ, or the Trinity, and it imposed lesser penalties for profaning the Sabbath or for reproaching the Virgin Mary or the Apostles. Another clause anticipated group libel laws (statutes prohibiting the holding up of a group to ridicule, scorn, or contempt to a significant segment of the community) by penalizing the reproachful use of any name or term such as "heretic," "puritan," "popish rites," "anabaptists," "separatist," or "antinomian."

At a time when intolerance was the law in Europe and most of America, Maryland established no church and tolerated all Trinitarian Christians, until Protestants, who had managed to suspend the Toleration Act between 1654 and 1658 gained political control of the colony in 1689. In 1691 the Calvert charter, issued by the second Lord Baltimore in 1632 establishing the colony, was annulled and in 1702 the Church of England was officially established in Maryland. Catholics were not granted religious toleration under this new regime. The Maryland constitution of 1776 guaranteed that "all persons professing the Christian religion, are equally entitled to protection in their religious liberty."

MASSACHUSETTS BAY COLONIAL CHARTERS (1629, 1691)

In 1629 King Charles I of England granted a royal charter to Puritan leaders of the New England Company, incorporating them as the Massachusetts Bay Colony. The charter became the colony's basic instrument of government. In the same year, Puritan leaders received authorization to migrate to New England and take the charter with them. As a result, the Puritans controlled Massachusetts and sought to create a Bible commonwealth or theocracy. The charter authorized the freemen of the company to meet in a general court or legislature, and to choose a governor, a deputy governor, and assistants, seven of whom could function as the General Court. The charter vested power in these men to govern Massachusetts Bay in every respect and guaranteed that all inhabitants "shall have and enjoy all liberties and immunities of free and natural subjects . . . as if they . . . were born within the realm of England." The Puritans, who governed themselves, enjoyed the rights of Englishmen. However, they distanced themselves from England and became firmly independent.

Massachusetts admitted only church members for freemanship, but the small oligarchy in control refused to allow all freemen a right to participate in governing—a violation of the charter. In 1634 the freemen, on seeing the charter for themselves, demanded full participation in government. From then on the freemen in the town chose two deputies from each town as members of the General Court, making it a representative body. Conflict between the freemen and the assistants led to an agreement that laws could be passed only by a majority vote of both the freemen and the assistants. Bicameralism—that is, a legislature composed of two chambers, emerged from this practice.

Growing estrangement between the colony and England resulted in the annulment of the company's charter in 1684 and the substitution of royal government under a new charter granted in 1691. The charter of 1691 turned Massachusetts from comparative autonomy into a royal colony. The king appointed its governor and his deputy and the governor could veto legislation—a model for a strong executive in later American history. The government established by the second charter recognized a clear separation of powers between the three branches. The charter also embodied the principle of liberty of conscience for all Christians (except "papists") and like the first charter, also guaranteed the rights of Englishmen.

📖 MCCOLLUM V. BOARD OF EDUCATION (U.S. 1948)

During the late 1940s and 1950s released-time programs were popular around the country. Under these programs public school students were "released" from school to spend time in religious studies in accordance with their families' wishes. Public school boards and administrators cooperated with churches and synagogues to provide this religious education. More than 3,000 communities in 46 states had such programs.

In Champaign-Urbana, Illinois, public school students whose parents had signed a "request card" were released during school hours to attend religious instruction within the school building. The classes were taught by outside teachers furnished by a local interdenominational religious council. Attendance records were kept, and the outside teachers were subject to approval by the school superintendent. Students who did not enroll were sent from their classrooms to other rooms where they continued their secular education.

Mrs. Vashti McCollum, an atheist whose child, Terry, attended a public school in Champaign, Illinois, challenged the Illinois practice, claiming that it violated the Establishment Clause of the First Amendment. The case was the first church-state controversy to reach the Court since *Everson v. Board of Education* (U.S. 1947) was decided. In striking down the program as a violation of the Establishment Clause, Justice Hugo Black delivered the opinion for the majority. Referring to the theory of strict separation announced as *obiter dictum* (an incidental remark, not part of the holding) in his *Everson* opinion, Black held that the Illinois arrangement fell squarely within the First Amendment's ban on government action tending to "establish" a religion. He stressed particularly the utilization of tax-supported facilities to aid religious teaching.

Justice Felix Frankfurter concurred in an opinion in which Justices Robert Jackson, Wiley Rutledge, and Harold Burton joined. These four had dissented from *Everson*'s approval of state aid.

Justice Jackson also concurred separately, rejecting the sweeping separationism of the Black opinion. Arguing that there was little real cost to the taxpayers in the Illinois program, he agreed that the Court should end "formal and explicit instruction" such as that in the Champaign-Urbana schools, but cautioned against inviting ceaseless petitions to the Court to purge school curricula of materials that any group might regard as religious.

Justice Stanley F. Reed, the lone dissenter, had concurred in the result in *Everson*. In *McCollum* he argued that the majority was giving "establishment" too broad a meaning: unconstitutional "aid" to religion embraced only purposeful assistance directly to a church, not cooperative relationships between government and religious institutions. He argued against "a rigid interpretation . . . that conflicts with accepted habits."

The *McCollum* case was the first to hold a state or federal legislative enactment unconstitutional on the basis of the newly incorporated Establishment Clause. The "incorporation" doctrine allowed the Supreme Court to apply the protections in the Bill of Rights, which originally constrained only the federal government, to the state governments as well through the operation of the Fourteenth Amendment. The *McCollum* opinion was criticized for its historical analysis, its reliance on Madison's absolute conception of church and state, and for Justice Frankfurter's attempt to use the public school system as a "symbol of our secular unity." Many Roman Catholic Church theorists, for example, had long contended that the state must support the church when its aid was needed or when temporal and spiritual matters converge, such as in education and marriage, and opposed the "American" approach to issues of church-state relations, which emphasized a strong separation of church and state. This opposition largely diminished following the Second Vatican Council's Declaration on Religious Freedom in the early 1960s, which announced a change in the Church's position. The Declaration repudiated all coercion in religious matters as contrary to the dignity of man.

Critics of the decision also contended that it increased, rather than dissipated, uncertainty about the constitutionality of released-time programs.

McCollum seemed to represent a deepening Supreme Court commitment to the theory of strict separation of church and state, but it was significantly limited by another released-time case, *Zorach v. Clausen* (U.S. 1952).

MCDANIEL V. PATY (U.S. 1978)   In this case the U.S. Supreme Court held that a Tennessee statute that prohibited members of the clergy from holding public office was unconstitutional. Such statutes were once common, but eventually were repealed everywhere but Tennessee. The statute also prohibited ministers and priests from service in a constitutional convention. A Baptist minister, Paul A. McDaniel, had contested the law after he was prohibited from taking part in a state constitutional convention to which he had been elected.

McDaniel's case reached the Supreme Court. Although the Court was unanimous in its verdict, the justices divided four ways in their reasoning behind the result. The plurality opinion by Chief Justice Warren E. Burger, joined by Justices Powell, Rehnquist, and Stevens, maintained that the Tennessee statute violated the Free Exercise Clause of the First Amendment.

These justices found the case to be governed by *Sherbert v. Verner* (U.S. 1963), which required strict scrutiny of governmental restrictions upon the free exercise of religion. Tennessee had failed to show any validity to supposed dangers of clergy participation in the political process. The Court distinguished the case of *Torcaso v. Watkins* (U.S. 1961), which involved a provision of the Maryland constitution stating that "no religious test ought ever to be required as a qualification to any office . . . other than a declaration in the belief of God." Justice Black, for the Court, found that this requirement contradicted the Establishment Clause of the First Amendment. *Torcaso* was different from the case at hand because the state in this instance was acting on the basis of one's status as a clergyman rather than on the basis of one's beliefs. Justice William E. Brennan, joined by Justice Thurgood Marshall, found *Torcaso* controlling because imposing a restriction upon one's status as a clergyman does penalize religious belief—the freedom to profess or practice that belief. Justice Potter Stewart also found *Torcaso* was the controlling decision in this case. Justice

Byron R. White contended that the Tennessee law was invalid as an equal protection violation because of the restraint upon clergy members who wish to seek political office.

IIII MEDICAL TREATMENT   Some religious groups, such as the Christian Scientists, reject all or most forms of conventional medical treatment, believing instead in the power of prayer and faith to cure medical problems. Other groups, such as the Jehovah's Witnesses, oppose one specific type of treatment, such as blood transfusions.

A competent adult patient has a generally acknowledged right to refuse medical treatment. [*Werth v. Taylor* (Mich. Ct. App. 1991); *Schloen-dorff v. Society of New York Hospital* (N.Y. 1914)] The U.S. Supreme Court has issued several historically significant opinions on many of the crucial legal issues involving religion and medical treatment. [*See, e.g., Prince v. Massachusetts* (U.S. 1944); *United States v. Ballard* (U.S. 1964); *Cruzan v. Missouri Department of Health* (U.S. 1990)]

It should, however, be noted that all of these issues were resolved prior to either the balancing test under the Free Exercise Clause announced in *Sherbert v. Verner* (U.S. 1963) or the repudiation of the "compelling interest" standard of *Employment Division v. Smith* (U.S. 1990). It is always possible that the Supreme Court could reverse its position on these issues under the modern approach. Despite the possibility of contrary rulings in the future, however, it must be remembered that the following cases do reflect the current position of the Court.

American courts have upheld the right of the state to protect the health and safety of minor children over the religiously based objections of the child or of the parents. The broad principle has been enunciated in a wide range of cases that a state may, through a court order, intervene to ensure that a child is given medical treatment necessary for the protection of life or limb—including treatment for mental or emotional ills—where the custodian of the child has unreasonably refused to allow such treatment. In certain circumstances the exercise of the state's power to protect the lives and health of its children over the objections of their parents is not violative of the constitutional right to freedom of religion. Thus, courts have appointed guardians to consent to necessary medical treatment (such as blood transfusions) for children even though the treatment violates the child's or parent's religion. [*In re Sampson* (N.Y. 1972); *People ex rel. Wallace v. Labrenz* (Ill. 1952); *Jehovah's Witnesses v. King County Hospital* (W.D. Wash. 1967)] In a few cases a court has refused to order medical treatment that was beneficial but not related to the preservation of the child's life. [*In re Green* (Pa. 1972)]

Appropriate legal action may also be taken against parents for neglecting the health or safety of their children, regardless of whether the parent acted on the basis of religious principles. [*State v. Perricone* (N.J. 1962)]

One of the more difficult balancing acts that a court must undertake is determining when to order that a child be given over to the custody of a health services agency for the purpose of administering medical treatment when the parents object on religious grounds. Far from being neglectful or otherwise unfit parents, most such parents are deeply involved with their children's needs and seek to transmit their religious and spiritual values to them. Nevertheless, the state has a responsibility not to allow the children to suffer because of such beliefs. In *Newmark v. Williams* (Del. 1991), the court refused to order a 3-year-old child suffering from cancer to undergo medical treatment over the religious objections of his Christian Science parents. Despite evidence that the child would die within six to eight months if left untreated, the court took into account that the medical treatment itself was extremely invasive, risky, toxic, and dangerously life threatening, and offered less than a 40 percent chance for success. In other circumstances courts have authorized treatment where a child's condition was not an emergency or otherwise immediately life threatening. Many jurisdictions have rules, regulations, constitutional provisions, or legislative enactments directly addressing the issue of when medical treatment may be ordered for a child.

Through legislative activity at the federal and state levels, some religious groups have sought, and in many cases attained, government recognition in the form of approved payment from the state for "nonmedical therapy" and exemption from child abuse and neglect laws when children do not receive conventional medical care. Forty-two states and the District of Columbia have enacted statutes to exempt parents who decline to provide children with medical treatment for religious reasons from liability for child neglect. There is an argument that religious exemptions from child immunization laws violate the equal protection rights of children, along the lines that statutes providing exemptions from child abuse and neglect laws for religiously motivated parents who provide spiritual treatment rather than conventional medical care for their severely ill minor children violate the Establishment Clause. A contrary argument maintains that the very existence of such exemptions is supported by the Free Exercise Clause as a safeguard against the persecution of religious minorities.

More current caselaw involves claims by individuals that the Free Exercise Clause entitled them to an exemption from a health or medical regulation. Today, the Supreme Court uses a Free Exercise Clause test that would make it difficult, if not impossible, for an individual to prevail in such a case. The Court summarized its standards as follows:

A law that is neutral and of general applicability need not be justified by a compelling government interest even if the law has the incidental effect of burdening a particular religious practice. . . . [A] law failing to satisfy [the neutrality and general applicability] requirements must be justified by a compelling governmental interest and must be narrowly tailored to advance that interest. [*Church of the Lukumi Babalu Aye v. Hialeah* (U.S. 1993)]

So long as the health regulation at issue in a Free Exercise Clause case is a generally applicable law that is religiously neutral, the Court would not require the government to grant religiously based exemptions from it.

Some justices believe that the Court should apply a balancing test or a compelling interest test in all free exercise cases. If a majority of the justices in the future were to adopt any type of case-by-case approach to Free Exercise Clause claims, the Court might find that in some circumstances the social benefits of a particular health law are so slight that the government must grant an exemption for persons whose religious beliefs prevent them from complying with the law. However, such an approach to these cases would represent a major departure from the U.S. Supreme Court's most recent free exercise rulings.

MILITARY SERVICE, EXEMPTIONS FROM   *See* CONSCIENTIOUS OBJECTOR

MINERSVILLE SCHOOL DISTRICT V. GOBITIS (U.S. 1940)

In this case the Supreme Court found that a state regulation requiring pupils in the public schools (on pain of expulsion) to participate in a daily ceremony of saluting the national flag while reciting in unison a pledge of allegiance to it was within the scope of legislative power, and consistent with the Fourteenth Amendment. Thus it could be applied to children brought up in, and entertaining, a conscientious religious belief that such obeisance to the flag is forbidden. The children in this case were Jehovah's Witnesses who believed that oaths to "images" such as the flag were sinful.

Justice Frankfurter delivered the opinion of the Court, which found that religious convictions do not relieve the individual from obedience to an otherwise valid general law not aimed at the promotion or restriction of religious beliefs. As far as the federal Constitution is concerned, the Court held, it is within the province of the legislatures and school authorities of the states to adopt appropriate means to evoke and foster a sentiment of national unity among the children in the public schools.

The Court said it could not exercise censorship over the conviction of legislatures that a particular program or exercise would best promote in the minds of children who attend the public schools an attachment to the institutions of their country, nor overrule the local judgment against granting exemptions from observance of such a program.

Thus, *Gobitis* upheld the practice of compulsory pledging of allegiance to the flag against a free exercise challenge on the grounds that coercion of this sort is part of the price to be paid for living in a free society. *Gobitis* was reversed in *West Virginia Board of Education v. Barnette* (U.S. 1943), but controversies over official rituals involving the flag have not completely subsided. In *Lipp v. Morris* (3d Cir. 1978), a high school student successfully challenged a requirement that she show "full respect" to the flag by standing at attention during the recitation of the pledge of allegiance.

MORMON CASES

The Supreme Court's first challenge on the grounds that a law conflicted with the First Amendment's guarantee of free exercise of religion occurred in a series of cases in which the federal and territorial governments moved against the Members of the Church of Jesus Christ of Latter-Day Saints (the Mormons) because of their practice of polygamy, or having multiple wives. Actual prosecutions and convictions for bigamy presented little problem for the Supreme Court, because it could distinguish between beliefs and acts. [*Reynolds v. United States* (U.S. 1879); *Cleveland v. United States* (U.S. 1946)] Nevertheless, the presence of large numbers of Mormons in some of the territories made local convictions on polygamy charges difficult to obtain. In 1882 Congress passed the Edmunds Act. The Edmunds Act amended the Anti-Bigamy Act of 1862 by declaring polygamy a felony, disenfranchising polygamists, defining unlawful cohabitation, and prohibiting polygamists from serving in public office or as jurors. After the passage of the statute, the first sustained effort to eradicate polygamy in Utah began. The Supreme Court approved the effort, even as it applied to persons who had entered the state before enactment of the original law prohibiting polygamy and as to persons for whom the statute of limitations had run. [*Murphy v. Ramsey* (U.S. 1885)]

In *Cannon v. United States* (U.S. 1885) the Supreme Court upheld a conviction for unlawful cohabitation despite a lack of any evidence of sexual relations between the defendant and his second wife. Justices Samuel

Miller and Stephen Field dissented on the ground that the lack of evidence of a sexual relationship prohibited a conviction.

Subsequently, the Court upheld an act of a territorial legislature that required prospective voters not only to swear that they were not bigamists or polygamists, but as well that they did not belong to any organizations that encouraged such practices. The opinion of the Court was devoted to the condemnation of plural marriage and its advocacy as equal evils. [*Davis v. Beason* (U.S. 1890)]

Then ultimately, the Supreme Court sustained the revocation of the charter of the Mormon Church and confiscation of all church property not actually used for religious worship or for burial. [*Church of Jesus Christ of Latter-Day Saints v. United States* (U.S. 1890)] The Court in that case ruled that "[t]he property of the said corporation . . . is to be used to promote] the practice of polygamy—a crime against the laws, and abhorrent to the sentiments and feelings of the civilized world. . . . The organization of a community for the spread and practice of polygamy is, in a measure, a return to barbarism. It is contrary to the spirit of Christianity and of the civilization that Christianity had produced in the Western World."

Congress enacted the Edmunds-Tucker Act in 1887, which further restricted the privileges of people practicing polygamy. In 1890 the Mormon church officially disavowed polygamy and advised its members to abide by the laws of the United States in regard to it. When they voted to accept LDS President Wilford Woodruff's manifesto, in addition to giving up polygamy (or plural marriage), the members of the Mormon church also disavowed "economic communitarianism" and the political kingdom. The first concept referred to the religion's emphasis on sharing property in common. The latter referred to the fact that temporal government was placed in the hands of ecclesiastical leaders under the auspices of a political kingdom of God whose theocratic model was Israel. The manifesto represented the beginning of the reconnection of the LDS church with the world, a joining into the American cultural mainstream that ensured the survival of the religion. The religious commitment of LDS church members since that time has facilitated their social and economic success in the world.

Shortly thereafter, in 1896, Utah was admitted to the Union with a constitutional provision forbidding the practice of polygamy. Four other western states subsequently were admitted to the Union that also forbade the practice of polygamy in their constitutions (Oklahoma, Idaho, Arizona, and New Mexico). In 1898, the Utah legislature adopted a statute declaring the common law to be the "rule of decision in all courts of this state."

IIIIII *Mueller v. Allen* (**U.S. 1983**)   This major case on the issue of separation between church and state altered constitutional law on government aid to parents of parochial school children. The U.S. Supreme Court upheld by a five-to-four vote a Minnesota program permitting parents to deduct from their state income tax certain expenses incurred in educating their children. Justice William Rehnquist, writing for the Court, noted that the educational deduction was one of many deductions designed to equalize tax burdens and encourage desirable expenditures. Most important, unlike an earlier tax break program for parents of private school children that the Court invalidated (*Committee for Public Education v. Nyquist* (U.S. 1973)), the Minnesota tax break was available to all parents, including those whose children attended public schools. Justice Rehnquist commented: "[A] program that neutrally provides state assistance to a broad spectrum of citizens is not readily subject to challenge under the Establishment Clause." The argument that the bulk of the deductions would be claimed by parents who pay high tuition at sectarian schools was dismissed: "Such an approach would scarcely provide the certainty that this field stands in need of, nor can we perceive principled standards by which such statistical evidence might be evaluated." Further, Justice Rehnquist saw no significant danger of "comprehensive discriminating, and continuing state surveillance" in the religious schools that might excessively entangle the state in religion.

Justice Rehnquist placed special emphasis on the benefits provided to society by parents supporting private schools. Tax benefits to such parents serve the secular purposes of educating children and of assuring the continuing financial health of private schools. The private school system relieves the burden on public schools, serves as a benchmark for public schools, and provides an educational alternative promoting diversity. Any unequal effects of the program could be viewed as a "rough return for the benefits" provided to the state and taxpayers generally.

For Justice Thurgood Marshall, dissenting, the Minnesota law, like any tax benefit system subsidizing tuition payments to sectarian schools, had "a direct and immediate effect of advancing religion."

The *Mueller* case reflected a turnabout in the Court's thinking. Earlier precedents had established that a state may not aid parochial schools either by direct grants or indirectly by financial aids to the parents of the children; whether those aids took the form of tax credits or reimbursements of tuition expenses did not matter. In this case the statute allowed taxpayers to deduct expenses for tuition, books, and transportation of their children to school.

MUTUAL ABSTINENCE   Mutual abstinence embraces the notion that the state should not become involved in religious affairs and that sectarian differences should not be allowed to fragment the body politic. This ideal of mutual abstinence includes the principle that under no circumstances should religion be supported by public taxation. The separation principle involved in the theory of mutual abstinence operates in both directions. It was meant to keep religion from entangling with the state, as well as to keep the church free from the state influence that would have been the inevitable result of state financial support.

The Constitution is viewed, under the doctrine of mutual abstinence, as a pact to maintain civil peace in a society where political issues and values differ so as not to open religious conflict and arouse sectarian hostility. The purpose of the religion clauses in the First Amendment is to "ensure civil peace."

The justifications for First Amendment freedoms arise out of the political objective of establishing civil peace by means of toleration and the theory of the marketplace of ideas. John Locke's use of John Milton's phrase about truth winning out in a contest with falsehood has the intent to ensure that doctrinal division does not upset civil peace by becoming part of governmental strife. From their shared experiences, an understanding developed in the original 13 colonies that government should interfere in religious matters only when necessary to protect the civil peace or to prevent "licentiousness." In other words when religious beliefs conflicted with civil law, religion prevailed unless important state interests militated otherwise. Civil peace was one of the values, along with other values such as autonomy, that the supporters of the Bill or Rights used to justify making the religion clauses part of the U.S. Constitution. These values were neutral values that all reasonable people must accept, whose necessity were apparent to reasonable persons regardless of their particular sectarian beliefs or their atheism or agnosticism.

A civil peace justification is one that nearly everyone can accept because nearly everyone wants to avoid violence and a justification that the political order will reduce violence is one that nearly all can accept. On the other hand an autonomy justification is rejected by many religious believers.

Under one interpretation of the civil peace ideal, religion should be entirely private; it should not challenge or enliven one to seek to change the outside world. This philosophy promotes the view that religious discourse and civil discourse are incompatible, so that religious differences must be suppressed to promote civil peace. Under this view, because of the centuries of distrust and conflict, government institutions and religious institutions are unable to work together without one seeking to dominate the other.

In the United States the First Amendment intends that civil peace may be achieved even with religious diversity. In the American tradition, the religion clauses were not written as protection from religion, but as protection for religion. The Framer's intended that religion flourish vigorously and peaceably.

According to the holding in *Employment Division v. Smith* (U.S. 1990), a law that targets religion is subject to strict scrutiny to determine whether it is constitutional. This principle not only prevents petty harassment of religious institutions, but also serves the important structural goal of maintaining civil peace through a governmental stance of neutrality toward religion.

Accomodationists criticize separationist views of nonestablishment as a guarantor of civil peace. Many accommodationists view the basic controversy as boiling down to one question: Has religion divided and endangered political communities, or have political factions used religious symbols, affiliations, and authority to fight their political wars? They admit that world history supports to some extent the idea that religious conflict has often threatened civil tranquility. In U.S. history, however, almost precisely the opposite is true. Many accommodationists believe that Christianity has united, if not defined, the United States, and has supported political liberty.

As the United States enters the twenty-first century, large-scale outright religious violence is not a problem. The threat of violence is unfortunately not absent from the American scene. Each time a cross or church is burned, however, the assurance of civil peace in the United States is damaged. A loss of civil peace invariably translates into a loss of ordered liberty. Church burnings and cross burnings not only threaten the lives of African Americans and others, but are threats to the entire American system. Civil peace can not survive when racially motivated arson persists in American society.

Of course, civil peace could survive establishment of religion and serious inroads on free exercise. Therefore, our constitutional order on religion cannot be justified on simply preventing violence alone. An advocate of the civil peace justification might counter that more subtle forms of civil strife continue, and that were legal protections of religious freedom to disappear, outright violence might follow. The present strength of a civil peace justification depends on whether civil strife is a contemporary danger. And in some cases, with the presence of hate-motivated violence, it is.

The civil peace rationale for special protection of religious freedom may not go far enough. It does not justify protecting groups too small or fringe to fight back or muster widespread sympathy. Moreover, more ruthless religious suppression must be even more productive of civil peace than toleration.

In a pluralistic community, civil peace and inclusiveness can be achieved only imperfectly and only through compromise, cultivated tolerance, mutual forebearances, and strategic silences. In this context, the judicial imposition of any set of consistent and explicit principles is likely to undermine the possibilities for compromise and forbearance, and hence to aggravate the dangers of civil strife and alienation. Civil peace, in short, must be the product of prudence, not of principle imposed from above.

Critics of the general notion of nonestablishment as a guarantor of civil peace argue that the Supreme Court ignores the basic controversy in the area: has religion divided and endangered political communities, or have political factions used religious symbols, affiliations, and authority to fight their political wars? Although the issue undoubtedly permits no categorical answer, the justices offer no analysis at all. More important, although there is indeed a history to the idea that religious conflict threatens civil tranquility, the Court overstates it and in the process denies the overwhelming evidence in U.S. history of almost precisely the opposite. Christianity has united, if not defined, the United States, and because political liberty presupposes a religious citizenry, government must set aside religion to ensure its own survival. That the generation that enacted the First Amendment held the latter, more favorable, view of religion and the polity is beyond question.

N

NATIONAL CHURCH   *See* ESTABLISHMENT CLAUSE

NATIVITY SCENES   *See* HOLIDAY DISPLAYS

NATURAL LAW   Natural law comprises an unwritten body of universal principles that underlie the ethical and legal norms by which human conduct is evaluated and governed. This law is supposedly of divine origin, and is accessible by reason to people of all races, classes, religions, and cultures. The primary precepts of natural law, to do good and to avoid evil, are universally recognized, despite differences with respect to understanding and application.

Although the roots of natural law theory extend to such classical theorists as Socrates, Plato, Aristotle, and Zeno, the Middle Ages were the heyday of natural law theory. In medieval Christendom, the laws of nature were thought to supplement Scripture as God's truth, and thus, both served simultaneously as the foundation for canon law and civil law, the respective bodies of law of the two partners in the medieval world: church and state. In the Middle Ages Saint Thomas Aquinas accorded to natural law an exalted position just below "Positive Divine Law" and above "Human Law." Positive law consists of the written rules and regulations enacted by the government. Positive divine law was the law given by God in addition to the natural law. Whereas the natural law is promulgated in the very structure of his being and is discernible by natural reason alone, the existence and content of positive divine law is known only by revelation.

The term *natural law* is derived from the Latin words *jus naturale*. Adherents to natural law philosophy are known as naturalists.

Naturalists believe that natural-law principles are an inherent part of nature and exist regardless of whether government recognizes or enforces them. Naturalists further believe that the government must incorporate natural law principles into the legal system before justice can be achieved. There are three schools of natural law theory: divine natural law, secular natural law, and historical natural law.

Divine natural law holds that law must be made to conform to the commands laid down or inspired by God, or some other deity, who governs according to principles of compassion, truth, and justice.

Secular natural law replaces the divine laws of God with the physical, biological, and behavioral laws of nature as perceived by human reason. This school theorizes about the uniform and fixed rules of nature to identify moral and ethical norms.

According to the school of historical natural law, law must be made to conform with the well-established, but unwritten, customs, traditions, and experiences that evolved over the course of history. Historical natural law has played an integral role in the development of the Anglo-American system of justice.

NEUTRALITY STANDARD   The United States Supreme Court has concluded that under the Establishment Clause of the First Amendment the proper relationship of government vis-a-vis religion and religious institutions in this country is not one of hostility, but of neutrality, and that the neutrality that is required need not stem from a callous indifference to religion, but may at times be benevolent. [*Committee for Public Education & Religious Liberty v. Nyquist* (U.S. 1973); *Gillette v. United States* (U.S. 1973)] State courts, too, have supported the requirement of government neutrality, or a "hands off" policy. Although the metaphor of a wall, or impassible barrier, between church and state, when taken too literally, may mislead constitutional analysis, nevertheless the Establishment Clause of the First Amendment stands at least for the proposition that when government activities affect the religious sphere, they must be secular in purpose, even-handed in operation, and neutral in primary impact. [See *Lemon v. Kurtzman,* U.S. 1971.]

Under the Establishment Clause government neutrality in matters of religion is not inconsistent with benevolence by way of exemption from onerous duties, so long as an exemption is tailored broadly enough that it reflects valid secular purposes. [*Gillette v. United States* (1971)]

NONPREFERENTIALIST   *See* ACCOMMODATIONIST

NONPROFIT CORPORATION   Corporations organized exclusively for religious, charitable, educational, or hospital purposes may be organized as nonprofit corporations. A nonprofit corporation is generally understood to be "a corporation, no part of the income or profit of which is distributable to its members, directors, or officers," [Model Nonprofit Corporations Act § 2(a)(1964)] A nonprofit corporation can be understood as a corporation that exists for, and applies any profits it makes to, charitable purposes, rather than for private gain. Nonprofit corporations cannot distribute profits or net incomes to their members, officers, or directors, and are prohibited from issuing shares of stock, or paying dividends to those who have contributed capital. All income must be retained and used to advance the purpose of the corporation.

The nonprofit form of incorporation is one of the most common organizational structures utilized by religious and religiously affiliated groups. As religious corporations, they are artificial constructions of the state designed to provide the congregations with an orderly procedural framework so as to ultimately permit them to exercise their religion freely, although the scope and application of the term may be defined and restricted, by the terms of the statute in which it is used.

A nonprofit corporation enjoys numerous advantages. They have been traditionally immune from tort liability. [*Hauser v. YMCA of Rahway* (N.J. Super. 1966)] Also, the nonprofit corporation can easily amend its corporate governing instruments. The corporation is an artificial entity that can sue and be sued, contract, and hold property in its own name. It has an indefinite existence, and a centralized management known as the board of directors. Directors of a nonprofit corporation are held to a lower standard of care than charitable trustees. Directors also enjoy the advantage of limited liability. The corporation offers more established patterns than the trust for determining the legal consequences in multiple operations (consolidations and mergers, and reorganizations). Nonprofit corporations enjoy special rights, including tax exemptions, because these corporations serve a social useful function that might otherwise fall on the government tax base and they do not otherwise compete with the profit sector.

Compared to the unincorporated association or charitable trust, the charitable corporation must conform to more formalities in its creation and dissolution but internal governance normally is more flexible, making it easier to react to changed circumstance such as the resignation or death of a director. A corporation can hold new elections for board members while a change in trustee for a charitable trust may require application to a court.

The requirements for nonprofit and charitable status vary from state to state. Some states have a general nonprofit law applicable to all nonprofit corporations; others, including Delaware, do not. Many states have statutes applicable to religious corporations, or to particular religions. Some states have statutes prohibiting indirect economic benefits from flowing to members and controlling persons. Religious corporations during the twentieth century have been assimilated into the nonprofit corporation statutes of many states and in many respects came to be required to fulfill the same formalities and standards as modern business corporations.

Most states now incorporate religious organizations primarily under a membership corporation model. A membership corporation is similar to a business corporation in that members of the former theoretically hold substantially the same power as the shareholders of the latter. The membership form of religious corporation comprises a subset of general nonprofit corporations because the form is being used for numerous other types of corporations as well.

The specifics of the nonprofit corporation law of the church or religious corporation's domicile should be consulted with respect to all matters relevant to its organization and structure: for example, matters of form, management, membership and voting rights, meetings, property rights, mergers, dissolution, and qualification as a "charity" for tax and other purposes.

The American Bar Association drafted a Revised Model Nonprofit Corporation Act in 1987. The Revised Act resulted from the efforts of the ABA to provide the states with a model of codified standards for nonprofit corporations. Under the Model Act, religious corporations are largely self-regulated. This may be due in part to the fact that the ability of the various state governments or of church members to regulate the fiscal decisions of the church's corporate directors or officers is made difficult by statutory limitations and constitutional questions. The Model Act continues the practice of recognizing religious corporations as both a subset and distinct from general nonprofit corporations.

The idea that the government might give benefits to religious groups so long as it acted in a neutral fashion is apparent in tax cases. Exemption of charitable organizations from taxation has a long tradition in English and American history. Charitable, religious, and educational organizations were exempt from taxation under the Revenue Act of 1894. This preferred status was later granted to other types of nonprofit organizations. *Walz v. Tax Commission* (U.S. 1970) held that the government could give property tax exemption to religious organizations, so long as they were included in a larger class of nonprofit corporations. What the court meant by this is substantive, rather than formal neutrality—an attempt to minimize government influence one way or the other on people's religious belief or practice. The Court explained that it must walk a "tight rope" between establishing religion and restricting religious freedom."

One variation of the religious corporation is the corporation sole, which is the device used in many American jurisdictions to allow for the incorporation of the Catholic Church as a distinct entity under state law. Some states, however, did not permit the corporation sole, therefore, a diocese would create a corporation to hold title to its assets under the states' nonprofit corporation law. Notwithstanding the existence of the corporation sole and nonprofit corporation statutes, many dioceses choose to operate through common law charitable trusts.

American law allows religious corporations to choose which persons will receive certain services they provide, which in other contexts may be construed as unlawful discrimination. The rationale for this is that if the corporate or group expression of religion is protected, for the state to intrude upon the group and say that the group, outside of organization within a church, may not have a special religious character, and may not enforce religious criteria upon its members, is a violation of that freedom.

A real, if not formal, relationship between the nonprofit organization and a church may allow the nonprofit to claim an exemption under § 702 of Title VII and the federal Fair Housing Act. The criteria for an exemption include: whether the entity's bylaws or articles of incorporation contain any statements of religious purpose, require approval by the church of any changes in the bylaws or articles of incorporation, or require that church appointees sit on the board of directors or other governing body; whether the entity is forbidden from deviating from any tenet of the members' religion; whether, on those grounds, the entity has reserved the right to discriminate in employment on the basis of religion; and whether it has succeeded in asserting such a right, if that assertion has been challenged. Close affiliation, however, by itself may not be enough if the organization's activities are not themselves sufficiently religious. In the absence of affiliation and significant religious activities, the organization will be denied an exemption. The Fourth Circuit held that a children's home that was funded by, and maintained close ties with, the Methodist Church, whose mission was to provide a "Christian home for orphans and other children," was not exempt from Title VII because the "direction given the day-to-day life of children [was] practically devoid of religious content or training."

The Fifth Circuit Court of Appeals held that a theological college would not lose its protection as a nonprofit organization even if it ceased to be owned and operated by a group of Southern Baptist churches. This is because, in addition to the general exemption under § 702, § 703 of Title VII, it has a religious curriculum exemption. The religious curriculum exemption allows a school "to hire and employ employees of a particular religion . . . if the curriculum of such school . . . is directed toward the propagation of a particular religion." In this case, the court found that the college was a religious corporation because its primary purpose was to serve the religious purposes of the Southern Baptist Convention [*EEOC v. Mississippi College* (5th Cir. 1980, *cert. denied*)]

Similarly, the publishing society of the Christian Science Church was held to be a religious corporation because its primary purpose was to promote, extend, and advance the Christian Science religion. [*Feldstein v. Christian Science Monitor* (D. Mass. 1983)]

The federal Fair Housing Act also contains an exemption for religious organizations, permitting a religious organization, or any nonprofit organization, operated, supervised, or controlled by, or in conjunction with, a religious organization, to limit "the sale, rental, or occupancy of dwellings which it owns or operates for other than a commercial purpose to persons of the same religion."

The courts have refrained from adjudicating doctrinal disputes within churches, but have adjudicated nonreligious disputes involving churches. Courts have applied neutral principles of law to resolve internal disputes on governance and other nonproperty issues in congregational religious organizations. For example, a federal district court mandated that resolution of membership disputes are limited to the identifying governing body and applying majority rule. [*First Baptist Church of Glen Este v. Ohio* (S.D. Ohio 1983)] In a case involving a religious corporation's records, a state court required the church to disclose financial information sought under the state's nonprofit corporation statute. [*Gipson v. Brown* (Ark. 1986)] Likewise, another state permitted church members to exercise their right to inspect church records under the state nonprofit corporation statute. [*Bourgeois v. Landrum* (La. 1981)]

NONPUBLIC SCHOOLS   *See* GOVERNMENT AID TO RELIGIOUS INSTITUTIONS

***NORWOOD V. HARRISON* (U.S. 1973)**   The issue in this case was how courts should apply principles forbidding racial discrimination to prohibit the government from subsidizing religious schools that are segregated, including those that are segregated for religious reasons. The U.S. Supreme Court unanimously held that the state of Mississippi could not lend textbooks to students of a school that discriminated on the basis of race, based on the Fourteenth Amendment to the U.S. Constitution. This was true even though the program was identical to one under which the Court had allowed textbooks to be lent to students of religious schools. Such a textbook program may aid religious schools, as they represent a value in the free exercise of religion that offsets any slight aid to religion. There is, however, no countervailing constitutional value that could justify state aid to a racially discriminatory school. Although the form of state aid to each set of schools was identical, the Court found that the practice constituted an unconstitutional subsidy solely because it subsidized the racially restricted schools. The Court held that state aid to racially discriminatory schools was not permissible even where the aid and the discrimination were not tied together. It said that racially discriminatory schools "exer[t] a pervasive influence on the entire educational process," outweighing any public benefit that they might otherwise provide. Thus, the aid to these students would violate the Equal Protection Clause of the Fourteenth Amendment.

In other words, while the sectarian schools represented the constitutionally recognized values of both free association and the free exercise of religion, the segregated schools represented no significant interest that could be accorded affirmative constitutional protection so as to sanction a disregard of the value of racial equality.

Significantly, the Court held that the state's practice of lending textbooks to this particular school did not constitute a promotion of religion for Establishment Clause purposes, even though it did constitute an encouragement of racism for Equal Protection purposes. *Norwood*, thus, indicated that the state may in a limited way assist in the education of students in religious schools in secular matters.

O

OATHS   *See* RELIGIOUS OATHS

O'LONE V. ESTATE OF SHABAZZ **(U.S. 1987)**   Regulations at a New Jersey prison forbade minimum security inmates who worked outside the main prison building from reentering the building during the day, thus preventing certain Muslim prisoners from attending their weekly worship service held on Fridays. Required by the Koran to attend the service, the prisoners filed suit, claiming violation of their rights under the Free Exercise Clause of the First Amendment. Adopting what was essentially a compelling state interest test, the court of appeals held that the prison had to prove "that no reasonable method exists by which [these persons'] religious rights can be accommodated without creating bona fide security problems."

In a five-to-four decision, the Supreme Court reversed, ruling that the court of appeals paid insufficient deference to prison officials, who have authority to enact any prison regulations "reasonably related to legitimate penological interests."

Justice William J. Brennan, writing for the dissenters, accused the majority of uncritically accepting the assertions of prison administrators. Brennan did not claim that the courts should never defer to the judgment of prison authorities, but he maintained that when a prison completely deprives prisoners of a right and the activity in question is not presumptively dangerous, prison officials should be required to show that the denial of the right is no greater a measure than necessary to achieve the government's objective.

Shabazz foreshadowed the Court's eventual abolition of the compelling state interest test for all free exercise cases in *Employment Division v. Smith* (U.S. 1990).

ORIGINAL INTENT   Original intent refers to the intent of the Framers of the U.S. Constitution in writing the various provisions of that document. Many legal professionals, commentators, scholars, and politicians alike believe that original intent should be the sole or most significant consideration when interpreting the Constitution.

There is a seemingly irresistible impulse to appeal to history when analyzing issues under the religion clauses of the First Amendment to the U.S. Constitution. In no other area of constitutional law has the study of the historical record been so driven than in the search for the meaning of the text of the First Amendment. There is, unfortunately no clear history as to the meaning of the clauses.

In addition, the Supreme Court has been rather selective in its use of history as a device to give content to the constitutional norms protecting religious liberty. The "original intent" of the nonestablishment guarantee has generally been considered quite relevant to its interpretation. There is by contrast, little discussion of the original intent behind either the Free Exercise or Religious Test Clauses.

Selective use of history has a profound effect on the Supreme Court's understanding of the religious liberty guarantee. The most obvious problem is conceptual. To the extent that a historical perspective is used as the grounding for the Court's interpretation of any constitutional provision, it is necessary to have a complete (or as near to complete as possible) understanding of the evil at which that provision was directed. If the historical understanding is incomplete, so too will be the vision of what that provision of the Constitution requires or prohibits. Without historical grounding, the language will be infused with whatever meaning seems appropriate to the time and circumstances.

P

PEOPLE FOR THE AMERICAN WAY FOUNDATION

People for the American Way Foundation (PFAWF) is an organization dedicated to supporting the religious freedom guaranteed to all Americans. The organization stands for the principle that America must sustain a public life that can accommodate as many different faiths as there are people. The organization believes this is only achievable when religion and government are kept separate. Taking a strict separationist stance, PFAWF tries to defend the fundamental constitutional principle of the separation of church and state throughout the United States.

The PFAWF has often used litigation to focus public attention and increase public awareness on religious issues, to oppose the efforts of religious conservative groups, to achieve PFAWF's substantive objective, and to assist individuals. The organization's legal department helps PFAWF defend constitutional and civil liberties and oppose religious conservatives throughout the country.

The PFAWF comprises 300,000 members nationwide who support the values of freedom of conscience and expression, civic participation, equality, justice, tolerance, and diversity.

The People for the American Way Foundation assists members, activists, concerned citizens, local school boards, and other organizations with problems involving freedom of religion, separation of church and state (e.g., school prayer, creationism, vouchers), school censorship and other education issues, civil rights (for example, discrimination against gay men and women, affirmative action), art censorship, Internet censorship, and other freedom of speech and expression issues.

The PFAWF has actively opposed school prayer in the following cases: *Ingebretsen v. Jackson Public School District* (S.D. 1994); *Committee for Voluntary Prayer v. Wimberly* (D.D.C. 1997); *Herdahl v. Pontotoc County School District* (N.D. Miss. 1996); and *Chandler v. Jones* (D. Ala. 1997). It has opposed school vouchers and tax credits in *Kotterman v. Killian* (U.S. 1999); *Simmons-Harris v. Goff* (Ohio 1999); and *Giacomucci v. Southeast Delco School District* (Pa. C.P. 1999).

PEYOTE, RELIGIOUS USE OF   *See* EMPLOYMENT
DIVISION V. SMITH (U.S. 1990)

PIERCE V. SOCIETY OF SISTERS **(U.S. 1925)**   An
Oregon law required children between the ages of eight and 16
years to attend public school. The law was passed as a result of an initiative campaign organized primarily by the Ku Klux Klan and Scottish Rite Masons. Supporters urged that the separation of children of different religions in private schools would cause dissension and discord. Anti-Catholicism also played a major role in the campaign. The plaintiffs were two Oregon religious orders that owned and operated schools.

In this major due process case, the Supreme Court held that the Oregon statute was an unreasonable interference with the liberty of parents and guardians to direct the upbringing of their children, and thus that it violated the Fourteenth Amendment. The court explained that a statute requiring children to attend public schools unconstitutionally restricted the freedom of both parents and students. Moreover, the fundamental theory of liberty upon which all governments in the United States are based prohibits the states from standardizing education by forcing children to receive instruction from public schools only.

The religious orders that owned the schools also had standing to invoke the liberty interests guaranteed by the Fourteenth Amendment against the state's action because they were threatened with destruction of their business and property through the improper compulsion exercised by the statute upon parents and guardians. The Court found that the interest of the religious orders was direct and immediate, and thus, they were entitled to an injunction, based on *Truax v. Raich* (U.S. 1915).

Today, *Pierce* represents the right of children to attend private (including religious) schools, provided such schools meet basic educational standards. The state cannot control the subjects taught in those schools beyond ensuring that children are given competent instruction in specified secular subjects and that they are in a safe and healthy environment. *Pierce* is also notable because it held that religious minorities are entitled to due process protection under the Fourteenth Amendment.

The *Pierce* decision has profoundly affected the evolution of civil liberties in contemporary America. In its emphasis on fundamental rights not expressly articulated in the Constitution and on family autonomy, it was the forbearer of later privacy decisions.

PLACE OF WORSHIP   From a legal viewpoint, a location's status as a "place of worship" is crucial in determining whether it is entitled to a tax exemption, whether local liquor control ordinances can be invoked in its vicinity, or whether the Establishment and Free Exercise Clauses of the First Amendment have been violated.

In addition to the federal constitutional provisions, some state constitutions provide that no individual may be compelled to erect or support any "place of worship."

In the following cases, the court found that a certain building or place was used as a place of worship. In *Dougherty v. Kentucky Alcoholic Beverage Control Board* (Ky. 1939) a building in which preaching services and an organized Sunday school were regularly held, and a series of revival services was conducted, and that was used for no other purpose, was a "place of worship" under the law, even though it had no church organization with a pastor, board of stewards, deacons, or similar officers. Thus denial of a liquor license to a tavern located within 200 feet of the building pursuant to a state statute prohibiting liquor sales within the vicinity of churches was proper.

On the other hand, a private chapel, which merely offered a generalized opportunity to the public for use for meditation, Bible study, and prayer, was not a "church or other place of worship" within requirements needed to sustain a 200-feet zone set up by New York's Alcohol Control law. [*Jane Street Seafood Corp. v. New York State Liquor Authority* (N.Y. 1980)]

The following were also not considered "places of worship": a city's displays of a nativity scene and menorah at the front entrance to city hall [*ACLU v. Schundler* (D. N.J. 1995)]; a mausoleum in which there was a chapel where funeral services were conducted [*Foster v. Harding* (Okla. 1967)]; and buses used to transport students to and from nonpublic schools [*Honohan v. Holt* (Ohio 1968)].

In Georgia a building with the outside appearance of a residence that served as the headquarters of a religious association and contained a kitchen, an office for the association's employees, and a chapel occupying 25 percent of its space at which were held some religious exercises but no church or Sunday school services on Sunday morning, was also found not to be a "place of worship." The building was primarily used for coordination, training, and promotional work in furtherance of the religious association's administrative duties and was not open as a public place of worship. Thus it was not entitled to a tax exemption. [*Leggett v. Macon Baptist Association* (Ga. 1974)]

PLEDGE OF ALLEGIANCE   Public schools have long been embroiled in controversies over public rituals, and religious belief (including nonbelief) has been at the heart of most of them. In *Minersville School District v. Gobitis* (U.S. 1940) the Supreme Court upheld the practice of compulsory pledging of allegiance to the flag against a free exercise claim on the grounds that this type of coercion is a price to be paid for living in a democracy. *Gobitis* was reversed in *West Virginia Board of Education v. Barnette* (U.S. 1943).

The controversy over official rituals involving the flag has not subsided. A high school student successfully challenged the requirement that she show "full respect" to the flag while the pledge was being given by standing at attention during the flag salute and recitation of the pledge of allegiance. [*Lipp v. Morris* (3d Cir. 1978)]

It is almost certainly not unconstitutional for schools to conduct official ceremonies and rituals that contain occasional references to God, as these references are merely incidental. For instance, a majority of the Supreme Court has indicated that the use in public schools of the pledge of allegiance, with its reference to "one nation under God," does not violate the Establishment Clause of the First Amendment, because this is merely a "reference to our religious heritage," rather than an endorsement of religion. [See *Lynch v. Donnelly* (U.S. 1984)(dicta)]

Critics of the reference to God have asserted that in situations involving the pledge of allegiance, the threat of indirect compulsion is much greater than in cases involving individual prayers because when the pledge is said the individual dissenter is made to stand out as one opposed to patriotism.

Also, the reference to God was not originally part of the pledge. The pledge is incorporated in the "flag code" of the United States Code, the code of federal laws. The pledge originally appeared, with two minor differences in the wording, in the magazine *Youth's Companion* in 1852. Authorship of the pledge was disputed between Francis Bellamy and James B. Upham until a committee of the U.S. Flag Association decided in 1939 to accept the claims of the former. The words "flag of the United States of America" were substituted for "my flag" in 1923. The phrase "under God" was added in 1954.

In *Sherman v. Community Consolidated School District 21* (7th Cir. 1992), the panel opinion by Judge Frank Easterbrook rejected a claim that daily recitation of the pledge of allegiance, led by the school principal, is inherently coercive. In *Sherman*, Easterbrook proposed the "coercion test" and proclaimed the death of the *Lemon* test.

▥ POLYGAMY   Congress criminalized Mormon polygamy in
the United States territories by statutes, including the Morrill
Act of 1862, the Edmunds Act of 1882, and the Edmunds-Tucker Act of
1887. The legislative history of the Morrill Act reveals that religious beliefs clearly played a major role, if they were not the motivating factor, in
the congressional ban of Mormon polygamy. The rise of Mormonism
brought "our holy religion into contempt, [defied] the opinions of the
civilized world, and [invoked] the vengeance of Heaven by a new
Sodom and a new Gomorrah to attract its lightning and appease its
wrath." Congress concluded that the Morrill Act "was a law respecting
an establishment of religion," but added with open contempt "if the odious and execrable heresy of Mormonism can be honored with the name
of religion." [House Report 83–86, cmt 4 (1860)] Religious issues were,
thus, clearly central to the legislators' purpose when they outlawed
polygamy. Some commentators believe that the background of the Morrill Act illustrated that when the federal government had legislated on
marriage forms in the past, the principle purpose was to achieve religious conformity.

That polygamy was almost universally considered immoral was taken
largely as a given. As few presumably needed convincing on the point,
the history of the Morrill Act, for instance, has very little discussion on
why polygamy is so evil. Following this social consensus, moreover,
some judges, such as James B. McKean, Chief Justice of the Utah Territorial Supreme Court from 1870 to 1875, regarded "cleansing the country of
polygamy" as a "religious cause."

The U.S. Supreme Court agreed with the Utah Supreme Court in
Reynolds v. United States (U.S. 1878) and held that George Reynolds, a
member of the Mormon Church, had violated the 1862 Morrill Act. The
federal government's right to make bigamy a crime in federal territories
was upheld in *Reynolds,* over the free exercise objection of Reynolds who
claimed that polygamy was his religious duty. The opinion reviewed the
widespread condemnation of polygamy in Western civilization, and accepted this opprobrium as determinative, but did not overtly consider
how Western civilization came to hold this opinion. The Court considered the practice of religiously related polygamy as similar to the practice
of religiously motivated human sacrifice; each was conduct "in violation
of social duties," and therefore prohibited by the state.

Some scholars believe that the antipolygamy law upheld in *Reynolds*
reflected widespread anti-Mormon feeling. Under the "least restrictive
means to a compelling end" standard, enunciated in *Sherbert v. Verner*
(U.S. 1963), some question would have arisen as to whether the goal supposedly being pursued by enactment of the ban (preservation of monog-
amous marriage) was sufficiently compelling, and whether the refusal to

exempt Mormons was sufficiently critical to the attainment of that goal to justify the burden placed on the religious liberty of Mormons.

Under the modern standard enunciated in *Employment Division v. Smith* (U.S. 1990), however, only statutes that expressly seek to regulate religious beliefs or conduct violate the Free Exercise Clause of the Constitution.

PRAYER IN PUBLIC SCHOOLS   *See* SCHOOL PRAYER

PRISONS AND PRISONERS   A prison regulation restricting inmates' constitutional rights (including First Amendment rights) is legal if the regulation is "reasonably related to legitimate penological interests." Applying this standard, the U.S. Supreme Court has upheld a prison regulation on the work duties of inmates that precluded Muslim inmates from attending a religious service held on Friday afternoons. [*O'Lone v. Shabbazz* (U.S. 1987)] The Court in *O'Lone* was applying the standard enunciated in *Turner v. Safley* (U.S. 1987). In *Turner*, the Court found that a restriction on the fundamental rights of prison inmates should be upheld so long as the restriction was reasonably related to legitimate penological interests. This standard seems to require a case-by-case approach to determine the reasonableness of all prison regulations that restrict fundamental rights. In *Turner*, for example, the Court upheld restrictions on the ability of prison inmates to send mail to each other, but invalidated a prison regulation that virtually prohibited all marriages between prisoners or between a prisoner and a person outside the prison facility.

PRIVACY   Privacy as a concept has no plain meaning for most Americans. "The right to be let alone," as U.S. Supreme Court Justices Earl Warren and Louis Brandeis called it, covers many situations and many abuses. Obviously, private life must shelter information, decisions, and behaviors of many different kinds. The question is, which ones are to be protected against regulation or governmental intrusion?

The right to privacy entails freedom from publicity about one's private affairs or the wrongful intrusion into one's private activities. It also encompasses the right to prevent the unauthorized appropriation or exploitation of one's personality. The U.S. Supreme Court has held that the First Amendment protects some rights to privacy in speech or association. The Court has also spoken on when a tort suit may be brought against a person whose speech has invaded the privacy of another.

In terms of due process and equal protection of the law, the right to privacy has come to include a right to engage in certain highly personal activities; specifically, freedom of choice in marital, sexual, and reproductive manners. Even this definition may be too broad, for the Supreme Court still has not recognized any general right to engage in sexual activities that are done in private. [See *Bowers v. Hardwick* (U.S. 1986)(state could criminalize homosexual acts done in privacy of home)] Instead, the justices have acknowledged the existence of a right and defined it by very specific application to laws on reproduction, contraception, abortion, and marriage. [*Griswold v. Connecticut* (U.S. 1965); *Roe v. Wade* (U.S. 1973)]

Nonetheless, the Court has been remarkably unclear about principles that do or ought to govern the elaboration of the unenumerated right of privacy. The justices have sometimes relied upon societal tradition, sometimes on precedent, and sometimes on a principle thought to underlie constitutional privacy. The justices, moreover, have characterized the relevant tradition, precedent, or principle differently and sometimes inconsistently.

Tort principles on privacy rights have been applied in cases brought against a clergyman, church, or religious organization. Courts have held that no cause of action for invasion of privacy exists in cases involving employment discrimination by a church or the practice of shunning, with the latter court holding that the First Amendment protected such religious practices. [*See Ventimiglia v. Sycamore View Church of Christ* (Tenn. App. Ct. 1988)] In another shunning case, *Paul v. Watchtower Bible and Tract Society* (9th Cir. 1987), the Ninth Circuit Court of Appeals held that a former Jehovah's Witness could not recover for injuries arising from that church's use of shunning as a disciplinary method. Janice Paul was raised as a Jehovah's Witness. In 1975 when she withdrew from the church, it did not shun people who left voluntarily. However, this policy changed in 1981. As a result, many of Paul's childhood friends began shunning her. Paul subsequently filed a lawsuit, including among her allegations a claim for outrageous conduct and intentional infliction of emotional distress caused by the shunning. The Ninth Circuit held that the First Amendment prevented Paul from recovery. The court found that the shunning was religiously motivated and that allowing tort damages for it would directly burden the free exercise of religion: "Imposing tort liability for shunning on the church or its members would in the long run have the same effect as prohibiting the practice and would compel the church to abandon part of its religious teachings."

One court, in a case involving two church superiors who induced a minister's psychiatrist to breach the physician-patient privilege, has held that, even assuming there was a right to privacy at a common law, such right would not allow any greater recovery than that already allowed for inducing a breach of the confidentiality privilege. [*Alberts v. Devine* (Mass. 1985), *cert. denied* (U.S. 1980)]

Reasoning that the behavior of the church officials and clergy was unreasonable, two courts have held that allegations that a church or clergyman intentionally interfered with the marital and family relationships of another stated a cause of action for invasion of privacy. [*O'Neil v. Schuckardt* (Idaho 1986)] In O'Neil, for example, the court held that a husband had proved his claims of invasion of privacy against a church for interfering with his relationship with his wife and five children. The wife had become involved with a fundamentalist sect of the Catholic Church that believed that marriages between Catholics and non-Catholics were invalid in the eyes of God. Because the plaintiff husband was not Catholic, the church convinced the wife that her marriage to him was invalid and that she would be committing a sin if she had sexual relations with him (although she could continue to live with him as though he were her "brother"). The church's interference led to a divorce. In the husband's tort action the court found that the evidence supported a finding of an intentional and wrongful invasion of the couple's domestic privacy by the church.

One court has found the elders of a church liable for invasion of privacy when they wrongfully publicized private facts about a former parishioner's life, including sexual relations with a nonmember. [*Guinn v. Church of Christ* (Okla. 1989)] In that case, the plaintiff had joined a church with an extremely strict and public disciplinary process. When she realized that the church elders intended to denounce her publicly for fornication, she tried to quit the church to avoid exposure of her private life. The elders of the church, however, believed that members could not withdraw from the congregation and proceeded to "disfellowship" the plaintiff by publicly announcing her "sins" and reading the biblical passages she had allegedly violated.

PRIVATE EDUCATION

PRIVATE EDUCATION   Under current law, there is very little state aid that may go to religious primary and secondary schools without violating the Establishment Clause. Because the U.S. Supreme Court has held that these schools are permeated by religious teaching, any significant aid probably has the effect of aiding religion. The only way to avoid such an effect would be the imposition of so many procedural checks that the program would result in excessive entanglement between government and religious entities. Additionally, these aid programs have a history of causing serious political divisions. For these reasons the Court has been quite strict in applying the purpose-effect-entanglement test to these programs. The First Amendment principles that govern this area are the result of a series of Supreme Court decisions on very specific types of aid to religiously affiliated schools, including public aid for student transportation, textbooks, and tuition tax credits.

The Supreme Court has not adopted a constitutional test that would separate unconstitutional aid to religiously affiliated schools from constitutional aid going to students or the parents of students who attend religiously affiliated schools. Instead of using a "student aid" versus "aid to religious schools" distinction, the U.S. Supreme Court has used the so-called *Lemon* test from *Lemon v. Kurtzman* (1971)(also known as the purpose-effect-entanglement tests) to determine the validity of each type of government aid that is given to religious schools or their students. The *Lemon* test focuses on three factors when evaluating government aid programs: purpose, effect, and entanglement. Under the *Lemon* test, a law or government practice is invalid if it lacks a secular purpose, has a primary effect of advancing or inhibiting religion, or unduly entangles government with religion. The *Lemon* test has directed the Supreme Court's analysis in many of its modern Establishment Clause decisions. The test has led to a policy of allowing no substantial government aid to religious institutions.

The Supreme Court is most likely to uphold government assistance programs if those programs are viewed primarily as aid to the individual students and their parents rather than a form of aid to the religious schools. [*Mueller v. Allen* (U.S. 1983); *Witters v. Washington Department of Services for the Blind* (U.S. 1986); *Zobrest v. Catalina Foothills School District* (U.S. 1993)]

The public school is the place in which child and state (parties vastly unequal in power) encounter each other. The same skewed balance of power is true in the context of a religiously affiliated school; this is a place in which the child encounters the church as an institution. In the public school context, the problem seems to be how to keep the schools nonreligious but still permit them to impart values, while in the private school setting the problem is how to differentiate between the teaching of moral values and the teaching of religious doctrine.

The importance of these questions to the development of the law on religion and education cannot be overstated. Dissenting in *Everson v. Board of Education* (U.S. 1947), Justice Robert Jackson argued that public schools are "organized on the premises that secular education can be isolated from all religious training," and raised the question of "whether such a disjunction is possible, and if possible, whether it is wise."

There are two basic positions within the Supreme Court on state support for students enrolled in religiously affiliated schools. Some justices believe that the First Amendment requires the state to remain neutral between and among religions, and between religions and secular viewpoints on the role of religion in education. This faction generally permits the state to allocate educational benefits to all students, regardless of where they go to school, so long as the assistance is provided in a religiously neutral public benefits program. Their view is best described as one that permits "formal" neutrality in the distribution of public benefits. Such an approach favors the decentralization of control over education.

Other justices believe that the Establishment Clause was intended to eliminate any form or vestige of official government support for religion, and to eliminate the possibility that the body politic will be divided along religious lines. In their view, the public schools are to be viewed as a religiously neutral educational setting, and that, to the extent children or parents desire to take advantage of publicly funded educational opportunities, they must do so in the public schools. This approach views education as a state function, and federalizes a set of philosophical norms on the role of religion, religious training, and religious ritual, in the education of primary and secondary school children.

PROPERTY TAX EXEMPTION

For many reasons, many rooted in colonial American history, churches and religious organizations have enjoyed special tax considerations. Legislatures have traditionally provided special tax treatment to groups and organizations whose influences or services are thought to be beneficial to the life of the community. Thus, houses of religious worship, nonprofit schools and colleges, public museums, libraries, and nonprofit hospitals are generally exempt from property taxes in all states. Similarly, the federal government exempts organizations operated exclusively for religious purposes from payment of income and gift taxes. Churches and their associations are subject to the unrelated federal business tax—that is, to taxes on income-producing property unrelated to the church, such as a commercial rental property or business enterprises.

Although there is little doubt that the tax structure often benefits religious organizations and in effect offers them a tax subsidy, the issue has not been widely litigated. The U.S. Supreme Court has considered the constitutional issue of establishment and a church property tax exemption on only one occasion. In *Walz v. Tax Commission* (U.S. 1970), the Court upheld a New York tax exemption for properties of religious organizations when the properties were exclusively for religious purposes. Conceding that such an exemption gives churches an economic benefit, the Court nevertheless ruled that the granting of property tax exemptions to churches does not violate the Establishment Clause of the First Amendment. To answer the contention that such an exemption is indirect tax support of religion, the Court noted, "The general principle deducible from the First Amendment and all that has been said and done by the Court is this—that we will not tolerate either governmental established religion or governmental interference with religion. Short of those expressly proscribed governmental acts there is room for play in the joint product of a benevolent neutrality which will permit religious exercise to exist without sponsorship and without interference."

Furthermore, the Court pointed out that such tax exemptions assist in guarding against the latent dangers to the free exercise of religion inherent in the imposition of taxes. The exemption transfers no public revenue to a church and there is not real connection between the exemption and the establishment of religion. Indeed, it has been argued that exempting religious property may promote separation by restricting fiscal contact between church and state. The Court noted that the problem of entanglement between church and state might actually be worse without an exemption scheme than with one, because the government would then have to be involved in "tax valuation of church property, tax liens, tax foreclosures, and the direct confrontations and conflicts that follow in the train of those legal processes."

 PUBLIC AID TO RELIGION   *See* GOVERNMENT AID TO RELIGIOUS INSTITUTIONS

 PUBLIC EDUCATION   *See* PUBLIC SCHOOL CURRICULUM

 PUBLIC FORUM   The courts have created a qualified right to a public forum in order to give meaning to the protection of freedom of speech, freedom of the press, and the right to assemble, and the right to assemble for redress of grievances given by the First Amendment.

The First Amendment serves two essential values. First, freedom of communication and assembly serve the public good by allowing all ideas relevant to an issue of public policy to be freely discussed without governmental censorship and with every citizen free to contributes his or her opinion.

The U.S. Supreme Court established the doctrine of the public forum in 1939, when it ruled in *Hague v. Congress of Industrial Organizations* (U.S. 1939) that government may not prohibit speech-related activities such as demonstrations, leafletting, and speaking in public areas traditionally provided for speech. Such places have historically served as an essential means of communication, especially for groups who lack power or access to alternative channels of communication.

Government may close public forums it designates as such, but it must adhere to neutral standards while such forums remain open. In *Widmar v. Vincent* (U.S. 1981), for example, the Supreme Court ruled that once it had opened its facilities for use by student groups, a state university had created a public forum. It was then required to justify any content-based exclusions. Such exclusions would be upheld only if they were necessary to serve a compelling state interest and if they were narrowly drawn to achieve that end. The university was unable to meet this standard with regard to student religious groups and, thus, was required to permit them to use its facilities under the same terms as those applicable to other student groups.

In recent years the U.S. Supreme Court has elevated the distinction between public and nonpublic forums into a fundamental principle of First Amendment doctrine. Apart from rules of time, place, and manner, government regulation of speech within a public forum is especially subject to the strict scrutiny ordinarily required by First Amendment jurisprudence. Government regulation of speech within a nonpublic forum, however, is accorded wide latitude and presumptive constitutionality. The Court has increasingly relied upon public forum doctrine to insulate from judicial review restrictions on speech in such settings as schools, prisons, military establishments, and state bureaucracies.

The most controversial aspect of contemporary public forum doctrine has been the Supreme Court's tendency to defer to institutional authorities on the question of whether the regulation of speech is truly necessary to achieve institutional objectives. In *Hazelwood v. Kuhlmeier* (U.S. 1988), for example, the Court concluded that determinations of the educational propriety of speech should properly rest with the school board rather than with the federal courts, and that therefore judges should defer to the decisions of the school officials. However, such deference in effect cedes to the states enormous discretion to regulate speech and hardly raises the question of the circumstances under which courts ought to relinquish careful supervision of governmental curtailments of speech.

PUBLIC OFFICE   Early in American history, 13 states by statute or constitutional provision prohibited members of religious orders or ministers from holding public office. The purpose was to avoid the entanglement of church and state in the civil law-making function of the legislature. By the turn of the twentieth century it was generally recognized that these laws conflicted with both the Free Exercise and Establishment Clauses of the First Amendment, and accordingly, they were repealed or annulled in all but two of the states that had adopted them. Only Maryland and Tennessee still had these laws. Maryland's disqualification law was declared unconstitutional in *Kirkley v. Maryland* (D. Md. 1974). Tennessee had by statute barred "ministers of the gospel, or priest[s] of any denomination whatever," from serving as delegates to the state's constitutional convention. This statute mirrored a provision of the state constitution barring such persons from membership in the state legislature. The U.S. Supreme Court unanimously found that the statute was unconstitutional in *McDaniel v. Paty* (U.S. 1978). There was no majority opinion in *McDaniel*, however, because the justices could not agree on exactly why the statute was unconstitutional. Chief Justice Burger, in his opinion joined by Justices Powell, Rehnquist, and Stevens, concluded that the disqualification statute violated the Free Exercise Clause because it conditioned McDaniel's right to the free exercise of his religion on the surrender of his right to seek public office. The opinion by the chief justice found that the law was not one that infringed the "freedom to believe," and therefore, was not automatically invalid under *Torcaso v. Watkins* (U.S. 1961). In *Torcaso* the Court held that persons may not be disqualified from government service (in this case, service as a notary public) on the grounds of religion. The chief justice noted that the history of such disqualification clauses in the original states indicated that such laws had been aimed merely at restricting acts of religious groups that would have further entangled the states with religion. The Tennessee law, however, regulated actions that related to the individual's religion, and therefore, it was to be tested by the Free Exercise Clause balancing test. Under this test, the state's failure to demonstrate that participation by clergy in the political process would bring about further "establishment" problems indicated that this law in fact did not promote a strong state interest. Thus, the law was invalid because it burdened religious practices without advancing overriding state interests. The Court found that the state's interest was not sufficiently important without a showing of current validity to justify an infringement of the minister's free exercise rights. In other words, given Tennessee's failure to demonstrate the reality of the alleged dangers of clergy participation in the political process, the state's infringement on free exercise could not withstand the constitutional challenge. Burger found no reason to examine whether the state's asserted interest in furthering separation of church and state under other circumstances might constitute a permissible legislative goal.

Justice William Brennan, joined by Justice Thurgood Marshall, found that the statute violated both the Free Exercise and Establishment Clauses of the First Amendment, which applied to the states through the Fourteenth Amendment. Unlike the chief justice, Justice Brennan found that this law disadvantaged a person because of his or her religious belief. So construed, the law was a per se violation of the Free Exercise Clause; there was no reason to employ the balancing test in such a case. Justice

Brennan noted that requiring a minister to forego either his ministry or public office constituted a sufficient burden to invoke the Free Exercise prohibition against burdening religious beliefs.

PUBLIC PLACES   *See* PUBLIC FORUM

PUBLIC SCHOOL CURRICULUM   The fundamental power to select the system of instruction and course of study in the public schools belongs to the state legislature, although, for practical reasons, the selection of courses of study is often delegated to local authorities under general limitations and rules laid down by the legislature. The legislature, however, cannot prescribe courses of study without regard to constitutional principles. The caselaw is in some conflict as to the limits of the respective powers of parents and school authorities over the course of study to be pursued by a particular student, and the right of a parent to control his or her child's education, and particularly religious training. The interest of the school in universal education is subject to a balancing test when it comes into conflict with the Free Exercise Clause of the First Amendment.

Parents often charge that the teaching in public schools is inimical to their religious beliefs and therefore violates their right to free exercise of religion. The Supreme Court has not yet dealt with this issue, and its pronouncements elsewhere offer little guidance. The Court has often stated that a substantial burden on free exercise can be justified only by a compelling state interest, pursued by the least restrictive means. Public schools have denied that their teaching burdens free exercise at all because their teaching is secular, not religious. Children need not accept what is taught, and children are not compelled to attend public schools, but are free to attend private schools. Dissatisfied parents reply that free exercise is burdened if their children are taught that their religion is wrong, although the children do not have to profess acceptance of the school's teaching, and although others consider the issues in question secular. These parents stress that young impressionable children may not understand that they should reject the school's teaching, or may be too intimidated to express their disagreement. They also argue that the option of attending private schools is too expensive for most parents to remove the burden on free exercise.

However, even if a public school's curriculum does burden free exercise, public schools claim a compelling state interest in giving all children this education. Most observers concede that states have an interest in teaching basic skills such as reading and writing. However, it is debatable how important the state's interest is in other areas, including moral values and sex education. If a public school does burden free exercise without compelling justification, some accommodation of the religious students may be necessary as a remedy. Thus, many schools excuse students from certain programs to which they have religious objections, and some schools provide students with alternative instruction. The latter approach can be expensive and administratively burdensome; the former may prevent the child from obtaining essential skills. Suggestions that children be given vouchers to attend private schools meanwhile have been attacked as both violative of the Establishment Clause and destructive of the objectives of public education.

The legal need for accommodation may no longer be as pressing as it once was, however. The Supreme Court recently indicated in *Employment Division v. Smith* (U.S. 1990) that it has abandoned the "compelling state interest" standard. If the Court adheres to this position, public schools would not be constitutionally required to show a compelling reason for subjecting children to teaching that is hostile to their religion.

In 1983 a group of fundamentalist parents in Tennessee sought to have their children exempted from a school reading program because they believed the content of the textbooks disparaged their religious beliefs. The Tennessee parents did not want to change school curriculum, they simply wanted their children to have an alternative reading program, while allowing their children to participate in the rest of the school's academic program. The district court found for the parents. [*Mozert v. Hawkins County Public Schools* (E.D. Tenn. 1984)]

A three-judge panel on the Sixth Circuit Court of Appeals unanimously reversed. However, the judges could not agree on the reasons for reversal. One judge argued that the reading program did not burden the children's free exercise rights because it did not tell them what to believe. A second judge maintained precisely the opposite, arguing that a broader purpose of the reading was to inculcate "values." This purpose gave the school district a compelling state interest in not allowing exemptions to the program. The third judge, meanwhile, claimed that the reading program did not burden free exercise, but he did not want to issue a new precedent in this area without express guidance from the Supreme Court. The Supreme Court declined to follow this course of action, although it later made clear in *Employment Division v. Smith* (U.S. 1990) that it had no intention of broadening free exercise rights. *Smith* suggests that further litigation using the free exercise approach is likely to fail. In several cases religious parents have tried to turn the Supreme Court's expansive interpretation of the Establishment Clause ban on religion in the public schools to their advantage by alleging that the schools are unconstitutionally establishing a religion they term *secular humanism* through the teaching of other subjects—most notably the theory of evolution and other scientific postulates. Although the Supreme Court has not addressed this issue, the lower federal courts have uniformly rejected these claims. [*Wright v. Houston Independent School District* (D. S.D. 1972); *Daniel v. Waters* (6th Cir. 1975); *McLean v. Arkansas Board of Education* (E.D. Ark. 1982)] These results seem appropriate. The Supreme Court has stated that nontheistic faiths, including secular humanism, can qualify as religions under the First Amendment. However, if secular humanism is defined narrowly enough to be considered a specific religion, the public schools are certainly not establishing it, because they promote no particular dogma or rituals. In contrast, if secular humanism is defined so broadly as to include all the education given in public schools, it ceases to be a religion for First Amendment purposes. A contrary conclusion would impel the untenable result that virtually any secular enthusiasm, such as music, art, or sports, could be considered a religion and thus barred from the public schools. Although a violation of the Establishment Clause of the First Amendment need not be attended by coercion, objections that sex education programs in the public schools violate that Clause by tending to establish a secular religion have been rejected when it appeared that the subject was not covered from a religious point of view; but simply as a public health matter. [*Cornwell v. State Board of Education* (D. Md. 1969)]

The designation of sex education as an independent topic of study and discussion in the public schools appears to be a relatively recent development. There is no truly relevant case prior to 1969. When provision has been made that students whose parents object to courses in sex education can be excused, the giving of such a course has been uniformly upheld in which the matter has been adjudicated. [*Cornwell v. State Board of Education* (D. Md. 1969, aff'd (4th Cir. 1970)(rejecting free exercise challenge to compulsory sex education program); *Citizens for Parental Rights v. San Mateo County Board of Education* (Cal. App. Ct. 1975)]

Decisions holding that a system for excusing students whose parents object was not sufficient to meet constitutional objections to other public school programs, such as Bible reading or prayer, have been distinguished as involving the direct use of tax-supported public school systems for religious instruction in violation of the Establishment Clause. [See *Medeiros v. Kiyosaki* (Haw. 1970)] One court has even held that when a program has no compulsory feature, constitutional objections based on the rights of parents need not be considered. [*Hobolth v. Greenway* (Mich. 1974)] No court has yet held a sex education program invalid, even when attendance is compulsory.

Objections that sex education programs in the public schools violate the right of objecting parents to the free exercise of religion have been rejected when attendance is not compulsory, because a violation of the Free Exercise Clause must be predicated on coercion. [*Citizens for Parental Rights v. San Mateo County Board of Education* (Cal. 1975)] One court has held that mandatory attendance could represent coercion against the practice or exercise of religious beliefs. [*Hopkins v. Hamden Board of Education* (Conn. 1971)] Moreover, a sex education program that puts some burden on the free exercise of religion may be justified by a compelling state interest, although one court has held that facts must be proven or stipulated before the balance can be struck. [*Valent v. New Jersey State Board of Education* (N.J. 1971)] A compelling state interest is one that the state is obligated to protect. The concept would uphold the state's action in the face of a challenge based on the right to equal protection or First Amendment rights because of a serious need for such state action. Objections to such programs can arguably be based on a parental right to direct the upbringing of children that is clearly supported by precedent, and such a right can be infringed when the state establishes compulsory sex education programs involving sexually explicit materials.

Objections to sex education courses based on the Free Exercise Clause have also been rejected when the parents failed to satisfy the court that their objections to the program were based on religious, rather than merely philosophical or personal grounds. [*Davis v. Page* (D.N.H. 1974)]

In a related issue, there have been efforts by evangelical Christians to have so-called creationism taught in the public schools. Creationism, or creation "science," is the fundamentalist Christian belief in the literal truth of the biblical story of creation. Unlike fundamentalists from an earlier era, the new creationists do not argue that evolution should not be taught; they only contend that whenever evolution is taught, scientific creationism must also be taught in order to protect the students' right to study different points of view. Hence, they argue their case in terms of academic freedom. In *Edwards v. Aguillard* (U.S. 1987), however, the Supreme Court struck down a Louisiana law that adopted this approach as violative of the Establishment Clause.

PUBLIC SCHOOL FACILITIES, ACCESS OF RELIGIOUS GROUPS TO

In addition to controversies over the school curriculum, disputes have also multiplied over the use of public school facilities by student religious groups. In *Widmar v. Vincent* (1981), the Supreme Court insisted that public university facilities generally available to student groups and speakers must also be open to student religious groups. Although government may not promote religion through its educational facilities, it may not, in pursuit of neutrality, bar groups of students seeking voluntarily to meet to engage in religious activities from doing so on school property, at least in institutions of higher learning. So long as an institution permits nonreligious groups to meet on a nondiscriminatory basis, to allow religious groups access to the same facilities would not constitute an impermissible benefit to religion, the purpose in allowing access would be secular, and little hazard of entanglement was likely. Whether the case would apply similarly to secondary and perhaps elementary schools is unclear. The Court noted that university students "are less impressionable than younger students and should be able to appreciate that the University's policy is one of neutrality toward religion."

In 1984 Congress tried to extend this principle to secondary schools by adopting the Equal Access Act, which forbids secondary schools from discriminating on the basis of the content of speech when affording student groups access to school facilities outside school hours. However, the school may not sponsor, and school employees may not participate in, student religious groups.

In one of the first cases the U.S. Supreme Court heard after the Equal Access Act was passed, *Bender v. Williamsport Area School District* (U.S. 1986), a school district refused to let a voluntary student religious group meet on school premises. The Reagan administration strongly supported the student group, claiming that permitting such meetings was wholly consistent with—indeed required by—the religion and speech clauses of the First Amendment. But rather than resolve the substantive issue, the Supreme Court decided the case on standing grounds. The Court ruled that because a school board member—not the school board—had appealed a district judgment against the school system, the district court judgment must be preserved. Justices Burger, Powell, Rehnquist, and White dissented, claiming that the substantive issue should have been resolved in favor of the student group.

Some critics of the Equal Access Act believed that the Act was unconstitutional because of the possibility that school employees would become involved and that students would perceive the provision of facilities to student religious groups as endorsing religion. The Court disagreed in *Board of Education v. Mergens* (U.S. 1990), which held that the Equal Access Act did not violate the Establishment Clause.

Mergens is significant because the Court placed the decision whether to allow student religious groups to meet during noninstructional hours in the schools, rather than the courts. Schools may reflect more accurately the sentiments of their communities if they are free to create or deny a "limited open forum" as defined in *Mergens*. The decision also provided clearer guidance as to what path schools can follow to preserve the rights of all their students.

R

RACIAL DISCRIMINATION   Problems of race and race relations—particularly issues concerning the status of African Americans—have played a prominent role in American life since the colonial era. Given the place of the U.S. Supreme Court in the political structure, it was almost inevitable that the Court would be called upon to take an active role in resolving issues of race in American life.

Although state aid to private schools does not necessarily violate the Establishment Clause, the government may not aid a school that discriminates on the basis of race. In *Bob Jones University v. United States* (U.S. 1983), the Supreme Court upheld the validity of an IRS ruling that denied tax exemptions to schools with racially discriminatory policies. Bob Jones University, dedicated to the teaching of fundamentalist Christian beliefs, objected to the revocation of its tax exempt status based on its policies prohibiting interracial marriage and dating. The University claimed its policies were based on the Bible and, therefore, governmental interference with them violated its free exercise rights. The Court, however, per Chief Justice Burger, held that the government had a "fundamental, overriding interest in eradicating racial discrimination in education." That interest substantially outweighed the burden on free exercise and there were "no less restrictive means" available to achieve the government's interest.

In *Allen v. Wright* (U.S. 1984) the Supreme Court held that private individuals have no standing to challenge the tax exempt status of racially discriminatory private schools, thus severely limiting the potential reach of the holding in *Bob Jones University*. The plaintiffs in *Wright* were parents whose children were enrolled in school systems subject to desegregation decrees. They alleged two direct harms: (1) the fact of government financial aid to discriminatory private schools; and (2) that federal tax exemptions to racially discriminatory private schools in their communities allegedly impaired the ability of the communities in which they lived to desegregate their public schools. The Court rejected both assertions, holding that "neither [harm] suffices to support respondents' standing. The first fails under clear precedents of this Court because it does not

265

constitute judicially cognizable injury. The second fails because the alleged injury is not fairly traceable to the assertedly unlawful conduct of the IRS."

REGISTRATION OF RELIGIOUS ORGANIZATIONS

A state may not exempt certain religions from regulations requiring organizations (including religious organizations) to register with the state because the primary purpose and effect of such action advances religion in violation of the Establishment Clause of the First Amendment. [*Larson v. Valente* (U.S. 1982)] The Supreme Court held in *Larson* that legislation demonstrably intended to disadvantage particular religious denominations violated the Establishment Clause.

RELEASED-TIME PROGRAMS

The arrangement by which public primary and secondary schools permit students to be dismissed from classes prior to the completion of the regular school day in order to take religious instruction is sometimes called a released-time program.

The First Amendment of the Constitution guarantees freedom of religion in both belief and practice under the Free Exercise Clause, but prohibits the government from aiding and recognizing any religion under the Establishment Clause. These constitutional provisions are binding on the states through the Due Process Clause of the Fourteenth Amendment.

Since their creation in 1914 in Gary Indiana, release-time programs have provided a means by which students who would otherwise be deprived of an opportunity to receive religious instruction can learn about their religion. Such programs have come under judicial scrutiny because of the claim that the involvement of public school boards in religious concerns violates the Establishment Clause.

The U.S. Supreme Court has considered public school programs involving the exemption of public school students from class so that they could receive religious instruction. The Court has held that students may not be given religious instruction on public school premises, because such a program has the direct effect of aiding the establishment of religious beliefs. [*McCollum v. Board of Education* (U.S. 1948)] The state, however, may release students from school so that they may attend religious instruction away from the public school. [*Zorach v. Clausen* (U.S. 1952)] This early release of students is intended to accommodate individual religious group preferences, rather than as an aid to the religions.

When the Court first considered the issue, it ruled that released-time programs in which regular classes end an hour early one day a week and religious instruction is given in public classrooms to students who request it are invalid. [*McCollum v. Board of Education* (U.S. 1948)] The Court held that the superintendent's approval of the teachers, the use of public school classrooms, and the assistance provided by compulsory attendance laws breached the separation of church and state.

Justice Hugo Black gave the Court's opinion as follows: "[P]upils compelled by law to attend school for secular education are released in part from their legal duty upon the condition that they attend religious classes. This is beyond all question a utilization of the tax-established and tax-supported public school system to aid religious groups to spread their faith."

Four years later the Court upheld New York City's released-time program in which religious instruction was given during the school day but not in the public schools. The Court ruled that programs in which participating children attend religious classes conducted at religious centers away from the public schools do not violate the Establishment Clause. [*Zorach v. Clauson* (U.S. 1952)] The Court also considered the fact that the school did not approve the teachers, public school classrooms were not used, and no public funds were expended in the program.

The Supreme Court found that the New York program did not significantly aid religion; it simply required that the public schools "accommodate" a program of outside religious instruction. "Government," wrote Justice William O. Douglas, "may not coerce anyone to attend church, to observe a religious holiday, or to take religious instruction. But it can close its doors or suspend its operations as to those who want to retire to their religious sanctuary for worship or instruction. No more than that is undertaken here."

In their dissent, Justices Black, Frankfurter, and Jackson argued that the program was coercive and a direct aid to religion.

The key concept in *Zorach* is the neutral principle of "accommodation." If there had been proof that the city's program coerced students into attending religious classes, the state support of those programs would violate both the Free Exercise Clause and the Establishment Clause. The line is drawn according to the degree of interaction between religious and government institutions. Both *McCollum* and *Zorach* were precursors to the "excessive entanglement" test set out in *Lemon v. Kurtzman* (U.S. 1971). *Zorach* modified the strict separationist approach of *McCollum* to allow some accommodation of church and state cooperation. *Zorach* also opened up the possibility that some government aid to religious educational institutions might be constitutionally permitted.

≡≡≡ Religion   Religion may be viewed as consisting of (1) a belief in a deity or in a power beyond the individual, (2) a doctrine (an accepted body of truth that is believed), (3) a code of morality for the guidance of conduct, (4) the use of sacred stories, and (5) rituals.

The Constitution does not define the term *religion*. In order to ascertain its meaning in reference to that document, one must refer to other sources. No source is more appropriate than the history of the period during which the provision for the protection of religious liberty was adopted. The Supreme Court has stated that the term *religion* refers to "one's views of his relationship to his Creator and to the obligations they impose of reverence for his being and character and of obedience to his will." [*Welsh v. United States* (U.S. 1970); *United States v. Seeger* (U.S. 1965)] The *Welsh* and *Seeger* cases so expanded (or diluted) the notion of "Supreme Being" that only ardent atheists or the completely uncommitted could not claim free exercise protection.

Religion is often confused with the form of worship of a particular sect, but is distinguishable from the latter. Religion does not mean merely the Christian religion, although as distinguished from non-Christian religion, it was realized that because of the number, influence, and social standing of its adherents in the United States, Christianity is the prevailing religion of the country.

Religious believers create lives for themselves around certain kinds of beliefs and values. They usually join a community of like-minded people (a church). They typically have ideas about their relationship to God that orient them in their daily life.

If the belief asserted is philosophical and personal rather than religious, or merely a matter of personal preference, and not one of deep religious conviction, shared by an organized group, it will not be entitled to First Amendment protection. It has been held that so-called New Age concepts do not implicate the Establishment Clause of the First Amendment, inasmuch as they do not demonstrate any shared or comprehensive doctrine or display any structural characteristics or formal signs associated with traditional religions, given the absence of any organization, membership, moral or behavioral obligations, comprehensive creed, particular texts, rituals, or guidelines, particular object or objects of worship, or any requirement that anyone give up religious beliefs he or she already holds.

The term *secular humanism*, often used by conservative Christians, refers to a world view that they believe eclipses God and elevates the worship of humanity itself. According to those who use the term, it is a pernicious ideological viewpoint undercutting modern American society. Throughout the 1980s, conservative religious political coalitions sought to mobilize public opinion in a campaign to oppose the influence of secular humanism on public life. One argument has been to cast secular humanism as a religion in itself and then to complain that government actions that are neutral with regard to traditional religious activities are actually aiding the new "religion" of secular humanism in violation of the Establishment Clause. Courts have uniformly rejected this argument. [See *Fleischfresser v. Directors of School District 200* (7th Cir. 1994)(discussing problems with defining religion and holding that elementary reading series in public school that included stories of "fantasy and make-believe" was not "impermissible establishment of pagan religion"); *Smith v. Board of School Commissioners* (S.D. Ala. 1987); *Mozert v. Hawkins County Public Schools* (6th Cir. 1987); *Panarella v. Birenbaum* (N.Y. 1969); *Doe v. Human* (W.D. Ark. 1989)]

While the Supreme Court has never formulated a lasting definition of what constitutes "religion," how the Court characterizes the conduct alleged to be "religious" goes a long way to determining the outcome of any Establishment Clause challenge. For example, Scientologists established the Church of Scientology in part to protect the organization's therapeutic devices from regulation by the federal Food and Drug Administration. Scientology was held to be a "religion" because the group's beliefs are decribed as a theory of "man's nature or his place in the Universe," analogous to beliefs held by recognized religions. The court also held that the Science of Dianetics is a religion for purposes of the Free Exercise Clause. [*Founding Church of Scientology v. United States* (D.C. Cir. 1969, *cert. denied*)] Transcendental Meditation, whose practices are derived from the Hindu religion, sought classification as a "therapeutic science," partially so that the group's meditation techniques could be taught in the public schools. The court found transcendental meditation to be a religion under the Establishment Clause. [*Malnak v. Yogi* (3d Cir. 1977)] One court found that a "religion" includes "devotion to some principle; strict fidelity or faithfulness; conscientiousness; pious affection or attachment." [*Washington Ethical Society v. District of Columbia* (D.C. Cir. 1957)]

The U.S. Supreme Court has found beliefs to be "religious" in several cases for First Amendment purposes. The Court found the proselytization requirements of the Krishna sect to be religious in *Heffron v. International Society for Krishna Consciousness* (U.S. 1981), as well as the practice of the Amish not to send their children to high school. [*Wisconsin v. Yoder* (U.S. 1971)] The Court suggested that, if sincerely held, the beliefs of members of the "I AM" movement would be protected, even if they seemed "preposterous." [*United States v. Ballard* (U.S. 1944)] And the Court acknowledged the religious character of Mormon beliefs about polygamy. [*Reynolds v. United States* (U.S. 1878)]

▥ **RELIGION AND POLITICS**   Throughout American history, religious values, ideas, and advocates have played a role in the political development of the nation, including the abolition of slavery, the women's suffrage movement, and the civil rights movement. All were supported largely with the advocacy of faith communities (and often against the wishes of others in those same faith communities).

The rise of the religious conservative movement (referred to as the Religious Right by its detractors) in the 1980s made uncomfortable those who opposed the blending of religion and politics in the United States. The reality, however, is that the two have rarely strayed far from each other in the American system. As observers such as Hector St. John de Crevecoeur and Alexis de Tocqueville observed early in American history, religion had a paramount role in the political life of the United States in the nineteenth century. More recently, Garry Wills observed that politicians in the late twentieth century who ignore the influence of religion in American politics find themselves on politically tenuous grounds. Many religions in the United States joined in support of the civil rights movement in the 1960s. During the late 1970s and 1980s, the Moral Majority, and later the Christian Coalition advocated a conservative political program based on conservative Christian principles.

Despite the considerable influence of religion on American politics, Christian political parties have managed only very limited successes in the United States. The American Party of the 1840s and 1850s nominated a presidential candidate in 1856 (former President Millard Fillmore) and held a few seats in Congress, but faded as the Civil War drew nearer. Further, that party left an unsavory legacy of nativism (originally meaning a hostility to immigrants, especially non-Protestant ones) to those who dreamed of a Christian party in the United States.

Various Christian organizations that have sought to organize as a political movement have tended to revolve around a single issue of great importance, such as prohibition. In fact, a Prohibition Party regularly nominated candidates for office, including the presidency, throughout the latter third of the nineteenth century and into the twentieth century. However, religious influences have centered more on attempts to persuade mainstream candidates and office holders to take certain stances on particular issues or for particular causes.

The formation of the Moral Majority by the Reverend Jerry Falwell in 1979 was not an attempt to create a party, but an attempt to create a pressure group. Falwell's organization hoped to persuade politicians to enact laws to overturn Supreme Court rulings on abortion and prayer in public schools and to permit tax credits for parents sending children to private church-based schools. Although Falwell claimed to have ensured Ronald Reagan's election in 1980, most commentators attribute it to other causes. Undoubtedly, however, Falwell's high visibility and his grass-roots appeals contributed to Reagan's victory.

The political activism by American religious leaders during the twentieth century usually involved the efforts of traditional Christians to reverse what they perceive as negative trends in society. Pleas to protect the environment, for example, are presented in terms of morality. Although the moral and religious overtones of the civil rights movement appear clear to commentators, appeals by women, gays, lesbians, and Native Americans, are similar moral appeals to politicians and the electorate. Although many commentators believe that religion is irrelevant in contemporary American politics, the moralistic tone of the rhetoric persists.

In contemporary America, religion is almost always seen as something primarily political, but this is because the political has claimed increasingly more of the lives of Americans. In the 1980s and 1990s, political scientists and journalists have reported an increased political activity on the part of religious Americans. The period has seen the rise of the Moral Majority, the creation of the Christian Coalition, and the presidential campaigns of the Reverends Jesse Jackson and Pat Robertson. Politics looks more like a religion than religion looks like politics. Conservative Christian groups, such as fundamentalists, contrary to a tradition of political noninvolvement, became politically active because they believed that American law was adopting principles and practices that were directly opposed to the tenets of religion, and of Christianity in particular. Beginning in the mid-1970s, fundamentalists were mobilized into political action in opposition to legalized abortion, the Equal Rights Amendment (ensuring equal rights to women), increased rights for homosexuals, and challenges to church-related schools. Separationists, including many in the American Civil Liberties Union (ACLU), argue that a political agenda inspired by religious beliefs is anathema to our democracy because it ultimately politically divides the nation on religious grounds. One example is that religious conservatives, evangelical Christians in particular, often have a difficult time articulating a public philosophy that is not ultimately based on the moral authority of the Bible.

RELIGION IN THE WORKPLACE GUIDELINES   In August 1997 President Clinton issued an executive order entitled "Guidelines on Religious Exercise and Religious Expression in the Federal Workplace." This order protects religious expression by workers in government agencies and was drawn up with the help of the Union of Orthodox Jewish Congregations of America, the American Jewish Congress, the National Council of Churches, the Center for Law and Religious Freedom, and People for the American Way. The guidelines uphold

the right of federal workers to wear religiously mandated clothing, conduct prayers in unused conference rooms, discuss religion, and decline assignments on religious grounds.

The guidelines stemmed from an effort launched in 1994 by the Equal Employment Opportunity Commission (EEOC) aimed at deterring workplace harassment. While the administration said it had been working on the guidelines since 1994, the issuance of the new rules highlighted the president's interest in restoring some of the protections that had been included in the Religious Freedom Restoration Act (RFRA) of 1993. The U.S. Supreme Court had overturned that act in *City of Boerne v. Flores* (U.S. 1997), ruling that Congress had exceeded its authority when it attempted in the Act to define the level of protection that the Constitution afforded to religious expression. President Clinton supported the RFRA, which said that the government could not enforce laws that "substantially burdened" individuals' rights to religious expression.

Some criticized President Clinton's guidelines for religious expression in the executive branch of the federal workplace because they took a narrower approach to protecting the freedom of religious expression than the approach taken by the EEOC's *Proposed Guidelines on Harassment Based on Race, Color, Religion, Gender, National Origin, Age, or Disability,* which it proposed in 1993 and withdrew in 1994. Others have criticized the president's *Guidelines* as an attempt to avoid having to face the public scrutiny that the regulations would go through if they had been promulgated by the EEOC.

RELIGIOUS BELIEF, DEFINITION OF   The U.S. Supreme Court has not defined the term *religious belief.* However, it has made clear that religious belief does not require recognition of a supreme being. [*Torcaso v. Watkins* (U.S. 1961)] Religious belief also need not arise from a traditional, or even an organized religion. [*Frazee v. Illinois Department of Employment Security* (U.S. 1989)] One possible definition is that the "belief must occupy a place in the believer's life parallel to that occupied by orthodox religious belief." [*United States v. Seeger* (U.S. 1965)] *Seeger* interpreted the statutory (§ 6(j) of the Universal Military Training and Service Act, governing conscientious objections), rather than the constitutional provision. In any case, the Supreme Court has never held an asserted religious belief to be "not religious" for First Amendment purposes.

The Supreme Court often is asked to determine whether particular state activities unconstitutionally affect issues of religion. In *Wisconsin v. Yoder* (U.S. 1972), the Court held that Wisconsin could not require members of the Amish faith to send their children to public school after the eighth grade. In finding a significant burden on the free exercise of religion imposed by the state's law, the Court had to decide whether the parents' refusal to send their children to school was based on religious beliefs. As the Court noted, a claim based on a personal or philosophical rejection of secular values would not be protected by the Free Exercise Clause. Thus, if the Amish refused to send their children to school merely to preserve a "traditional way of life," their claim would be denied. However, the Court found that the Amish lifestyle, educational practices, and refusal to send their children to school to further secular education were religious in nature.

This holding was based on the following facts: (1) this was a shared belief by an organized group rather than a personal preference, (2) the belief was based on certain theocratic principles and interpretations of religious literature, (3) the system of beliefs pervaded and regulated their daily lives, (4) the system of belief and lifestyle resulting from it had been in existence for a substantial period. It is not clear as to which, if any, of those factors determines the presence of a "religion" or a "religious belief."

The question of how one determines whether a belief is "religious" cannot be answered definitively, as this is the only case in which the U.S. Supreme Court has addressed the issue of defining religion apart from a statutory determination.

A narrow definition of religion, perhaps recognizing only very structured religions, should be employed in Establishment Clause cases because no real danger is posed to religious freedom by government aid to unusual or nonstructured groups, even if they could arguably be deemed religious. It would seem that the Supreme Court should be more lenient in defining "religious" or "religion" in cases under the Free Exercise Clause. These claims seek only to protect private individual liberty rather than to overturn governmental social welfare programs. Under the Free Exercise Clause one cannot allow individuals to grant themselves a "religious exemption" from laws that they don't like. As Chief Justice Burger stated for the majority, "although a determination of what is a religious belief or practice entitled to constitutional protection may present a most delicate question, the very concept of ordered liberty precludes allowing every person to make his own standards on matters of conduct in which society as a whole has important interests." [*Wisconsin v. Yoder* (U.S. 1972)]

Although courts may decide which beliefs qualify as "religious," they may not determine such beliefs to be "false." For example, if a person says he spoke to God and that God said the person should solicit money, he cannot be found guilty of fraud on the basis that God never said that. However, a court may determine whether such a person is sincerely asserting a belief in the divine statement. [*United States v. Ballard* (U.S. 1944), as described in *Employment Division v. Smith* (U.S. 1990)]

The majority opinion in *Thomas v. Review Board* (U.S. 1981) was written by Chief Justice Warren Burger. The chief justice avoided ruling on what type of beliefs were "religious," although the majority opinion indicated that judges had to accept an individual's assertion that his or her belief or motivation for actions was religious so long as the person asserts the claim in good faith and so long as the belief could arguably be termed "religious." In *Thomas* the state had denied unemployment compensation benefits to Eddie C. Thomas, a Jehovah's Witness, who had terminated his job because his religious beliefs forbade him to participate in the production of armaments. He claimed that the denial interfered with his free exercise rights.

Once Thomas's reasons were found to be religious, the case was easily disposed of under the First Amendment. Conditioning a significant benefit upon conduct prohibited by a religious belief places a substantial burden on the individual regardless of whether the burden can be labeled direct or indirect.

Religion is not understood as designating certain subjects, such as euthanasia, as "religious" for the purposes of the religion clauses. Under such a view, all beliefs on those matters would fit into the constitutional definitions of religion, whether or not those beliefs derive from a faith in a god. If euthanasia is an inherently religious subject matter, the beliefs of atheists and agnostics on euthanasia would also be "religious."

The Supreme Court's religion cases reject such a definition of religion, which denominates certain subject matters as religious for all persons, in favor of one that looks at the particular belief systems of each person. Under the Court's approach, courts examine the belief systems of persons on a case-by-case basis to determine which beliefs sufficiently implicate a person's faith in a god to qualify as religious for First Amendment purposes. In the conscientious objector cases, the Court broadened its definition of religion when it indicated that analogous beliefs of nonbelievers qualify as well. [*United States v. Seeger* (1965); *Welsh v. United States* (1970)] Since *Welsh* the U.S. Supreme Court has commented only twice on the definition of "religion," both times in dicta.

The Supreme Court has apparently retreated from the view that some beliefs of nonbelievers qualify. [*Wisconsin v. Yoder* (U.S. 1972)] The Supreme Court has offered a restricted definition of religion in which the protection of the religion clauses depends, at least to some extent, on an individual's membership in an organized, established sect. In *Thomas v. Review Board* (U.S. 1981), the Court stated that "[o]nly beliefs rooted in religion are protected by the Free Exercise Clause."

██ **RELIGIOUS BROADCASTING**   The First Amendment to the U.S. Constitution generally protects the rights of citizens to express their opinions publicly in the press. This includes opinions that are religious in nature. Thus, any citizen or group of citizens is privileged to write and publish for broad dissemination materials relating to religious beliefs or to proselytize on behalf of religious beliefs. However, it has long been held that broadcast media are subject to greater government regulation than other types of media because the broadcast spectrum—unlike printed media—is finite and limited. Therefore, the government has the obligation to ensure the greatest possible access to such media for the various diverse views held by the nation's citizenry. It therefore has the power to grant licenses for the use of discrete bands of the broadcast spectrum. Because of this power questions may arise regarding how the government allocates licenses to groups that wish to broadcast religious programs. For example, does the grant of a license to a religious group constitute a government "establishment" of religion? Or, on the other hand, does a denial of a license to a religious group constitute interference with that group's right to the "free exercise" of religion? Are religious broadcasters entitled to government subsidies normally given to broadcasters of secular information? These issues have been addressed as follows.

Religious broadcasting closely parallels the history of broadcasting. The parallel is seen both in technical development, from local radio to televised broadcasts via satellite, but also in its social role and importance. The first religious broadcast occurred in the United States less than two months after the first licensed radio station went on the air. Station KDKA, Pittsburgh, provided a remote broadcast from Calvary Episcopal Church. In 1924 the first religious station, St. Louis based KFUO ("Keep Forward, Upward, Onward") operated by the Lutheran Church Missouri Synod's Concordia Seminary, was up and running. By 1925, at least 63 stations were owned by church institutions. As radio frequencies became more valuable, many churches sold out to commercial interests, in some cases accepting a promise of free broadcast time in lieu of cash. By the 1930s church-owned stations had all but vanished, but many local stations continued to broadcast Sunday worship services for the churches in their community, either "remote" from a church sanctuary, or directly from the station's own studios.

The relationship between broadcasters and religious organizations has been controlled in part by federal regulation. When in 1934 the Communications Act was being debated in Congress, an amendment was proposed that would have allocated fully 25 percent of broadcast frequencies for the exclusive use of nonprofit agencies, including churches. The coalition of educators, religious groups, farm agencies, and other nonprofit organizations was strongly resisted by broadcasters who, during extensive hearings, assured Congress that they, the broadcasters, should be trusted to provide ample free time for nonprofit groups.

The Congress chose a compromise. While it rejected the proposal to give frequencies outright to nonprofit groups, Congress established the Federal Communications Commission (FCC) to regulate the broadcasters, and as a first order of business, mandated the new FCC to "study the proposal that Congress by statute allocate fixed percentages of radio broadcasting facilities to particular types or kinds of nonprofit radio programs."

The FCC recommended in early 1935 that, since the broadcasters were making their facilities available to nonprofits in a spirit of "unity and cooperation," therefore no fixed percentage of broadcast facilities should be allocated for the use of nonprofit activities. However the FCC said, "[I] n order for nonprofit organizations to obtain the maximum service possible, cooperation in good faith by the broadcasters is required. Such cooperation should, therefore, be under the direction of the Commission." Thus, while religious and other nonprofit groups did not get their frequency allocations, they were told that the FCC would make certain that the broadcasters would continue to give them the time to be heard on the commercial stations.

A basic policy difference began to develop among the religious broadcasters themselves. The larger, more established, "main line" denominations generally held the view that broadcasters should provide time on the air for a balanced presentation of all religious views, involving representative groups in the community, even if this required stations to supply the time without charges. The smaller, more "sect type" groups believed that they were being ignored by this policy, and accused the cooperative groups of attempting to silence them. They chose to purchase air time and in order to pay for the time, to make financial appeals over the air. Independents such as Charles F. Fuller, Aimee Semple McPherson, M. R. De Haan, and H. M. S. Richards put most of their funds into buying time. By 1933, conventional Protestant broadcasting accounted for only 28 percent of the total religious radio output.

Various Catholic religious orders became involved in broadcasting beginning in the 1930s, including the Franciscans and the Paulists. In 1968 the U.S. Catholic Conference established an Office of Radio and TV to represent it in all broadcasting matters.

In 1945, the Jewish Theological Seminary of America began "The Eternal Light," a weekly program that dramatized Jewish culture and religion on the NBC network.

In the United States during the 1970s, the Electronic Church emerged on both radio and TV. By the early 1950s, Billy Graham had brought television cameras and sophisticated advertising techniques to his mass meetings, and with the help of William R. Hearst's newspapers, he become an overnight celebrity.

While the FCC had always encouraged broadcasters to carry some religious programming, such television fare did not become influential or controversial until the advent of widespread cable television. Coupled with changes in broadcasting regulations, religious television has become much more visible during the past two decades.

The National Religious Broadcasters (NRB), established in 1944, with the encouragement of the National Association of Evangelicals has grown to be a coalition of many religious radio stations, television stations, and production companies and distributors related to the electronic evangelists. While the NRB lobbied for the deregulation of broadcasting, main-line churches complained that the electronic evangelists had become the captives of commercial broadcasting and its values, and that their emphasis on purchase of time played into the hands of commercial broadcasting and worked to drive religious diversity off the air. During the 1970s, the number of stations carrying main-line religious programs dropped by more than half, as stations sold time to Electronic Church syndicators in preference to carrying the free network programs.

Although easier access to electronic media has allowed increases in several different types of religious programming, the most visible and largest (in terms of audience) has been the segment of religious television associated with evangelical Protestantism. Programs such as the *Old Time Gospel Hour,* the *700 Club,* the *PTL Club,* and *Hour of Power* have combined an explicitly "old fashioned" evangelical religious message with the technology of modern mass communications.

The content of many of these programs has had an explicitly political message. The *Old Time Gospel Hour* was one important vehicle through which Jerry Falwell promoted the Moral Majority, and Pat Robertson used the *700 Club* to launch his bid for the 1988 Republican presidential nomination. Televangelism has been effective at providing religious and political messages to a relatively self-selected audience and religious television has been a potent means of fund raising as well.

A major crisis developed in early 1987, when sexual and financial scandals sullied the reputations of several leading televangelists. Listener confidence dropped sharply, and income for the TV ministries also decreased sharply. By the beginning of 1988 some of the Electronic Church ministries verged on bankruptcy.

On 25 February 1998 the Federal Communications Commission (FCC) modified its equal employment opportunity enforcement policies for religious broadcasters, allowing them to establish religious belief or affiliation as a bona fide job qualification for all station employees.

A federal district court held that the government's decision impacting religious broadcasters did not violate the Religious Freedom Restoration Act (RFRA), prior to the time that this statute was found unconstitutional. In *Fordham University v. Brown* (D.D.C. 1994), the court granted summary judgment in favor of the government in an action under RFRA that challenged the government's refusal to fund certain broadcast facilities that broadcast sectarian programs, such as the plaintiff's radio station, which had a weekly broadcast of a Catholic mass. The court found that the plaintiff radio station had not been sufficiently burdened by the lack of funding, because it continued to broadcast the mass, and concluded that the government had a compelling interest in upholding the Establishment Clause.

Broadcasts by a public television station of a Catholic mass program had a sectarian purpose and thus, the broadcast fell under a regulation prohibiting funding by the National Telecommunications and Information Administration (NTIA) through grants from the Public Telecommunications Facilities Program (PTFP). The NTIA did not mean to look to the essential mission of the station but instead to apply its regulations to facts at hand. [*Fordham University v. Brown* (D.D.C. 1994)]

RELIGIOUS CLOTHING *See* RELIGIOUS GARB

RELIGIOUS COLLEGES AND UNIVERSITIES   Although government aid to nonpublic institutions of higher education has been the subject of only a few U.S. Supreme Court decisions, it is clear that government programs aiding these schools must be tested under the same criteria that have been employed in the primary and secondary school cases. The aid must have a secular purpose, its primary effect must neither advance nor inhibit religion, and the aid must avoid creating an excessive entanglement between government and religion. [*Lemon v. Kurtzman* (U.S. 1971)]

Government grant programs have been held not to have a primary effect of aiding religion where there was at least some formal guarantee by college authorities that funds provided by the government would not be used for religious instruction or other sectarian activities. The Supreme Court does not assume that religious colleges are so permeated with religion that their secular functions cannot be separated from their religious mission. Thus a program that is tied only to secular instruction will not have an effect of advancing religion. [*Tilton v. Richardson* (U.S. 1971); *Hunt v. McNair* (U.S. 1973)]

However, if the institution to be aided is sectarian to the extent that the advancing of religious beliefs permeates its entire program, the institution would be similar to the parochial elementary and secondary schools that the majority of Supreme Court justices have deemed to have a primary function of propagating religious doctrine. In such a situation, the secular teaching function of the college could not be sufficiently separated from its religious mission to avoid the prohibited effect of government aid advancing religion.

In determining whether excessive entanglement exists, courts examine three factors: (1) the character of the institutions benefitted; (2) the nature of the aid provided; (3) the resulting relationship between government and church authorities. Additionally, the program must not be of a type that will cause political division along religious lines.

The Supreme Court was closely divided, and approved quite extensive public assistance. [*Tilton v. Richardson* (U.S. 1971)] On the same day that it first struck down an assistance program for elementary and secondary private schools in *Lemon v. Kurtzman* (U.S. 1971), the Court sustained federal construction grants to church-affiliated colleges and universities under the Higher Education Facilities Act of 1963. The specific grants in question were for construction of two library buildings, a science building, a music, drama, and arts building, and a language laboratory. The statute prohibited the financing of any facility for, or the use of any federally financed building for, religious purposes, although the restriction on use ran for only 20 years. The Court found that the purpose and effect of the grants were secular and that, unlike elementary and secondary schools, religious colleges were not so permeated with religious inculcation that every activity they sponsored was religious in nature. The supervision required to ensure conformance with the nonreligious-use requirement was found not to constitute "excessive entanglement," because the construction grants were one-time projects and did not continue as did the state programs.

The Supreme Court later, in *Hunt v. McNair* (U.S. 1973), sustained a South Carolina program under which institutions of higher education could enter into contracts with a state authority by which the authority would issue revenue bonds for construction of projects on an institution's campus. This provided a participating Baptist-operated college a better arrangement in terms of interest costs than it could make otherwise. Under the program the state authority held formal title to the project, while the principal and interest on the bonds, as well as the expenses of the authority, was paid by the college. The Supreme Court concluded that state financing of construction projects at religiously affiliated colleges would not create entanglement problems because the funding was clearly directed to the secular functions of the college. Justice Powell explained in his opinion that, " [a]id may normally be thought to have a primary effect of advancing religion when it flows to an institution in which religion is so pervasive that a substantial portion of its functions are subsumed in the religious mission or when it funds a specifically religious activity in otherwise substantially secular setting." The colleges involved, although affiliated with religious institutions, were not shown to be so permeated with religion as to fall under the former clause. First, no religious test existed for the faculty or student body. Second, a substantial percentage of the student body did not identify with the religion of the college's affiliation. And third, state law precluded the use of any project financed under the program for religious activities.

The kind of assistance permitted by *Tilton v. Richardson* (U.S. 1971) and by *Hunt v. McNair* (U.S. 1973) seems to have been broadened when the Court sustained a Maryland program of annual subsidies to qualifying private institutions of higher education. [*Roemer v. Maryland Board of Public Works* (U.S. 1976)] The grants were noncategorical but could not be used for sectarian purposes, a limitation to be policed by the administering agency. The Court's plurality opinion found a secular purpose to the grants. It found that the religiously affiliated institutions were not so pervasively sectarian that secular activities could not be separated from sectarian ones, and therefore that the limitation of funding to secular activities was meaningful. The plurality also thought the character of the institutions aided was not pervasively sectarian, which reduced the degree of public surveillance required to police the use of the funds to such an extent that excessive entanglement was improbable. The annual nature of the subsidy was a problem, but the plurality thought that the generally secular character of the institutions, again, permitted the relationship between the public agency and the recipient institution. The Court also saw much less likelihood of political divisiveness in controversies over annual funding because the student body was not local, and because many of the nonreligiously affiliated institutions also received aid. Thus, the Court upheld the law, asserting that it was narrowly drawn to avoid advancing religion and therefore did not violate the Constitution.

A still further broadening of governmental power to extend aid to religious institutions of higher education is suggested in the Supreme Court's summary approval of two lower court decisions upholding programs of assistance—scholarships and tuition grants—to students at colleges and universities as well as to those in vocational programs in both public and private (including religious) institutions. One program contained no secular use restrictions at all, and in the other one the restriction seemed perfunctory. [*Smith v. Board of Governors of the University of North Carolina* (U.S. 1977); *Americans United for the Separation of Church and State v. Blanton* (U.S. 1977)]

▥ RELIGIOUS DISCRIMINATION Since 1970, the Internal Revenue Service has denied tax-exempt status to schools

that discriminate on the basis of race. The Service was forced to adopt this policy in Mississippi as a result of litigation; thereafter, the administration temporarily abandoned this policy in January 1982. It explained that Congress had not included a nondiscrimination requirement in the law, and that the executive branch had no authority to impose such a requirement on its own.

The internal affairs of churches are an enclave in which the Free Exercise Clause must control; outside such enclaves, the policy against racial discrimination controls. When one seeks to affiliate with a church, or with a pervasively religious school, he or she must do so on the church's terms. Similarly, when the church ventures into secular society, it must do so on society's terms.

A religiously motivated citizen, who objects to racial equality, is not entitled to be excused from secular rules forbidding discrimination that apply to all. This includes not being permitted to discriminate as a landlord. The same result applies when the church acts collectively. For example, a church is not entitled to exclude African Americans from a public park during a church picnic, just because a religious belief mandates it. It is not entitled to discriminate in its disposal of a church building for sale in the open market, it cannot disseminate among potential buyers on the basis of race. Our societal commitment to racial equality is so important that the views of dissenting churches are regularly subordinated to it, whenever the church or an individual believer, ventures into the outside world.

Inside the church, however, the balance must be struck the other way. Churches must be free to select their own members on any terms they choose, and to discriminate among those members on any terms the faithful will accept. Despite the strong national policy against sex discrimination, Congress has no power to tell the Catholic Church it must ordain women. Similarly, Congress has no power to tell the Church of Jesus Christ of Latter Day Saints to admit African Americans into the priesthood before a change in that church's teachings on the subject. Ordering a church to admit black members is not much different. And when a church school is pervasively religious, operated as an integral part of the church itself, ordering it to accept African American students is also not much different. The Free Exercise Clause requires that pervasively religious schools not be penalized for discrimination in admissions or other internal policies.

A statute denying tax exemptions to schools that discriminate will seriously infringe the autonomy even of church schools that do not discriminate, because every school will face the risk of being required to prove its nondiscriminatory policy. Even nondiscriminatory churches with long and admirable records of educating minorities have reason to be concerned with the governmental intrusion required to enforce a nondiscrimination policy. One example is the injunction in *Green v. Miller*, ordering the Internal Revenue Service to adopt more vigorous procedures for identifying discriminatory schools. The district court ruled that an inference of present discrimination arises with respect to any private school that was established or expanded while the public schools in its locality were desegregating. That is not an unreasonable inference; many private schools were established expressly for creating a segregated alternative to forcibly integrated public schools. It is, however, a plainly overbroad inference. Desegregation cases can drag on for years, and many private schools have been established or expanded for innocent reasons during the local public school desegregation.

The U.S. Supreme Court has not specifically decided whether churches and church schools that discriminate may be denied a tax exemption available to all other churches and schools. It has decided cases in other contexts that strongly support the principles stated above. One line of cases restricts state entanglement in church affairs. This doctrine was developed in response to Establishment Clause challenges to aid to church schools, but it has recently been extended to government regulation of churches. Another line of cases restricts secular resolution of internal church disputes, especially in cases of schisms and disputed clerical appointments.

The Equal Employment Opportunity Commission (EEOC) of the federal government has promulgated guidelines regarding employment in religious institutions. These *Religious Discrimination Guidelines* state that the EEOC will define the statutory term "religious practices" to include moral or ethical beliefs as to what is right and wrong that are sincerely held with the strength of traditional religious views. Thus, a worker is required to show only that he or she took a position of conscience on the basis of beliefs that are sincerely held "with the strength of traditional religious views." It is irrelevant whether the teachings are "identifiably" those of the faith to which the worker subscribes. [*See, EEOC, Religious Discrimination Guidelines* (1966)] In this regard, the EEOC follows the broad definition of the concept of religion developed in conscientious objection cases.

⚖ RELIGIOUS DISCRIMINATION IN EMPLOYMENT

Laws prohibiting employment discrimination involve primarily the need to guarantee to all members of American society unfettered access to the labor market, and to all of the economic and social benefits that flow from active participation in it.

Religious discrimination in employment has been the subject of state as well as federal legislation and courts have been called upon to define the circumstances under which particular conduct constitutes illegal religious discrimination in employment under state statutes. For example, in *Finnemore v. Bangor Hydro-Electric Co.* (Me. 1994), the Maine Supreme Judicial Court concluded that a genuine issue of fact existed about whether sexually explicit comments directed at a fundamentalist Christian constituted illegal religious harassment violating state law. Other courts applying state antidiscrimination statutes have reached varying results, depending on the particular circumstances involved and the language of the statute in question.

Many states have enacted statutes to prevent employers from discriminating based on race, color, national origin, or religious creed, with respect to personnel decisions or the terms and conditions of employment. State laws barring employment discrimination based on religion, like state civil rights laws generally, vary considerably. These state laws sometimes closely follow the equivalent federal law contained in Title VII of the Civil Rights Act of 1964, although other state statutes differ significantly from the federal civil rights laws.

Title VII of the Civil Rights Act of 1964 prohibits employers covered by the Act from discriminating against persons because of their religion. This statute greatly impacts the employment market because it applies to most forms of private, as well as governmental, employment and the activities of labor unions.

The Act itself is fairly straightforward in its approach to this problem. It prohibits an employer from discriminating in the hiring, payment, or treatment of employees on the basis of their religion. Similarly, the statute makes it unlawful for a labor organization to exclude or burden a worker on the basis of religion.

In 1972 the Act was amended to include a definition of religion that also defines an employer's duties in this area. The Act now reads:

> The term "religion" includes all aspects of religious observance and practice, as well as belief, unless an employer demonstrates that he is unable to reasonably accommodate an employee's or prospective employee's religious observance or practice without undue hardship on the conduct of the employer's business.

The goal of Title VII is to reduce or eliminate most religion-based barriers to labor market participation. In 1966 the Equal Employment Opportunity Commission (EEOC) interpreted Title VII's antidiscrimination provision as imposing an affirmative duty upon employers to accommodate the religious practices of employees if accommodation did not cause a "serious inconvenience to the conduct of their business." A year later, the EEOC changed its position and required less from an employer. The amended guidelines required accommodation of an employee's religious practices if it did not impose an "undue hardship on [the employer's] business." Congress later amended Title VII to reflect the undue hardship requirement.

Courts, including the U.S. Supreme Court, have routinely construed Title VII broadly, understanding this provision to be a general expression of Congress's intention to eradicate all forms of invidious discrimination in the employment context. In applying Title VII, courts have recognized claims alleging that employers discriminated against employees by creating hostile working environments. Title VII also states, however, that employers must accommodate employees' religious beliefs, a rule that the courts have applied narrowly. Thus, employers are both forbidden to subject their employees to religiously hostile environments and required to make some accommodation to religious employees.

According to the Equal Employment Opportunity Commission, there has been a steady rise in recent years in religious discrimination complaints filed by employees—from 1,192 cases in 1991 to more than 1,560 in 1996.

The most common religion-related problems reported by human resources managers: employees who attempt to proselytize other workers (20 percent); complaints from employees who feel harassed by their coworkers because of expression of their religious beliefs (14 percent); and, employees refusing certain duties based on religious beliefs (9 percent). The most common kinds of religious accommodation offered by employers are: flexible scheduling that allows time off for religious observances (70 percent); allowing the display of religious materials in work areas (24 percent); providing space or time for religious observance, study, or discussion during work breaks (15 percent); and making exceptions in dress or personal appearance codes (13 percent).

 RELIGIOUS DISQUALIFICATION   *See MCDANIEL V. PATY*

RELIGIOUS EXEMPTIONS   The U.S. Supreme Court has held that no religious exemption was required from the following religiously neutral regulations, even though certain groups objected because the regulation interfered with sincerely held religious beliefs:

1. Prohibition against use of peyote [*Employment Division v. Smith* (U.S. 1990)(claimant argued use was part of sacred rite in Native American Church)]
2. Prohibition against polygamy [*Reynolds v. United States* (U.S. 1878)(claimant argued that multiple wives were required by Mormon faith)]
3. Denial of tax exempt status to schools that discriminate on the basis of race [*Bob Jones University v. United States* (U.S. 1983)(claimant argued that separation of races was part of religious creed)]
4. Prohibition against religious garb for members of air force while in uniform [*Goldman v. Weinberger* (U.S. 1986)(claimant wanted to wear yarmulke while on duty)]
5. Sunday closing laws [*Braunfield v. Brown* (U.S. 1961)(claimant, whose Sabbath was celebrated on Saturday, argued that Sunday closing requirement was undue burden on his religious practice)]
6. Requirement that employers comply with federal minimum wage laws [*Tony and Susan Alamo Foundation v. Secretary of Labor* (U.S. 1985)(employer argued that minimum wages interfered with members' religious desires to work without compensation)]
7. Requirement that employers pay social security taxes [*United States v. Lee* (U.S. 1982)(claimant argued that his religious beliefs prohibited payment and receipt of social security type payments)]
8. Draft laws and the selective service provision for exemption to conscientious objectors of all wars [*Gillete v. United States* (U.S. 1971)(claimant objected to specific war only)]
9. Denial of veterans' entitlements [*Johnson v. Robison* (U.S. 1974)(claimants were conscientious objectors who performed alternative civilian service)]
10. Denial of exemption from sales and use taxes [*Jimmy Swaggart Ministries v. Board of Equalization* (U.S. 1990)(claimant argued that denial of exemption to religious organization was impermissible discrimination)]
11. Development of federal lands [*Lyng v. Northwest Indian Cemetery Protective Association* (U.S. 1988)(claimants objected to logging of area that their religious belief held sacred)]

RELIGIOUS FREEDOM   The First Amendment to the Constitution of the United States forbids Congress to make any law "respecting an establishment of religion or prohibiting the free exercise thereof." Although technically and originally this was a restriction on Congress only, the First Amendment has been made applicable to the states by passage of the Fourteenth Amendment.

The constitutional restriction against legislation affecting religion has a double aspect. On the one hand it forestalls compulsion by law of the acceptance of any creed or the practice of any form of worship. On the other hand, it safeguards the free exercise of one's chosen form of religion. The interrelation of the Establishment and Free Exercise Clauses has been well summarized as follows:

> The structure of our government has, for the preservation of civil liberty, rescued the temporal institutions from religious interference. On the other hand, it has secured religious liberty from the invasion of the civil authority. Although the two clauses overlap in certain instances, and a general harmony of purpose exists between them, the limits of permissible state accommodation of religion under the "Establishment Clause" are not coextensive with the noninterference mandated by the "Free Exercise Clause." The Free Exercise Clause has a reach of its own. A distinction between the "Free Exercise" Clause and the "Establishment" Clause of the First Amendment is that a violation of the former clause is based on coercion, while a violation of the latter clause need not be so attended. [*Gillette v. United States* (U.S. 1971)]

RELIGIOUS FREEDOM AMENDMENT (1997)   Legislation known as the Religious Freedom Amendment was first introduced in the U.S. House of Representatives. Its purpose was to amend the Constitution to expand the right to religious expression in public settings and possibly allow government funding of religious institutions. The measure [House Joint Resolution 78], sponsored by Ernest Istook (R-Okla) is an expansion of the school prayer amendments that Congress started considering in 1966. Those measures sought to allow prayer in public schools. This proposal would cover school prayer and other forms of religious expression on public property, such as placing a nativity scene in front of a town hall.

The most controversial element, a provision that prohibits the government from denying "equal access to a benefit on account of religion," may result in public funding of religious schools and of churches involved in social welfare programs.

The benefits clause in the amendment could allow for school voucher programs, whose constitutionality has not yet been resolved by the U.S. Supreme Court. Vouchers provide tuition money for parents to use to send their children to a private or parochial school.

Separationist organizations, such as People for the American Way, assert that the amendment could be best characterized as a religious coercion amendment and is not only unnecessary, but if enacted would usher in a new wave of divisive government-sponsored religious activity. The proposed amendment was defeated.

RELIGIOUS FREEDOM RESTORATION ACT (1993)

The Religious Freedom Restoration Act (RFRA) was enacted by Congress in 1993 to prevent the government from restricting religious freedom, unless it has a "compelling state interest," that is, an interest that the state is forced or obliged to protect. Congress passed the RFRA to restore protections of religious liberty weakened by the Supreme Court's holding in *Employment Division v. Smith* (U.S. 1990). In *Smith* the Supreme Court held that Oregon could constitutionally withhold unemployment benefits from two former drug rehabilitation counselors who had lost their jobs for using peyote in a religious rite at the Native American Church. The use of peyote, a hallucinogen, violated Oregon's drug laws. The men sued, claiming the state's interest was not compelling enough to warrant infringement of their religious rights. The Supreme Court, however, ruled against them, effectively eliminating the compelling interest test.

The holding in *Smith* made it less difficult for states or the federal government to enact statutes that restrict individual religious rights, by ruling that the compelling state interest test applied only in cases in which a regulation directly discriminated against religious conduct. "Compelling state interest" is a legal concept invoked by a government to uphold a "state action" (an action by a government or governmental body) against claims based on equal protection of the law under the First Amendment.

As a result of the *Smith* opinion, as long as the government's policies were neutrally stated and generally applicable, they would hold up under constitutional attack, unless they were targeting a specific religious group. *Smith* made it more difficult to challenge incidental infringements on personal religious liberty.

Before *Smith* state laws restricting religious activities had to meet a stricter legal standard of serving a "compelling" government interest in a way that posed the least possible burden on religious freedom. Federal courts could strike down a law if the state could not prove such a compelling interest. Starting in 1986 exceptions to this standard had been created for the military and prisons.

On 27 June 1991 Congressman Stephen Solarz (R-NY) harshly criticized *Smith* as a "dastardly and unprovoked attack on our first freedom" and declared that *Smith* "must not be permitted to stand unchallenged." To counteract the effects of *Smith,* Solarz introduced a bill entitled the Religious Freedom Restoration Act. Specifically, the RFRA stated:

> Government shall not substantially burden a person's exercise of religion even if the burden results from a rule of general applicability unless the government can prove that application of the burden to the person (1) is in furtherance of a compelling governmental interest; and (2) is the least restrictive means of furthering that compelling governmental interest.

As a legislative effort to overrule the *Smith* decision, the RFRA's express purpose was to restore the compelling interest/least restrictive means analysis to regulations that affected citizens' free exercise rights, as provided by the U.S. Supreme Court's *Sherbert v. Verner* (U.S. 1963) and *Wisconsin v. Yoder* (U.S. 1972) decisions. *Sherbert* and *Yoder* were part of a series of free exercise cases that rigorously enforced the compelling interest test. Most legitimate governmental interests are not compelling. "Compelling" does not mean merely a "reasonable means of promoting a legitimate public interest." Nor does it mean merely important. Rather, "compelling" interests include only those few interests "of the highest order," or similarly "only the gravest abuses, endangering paramount interests." Some examples of compelling state interest include the nation's need to maintain order in its military and the integrity of its system of taxation. [*Goldman v. Weinberger* (U.S. 1986)]

Specifically, the RFRA prohibited the state and federal governments from restricting a person's exercise of religion without showing both a compelling governmental interest in the restriction and that the restriction is the least restrictive means of achieving the governmental interest.

The RFRA was introduced with bipartisan sponsorship in both houses of Congress and was supported by President Clinton. The Act enjoyed its wide bipartisan support only after sponsors included language to ensure that it would not be used to challenge state abortion restrictions. Similar legislation introduced in 1990, 1991, and 1992 had become ensnared in the abortion debate.

When it was enacted in 1993, the RFRA effectively overruled the *Smith* holding. In so doing, the RFRA made it more difficult for government to infringe on religious practices. By explicitly applying itself to all cases in which the government burdens religion, the RFRA essentially returned the law not to the status quo before *Smith* but to the status quo before 1986. Under the RFRA, all government burdens on religious conduct became subject to the *Sherbert* test.

Once it passed, the RFRA unquestionably withdrew the power of state legislatures to restrict free exercise rights. Supporters of the Act argued that this would prevent both the discriminatory regulation and the pervasive state regulation of religion. At first, the RFRA was upheld as constitutional in several cases, including by the Fifth Circuit Court of Appeals in *Flores v. City of Boerne* (5th Cir. 1996).

In 1997, however, the U.S. Supreme Court, by a six-to-three vote, invalidated the RFRA in *City of Boerne v. Flores* (U.S. 1997). The Court ruled that Congress had unconstitutionally attempted to rewrite the U.S. Constitution's Free Exercise Clause by setting a higher legal standard of review for any law alleged to impose a restriction on religious practice. In so ruling, the Court dramatically asserted its prerogative as the final arbiter of constitutional questions and as the interpreter of constitutional norms.

The *Agostini v. Felton* (U.S. 1997) and *Flores* decisions make it clear that protection of religious rights has moved from the courtroom to the political area. Arguing that a law treads on constitutional rights under the First Amendment Religion Clauses will be harder and harder. Only government laws or policies that truly coerce acceptance of, or specifically endorse, religion will be found unconstitutional. Rather, our historical separation of church and state means that as a matter of good public policy the government should not impose a rule that will be necessary or entangle itself with religion.

RELIGIOUS FUNDAMENTALISM   One of the greatest achievements of American constitutionalism was how it resolved the paradox that the intolerance of religious fundamentalists may destroy republican government, but their rigorous attachment to moral principle may be needed to defend it. American constitutionalism harnessed the moral idealism of religious fundamentalism, while restraining its potential for bigotry. The Founders harnessed fundamentalism's moral idealism by stressing the importance of morality in civil life and by acknowledging the crucial role that churches play in fostering this morality. At the same time, the Founders sought to temper fundamentalism's intolerance by removing religious questions from the political arena, which in reality reduced the consequences of religious intolerance by ensuring that government power would never be used to resolve religious controversies.

The Founders' arrangement produced an institutional separation between church and state even while forging a practical tie between religion and politics on the basis of morality. Religious fundamentalists were discouraged by the nature of politics from using the government to promote their theological belief, but the door was open for them to enter the political arena as citizens in order to promote government policies in accord with both the principles of the Constitution and the "laws of nature and nature's God" on which those principles are premised.

In the late twentieth century, major changes occurred in the perception of church-state relationships. The new emphasis on individual religious freedom was due in part to the changing nature of church-state jurisprudence in the 1970s and 1980s. Whereas previous church-state legal conflicts had focused on how much the government could do to promote religion while complying with the Establishment Clause, new controversies concerned how far the state could go in restricting individual religious expression. Public high school students were forbidden by school authorities from meeting on their own during lunch or before school for prayer and Bible study. Churches were prevented form utilizing public facilities readily available for use by other community groups, and zoning laws were invoked to curtail religious activities in private homes. In addition, many parents faced the choice of either removing their children from public schools or allowing their children to be taught the permissibility of behaviors they found morally unacceptable. Some religious parents who tried to teach their children at home were jailed. These new conflicts caused many evangelicals to see the government as the problem rather than the solution, and they accordingly sought ways to curb what they regarded as state-sponsored persecution of their religious beliefs and practices.

One new rationale that has not been invalidated by the Supreme Court is equal access, which calls for religious expression to be protected as speech under the First Amendment. The primary idea behind equal access is that religious individuals and groups should be accorded the same access to public facilities as nonreligious individuals and groups. For example, if a public library rents rooms to community groups for meetings, it should not be able to forbid religious groups from renting the rooms for religious meetings because this would be discriminating against certain groups on the basis of the content of their speech. Similarly, if high school students have the right to distribute political leaflets to their classmates on school grounds, they must also have the right to pass out religious leaflets. The equal access rationale has been applied by evangelicals with particular success in the public high school setting, where many schools previously had denied religious student groups the same right to meet on school property routinely afforded to other student groups. The Supreme

Court sustained federal legislation providing a limited statutory right to equal access in public secondary schools in *Board of Education v. Mergens* (U.S. 1990).

The development of equal access is yet another indication of how successful the Founders were in establishing a system in which the political demands of religious fundamentalism would be framed in terms of generally applicable moral principles rather than petitions based on divine right. In the United States religious fundamentalists have increasingly recognized that the same laws that protect other citizens also protect them and that they do not need special privileges conferred by the government to do well.

RELIGIOUS GARB Statutes governing religious garb in the United States originated in the late nineteenth century, and were designed to prevent Catholic nuns from wearing their habits when teaching in public schools. Shortly after the Pennsylvania Supreme Court held that the wearing of religious garb did not constitute sectarian teaching in *Hysong v. Gallitzin School District* (Pa. 1894), the Pennsylvania legislature enacted a religious garb law statute. That law was sustained in *Commonwealth v. Herr* (Pa. 1910), on the ground that the regulation was not a "religious test," and was justified on the grounds that it was necessary to avoid all appearances of sectarianism in public schools.

The Pennsylvania law was similar to one enacted in Oregon almost 100 years later, which was likewise upheld in *Cooper v. Eugene School District No. 4J* (Ore. 1986). Under that law, teachers were prohibited from wearing distinctive garments with religious significance while teaching in the public schools. The plaintiff in the Oregon case was enjoined from wearing the garb of the Sikh faith to which she had recently converted.

In a remarkable series of cases, the state of New York requested orders forbidding a lawyer and Roman Catholic priest named Vincent LaRocca from wearing religious garb while defending persons accused of committing crimes. New York state courts issued the requested orders. After unsuccessfully appealing the orders in state court, LaRocca sued in federal court alleging a violation of his civil rights. [*LaRocca v. Gold* (2d Cir. 1981)]

Recently, Muslim women around the United States are allegedly being suspended, terminated, or barred from employment for wearing religious headscarves. In *United States v. Board of Education* (E.D. Pa. 1989) *aff'd* (3d Cir. 1990), the U.S. Department of Justice filed a lawsuit to enjoin the state of Pennsylvania and the Philadelphia Board of Education from enforcing a state statute proscribing the wearing of religious garb by teachers. Delores Reardon, a former teacher in the Philadelphia public school system, claimed that she was denied teaching assignments in 1984 because she wore a headpiece, which she believed, was required by her Islamic faith. The Justice Department argued that the Pennsylvania state law conflicts with Title VII of the Civil Rights Act of 1964, which requires employers to make reasonable accommodations to workers on the basis of religion. The district court held that allowing Reardon to teach in the public schools in her Muslim clothing would not violate the Establishment Clause. On appeal, the circuit court did not specifically address the Establishment Clause issue, but it did strongly hint that Reardon's practice would not violate the Establishment Clause. The Third Circuit Court of Appeals concluded that the Pennsylvania statute does not forbid teachers from wearing headscarves or dresses with sleeves, it forbids only headscarves or dresses that are distinctively "Muslim."

Bias against job applicants or employees on the basis of religion-based dress or personal appearance may violate state and federal equal employment opportunity laws. This is particularly so if the discrimination is based solely on the company's image (usually expressed in a dress code) or customer preference. Courts and administrative agencies are more likely to uphold an employer's restrictive dress policy, however, if an individual's religious garb or appearance raises safety or other compelling concerns.

The only dress code case to reach the U.S. Supreme Court through a Free Exercise Clause claim is *Goldman v. Weinberger* (1986). Goldman, an Orthodox Jew, ordained rabbi, and commissioned officer in the United States Air Force, brought suit against the U.S. secretary of defense and others. He asserted that air force dress code regulations prevented him from wearing his yarmulke (a small skullcap worn by Jewish men), thereby infringed upon his right to free exercise of religion in violation of the First Amendment. A divided Supreme Court held that the First Amendment permitted the air force to regulate Goldman's attire, even though the effect was to prohibit him from wearing a yarmulke as his religious beliefs required.

As the American workforce becomes more diverse and as religious fundamentalists grow more willing to fight to protect their right of religious expression, the potential for religion-based lawsuits challenging dress and appearance regulations will continue to rise. In light of this trend and the mandates of the civil rights laws, the prudent employer will educate its supervisors about the accommodation requirements of Title VII and make every effort to accommodate the religious-based dress and grooming requirements of applicants and employees. The employer need not make an accommodation if it would cause a demonstrable hardship on the operation of its business. Courts and administrative agencies require, however, that the hardship claim be based on more than speculation and unsupported statements.

▥ RELIGIOUS INSTRUCTION IN PUBLIC SCHOOLS

Although prayers and Bible readings had been common in American schools from the outset of public education, sectarian religious instruction has become uncommon during the twentieth century. In the rare nineteenth-century cases in which the judiciary did have occasion to confront denominational instruction in the public schools, the practice was banned, generally as a violation of state constitutional provisions prohibiting the use of public funds for sectarian instruction.

In *Board of Education v. Minor* (Ohio 1869), for example, the supreme court of Ohio addressed a dispute that arose out of complaints by Catholics over religious instruction and Bible reading in Cincinnati's public schools. Catholics objected particularly to the compelled instruction in the King James Bible. The Cincinnati school board responded by prohibiting further religious activity in school, but the trial court ordered the school board to resume the religious instruction. The Ohio Supreme Court disagreed and concluded that the constitution required the schools to end their religious instruction.

In the early part of the twentieth century, however, the weekday Sunday-school movement pressed school districts to allow the various denominations to provide voluntary religious instruction either outside the school or on the school premises. The Supreme Court continues to flatly prohibit states from requiring or permitting religious exercises in public schools.

During the 1970s, the study of religions in schools was becoming more common in Western countries, most noticeably in those with statutory provision for religious education, such as in the United Kingdom. In the United States, the decision in *Abington School District v. Schempp* (U.S. 1963) expressly allowed "teaching about religion" in public schools. Because, however, this comment of the justice is less widely known than the decision forbidding prayer and devotional reading of the Bible, only a minority of schools include the study of religions. Several attempts have been made to change this situation through teacher education programs, and the production of curriculum materials.

▥ RELIGIOUS LIBERTY

Religious liberty is protected in three provisions of the United States Constitution: the prohibition against religious tests for public office contained in Article IV and the Free Exercise and Establishment Clauses of the First Amendment. Because the first provision is self-executing and the last is involved mostly with issues of government aid, endorsement, or sponsorship of religious activities, the bulk of constitutional litigation over religious liberty has taken place under the Free Exercise Clause.

Religious liberty, as espoused by the U.S. Constitution, is an idea indigenous to the North American experiment in government that became the United States. When the English colonies were established in America, Great Britain had a state church and no real place for dissent. Under King James I those who rejected the Anglican Church were imprisoned and even killed.

Contrary to popular conceptions, neither the Puritans of Massachusetts nor the Anglicans in Virginia intended to alter the pattern of an established Christian church that they brought to the colonies. In some form or another all the colonies except Rhode Island had an established religion, some more stringently enforced than others. With numerous forms of establishment functioning in the eighteenth century, a kind of religious "tolerance" took shape by the time of the American Revolution.

In 1786 James Madison piloted Jefferson's religious freedom bill through the Virginia legislature, with his alternative language, calling for the "free exercise of religion." Thus, the theory of a free conscience in a free state was becoming a part of the American ideal. Madison would later work to make the "free exercise" language a part of the Bill of Rights, as passed by the First U.S. Congress in 1789. Originally, the First Amendment applied only to Acts of Congress. In the nineteenth century only one significant case arose for U.S. Supreme Court action, *Reynolds v. United States* (1879). The case dealt with the territory of Utah, under the direct authority of Congress, which had outlawed polygamy. Although admitting that the statute burdened the free exercise of the Mormon religion that allowed for multiple wives, the Supreme Court invoked a test of compelling state interest and upheld the legislation in order to safeguard the institution of marriage.

After the passage of the Fourteenth Amendment in 1868, the Supreme Court began to apply the Bill of Rights to state legislation. Under the incorporation doctrine, the Court made all state and local laws subject to federal judicial review in matters of constitutionality.

In recent history, there have been two general conceptions of the protections afforded by the Free Exercise Clause. The broad conception, which prevailed in the U.S. Supreme Court from 1963 (and arguably earlier) until 1990, held that no law or government practice could be allowed to burden the free exercise of religion unless it was the least restrictive means of achieving a governmental purpose of the highest order—that is, a "compelling" governmental purpose. The narrow conception, adopted by a five-to-four vote of the Supreme Court in 1990 in the case of *Employment Division v. Smith* (U.S. 1990), holds that the Free Exercise Clause prohibits only those laws that are specifically directed at religious practices.

The classic statement of the broad conception is found in *Sherbert v. Verner* (U.S. 1963). In that case the Supreme Court required the state of South Carolina to pay unemployment compensation benefits to a Seventh-

Day Adventist, not withstanding her refusal to accept available jobs that would have required her to work on Saturday, her Sabbath. According to the Court, denial of benefits was tantamount to a fine for following the tenets of her religion. Since *Sherbert*, the Court has required states to pay unemployment compensation to a Jehovah's Witness who refused to work on armaments in *Thomas v. Indiana Review Board* (U.S. 1981), to a convert to the Seventh-Day Adventist Church who refused to work on the Sabbath in *Hobbie v. Unemployment Appeals Commission* (U.S. 1987); and to a Christian who would not work on Sunday in *Frazee v. Illinois Department of Employment Security* (U.S. 1989). In *Frazee*, the Court unanimously held that the claimant was entitled to benefits, even thought his belief was not mandated by the particular religious denomination of which he was a member. The decision thus confirmed that the right of religious liberty extends to all sincerely held religious convictions and not just to those of established denominations.

In the years immediately following *Sherbert*, the Supreme Court extended free exercise protection to other conflicts between religious conscience and secular law, including compulsory education beyond the eighth grade in *Wisconsin v. Yoder* (U.S. 1972), and jury duty in *In re Jenison* (U.S. 1963). After 1972, however, the Court turned aside every claim for a free exercise exemption from a facially neutral law, outside the narrow context of unemployment compensation. Particularly noteworthy examples included *Goldman v. Weinberger* (U.S. 1986), in which the Court upheld an air force uniform requirement that prevented an Orthodox Jew from wearing his skullcap (yarmulke) while on duty indoors; *Tony and Susan Alamo Foundation v. Secretary of Labor* (U.S. 1985), in which the Court upheld imposition of minimum wage laws on a religious community in which the members worked for no pay; and *Lyng v. Northwest Indian Cemetery Protective Association* (U.S. 1988), in which the court allowed construction of a logging road through national forest lands that were sacred to certain northern California Indian tribes, even though the road would "virtually destroy the Indians' ability to practice their religion."

In each of these cases, the Court either held that the "compelling interest" test of *Sherbert* had been satisfied or that there were special circumstances making that test inappropriate to the particular case. Thus, during this period, the formal legal doctrine sounded highly protective of the rights of religious conscience, but in practice, the government almost always prevailed.

In 1990 the Court abandoned the compelling interest test in *Employment Division v. Smith* (U.S. 1990), holding that "the right of free exercise does not relieve an individual of the obligation to comply with a 'valid and neutral law of general applicability on the grounds that the law proscribes (or prescribes) conduct that his religion prescribes (or proscribes).'" The

Smith case involved the sacramental use of peyote by members of the Native American Church. Although 23 states and the federal government specifically exempt Native American Church ceremonies from their drug laws, Oregon does not. The U.S. Supreme Court held that the Free Exercise Clause does not require an exemption.

After *Smith,* the only governmental actions that can be challenged under the Free Exercise Clause are those in which this clause applies "in conjunction with other constitutional protections," such as cases involving free speech or childbearing, or those in which the law is specifically directed at a religious practice. Thus laws discriminating against religion as such would be subject to constitutional challenge. Such cases are unusual in the United States. The only example in recent decades was *McDonald v. Paty* (U.S. 1978), which involved a Tennessee law barring members of the clergy from service in the state legislature or a state constitutional convention. Because Tennessee had singled out religious leaders for a special disability, its statute was struck down. Another case of discrimination against religion was *Widmar v. Vincent* (U.S. 1981), in which a public university attempted to bar student religious groups from campus facilities. *Widmar,* however, was decided under the Freedom of Speech Clause, not the Free Exercise Clause. Except for *McDaniel* and *Widmar,* almost every free exercise case to come before the Supreme Court involved an ostensibly neutral law of general applicability, now resolved under *Smith* without inquiry into the strength of the governmental purpose behind the law.

The debate between the broad and narrow readings of the Free Exercise Clause goes back even before the proposal and ratification of the First Amendment from 1789 to 1791. John Locke and Thomas Jefferson both apparently opposed special religious exemptions from laws of general applicability; James Madison favored them, at least in some circumstances. The same issue arose under several of the state constitutions, yielding conflicting results. The majority of the state constitutions adopted before the First Amendment contained language that suggests the broad reading. Georgia, for example, guaranteed that "all persons whatever shall have the free exercise of their religion; provided it be not repugnant to the peace and safety of the State" [Georgia Constitution of 1777, Article LVI] Although it is perilous to draw firm conclusions from abstract legal language, the "peace and safety" provision would appear to be unnecessary unless the free exercise guarantees were understood to entail some exceptions from otherwise valid laws. Moreover, in actual practice, conflicts between minority religious tenets and general law in colonial and preconstitutional America were not infrequently resolved by crafting exemptions. Examples included exemptions from oath requirements and military conscription. The evidence, however, is thin because eighteenth-century America gave rise to few conflicts between religious and civil dictates.

If the narrow reading of the Free Exercise Clause announced in *Smith* remains in force, it will cause major changes in the constitutional rights both of religious individuals and of institutions. It is not uncommon for minority religious practices to conflict with "generally applicable" rules or regulations, and henceforth, any relief from such conflicts must come from the legislatures. Some religious groups—those more numerous or politically powerful—will be able to protect their interests in the political process; some will not. The Supreme Court commented in *Smith* that "[i]t may fairly well be said that leaving accommodations to the political process will place at a relative disadvantage those religious practices that are not widely engaged in; but that unavoidable consequence of democratic government must be preferred to a system in which each conscience is a law unto itself."

For many years, some justices maintained that laws or government policies that exempted religious organizations or religiously motivated individuals from laws applied to others were themselves suspect under the Establishment Clause. For example, Justice John Marshall Harlan, in the conscientious objection cases that came before the Court during the Vietnam War, concluded in *Welsh v. United States* (1970) that it would be unconstitutional to recognize religious objection to military service without also recognizing nonreligious conscientious objection. More recently the Court, in *Wallace v. Jaffree* (U.S. 1985), struck down state efforts to accommodate the religious needs of some school children for voluntary prayer through an officially declared moment of silence, and in *Thornton v. Caldor, Inc.* (U.S. 1985), the Court invalidated a statute that required private employers to honor the needs of Sabbath observers in determining days off.

In *Corporation of Presiding Bishop v. Amos* (U.S. 1987), however, the Supreme Court unanimously upheld a federal statute exempting religious organizations from the prohibition on discrimination on the basis of religion in employment. The Court reasoned that it is permissible for the government to remove government-imposed obstacles to the free exercise of religion, even if, in some sense, this gives preferential treatment to religious organizations. And in *Texas Monthly, Inc. v. Bullock* (U.S. 1989), when a fragmented Court struck down a Texas law exempting religious magazines from paying sales tax, the plurality was careful to note that benefits conferred exclusively on religious organizations are constitutionally permissible if they "would not impose substantial burdens on non-beneficiaries" or if they "were designed to alleviate government intrusions that might significantly deter adherents of a particular faith from conduct protected by the Free Exercise Clause."

Thus, although individuals or religious bodies can no longer challenge generally applicable government actions under the Free Exercise Clause, the courts have also become more likely to uphold legislation designed to accommodate religious exercise.

The principle of religious liberty, while an American ideal, is often said to be in a serious and immediate threat. One overriding problem exists in a liberal democracy: How can religion be treated neutrally? To protect religion, we must define it: We are already entangled.

RELIGIOUS LIBERTY PROTECTION ACT   After the Religious Freedom Restoration Act (RFRA) was declared unconstitutional by the U.S. Supreme Court in 1997 [*City of Boerne v. Flores* (U.S. 1997)], RFRA supporters sought to draft a bill that could withstand a constitutional challenge. It is known as the Religious Liberty Protection Act (RLPA). In *Boerne,* the justices struck down the RFRA, concluding that the lawmakers did not have the authority under the Fourteenth Amendment's Enforcement Clause to grant greater protection to religious groups than provided by the Court's own precedents. Instead of the Enforcement Clause of the Fourteenth Amendment, the RLPA is premised on powers inherent in the Constitution's Commerce and Spending Clauses.

The new bill is motivated by recent court cases that religious groups believe eroded the free exercise of religion as enunciated in the Bill of Rights. Supporters of the Religious Liberty Protection Action (RLPA) have sought to legislate stronger protections for religious freedom by developing the standard that prohibits state interference with religious practice unless there is a "compelling government interest." Also, governments must act in the least restrictive manner in cases involving religious practice. The RLPA is supported by more than 80 organizations from the Christian Coalition to the American Civil Liberties Union. Some Christian groups have opposed the legislation, arguing that it inappropriately links religious liberty with interstate commerce, expanding federal power. The bill, they believe, denigrates religion by associating it with commercial enterprise.

The RLPA attempts to regain as much of the RFRA's scope as possible. It mandates the same "compelling interest" and "least restrictive means" test (also called superstrict scrutiny) in cases in which government substantially burdens religious conduct. In a nod to the Supreme Court's declaration that Congress may not create new constitutional rights against the states, the RLPA is tied not only to the Fourteenth Amendment but also to Congress's powers to spend and govern commerce. Hence, the RLPA mandates superstrict scrutiny when religious conduct is substantially burdened in cases involving an activity that receives government financial assistance or cases involving commerce. In other words, wherever the federal government's dollars go, and wherever commerce exists, the RLPA would follow.

In 1999 the U.S. House of Representatives passed the Religious Liberty Protection Act and the Senate as of this writing has held hearings, but has not yet voted on the legislation as of this writing.

RELIGIOUS OATHS   A religious oath is calling upon God to witness the truth of a statement. Violating an oath (for example, by perjury in court) or even taking an oath is considered by many a violation of the honor due to God.

The federal government may not require anyone to take an oath based on a religious belief as a condition for receiving federal employment, because Article VI of the Constitution prohibits such a requirement. State and local governments are prohibited from requiring such oaths by the Free Exercise Clause. [*Torcaso v. Watkins* (U.S. 1961)]

RELIGIOUS ORGANIZATION   The term *religious organization* is broader than the term *church*. Churches are undoubtedly religious organizations, but not all organizations whose central purpose is religious are churches. Conventions and associations of churches and the "integrated auxiliaries" of churches are given the same tax treatment as churches, but there are many groups that are closely associated with churches that do not qualify as churches under the Internal Revenue Code. Among these are religious orders, apostolic and missionary groups, religious broadcasting stations and production companies, religious publishing houses, Bible and tract societies, church-run schools, colleges, universities, and seminaries, hospitals, nursing homes, orphanages, homes for unwed mothers, soup kitchens and food pantries, charitable funds for the support of the poor and homeless, fraternal societies, and cemeteries. Organizations such as the Young Men's and Women's Christian Associations are considered charitable societies.

RELIGIOUS PLURALISM   Religious pluralism refers to the increasingly common experience of living in communities in which several faiths coexist. It also is used to describe one of the theological responses within Christianity to the issues raised by such an experience. Such responses are frequently classified in three ways: Exclusivism stresses the radical uniqueness of Christianity. Inclusivism was adopted by the Second Vatican Council and by Pope John Paul II. It gives primacy to Christianity, but also sees Christ's saving work as at least partially present in other traditions that have many spiritual values. Pluralism sees each of the great traditions as comparable in value and of probably equal significance.

RELIGIOUS PURPOSES   Many states offer tax exemptions or incentives to property or organizations that have "religious purposes." Thus it is often an issue whether a certain activity qualifies as sufficiently "religious" to claim these benefits.

Generally speaking, the words "educational, literary, scientific, religious or charitable purposes," as used in contexts such as a tax exemption statute are to be defined and understood in their broad constitutional sense. [*Indianapolis Elks Building Corp. v. State Board of Tax Commissioners* (Ind. App. Ct. 1969)]

Some theological inspiration or spiritual content does not automatically imbue an activity with "religious purpose," within the meaning of a statute exempting from zoning regulations the use of land or structure for religious purposes. [*Needham Pastoral Counseling Center, Inc. v. Board of Appeals of Needham* (Mass. 1990)]

Courts have recognized the following as religious purposes for the purpose of state tax exemption statutes: Bible camps [*Appeal of Mount Shepherd Methodist Camp* (N.C. App. Ct. 1995); *In re Worley* (N.C. App. Ct. 1989)]; and a cemetery association organized for burial of deceased Roman Catholics. [*O'Leary v. Social Security Board* (3d Cir. 1946)] However, courts have not recognized the following as "religious purposes" for the purpose of a state tax exemption statute: a parsonage [*Church of the Redeemer v. Axtell* (N.J. Super. 1879)]; furnishing residential facilities to aged persons regardless of their religion [*Presbyterian Homes v. Division of Tax Appeals* (N.J. 1970) and *Yakima First Baptist Homes Inc. v. Gray* (Wash. 1973)]

RELIGIOUS SOLICITATION, REGULATION OF   Although cases involving the regulation of religious solicitation have generally been decided under the Free Exercise or Free Speech Clauses of the First Amendment, in *Larson v. Valente* (U.S. 1986), the Supreme Court, intertwining establishment and free exercise principles, voided a provision in a state charitable solicitation law that required only those religious organizations that received less than half their total contributions from members or affiliated organizations to comply with the registration and reporting sections of the law. Applying strict scrutiny and

equal protection principles, the Court held that by distinguishing between older, well-established churches that had strong membership and financial support and newer bodies lacking a contributing constituency or that may favor public solicitation over general reliance on financial support from the members, the statute granted denominational preference to the former organizations that was forbidden by the Establishment Clause.

RELIGIOUS SYMBOLS AND LANGUAGE   Given
America's religious heritage, it would be unusual not to anticipate the occasional government use of religious symbols and language in public areas. Thus, calling for God's protection and deliverance has been a part of American public life from the Declaration of Independence to the present. Indeed, since 1864 all coins of the United States have had imprinted on them the phrase "In God We Trust," and since 1955 all currency has carried this national motto. On the rare occasions when the federal courts have confronted the use of use of religious language and images on currency and stamps they have consistently upheld their use. [*Lynch v. Donnelly* (U.S. 1984); *Abington v. Schempp* (U.S. 1963)(Brennan, J., concurring); *Aronow v. United States* (9th Cir. 1970); *Snyder v. Murray City Corp.* (10th Cir. 1996)]

In the currency cases, the courts concluded that there is no religious coercion inherent in the symbols and that the language is purely ceremonial and not a religious exercise.

A somewhat more difficult problem arises when religious monuments and symbols are displayed or used on public property. A common problem has been the placing of Christian crosses on public property or the use of a nativity scene as a part of a Christmas display on public property. In the situations in which courts have upheld Christian crosses on public property, the courts have concluded either that the commercial setting of the display negated any religious message of the cross [*Meyer v. Oklahoma City* (U.S. 1972)] or that the cross was used in conjunction with an otherwise valid secular purpose, such as a war memorial [*Eugene Sand and Gravel v. City of Eugene* (U.S. 1976)]. When courts concluded that such crosses were intended as a religious message, they have disallowed their use. [*Fox v. City of Los Angeles* (U.S. 1978); *ACLU v. Rabun County Chamber of Commerce* (U.S. 1981)]

RELIGIOUS SYMBOLS IN PUBLIC PLACES   *See*
HOLIDAY DISPLAYS

RELIGIOUS TESTS   The original text of the U.S. Constitution prohibits religious tests as a prerequisite to holding public office. Article VI, Clause 3 states that "[n]o religious Test shall ever be required as a Qualification to any Office or public Trust under the United States." A similar provision is written into the constitutions of most states.

Article VI's prohibition of religious tests was the only religiously related issue dealt with when the U.S. Constitution was drafted by the Constitutional Convention in 1787. North Carolina and Connecticut voted against the ban, and the Maryland delegation was divided. At least one source of Maryland's indecision was the viewpoint of Luther Martin, the most powerful and outspoken critic of the Constitution in that state. In his antifederal treatise, *Genuine Information,* which he brought to the Maryland legislature on 29 November 1787, Martin attacked Article VI, sarcastically relating that some delegates were "so unfashionable" as to think an oath undesirable. Martin believed that "in a Christian country, it would be at least decent to hold out some distinction between the professors of Christianity and downright infidelity or paganism." Dr. Benjamin Rush, the Philadelphia physician and advocate of higher education, stated the objection more broadly in a letter to John Adams. "Many pious people wish the name of the Supreme Being had been introduced somewhere in the new Constitution. Perhaps an acknowledgment may be made of His goodness or of His providence in the proposed Amendments."

That the proffered Constitution was a "pagan" document, or at least insufficiently infused with Christian orthodoxy, was a theme resounding throughout the new nation and accounted for perhaps half of all the popular criticism of the new government's relationship with religion.

Although it is true that Article IV, Clause 3 prohibits religious qualifications for holding public office, this provision merely ensures that positions of authority will be open to all persons, and therefore to the influences of every faith—and of none. Public servants are expected to bring their personal judgments to bear, including judgments as to what is right, or moral, or appropriate. Of course, the views of religious individuals inevitably reflect their religious beliefs. It would be unreasonable to suppose that a public official can check the religious components of his or her convictions at the door before entering government service.

In the United States, the Test Clause is the nation's oldest employment antidiscrimination law. The caselaw on the Test Clause is sparse. [See, for example, *Girouard v. United States* (U.S. 1946)(relying in part on Test Clause as guide for construing obligation of applicant for naturalization to swear to "defend" United States); *Ex parte Garland* (U.S. 1866)(distinguishing test oath from other forms of oath taking)]

In fact, the two Supreme Court cases to which the Test Clause would most clearly apply are not within its scope, because they involved state statutes. [See, *McDaniel v. Paty* (U.S. 1978), *rev'g Paty v. McDaniel* (Tenn. 1977)(holding unconstitutional Tennessee constitutional provision excluding ministers from state legislature); *Torcaso v. Watkins* (U.S. 1961)(holding unconstitutional state constitutional provision that prohibited religious tests for public office, "other than a declaration of belief in the existence of God" as applied to state notary public)] As a result, it is difficult to state definitively whether the Test Clause forms a part of the religious liberty guarantees "incorporated" by the Fourteenth Amendment such that it applies to the states, or whether it stands as a limit on federal power only. In *Torcaso* Justice Hugo Black's opinion expressly stated that the Court "[found] it unnecessary to consider [the] contention that this provision applies to state as well as federal offices."

Given the large numbers of persons employed at the federal, state, and local levels of government, and the large number of projects funded in whole or in part by government money, the Test Clause is an underappreciated tool for those who believe they have been discriminated against because of religion.

An inquiry into a regulation's constitutionality under the Test Clause has several parts. First it must be determined whether a condition to taking office is, in fact, a "religious test." Second, an inquiry will be made as to whether the "test" is required as a condition of receiving a benefit such as the holding of office. Finally, a court will decide whether the position for which such a test is required is an "office or public trust under the United States" or under the laws of any state. Religious tests required for private employment may be allowed. However, private employers must still comply with Title VII of the Civil Rights Act of 1964.

RELIGIOUSLY AFFILIATED GRADE SCHOOLS OR HIGH SCHOOLS, AID TO   *See* GOVERNMENT AID TO RELIGIOUS INSTITUTIONS

RELIGIOUSLY AFFILIATED PRIMARY AND SECONDARY SCHOOLS OR HIGH SCHOOLS, GOVERNMENT AID TO   *See* GOVERNMENT AID TO RELIGIOUS INSTITUTIONS

REYNOLDS V. UNITED STATES (U.S. 1878)   This case was the Supreme Court's first direct pronouncement on the First Amendment's protection for the free exercise of religion. The

Court held that polygamy was a crime, not a religious practice. *Reynolds* brought before the Court a Mormon's challenge to the constitutionality of the federal law prohibiting plural marriages in Utah territory.

Observing that bigamy and polygamy were considered punishable offenses in every state, the Court found it "impossible to believe that the constitutional guaranty of religious freedom was intended to prohibit legislation in respect to this most important feature of social life."

S

SCHOOL CHOICE The term *school choice* covers many programs and plans designed to allow children and their families a choice in where they will attend school. Although the terms *school vouchers* and *school choice* are often used interchangeably, they are not synonymous terms. Public school choice, for examples, involves changes that exclusively occur within the existing structure of public education. Magnet schools, charter schools, and open enrollment are all such reforms. Vouchers involve providing parents with a certificate that they can use in place of money to pay for their children's tuition at the private school of their choice. Vouchers are founded on the theory that quality will improve if competition is introduced into the education system. Opinion polls indicate about 70 percent of those queried express support for some form of greater school choice for students.

Viewed from the perspective of those who consume educational services (parents, children, and taxpayers), American education is not a matter of "choice"; it is compulsory. Every state requires children to attend school and prosecutes parents who refuse or neglect to send their children to school. As a result, the first choice is not whether to educate the children (which is already required), but how.

Two choices are widely available: schools operated by the government and funded by tax dollars, or schools operated, either in whole or in part, by the private sector (including home schooling). A third alternative, cross-registration or "shared time," is not widely available. One of the most popular, yet controversial for education is the school choice voucher. One of the school choice alternatives is called controlled choice, which includes interdistrict, intersectional, or magnet school choice. In controlled choice, the student or parent is restricted in choosing the other public schools either within or outside their district. Alternatively, open enrollment choices, such as school vouchers, allow parents to choose with virtually no restrictions by area or whether the school is public or private.

The most controversial school choice plans include the option of selecting a private school, especially one that teaches religion as a part of its curriculum, with support from taxpayer funding. In some cases, funded choice at private schools is regarded as an attack on the very concept of a "common school." In this context, the sparse caselaw reflects long-standing divisions on the role of the state in education, the proper relationship of religion to education, and the need to avoid the close relationship between church and state, especially those that involve the transfer of money from one to the other.

Special problems would arise if a private school decides to exclude a protected class under equal protection analysis, such as based on race or religion. State constitutional law is implicated when religious schools are permitted to participate. Opponents claim their inclusion contravenes the Establishment Clause of the First Amendment. Supporters of school choice argue that this argument is merely an attempt to dilute the efficacy of school choice proposals. For example, the argument to exclude religious schools from a voucher plan is really an effort to diminish the supply of competing institutions, thus making school choice exist only in theory and not in practice.

School choice proponents argue that these programs can create equity in education because they are a more efficient way to run the school system. Opponents of school choice argue that such a policy could at the minimum lead to the impoverishment of the public schools and the establishment of a two-tiered educational system. They fear that school choice politics would increase education inequality and school segregation by class and race.

SCHOOL PRAYER   Since the U.S. Supreme Court decision in *Engel v. Vitale* (U.S. 1962), *school prayer* has been a phrase almost exclusively used to describe various forms of prescribed prayer in public schools. Few constitutional issues have generated as much public controversy, and as much confusion, as this one.

The use of officially authorized prayers or Bible readings for motivational purposes in the public schools is considered a direct violation of the Establishment Clause of the First Amendment. Even though a practice may not be coercive, active support of a particular belief raises the fear of eventual establishment of state-approved religious views.

The Supreme Court has twice held the official reading of prayers in the public schools to violate the Establishment Clause.

The first instance came in *Engel v. Vitale* (U.S. 1962). That case concerned an official prayer that had been composed by state-appointed officials of the New York State Board of Regents. The New York school districts required this prayer to be recited by students in unison in every classroom at the beginning of each school day. The Supreme Court found that the practice violated the Establishment Clause, which had been made applicable to the states through the Fourteenth Amendment. The Court's opinion by Justice Hugo L. Black held that the practice violated the Constitution even though the prayer was denominationally neutral and pupils who wished to do so could remain silent or be excused from the room while it was being recited.

One year later the Courts applied the principle of *Engel* to religious readings selected, but not written, by public officials. Statutes in Pennsylvania and Maryland required every public school to begin each day with the reading of verses from the Bible and group recital of the Lord's Prayer. Students were permitted to be excused from participation upon the written request of a parent or guardian. In *Abington School District v. Schempp* (U.S. 1963), the Court held these programs also violated the Establishment Clause, which the Court interpreted to preclude actions by state or federal governments that had the purpose or primary effect of either advancing or inhibiting religion. The Court noted that, although the First Amendment permits the study of the Bible or religion as part of a school's program for education, it does not permit government to organize devotional religious exercises. The fact that the particular devotionals had been selected by government officials, rather than composed by them as in *Engel*, was not a difference of constitutional importance.

The decisions in *Engel* and *Schempp* unleashed a substantial public protest, and repeated, unsuccessful efforts were made in the 1960s to overturn the rulings by amending the U.S. Constitution. The search for acceptable language for such an amendment dominated the debate in Congress. Some in Congress urged support for prayer in public schools, while others suggested adding restrictive adjectives such as "nonsectarian," "nondenominational," or "voluntary" to the calls for prayer. The intent appeared to be to make prayer as inoffensive as possible in order gain maximum support. Some leaders would have been satisfied with the term "meditation," rather than "prayer." All efforts to pass constitutional amendments failed, in large measure because of the strong opposition by the National Council of Churches, individual Protestant denominational leaders (including Presbyterian and Southern Baptist leaders), and various Jewish groups.

The Supreme Court's decisions meanwhile were misinterpreted by some to mean that even the utterance of a private prayer by an individual student while at school is unconstitutional. What the Establishment Clause actually prohibits is action by government officials that endorses or inhibits religion, and not religious activity initiated by students. Although *Engel* declared unconstitutional all forms of organized classroom prayer, the Court has never banned individual acts of devotion initiated by a student, so long as they are not disruptive of good order.

With the election of President Ronald Reagan in 1980, school prayer again became a major public issue and was made a part of the Republican Party's agenda, both in Congress and in court appointments. Throughout the 1980s several serious efforts were launched in the Senate to produce a constitutional amendment on school prayer. There was also a movement to authorize a moment of silence in public schools in several states.

In *Wallace v. Jaffree* (U.S. 1985), the U.S. Supreme Court invalidated an Alabama law providing for a moment of silence in the schools "for meditation or voluntary prayer," because the intent of the legislature in passing the law was found to be to support prayer. Although the Court struck down the particular law in *Jaffree*, a majority of the Court strongly suggested that some laws providing for a moment of silence would be constitutional. In this case Alabama had previously enacted a statute that authorized a one-minute period of silence for meditation. This law had passed review by lower courts. However, the new statute before the Supreme Court in *Jaffree* added the word "prayer" in its list of expressly approved activities during the moment of silence. Because students were allowed to pray under the earlier moment-of-silence statute, the new law's only additional purpose appeared to be "the State's endorsement and promotion of religion and a particular religious practice." This, the Court held, constituted impermissible endorsement of religion by the government. A majority of the justices indicated, however, that they would sustain moment-of-silence laws that did not expressly single out prayer as one of the officially preferred activities.

The Court explained:

When a statute creates an open, undesignated silent time, government itself has not undertaken action to favor or disfavor religion. The seemingly trivial addition of the words "for prayer" to a moment-of-silence law is unconstitutional precisely because it is unnecessary to the goal of creating an opportunity for students to choose to pray. If a simple moment-of-silence law crosses the line of constitutionality precisely . . . If a simple moment of silence is created at school, parents and religious leaders, may, if they wish, suggest to their children or parishioners that they use the moment of silence for prayer. Expressly providing in the state's code of laws that "prayer" is a designated activity unnecessarily takes the state itself into the improper business of official endorsement and promotion of a religious exercise.

Ideally, a simple moment of silence is functionally a one-minute "open forum" that each student can use as the student wishes. Implementing this in a truly neutral fashion is, however, difficult in practice. The facts of some lower court cases suggest that teachers and school officials in some districts have encouraged or coerced students to pray during the silent moment. Teachers may appropriately ask students to remain quiet during the moment of silence; if teachers suggest or insist that students pray or adopt a prayerful attitude, they have invoked the authority of the state for an impermissible end.

The Supreme Court has also used the concept of the open forum to permit students at school to engage in spoken group prayers as long as the religious activities are not encouraged, endorsed, or promoted by government or school officials. In *Widmar v. Vincent* (U.S. 1981) the Court held that a state university that allowed a diverse range of voluntary student activity groups to meet in university facilities was not required by the Establishment Clause to deny access to student-initiated religious clubs whose meetings on school property included prayer and other devotionals. Indeed, such clubs had a free speech right of equal access to the school's facilities on the same basis as volunteer student groups engaged in other speech activities.

President Reagan signed into law the Equal Access Act in 1984, which requires high schools receiving federal financial assistance to allow student religious groups to hold meetings before and after school hours, if other extracurricular groups are given similar rights. The Act applies only to meetings that are student initiated, voluntary, and carried out without sponsorship by the school or its employees (who may be present only as nonparticipants).

In *Board of Education v. Mergens* (U.S. 1990) the Supreme Court sustained the federal Equal Access Act that extended this principle to public secondary schools. The Act provides that when a public school creates a "limited open forum" by allowing student-initiated, noncurriculum groups to meet at the school, it may not deny access to the school for meetings of other student-initiated groups based on the "religious, political, philosophical, or other content of the speech at such meetings."

Even though many Americans remain unreconciled to the original school prayer and Bible-reading decisions in *Engel* and *Schempp*, and even though some recent decisions suggest that the Supreme Court is growing more tolerant of some governmental promotion of religion, it seems unlikely that the Court's original decisions will soon be overturned either by the Court or by constitutional amendment. The constitutional principle remains for now as it was when Justice Hugo Black wrote for the Court in *Engel*: "it is not part of the business of government to compose official prayers for any group of the American people to recite as part of a religious program carried on by the government."

In the final year of President George Bush's term the administration directed Solicitor General Kenneth Starr to defend a Providence, Rhode

Island, public school that had invited a rabbi to pray at a middle school graduation. Starr's approach was to admit at last that, while *Engel* and *Schempp* were properly decided, graduation ceremonies were distinguishable from other school programs because they did not involve compulsory attendance and were not held in the classroom. However, in a somewhat surprising turn of events, two new Republican appointees to the U.S. Supreme Court voted with the majority to declare the graduation prayer unconstitutional by a five-to-four vote in *Lee v. Weisman* (U.S. 1992).

By 1993 religious fundamentalists were leading a movement for what was described as "student-initiated prayer" at ceremonies such as graduation. As of 1997 the U.S. Supreme Court had still rendered no decision on that subject and circuit courts have been divided.

In the spring of 1996 two new constitutional amendments were introduced into Congress by Republican sponsors. One by Representative Ernest Istook (R-Okla) stated that "nothing in the Constitution shall prohibit student-sponsored prayer in public school." The other amendment, offered by Representative Henry Hyde (R-Ill) and Senator Orrin Hatch (R-Utah), abandoned the school-prayer issue and instead endorsed the agenda of the Christian Coalition to seek vouchers for religious schools. That amendment read in part that no law "shall deny benefits to or otherwise discriminate against any private person or group on account of religious expression, belief, or identity." The word "benefits" was intended to establish religious schools through state funding.

In 1998 the U.S. House of Representatives failed to approve by the required margin a controversial constitutional amendment, the Religious Freedom Amendment (H.J. Res. 78) strongly supported by Christian conservatives that would have allowed organized prayer in public schools. It was substantially the same amendment as that offered in 1996, with regard to school prayer. The vote was 61 votes short of the two-thirds vote necessary for passage of a constitutional amendment. The bill was not even considered by the U.S. Senate. Supporters of the bill argued that it was necessary to reverse three decades of U.S. Supreme Court decisions that they say weakened the nation's religious freedoms, including the outlawing of state-sponsored organized prayer in public school settings.

Opponents of the measure, including liberal religious organizations and civil libertarians, opposed the measure. They maintained that the amendment would breach the constitutional wall separating church and state and inevitably lead to the imposition of majority religious views on members of religious minorities. They also believe the amendment was unnecessary because students already may pray individually in school, read religious texts during study hall or other free-time periods, and assemble in groups for religious activities before or after regular school hours while in public school buildings.

Advocating organized school prayer remains one of the leading causes of religious conservatives in the late twentieth century, and opposing these activities remains a major concern of liberal organizations such as People For the American Way Foundation and the American Civil Liberties Union.

SCHOOLS   *See* SCHOOL PRAYER

SCOPES TRIAL

Also called the *Monkey Trial*, this refers to the well-publicized 1925 trial in Dayton, Tennessee, of John Scopes, a high school biology teacher, who was accused of violating a state statute prohibiting the teaching in public schools of Darwin's theories of the biological evolution of human beings. The case became a symbol of fundamentalist opposition to the teaching of evolution.

Soon after Charles Darwin published *On the Origin of Species* in 1859, American Protestants began to address the theory of biological evolution and its implications for the Christian faith. Although some theological conservatives, such as Charles Hodge, believed that evolution was utterly incompatible with the biblical record and the doctrine of creation, others such as Benjamin Warfield, came to accept some form of evolutionary development. Theological liberals, such as Lyman Abbott and Henry Ward Beecher, enthusiastically embraced evolution as God's way of working in the world.

Following World War I many theological conservatives, most notably Presbyterian layman and three-time presidential candidate William Jennings Bryan, became convinced that a Darwinist "might-makes-right" philosophy provided the basis for Germany's military aggression and threatened to undermine the foundation of American civilization. Fundamentalists, led by Bryan, urged states to enact laws forbidding the teaching of human evolution in public schools.

These efforts led Tennessee to pass its antievolution law. John Scopes, encouraged by the American Civil Liberties Union (ACLU), decided to test the recently passed legislation. He deliberately taught the evolution theory and was charged with violating the statute. Clarence Darrow, a renowned agnostic lawyer, represented Scopes. William Jennings Bryan represented the state, defending the antievolution law by insisting that "it is better to trust in the Rock of Ages than to know the age of rocks; it is better for one to know that he is close to the Heavenly Father than to know how far the stars in the heavens are apart." He conceded, however, that the "day" of creation might mean a million years. Darrow did not spare the elderly Bryan on cross-examination, telling him, "I am examining you on your fool ideas that no intelligent Christian on earth believes."

The trial was quickly transformed into a major media event, with over 100 reporters descending on the town to wire news of the trial across the country. The case allowed journalists like H. L. Mencken to ridicule Bryan (who died immediately after the trial) and fundamentalists generally.

Because Scopes made no pretense of denying his "guilt," no one was surprised when the court ruled against him. The ruling, however, was overturned on a technicality. The antievolution law remained on the books for 42 more years.

The trial left a lasting impression that fundamentalism was a rural, anti-intellectual movement that would fade away with the emergence of an educated, urban society. In the years immediately following the trial, antievolution efforts tended to be confined mostly to the South. By the 1960s, however, the rise of "creation science" revived the debate over evolution. Creation science is the academic theory based on the principle that all forms of life were created literally in the manner described of in the biblical Genesis creation accounts.

In 1987 the U.S. Supreme Court struck down a Louisiana law that required the teaching of "creationism" in public schools if the theory of evolution was also taught. [*Edwards v. Aguillard* (U.S. 1987)] The Court found that the requirement to teach "creationism" was a thinly disguised state attempt to establish a religious doctrine at the expense of genuine science.

SEPARATION OF CHURCH AND STATE   *See* "WALL OF SEPARATION" METAPHOR

SEPARATIONIST
Those who interpret the separation of church and state doctrine of the Establishment Clause as strongly prohibiting any aid to religion are known as separationists. Separationists tend to assume that religion is a dangerous source of social division and factionalism, and that certain behavioral consequences of religious belief (such as self-righteousness, intolerance, and anti-intellectualism) are undesirable in democratic politics. Absolute separationists believe that the realm of religion should be totally distinct from that of the state, prohibiting any public funding for religion.

Absolute separationists believe that a total separation of church and state is not only a constitutional requirement, but also a practical necessity. They believe that churches seeking government money (and money they believe is the moving force for breaching the wall of separation) are surrendering something more valuable: their freedom. Absolute separationists believe that government financial support of religious schools would involve partisan politics, political contributions, and church versus government antagonisms. This view is criticized on the basis that it was almost certainly not intended by the framers of the Constitution and might violate the Free Exercise Clause of the First Amendment.

Generic separationists recognize that religiously motivated citizens may be involved in political affairs, but believe that both the state and the church will be stronger if they coexist separately. This view compels a detachment from religion that neither advances nor harms religion and prohibits laws that aid or inhibit religion; this has been the official position of the U.S. Supreme Court since *Everson v. Board of Education* (U.S. 1947). The most enduring legacy of *Everson* was its lavish use of strict separationist rhetoric in both the majority and minority opinions. The justices relied on history, especially Thomas Jefferson's and James Madison's role in the dramatic disestablishment struggle in postrevolutionary Virginia, to support a separationist interpretation of the First Amendment.

Since *Everson*, the course of Establishment Clause jurisprudence has been directly affected by the efforts of Protestants, Catholics, Jews, and others to mark the boundary between permissible and impermissible governmental actions affecting religion.The conflict has largely been defined as one between separationists and so-called accommodationists. Although this is not universally true, Protestants and Jewish organizations involved in issues of the relation of religion and government have historically favored a separationist approach, and Catholic organizations have favored an accommodationist approach.

Organizations favoring a separationist approach include: Americans United for the Separation of Church and State, the National Council of Churches, and the American Jewish Congress. Organizations favoring an accommodationist approach include the United States Catholic Conference and the Catholic League for Religious and Civil Rights.

Despite the separation of church and state enshrined in the U.S. Constitution, remnants of the old state-church system remain in the form of the exemption from most taxation for religious organizations, the exemption for clergy from military service, and the remnants of financial support still allowed to religious schools and educational systems. These modest privileges, however, have been questioned and even attacked by certain groups in American society.

SHARED-TIME PROGRAMS Shared-time programs either provide secular education at private schools by sending teachers and other materials to the children, or by physically moving the children between public and private school premises, as in *Lanner v. Wimmer*.

Cross-registration programs, in which a student can be registered in both a public and private school, have been controversial for several reasons. First, they increase the costs incurred by the public schools, and add another issue to debates over the adequacy of public school budgets. Second, they are often considered an unwarranted attempt to "pick and choose" from a "menu" of public educational services, and are an implicit rejection of the state's authority in educational matters. And finally, there is the issue of government support for religious education. In those states in which entitlement to education at public expense is a right, it has been argued that exclusionary policies are an unconstitutional imposition on the exercise of one's constitutionally protected right to opt out of the public school system. In states where the constitution specifically forbids state support of schools that teach "sectarian doctrine," any assistance that "frees up" resources for the teaching of religion is perceived as support of such a school's religious mission.

The Supreme Court in *Grand Rapids School District v. Ball* (U.S. 1985) determined that shared-time programs violated the Establishment Clause. *Ball*, however, was overruled by *Agostini v. Felton* (U.S. 1997). In the majority opinion, Justice O'Connor wrote that, "[w]e no longer presume that public employees will inculcate religion simply because they happen to be in a sectarian environment." In *Agostini*, the Court ruled five to four that the Establishment Clause did not prohibit public school teachers from entering parochial schools to provide remedial education and guidance counseling to poor children who were struggling academically.

Justice Souter, in his dissenting opinion, criticized the holding, asserting that it would permit direct governmental funding of religious schools. Justices John Paul Stevens and Ruth Bader Ginsburg joined Souter's dissent. Justice Stephen G. Breyer joined in most of Souter's dissent.

▥ *SHERBERT V. VERNER* (U.S. 1963) In this case a member of the Seventh-Day Adventist Church was discharged by her employer because she would not work on Saturday, the Sabbath day of her faith. She was unable to obtain other employment, also because she would not work on Saturday, and her claim for state unemployment compensation benefits was denied under a provision that made claimants ineligible if they failed to accept suitable work when offered. The South Carolina Supreme Court upheld the denial of unemployment benefits to the claimant. An appeal reached the United States Supreme Court.

The Court held that the South Carolina unemployment compensation statute denied the claimant's right to the free exercise of her religion in violation of the First Amendment, as applied to the states by the Fourteenth Amendment.

The Court found no "compelling state interest" in enforcing the eligibility provisions of the South Carolina statute that would justify the substantial infringement of the claimant's right to religious freedom under the First Amendment. Moreover, allowing the claimant's eligibility did not foster an impermissible "establishment" of the Seventh-Day Adventist religion in South Carolina in violation of the First Amendment.

The Supreme Court held that the state unemployment benefits could not be denied to a Seventh-Day Adventist because she refused to work on Saturday due to her religious beliefs. Justice Brennan, writing for a seven-member majority, stated that for the denial of benefits to withstand scrutiny under the Free Exercise Clause, "it must be either because her disqualification as a beneficiary represents no infringement by the state of her constitutional right of free exercise, or because any incidental burden on the free exercise of appellant's religion may be justified by a compelling state interest in the regulation." Thus the majority endorsed a two-part balancing test of constitutionality: First, the plaintiff had to show a substantial burden on the exercise of her religion from the law under review. Second, such a burden would be valid only it was necessary to further a "compelling state interest" that outweighed the degree of impairment it imposed on the plaintiff's free exercise rights. This test implied that the degree of burden on religious activity must be balanced against the importance of the state interest and the degree to which it would be impaired by an accommodation for the religious practice. Relevant to such an inquiry is the importance of the state's interest and the degree to which there are alternative means to achieve it that do not burden religious practices.

In *Sherbert*, the majority found that the denial of unemployment benefits was invalid under this two-part test. First, there was a significant coercive effect on the practice of religion as the Sabbatarian was forced to make a choice between receiving state benefits or following her beliefs. Second, the state failed to prove a "compelling or overriding interest in the regulation," claiming only that this restriction avoided fraudulent claims. The state, however, did not raise this argument.

Sherbert is the most significant case for enunciating the compelling state interest test. The Supreme Court in that case held that government could burden a fundamental right like the free exercise of religion only if it was protecting a compelling interest by the least intrusive means possible, and found the state's interest insufficient to justify the infringement. *Sherbert* was controlling precedent until it was abandoned in *Employment Division v. Smith* (U.S. 1990). *Smith* reaffirmed the belief-action doctrine of *Reynolds v. United States* (U.S. 1879). That doctrine allows the government to require compliance with laws of general applicability regardless of their impact on religious conduct. However, the right to religious belief, as distinct from conduct, may not be infringed.

STANDING TO SUE   Standing to sue means that a party has a sufficient personal stake in an otherwise justiciable controversy to obtain judicial resolution of that controversy. Generally, a person must show that he or she was directly injured, or would be injured, by the conduct complained of in the lawsuit. In the context of constitutional challenges to laws that affect religious practices, issues involving standing have most often arisen in cases in which public funding has been extended to private sectarian schools.

In *Flast v. Cohen* (U.S. 1968), for example, the Supreme Court faced a challenge by federal taxpayers to the Elementary and Secondary Education Act of 1965, which would have permitted federal financing of textbooks, and the teaching of reading, arithmetic, and other subjects in both public and private schools. Holding that the taxpayers had standing, the Court announced a two-part test to determine whether a "logical nexus" existed between the plaintiff's status (as a taxpayer) and the claim to be adjudicated (support for students at religiously affiliated schools): First, the plaintiff must establish a logical link between the status as a taxpayer and the type of legislative enactment attacked, and second, the taxpayer must establish a nexus between that status and the precise nature of the constitutional infringement alleged.

The Court held that the challenge in *Flast*, and by implication all challenges to direct expenditures by federal or state authorities for religiously affiliated schools, met the nexus requirement. The effect has been to permit, since the mid-1960s, a wide range of federal cases challenging state and federal funding designed to defray part of the costs associated with religiously affiliated education.

Significantly, however, the Court has consistently refused to find standing under the *Flast* rationale in controversies other than those challenging government spending powers under the Establishment Clause. For example, the Court dismissed for lack of standing a case challenging a mandated moment of silence in public schools. [*Karcher v. May* (U.S. 1987)] The Supreme Court avoided ruling on whether students in a student-initiated non-denominational prayer club had a constitutional right to meet in a public school. The Court also dismissed for lack of standing a case involving equal access to high school facilities. [*Bender v. Williamsport Area School District* (U.S. 1986)] Similarly, it dismissed for a lack of standing a case challenging the government's turning over property to a parochial college. The Court ruled that standing requires injury, causation, and repressibility. [*Valley Forge Christian College v. Americans United for Separation of Church and State* (U.S. 1982)]

In *Valley Forge*, the Court found that the taxpayers had not met their burden to show that they had standing to sue, even though the Establishment Clause was alleged to control the outcome. The issue involved the transfer of surplus federal property. Holding that the plaintiffs had not satisfied the first prong of the *Flast* nexus requirement, the Court found it significant that the challenge was to the transfer by the secretary of the Department of Health, Education, and Welfare, rather than to the substance of the Congressional enactment on which it rested.

STONE V. GRAHAM (U.S. 1980)

In this case the Supreme Court considered a Kentucky statute that required the public schools to post the Ten Commandments in each classroom. The state claimed that the statute had a secular purpose, which was the highlighting of the Decalogue's role in the formation of Western civilization. However, the Supreme Court ruled that an "avowed" secular purpose is not sufficient to avoid conflict with the First Amendment and that "no legislative recitation of a supposed secular purpose can blind [the Court] to the plainly religious nature of the Ten Commandments." Therefore, the Court held that the Kentucky statute violated the first part of the test the Court announced in *Lemon v. Kurtzman* (U.S. 1971), which invalidated any law that did not have a secular purpose as a violation of the Establishment Clause of the Constitution.

The *Stone* case established that the U.S. Supreme Court is not bound to accept without scrutiny a legislature's routine assurances that a law is not religiously motivated. The Court, instead, is free to probe deeper into relevant evidence regarding a legislatures intent in passing the law.

SUICIDE

Suicide is the taking of one's own life. Moral questions associated with suicide go back to the earliest traditions of Western civilization. Pythagoras, Plato, and Aristotle held suicide to be a crime against the community, and Plato even argued that it was tantamount to a crime against God. In the classical world of Greece and Rome, suicide was often idealized as a noble form of death, but from the second century onwards Christian teaching has condemned it. Judaism condemns any active and deliberate hastening of death as the equivalent of murder and suicide is regarded as worse than murder in some respects, inasmuch as there can be no atonement by repentance for killing oneself. Saints Cyprian, Ambrose, Irenaeus, and Athanasius all contributed to the Christian doctrine on the subject, but it was St. Augustine who succinctly formulated the Christian position and named the three grounds on which suicide is renounced: (1) it violates the commandment "Thou shalt not kill"; (2) it precludes any opportunity for repentance; and (3) it is a cowardly act. St. Thomas Aquinas articulated the Christian thought on the subject in the thirteenth century, very similar to the Jewish reason for proscribing suicide: "Suicide is the most fatal of sins, because it cannot be repented of." Richard Hooker and Jeremy Taylor added the condition that no one can claim a right to death because human life belongs to God. All of the Christian churches oppose suicide.

Islam, like Judaism and Christianity, prohibits suicide, while glorifying those who die as martyrs for the faith. Hinduism affirms that suicide must be a thoughtful act—as in the resolve of the person to end the suffering of old age—or that it must be a religiously motivated act. Both Buddhism and Confucianism legislate against suicide, however, there are notable exceptions, as in the case of religiously motivated suicide. Under certain extraordinary circumstances, Buddhists view religiously motivated suicide as an act of sacrifice and worship.

Currently, the religious controversy mostly closely aligned with this topic focus on physician-assisted suicide, which some have argued is appropriate in the case of medical futility. The Hippocratic pledge, however, requires physicians to swear that "I will give no deadly drug to any, though it be asked of me, nor will I counsel such." Further among the ancient moral traditions in Western medicine is the maxim that requires physicians to preserve (some versions say prolong) life and to relieve pain (some versions include "suffering"). Today, these duties sometimes appear not as complementary but as antagonistic—sometimes life can be preserved only with great personal distress, or intractable pain can be relieved only at the expense of life itself.

With the advent of "living wills," "durable power of attorney for health care decisions," and other procedures intended to address end-of-life issues, several churches have adopted position papers. Some of these speak generally of "death with dignity" and individual prerogative. The United Methodist Church asserts the right of every person to die in dignity; the United Church of Christ affirms additionally the right of individuals to not have their lives unnecessarily prolonged; and the Presbyterian Church U.S.A concurs, adding "it is best to safeguard autonomy in medical decision making by whatever means." Other churches, like the Roman Catholic Church, the Episcopal Church, the Evangelical Lutherans in America, and the Assemblies of God, articulate a clear distinction between actions that deny extraordinary measures to prolong life and actions that directly cause death. While there is no duty to continue the former in treatment that is nonbeneficial, "it is morally wrong and unacceptable to take a human life in order to relieve the suffering caused by illness." Still others, like the Presbyterian Church in America and the Lutheran Church Missouri Synod address only the matter of physician-assisted suicide and condemn it as an "affront to the Lord who gives life," which also "opens the door for future abuse."

Under common law, suicide was a felony that was punishable by forfeiture of all the goods and chattels of the offender. Under modern American law, suicide is no longer a crime. Some states, however, classify attempted suicide as a criminal act, but prosecutions are rare, especially when the offender is terminally ill. Instead, some jurisdictions require a person who attempts suicide to undergo temporary hospitalization and psychological observation.

More problematic is the situation in which someone helps another to commit suicide. Aiding or abetting a suicide or attempted suicide is a crime in all states, but prosecutions are rare. Since the 1980s, the question of whether physician-assisted suicide should be permitted for persons with terminal illnesses has been the subject of much debate and continues to be a very controversial subject.

The debate over physician-assisted suicide concerns persons with debilitating and painful terminal illnesses. Under current laws a doctor who assists a person's suicide could be charged with aiding and abetting suicide. Opponents of decriminalizing assisted suicide argue that decriminalization would lead to a "slippery slope" that would eventually result in doctors being allowed to assist persons who are not terminally ill to commit suicide.

SUNDAY CLOSING LAWS

Commonly, Sunday closing laws require commercial activity to cease in observance of the Christian Sabbath as a day of rest. These laws are often called blue laws, a term of uncertain origin in the United States. It may have been derived from a list of Sabbath regulations that were published in 1781 in New Haven, Connecticut, and printed on blue paper. Sunday observance acts and sumptuary regulations (rules made for the purpose of restraining luxury or extravagance, which were enacted on religious grounds) were transplanted from or modeled on seventeenth-century English legislation. They were most common and most strict in Puritan communities, and usually forbade work or sport on Sundays.

In the mid-nineteenth century the maxim that Christianity was a part of the common law was cited by several state courts in opinions upholding the constitutionality of Sunday closing laws. In South Carolina, for instance, when a Jewish merchant challenged the constitutionality of his prosecution for selling clothing on Sunday, the court spent the first half of its opinion explaining that Christianity was part of the common law. When the issue arose in Arkansas and New York, the opinions of the courts read similarly. [*Charleston City Council v. Benjamin* (S.C. 1846); *Shover v. State* (Ark. 1850); and *Lindenmuller v. People* (N.Y. 1861)]

In nearly every case in which the issue came up, courts affirmed the constitutionality of Sunday closing laws. These laws were not always upheld on the grounds that Christianity was the common law of the jurisdiction in question. The cases concerning the constitutionality of the Sunday closing laws instead generally rested on determinations that these laws were enacted to enforce a day of rest to protect the public health, rather than for religious purposes. Thus, in South Carolina, for example, where the state supreme court discussed the maxim at great length, the case came down to the court's rhetorical question: "What has religion to do with a . . . regulation for Sunday? It is, in a political and social point of view, a mere day of rest."

The Supreme Court has ruled that laws requiring merchants to be closed on Sundays do not violate the Establishment Clause of the First Amendment. [*McGowan v. Maryland* (U.S. 1961)] The Court reasoned that as these statutes are administered today, they have a secular purpose and effect: providing a uniform day of rest for all citizens. In *McGowan*, the Court acknowledged that historically the laws had a religious motivation and were designed to effectuate concepts of Christian theology. However, "[i]n light of the evolution of our Sunday Closing Laws through the centuries, and of their more or less recent emphasis upon secular considerations, it is not difficult to discern that as presently written and administered, most of them, at least are of a secular rather than of a religious character, and that presently they bear no relationship to establishment of religion." That is, the Court determined that more recent history reveals a secular state interest in the promotion of the health, safety, recreation, and general well-being of its citizens, which may be effectuated by many types of law, including the requirement of a day of rest. "[T]he fact that this day is Sunday, a day of particular significance for the dominant Christian sects, does not bar the State from achieving its secular goals. To say that the States cannot prescribe Sunday as a day of rest for these purposes solely because centuries ago such laws had their genesis in religion would give a constitutional interpretation of hostility to the public welfare rather than one of mere separation of church and State." In other words, the choice of Sunday as the day of rest, while originally religious, now reflects simple legislative inertia or recognition that Sunday was a traditional day for the choice.

In *Estate of Thornton v. Caldo, Inc.* (U.S. 1985), the Supreme Court ruled that a state law affording employees an absolute unqualified right not to work on the Sabbath of their choice "has a primary effect that impermissibly advances a particular religious practice" in violation of the Establishment Clause. The law in *Thornton* did not relieve the Sabbatarian from any government-imposed obligation. Instead "[t]he employer and others must adjust their affairs to the command of the State whenever the statute is invoked by an employee."

T

TAX EXEMPTION The Internal Revenue Code treats religious activity as an exempt function under §§ 170, 501(c)(3), and 6033, and recognizes a wide range of religious organizations as exempt from taxes. It also draws a rather clear line between churches and the many kinds of organizations that operate either as a part of, or in conjunction with them. Churches are not only exempt from taxes on the income generated by their exempt functions, they are also exempt from a number of critical filing requirements. Churches need not file tax returns and are presumed to be exempt. All other religious organizations must demonstrate their eligibility for exempt status by filing an application on a form prescribed by the Treasury Department, but "churches, their integrated auxiliaries, and conventions or associations of churches" are given a "mandatory exemption" from the filing requirements under § 508(a) and (b) of the Internal Revenue Code.

The IRS may deny tax exemptions claimed for religious donations when the sums were paid to the church in exchange for services (for example, classes) because this is a general rule that applies to all charities. [*Hernandez v. Commissioner of Internal Revenue* (U.S. 1989)]

The Internal Revenue Code does not define the term *church*. Congress has not defined it, and regulators have taken the position that a rigid regulatory definition of the term would undoubtedly be unconstitutional.

To the extent that a working definition exists, it has developed over time and must be extracted from many statutory, regulatory, and judicial sources. It is more fruitful to focus, not on the term *church* itself, but rather on the categories of entities that are eligible for designation as churches under the Internal Revenue Code.

In order to qualify as a church under the Code's working definition, an organization must be able to demonstrate that it has at least some of the following characteristics:

1. Self-identification as a church from its inception. The term "church" has been interpreted to also include temples, mosques, synagogues, and other places of worship

2. A distinct legal existence
3. A recognized creed and form of worship
4. Some form of distinct ecclesiastical government
5. A formal code of doctrine and discipline
6. A distinct religious history
7. A membership not associated with any other churches or denominations
8. Ordained ministers who minister to their congregations and who are selected after completing a prescribed course of study
9. Its own literature
10. Established places of worship
11. A distinct congregation
12. Regular religious services
13. Schools for the religious instruction of children
14. Schools that train its ministers. [Internal Revenue Manual § 321.3; Rev. Rul. 59- 129, 1959 C.B. 58]

Few organizations of any denomination are described by all these criteria, but the listing does serve two basic services. First, it provides the IRS with a list of "objective criteria" against which it can measure a claim that an organization is a church. Second, and perhaps more importantly for statutory and constitutional purposes, it provides IRS examiners with a high degree of flexibility. In fact, the IRS has stated that it will also consider "any other facts and circumstances that may bear upon the organization's claim to church status."

In *Murdock v. Pennsylvania* (U.S. 1943), a tax immunity claim was based on the First Amendment. The putative taxpayers in *Murdock* were Jehovah's Witnesses who evangelized door to door. During their visits, they preached, delivered religious literature, and sought donations to cover the costs of that literature from those who were willing to accept it. Local tax authorities believed that their activities involved the "sale" of literature, and the tax authorities accordingly sought to collect the appropriate license tax. An excise tax was imposed on all individuals who engaged in the privilege of "canvassing for or soliciting . . . orders for goods, paintings, pictures, wares, or merchandise of any kind, or . . . delivering such articles under orders so obtained or solicited."

Novel cases in this area are quite common. In *Institute in Basic v. Watersmeet T.P.* (Mich. Ct. App. 1997) the Michigan Court of Appeals ruled that a corporation qualified as a religious society exempt from real property taxes even though it had no members. The court concluded that an organization or association qualifies as a religious society for the purposes of a tax exemption for houses of public worship if its predominant purpose and practice include teaching religious truths and beliefs.

In *Droz v. Commissioner* (9th Cir. 1995) the court affirmed denial of a So-cial Security tax exemption to a self-employed party who did not belong to any religious organization on the basis that Congress desired to main-tain a fiscally sound Social Security System to ensure that people were cared for, constituting a "compelling interest" that complied with the First Amendment and the Religious Freedom Restoration Act. Permitting the Plaintiff to "opt out" of the Social Security system would interfere with a compelling government interest.

TEN COMMANDMENTS   The Ten Commandments, also known as the Decalogue, supposedly came to Moses while on Mount Sinai. They were the guiding influence on the lives of the ancient Israelites, and play a major role in the moral conduct of Christians and Jews today.

The U.S. Supreme Court has ruled that posting the Ten Command-ments on the walls of public school classrooms plainly serves a religious purpose and is unconstitutional as an establishment of religion. [*Stone v. Graham* (U.S. 1980)]

Several recent controversies involve judges posting the Ten Com-mandments in their courtrooms. These include Judge Roy Moore in his Etowah County, Alabama, courtroom in 1997. Judge Moore had placed an 18-inch-tall, hand-carved plaque of the Ten Commandments above his head. In 1995, the Alabama Freethought Association filed a complaint against Judge Moore in the U.S. District Court for the Northern District of Alabama. The complaint sought an order requiring Judge Moore to re-move the plaque of the Ten Commandments from his courtroom wall. In 1995, the federal district court dismissed the lawsuit, holding that the plaintiffs could show no harm caused by the display of the Ten Com-mandments. [*Alabama Freethought Association v. Moore* (N.D. Ala. 1995)] The Alabama Supreme Court dismissed the case brought in state court in order to remove the Decalogue from Judge Moore's court in 1998.

It is unclear what the law is in this area. The federal courts, in the past, had ordered the Cobb County, Georgia, County Commissioners to re-move the Ten Commandments from display in their meeting room in 1994. [*Harvey v. Cobb County* (N.D. Ga. 1993, aff'd, 11th Cir. 1994). Col-orado was, however, allowed to keep a monument to the Decalogue, which included a bald eagle and a flag, in a public park near the state capitol. [*Freedom From Religion Foundation v. Colorado* (Colo. 1995)]

Salt Lake City was allowed to retain a granite monolith installed on public grounds and inscribed with the Ten Commandments and symbols representing the Star of David and Jesus Christ. The court recognized both their secular and religious aspects. The court stated that the monolith was an acceptable passive presentation of America's legal foundation in view of the Ten Commandments' influence on Western law. [*Anderson v. Salt Lake City Corporation* (10th Cir. cert. den.)] It is interesting to note that the chambers of the Supreme Court itself are adorned with a mural of Moses descending Sinai with the Ten Commandments.

TEXAS MONTHLY INC. V. BULLOCK (U.S. 1989)

The decision in this case affected the 15 states whose statutes on sales and use taxes exempted religious publications. Texas exempted periodicals that consisted entirely of writings promulgating a religious faith from sales and use tax. Voting six to three, the Supreme Court held the Texas law unconstitutional. The Court held that, although religious schools or religious associations may be included in tax exemptions available to many secular and religious organizations, a tax exemption that is available only for religious organizations or religious activities violates the Establishment Clause.

A bare majority of the justices believed that the statute violated the Establishment Clause. Justice William J. Brennan, writing for the Court, concluded that the statute failed to serve the secular purpose of maintaining the separation of church and state, but rather, had the purpose of advancing the religious mission of a particular faith. The exemption for religious periodicals in effect subsidized their teachings at the expense of taxpayers who were not exempt from the tax.

Brennan went further, thereby losing the support of Justices Harry A. Blackmun and Sandra Day O'Connor, when he also declared the statute violative of the Free Exercise Clause. Blackmun and O'Connor preferred to rest exclusively on the Establishment Clause, believing that Brennan's free exercise argument subordinated religious liberty to the Establishment Clause. They said that Texas engaged in "preferential support for the communication of religious messages."

Justice Byron White believed that because the statute discriminated on the basis of the content of publication, it violated the Free Press Clause because Texas discriminated on the basis of the publication's content, that consisted "wholly of writings promulgating the teachings of the faith."

In dissent, Justices Antonin Scalia, William H. Rehnquist, and Anthony Kennedy protested that the Court had mangled its own precedents and diminished the Free Exercise Clause. Justice Scalia concluded that with regards to the tax exemptions, that the constitution sometimes permits accommodation despite the Establishment Clause, the Free Press Clause, and the Free Speech Clause of the Constitution.

▦ **TEXTBOOKS**   In the area of public aid to religiously established schools, the consensus has largely been that direct financial aid to a religious school is unconstitutional. On the other hand various types of aid may be extended to the students of religious schools without violating the Constitution.

Accordingly, the debate in the textbook area has tended to focus on the problem of whether the furnishing of textbooks is to be regarded as aid to the school or to the pupil. The decision could obviously turn to some degree on the manner in which such aid is extended, and on the particular constitutional provision under discussion, so that it is unlikely that any categorical answer will be found in the cases, which have always gone both ways. The issue has been before the U.S. Supreme Court in several cases.

In *Board of Education v. Allen* (U.S. 1968) the Supreme Court ruled that a New York statute that required local public school authorities to lend textbooks free of charge to all students in grades 7 through 12, including students attending private and parochial schools, did not violate constitutional provisions as to establishment and free exercise of religion.

In *Lemon v. Kurtzman* (U.S. 1971) the Court held that a Pennsylvania statute that provided, among other things, for state reimbursement to private elementary and secondary schools for the cost of textbooks in specified secular subjects was unconstitutional under the Establishment Clause of the First Amendment.

On the other hand, in *Meek v. Pittenger* (U.S. 1975) a state law providing for the loan of textbooks to children attending nonpublic schools did not have the primary effect of advancing religion and did not involve the state in an impermissible entanglement with religion. The textbooks involved were approved for use in public schools, religious books could not be obtained, the expenditures were for a clearly identifiable secular purpose, and the only contact between the nonpublic schools and state authorities was in processing individual student book requests. [See also *Wolman v. Walter* (U.S. 1977)]

▦ ***THOMAS V. REVIEW BOARD* (U.S. 1981)**   This case involving conscientious objection stands for the principle that an exemption from a law of general application may be granted if the individual objecting acts from an honest conviction that springs from his or her religion, even though coreligionists may disagree.

In *Thomas* the state of Indiana denied unemployment compensation to a Jehovah's Witness who voluntarily quit his job because of his religious belief. Thomas quit because he was required to work on armaments and he believed his religion forbade participation in such work. The state refused to pay him unemployment benefits and ruled that he quit because of personal philosophical convictions rather than religious belief. Even though many Jehovah's Witnesses did not share his views of working on armaments, the religious sincerity of his belief was accepted by the Supreme Court.

Chief Justice Burger, for the Court, acknowledged that Indiana had not compelled any violation of Thomas's religious conviction. But, as in *Sherbert v. Verner* (U.S. 1963), the indirect character of the burden only began the inquiry. Even though the law was religiously neutral on its face, it unduly burdened the free exercise of religion: "Where the State conditions receipt of an important benefit upon conduct proscribed by a religious faith, or whether it denies such a benefit, because of conduct mandated by religious belief, thereby putting substantial pressure on an adherent to modify his behavior and to violate his beliefs, a burden upon religion exists. While the compulsion may be indirect, the infringement upon free exercise is nonetheless substantial." Just as in *Sherbert*, the state had coerced Thomas in the free exercise of his religion.

Having found a substantial burden on free exercise, Chief Justice Burger considered whether an exemption accommodating religion was required: "The State may justify an inroad on religious liberty by showing that it is the least restrictive means of achieving some compelling state interest." But in this instance the state could not meet the compelling state interest standard. First, there was no evidence in the record indicating that granting an exemption based on religious belief would produce widespread unemployment. Second, there was no evidence that employers would engage in detailed inquiries into the religious beliefs of job applicants.

Finally, as in *Sherbert*, the *Thomas* Court denied that recognizing an exemption would foster a religious faith in violation of the Establishment Clause. Indeed, any incidental benefit to religion by granting an exemption to the general unemployment compensation law only reflected the tension between the two religion clauses. The state must seek neutrality, neither advancing nor inhibiting religion.

Only Justice Rehnquist in dissent in *Thomas* sounded a theme that later [in *Employment Division v. Smith* (U.S. 1990)] would become dominant: "Where, as here, a State has enacted a general statute the purpose and effect of which is to advance the State's secular goals, the Free Exercise Clause does not require the State to conform that statute to the dictates of religious conscience of any group."

THORNTON V. CALDOR (U.S. 1985) In this case the

U.S. Supreme Court held that a Connecticut law providing employees with an absolute right not to work on their chosen Sabbath violated the antiestablishment guarantee. Chief Justice Burger took direct aim at what he considered the "primary religious purpose and effect" of the statute. "The State thus commands that the Sabbath religious concerns automatically control over all secular interests at the workplace. The statute does not consider the inconvenience or interests of the employer or those of other employees who do not observe a Sabbath. The employer and others must adjust their affairs to the command of the State whenever the statute is invoked by an employee. An employee who seeks a day off from his work for compelling, although secular, reasons can be denied, but the Sabbath observer cannot. The machinery of the state may not be harnessed to facilitate the religious convictions of a favored group."

TILTON V. RICHARDSON (U.S. 1971) In this case

the Supreme Court rejected an Establishment Clause challenge to federal construction grants for college buildings to be used solely for secular activities. Construction aid was given on a one-time basis, was religiously neutral, and did not require continuing government surveillance of the use of public money. Therefore, the grants were deemed permissible.

TIME, PLACE, AND MANNER RESTRICTIONS

Rights protected by the First Amendment are not immune from governmental regulations. A government may impose reasonable restrictions on the time, place, and manner in which such rights are exercised. To be valid regulations of expression in public fora must be content neutral; that is, they must be applied even-handedly regardless of the content of the speech at issue. These type of regulations are usually aimed at concerns such as reducing noise and traffic congestion. Instead of regulating what is said, they merely regulate such matters as when, where, and how loud things are said. [*MacDonald v. Chicago Park District* (N.D. Ill. 1997)]

Zoning ordinances excluding churches from residential districts have been upheld as reasonable time, place, and manner regulations. [*Corporation of the Presiding Bishop v. City of Porterville* (Cal. 1949); *Allendale Congregation of Jehovah's Witnesses v. Grossman* (N.J. 1959)]

In *Heffron v. International Society for Krishna Consciousness* (U.S. 1981), the plaintiffs were members of a religious sect that commanded its members to distribute religious literature in public places. They had challenged a

Minnesota statute that required all exhibitors at the state fair to sell and distribute materials only from fixed locations on the fair grounds. Plaintiffs argued that the city's denial of permission to mingle with the crowds to proselytize violated their constitutional rights. The Supreme Court rejected their challenge, holding that the regulation constituted a valid time, place, and manner restriction on their free speech rights, because it was not content based, served a significant governmental interest, was the least restrictive means of serving the government interest, and provided adequate alternative outlets for the free practice of the plaintiffs' religion. The Court stated that the interest protected by this rule, crowd control, was substantial, and reasonable restrictions that furthered this interest would be permissible so long as the content of the regulated speech was not at issue. Thus, the Court upheld the state's rule not on the basis that the rule inflicted no First Amendment injury, but on the basis that the rule was a valid "time, place, and manner" restriction and the injury was therefore justified.

Time, place, an manner restrictions on free speech by religious sects are considered valid if the ordinance neither discriminates against a religious use, nor favors one religion over another, and if the government provides alternative sites for churches and establishes an important government interest in the exclusion. [*Jehovah's Witnesses v. Grosman* (N.J. 1959)]

A zoning ordinance that limits where churches may be located does not violate a church's free exercise rights if, first, it is not content based. That is, the ordinance must not discriminate against religious uses nor favor one religious group over another. On that basis, an ordinance that excluded churches while allowing similar or more intensive uses would be impermissible. Second, the government must provide adequate alternative sites for the church. Thus, under either a standard free exercise analysis or under the doctrine of time, place, and manner restrictions on protected speech, the exclusion of churches from residential zones does not automatically violate the First Amendment.

Other activities that are subject to time, place, and manner restrictions include displaying a nativity scene in the park. The placing of the nativity scene, or any other speech activities in the park, could be subject to time, place, or manner restrictions. Student distribution of religious literature may be subjected to time, place, and manner restrictions in the interests of order and forwarding the school's educational goals. [*Hedges v. Wauconda School District* (7th Cir. 1993)]

Restrictions on prisoner's First Amendment rights may represent reasonable time, place, and manner restrictions. [*Pell v. Procunier* (U.S. 1974)]

One of the legitimate grounds for imposing reasonable time, place, and manner restrictions on free speech is to avoid the appearance of endorsing a particular religion.

▥ **TITHES**   American courts, in following the traditional understanding, have typically defined a *tithe* as a payment given as a voluntary contribution to support one's church or religious community. Usually, it consists of 10 percent of a specific sum, such as one's salary, or of an amount of in-kind goods, such as crops. [*Committee v. Cottam* (Pa.); *In re Whitney's Estate* (Cal.)]

▥ *TONY AND SUSAN ALAMO FOUNDATION V. SECRETARY OF LABOR* **(U.S. 1985)**   This case involved another unsuccessful effort to secure a religious exemption from a generally applicable law. Exemption from the minimum wage provisions of the Fair Labor Standards Act (FLSA) was sought by a nonprofit religious foundation. Most of the foundation's activities were conducted by associates who received no cash salaries for their labors, but who were given food, shelter, clothing, and other benefits.

The foundation had claimed that the receipt of "wages" by its associates would violate the associates' religious convictions. Justice White, responded that the FLSA does not require the payment of cash wages, so that the associates could continue to be paid in the form of increased benefits that would respect their religious beliefs. Further, if there was some religious objection to the increased benefits, the associates were free to return the "wages" back to the Foundation: "We therefore fail to perceive how application of the Act would interfere with the associates' right to freely exercise their religious beliefs."

▥ *TORCASO V. WATKINS* **(U.S. 1961)**   In this case the Supreme Court unanimously invalidated a provision in the Maryland constitution requiring that a person take an oath that acknowledged a belief in God in order to qualify for public employment. The Court found that the religious test for public office is an unconstitutional invasion of "freedom of belief and religion."

Justice Black, for the Court in *Torcaso*, concluded that the command of neutrality announced in *Everson v. Board of Education* (U.S. 1947) prohibited government favoritism towards traditional religions. As the justices found that aid could not be given to religion over nonreligion and that nonreligious beliefs could not be burdened, the law violated both of the religious clauses of the First Amendment, the Establishment Clause as well as the Free Exercise Clause. Government can neither "aid all religions against non-believers [nor] can [it] aid those religions based on a belief in the existence of God as against those religions founded on different beliefs." This principle extended protection not only to the secular humanist who challenged the Maryland law in this case but also to the adherents of other nontheistic religious beliefs such as Buddhism, Taoism, and Ethical Culture.

TORTS AND RELIGIOUS ORGANIZATIONS   A tort is either an intentional act that causes damage to a legally protected interest, or the breach of a legal duty that is the proximate cause of harm to a legitimate interests of another. There are at least three sets of interests that are involved in tort litigation in which legitimate First Amendment claims or defenses can be raised: (1) the legal interests of the tort plaintiff; (2) the First Amendment interests of the defendant; and (3) the regulatory interests of the state.

In a case in which First Amendment claims or defenses can be raised, however, the situation becomes complex. Although the state's interest in the enforcement of its tort and contract law policies is a strong one, the First Amendment requires that the courts take these important liberty interests into account. The litigation should be conducted in a manner that does not intrude on First Amendment rights, and the relationships must be defined in a way that does not intrude on constitutionally protected interests.

While some state courts have adopted the theory that since one who attends religious services or goes on the premises of a religious institution for any other purposes does so for his own benefit, such a person should be considered a guest or licensee (a person who has a privilege to enter land arising from the permission or consent, express or implied, of the possessor of the land but who goes on the land for his own purpose rather than for any purpose or interest of the possessor) who may not recover for injuries due to the mere negligent maintenance of the premises—regardless of whether the person was a member of the congregation or not. [*Huselton v. Underhill* (Cal. App.); *Coolbaugh v. St. Peter's Roman Catholic Church* (Conn.); *Jensen v. Grace Lutheran Church, Inc.* (Fla. App. D2,) *Holiday v. First Parish Church* (Mass.); *Williamson v. Wallace* (NC); *Glaser v. Congregation Kehillath Israel* (Mass)] Other state courts have held that the religious organization is liable for injuries on the church premises on the basis of negligence. These courts have ruled that the injured persons were invitees—people who enter by invitation, express or implied; whose entry is connected with the owner's business or with an activity the owner conducts or permits to be conducted on his land; and for whom there is mutuality of benefit or benefit to the owner. [*Price v. Central Assembly of God* (Col.); *Sullivan v. First Presbyterian Church* (Iowa);

Casey v. Roman Catholic Archbishop (Md.); *Manning v. Noa* (Mich.); *Schultz v. Webster Groves Presbyterian Church Assoc.* (Mo. App.,); *Gallagher v. St. Raymond's Roman Catholic Church* (NY App.)]

The issue of whether persons who were injured because of conditions on the premises of religious institutions may recover from such organizations or corporations may depend on whether the state follows the doctrine of "charitable immunity." It has been held that organizations directing their immediate activities to objectives other than religious worship can claim no immunity from tort liability by virtue of affiliation or control by a strictly religious or worshipping body, even granting that under the law of the particular jurisdiction the latter might be considered a "charity," or itself claim exemption upon some other theory. [*Vermillion v. Woman's College* (SC)]

One instance in which courts have sometimes found churches liable in tort is in the sounding of bells or carillons, which they found, in certain circumstances, to constitute a nuisance. This includes cases in which the ringing of a chime or bells from a church tower interfered with the physical comfort of ordinary persons living adjacent to the church. [See, for example, *Leete v. Pilgrim Congregational Society* (Mo. 1884); *Terhune v. Trustees of Methodist Episcopal Church* (N.J. 1917)]

TUITION TAX DEDUCTIONS OR CREDITS   A state

may not use a system of statutory grants, tax credits, or tax deductions to reimburse parents or students for tuition paid only to religiously affiliated schools. However, a tax deduction to all students or parents based upon the actual expenditures of attending any public or private school (including religious school) has been upheld. [*Mueller v. Allen* (U.S. 1983)] *Mueller* validated a tax statute allowing parents or private school students to deduct the expenses of tuition, textbooks, and transportation.

It would appear that a valid tax deduction statute must allow a deduction for: (1) expenditures for public as well as private schools; and (2) some expenditures other than tuition (such as expenditures for school supplies or books) so that public school students or their parents may benefit from the deduction.

Substantially similar tuition reimbursement programs in New York and Pennsylvania were declared unconstitutional by the U.S. Supreme Court. New York's program provided out of general tax revenues reimbursements for tuition paid by low-income parents to send their children to private elementary and secondary schools. The reimbursements were of fixed amounts and could not exceed 50 percent of the actual tuition paid. [*Committee for Public Education & Religious Liberty v. Nyquist* (U.S. 1973)] Pennsylvania provided fixed-sum reimbursements for parents who sent their children to private elementary and secondary schools, if the amount paid did not exceed actual tuition. The funds were derived from cigarette tax revenues. Both programs, the Supreme Court held, were public financial assistance to sectarian institutions with no attempt to segregate the benefits so that religious activities were not subsidized. [*Sloan v. Lemon* (U.S. 1973)]

New York had also enacted a program of tax relief for those parents sending their children to nonpublic schools; relief was available to parents not qualifying for the tuition reimbursements if they made less than $25,000 per year and the relief was in fixed sums bearing no relationship to the amounts of the tuition paid. "In practical terms there would appear to be little difference, for purposes of determining whether such aid has the effect of advancing religion, between the tax benefit allowed and the tuition grant allowed under section 2. The qualifying parent under either program receives the same form of encouragement and reward for sending his children to nonpublic schools. The only difference was that one parent receives an actual cash payment while the other is allowed to reduce by an arbitrary amount the sum he would otherwise be obliged to pay to the State." There was no answer to Judge Hays's dissenting statement that "[i]n both instances the money involved represents a charge made upon the state for the purpose of religious education." Some difficulty, however, was experienced in distinguishing this program from the tax exemption approved in *Walz v. Tax Commission* (U.S. 1970).

Two subsidiary arguments were rejected by the Supreme Court in these cases. First, it had been argued that the tuition reimbursement program promoted the free exercise of religion because it permitted low-income parents wanting to send their children to school according to their religious views to do so. The Court agreed that "tension inevitably exists between the Free Exercise and Establishment Clauses," but the government is required neither to advance nor inhibit religion and the tuition program inescapably advanced religion and was unconstitutional. In the Pennsylvania case, it was argued that because the program reimbursed parents who sent their children to nonsectarian schools as well as to sectarian ones, the section on the former parents was valid and parents of children who attended sectarian schools are entitled to the same aid as a matter of equal protection.

U

UNEMPLOYMENT COMPENSATION Many state unemployment compensation programs make payments only to persons who are involuntary unemployed (that is, those who were laid off, rather than resigned), and who are available to work (that is, willing to accept offered employment). Here, however, unlike other areas of regulation, the U.S. Supreme Court has held that the states must grant religious exemptions. Thus, if a person resigns from a job or refuses to accept a job because it conflicts with his or her religious beliefs, the state must pay him or her unemployment compensation if he or she is otherwise entitled to it.

A state cannot deny unemployment compensation merely because the applicant quit a job rather than work on a day on which religious beliefs forbid work. [*Sherbert v. Verner* (U.S. 1963)]

A state cannot deny unemployment compensation merely because a worker quits his or her job rather than work on the production of military equipment after a factory converts from nonmilitary to military production. [*Thomas v. Review Board* (U.S. 1981)]

A person does not have to be a member of a formal religious organization to receive an exemption from unemployment compensation requirements for religious reasons. All that is required is that the person sincerely holds religious beliefs that prevent him or her from working on a certain day or on certain products. [*Frazee v. Illinois Department of Employment Security* (U.S. 1989)]

The unemployment compensation cases do not give individuals a right to disregard criminal laws due to their religious beliefs. Thus, unemployment compensation laws may disqualify persons fired for "misconduct" (which includes any violation of criminal law).

A person who was fired from his job as a counselor at a private drug abuse clinic when it was discovered that he used peyote for religious reasons during nonwork hours claimed that denial of unemployment compensation to him was a violation of his right to free exercise of his religion. All use of peyote was illegal in the state (even if the use was for a

335

religious ceremony). The U.S. Supreme Court held that unemployment compensation could properly be denied here. [*Employment Division v. Smith* (U.S. 1988)]

UNENUMERATED RIGHTS   These are rights not explicitly stated in the U.S. Constitution. The starting point for interpreting the Ninth Amendment is its text: "The enumeration in the Constitution of certain rights shall not be construed to deny or disparage others retained by the people." The text and the rule of construction that requires plain meaning to be followed clearly establishes the existence of unenumerated rights.

In addition to rights known at the time of its inception, the Ninth Amendment probably was intended to provide the basis for unknown rights that time alone might disclose. Nothing in the thinking of the Framers of the Constitution foreclosed the possibility that new rights might claim the loyalties of succeeding generations.

The Ninth Amendment beckons us to look beyond its four corners for the enumerated rights of the people. It must and does have content. To interpret it as merely the converse side of the Tenth Amendment is to confuse the two amendments. An explicit declaration of the existence of unenumerated rights is an addition of unspecified rights to the Bill of Rights. Confusion between the Ninth and Tenth Amendments originated with proposals for the amendments by Virginia in 1788. Moreover, Madison himself argued that the line between a power granted and a right retained by the people amounted to the same thing as if a right were named. Unenumerated rights, however, are not named, and no affirmative power has been delegated to regulate or abridge them.

Undoubtedly, the Ninth Amendment and its problem of identifying unenumerated rights continue to be troublesome. Courts continue to discover rights that have no textual existence and might be considered enumerated, but for the judicial propensity to ignore the Ninth Amendment and imagine that some unspecified right under discussion derives from a right that is enumerated. Opponents of such rights often criticize judicial use of such rights as judicial activism.

So long as the government is instituted for the sake of securing the rights of the people and must exercise its powers in subordination to those rights, the Ninth Amendment should have the vitality intended for it. The problem is not so much whether the rights it guarantees are worthy of enforcement as are the enumerated rights; the problem, rather, is whether our courts should read out of the amendment rights worthy of our respect, which the Framers might conceivably have meant to safeguard at least in principle.

UNITED STATES V. BALLARD (U.S. 1944) In this case, the defendants were charged with using the mail to obtain money by fraud. The two defendants, Edna and Donald Ballard, claimed that they had been made divine messengers by "Saint Germain" who was Gary Ballard when he (Gary Ballard) was alive. They represented themselves as the divine messengers and teachers of the "I AM" movement with powers to heal many diseases, including some classified medically as incurable. The indictment charged that they "well knew" that these representations were false and that they made the representations to fraudulently collect donations from their followers for themselves. The district court had submitted to the jury the question of whether the defendants in good faith believed the representations. The trial judge, however, did not submit to the jury any issue as to the truth or falsity of the representations. The court of appeals reversed the defendants' convictions on the basis that it was necessary to prove that the representations were in fact false.

The U.S. Supreme Court, in a sharply divided and complicated decision, overturned the decision of the court of appeals, which had vacated the convictions and ordered a new trial. The justices had great difficulty in determining a standard to separate the issue of belief from the issue of truth. In an opinion by Justice Douglas, a majority of the justices declared that the Free Exercise Clause was created in order to ensure that even the most incomprehensible religious views would receive full constitutional protection. It said that, freedom of thought, "embraces the right to maintain theories of life and of death and of the hereafter which are rank heresy to followers of orthodox faiths." Individuals may believe what they cannot prove. The Court, instead, held that a jury could only determine whether or not a religious belief was sincerely held, not whether it was true. Thus, while the judges seem to have agreed that Ballard was guilty of fraud ("The religious views espoused by respondents might seem incredible, if not preposterous, to most people"), they ruled that the truth or falsity of the religious claims could not be subject to trial before a jury.

Justice Jackson dissented from the remanding of the case to the circuit court because he found that any inquiry into religious "fraud" was prohibited by the First Amendment. He argued that to allow inquiry into a defendant's good faith in asserting a belief was not materially different from a testing of the belief itself. Unless one proves that the asserted religion is not worthy of belief it is not likely that anyone will be convinced of a defendant's bad faith. Additionally, the possibility that government might begin testing when "preachers" lack true belief is in itself dangerous to religious freedom.

UNITED STATES V. LEE (U.S. 1982)   The Supreme Court in this case denied an Amish employer of Amish workers an exemption from compulsory participation in the Social Security System. The majority opinion, written by Chief Justice Warren Burger, first held that the employer could not claim the statutory exemption allowed self-employed individuals who had religious objections to payment of the tax. The chief justice went on to apply a balancing test, asking whether the payment of Social Security taxes by an Amish employer or the receipt of benefits by Amish employees from the System interfered with the free exercise of their religious beliefs. In accord with *Thomas v. Review Board* (U.S. 1981), the majority refused to decide the correct interpretation of any religious belief because such a decision was neither a function or a competency of the judiciary. The Court accepted Lee's claim that both payment of taxes and receipt of benefits were forbidden by the Amish faith. Therefore, because compulsory participation in the Social Security System violated Lee's and his employee's beliefs, such compulsion constituted a burden on their free exercise rights.

In the second part of the test, the chief justice asked if this burden on the free exercise of religion was justified by an overriding government interest and, if so, whether the religious belief could be accommodated without unduly interfering with the achievement of that interest. The chief justice found that the governmental interest in the Social Security System was compelling. This was a nationwide system of comprehensive insurance providing a variety of benefits and contributed to by both employers and employees. The government viewed compulsory payments as necessary for the vitality of the system because voluntary participation would undermine its soundness and would be difficult to administer.

The Court in *Lee* did not examine whether alternative means were available to achieve this compelling interest that would not burden the Amish. The chief justice stated that this complex taxing system was organized in such a way that it would be difficult to accommodate exceptions that might arise from a large spectrum of religious beliefs, except to the extent that such accommodation had already been made by the Congress in the statutory exemption. That exemption was narrow (self-employed members of a religious group that made sufficient provision for its dependent members) and readily identifiable.

The Court seemed to be concerned, as Justice Stevens recognized in his concurrence, that granting the exemption in this case would result in several other claims that would be difficult to administer. Thus, the government's interest in an efficient Social Security System justified forcing Lee to comply with the law in violation of his faith.

UNIVERSAL DECLARATION OF HUMAN RIGHTS

The Universal Declaration of Human Rights was drafted by the Human Rights Commission of the United Nations and was adopted by the General Assembly in 1948. At its inception the Declaration was viewed by the U.N. members as a nonbinding agreement. Article 2 of the Declaration provides that "everyone is entitled to all the rights and freedoms set forth in this Declaration, without distinction of any kind such as race, colour, sex, language, religion, other opinion, national or social origin, property, birth, or other status." Article 19 of the Declaration states: "Everyone has the right to freedom of opinion and expression, this right includes the right to hold opinions without interference, and to seek, receive and impart information and ideas through any media and regardless of frontiers." Along with the U.N. Charter and the International Charter on Economic, Social, and Cultural Rights, the Declaration is part of the International Bill of Rights. In addition to the Universal Declaration, the principal international human rights treaties require governments to prohibit "hate speech" based on race, religion, or nationality.

V

VACCINATIONS The U.S. Supreme Court very early in the twentieth century held that an individual could be required to receive a vaccination against disease. [*Jacobsen v. Massachusetts* (U.S. 1905)] Although submission to such a program might violate an individual's religious beliefs, vaccinations are an extremely important method of securing the public health. The Court's rationale recognized that the state had an interest in protecting children's health and well-being that would on occasion overcome a claim for religious freedom. The Supreme Court opinion, *Reynolds v. United States* (U.S. 1879), which was a controlling precedent in *Jacobsen*, had held that Congress was free to prohibit any action, regardless of its religious implications, so long as it did not formally prohibit a religious belief. Thus construed, the Free Exercise Clause would give no protection against the proscription of actions deemed central to a religion, unless the legislation formally outlawed the belief itself. Although the belief-action distinction was eliminated in *Sherbert v. Verner* (U.S. 1963), it was effectively reinstituted again in *Employment Division v. Smith* (U.S. 1990), and the holdings in *Jacobsen* and many other cases following *Reynolds* have remained unchallenged.

Although the chance of major health epidemics may have been small, the courts have continually upheld vaccination requirements as a precondition to a child's attendance at public school. [*Wright v. Dewitt School District* (Ark. 1965); *Vonnegut v. Baun* (Ind. 1934); *McCartney v. Austin* (N.Y. Sup. Ct., 1968)]

VIRGINIA STATUTE OF RELIGIOUS FREEDOM (1777) The adoption by the state of Virginia of the Statute of Religious Liberty was a pivotal episode in the long struggle for separation of church and state in America. The American colonies had inherited, through England, a social order that had governed Medieval Europe and that had survived the Protestant Reformation; there the church and state had been ideally regarded as parts of a greater and divinely sanctioned social order, and owed mutual support to each other.

341

The period of the American Revolution, however, accelerated a long-term evolution to a concept of society in which political and religious life existed in separate spheres and in which religion withdrew, theoretically, into the private sphere of activity. Part of the impetus behind the separation of church and state was itself religious. Some originally radical Protestant sects were early committed to separation, either because of their own experience with persecution, or out of more abstract considerations. In addition to these strains within American Protestantism, Enlightenment ideals emphasizing the sanctity of individual conscience were influential, most notably among Thomas Jefferson and other leaders of the disestablishment struggle in Virginia. Perhaps the overriding factor in deciding the general issue in the United States, however, was the practical consideration that the large numbers of sects in the country meant that, in the long run, the establishment of any one of them, or even of a combination, was not politically feasible.

Next to the Declaration of Independence, Thomas Jefferson took the greatest pride in his authorship of the Virginia Statute of Religious Freedom, which, as his friend James Madison said, "extinguished forever the ambitious hope of making laws for the human mind." Indeed, the statute included the immortal phrase, "Almighty God hath created the mind free."

Jefferson wrote this statute in 1777, when he had returned from the Continental Congress to begin a wholesale revision of Virginia's laws that would eradicate every trace of aristocratic privilege hidden in them. At the time, "the free exercise of religion, according to the dictates of conscience" was an established right in Virginia. Yet Jefferson's statute was bitterly opposed by those supporting the established church, and led to what he later called "the severest contest in which I have ever been engaged."

Although Jefferson first drafted his Bill for Establishing Religious Freedom in 1777, it was not enacted into law until 1786. The statute, nonetheless, firmly established the principles of religious freedom and the separation of church and state and provided the basis for the First Amendment's clause on religion.

The conclusive debates in Virginia took place in 1784–1785. Patrick Henry led a move in the legislature to establish a general assessment for the support of Christian worship, which would have effectively substituted for the Anglican establishment a more general Christian establishment. Initially passed in November 1784, this General Assessment Bill was sharply attacked by Madison, and defeated on its final reading in October 1785. Madison followed up this victory by securing a vote on the Bill for Establishing Religious Freedom, proposed by Thomas Jefferson and originally introduced in the legislature in 1779. It was adopted, and became law as the Statute of Religious Liberty in January 1786. The statute succeeded due to the political skills of James Madison and only after the assembly had deleted significant portions of Jefferson's original draft. With a preamble that is four times the length of the act itself asserting that "God had created the mind free" and that attempts to coerce it "tend only to begat habits of hypocrisy and meanness, and are a departure from the plan of the Holy Author of our religion," Jefferson's statute provided "that no man shall be compelled to frequent or support any religious worship, place, or ministry whatsoever, nor shall be enforced, restrained, molested, or burthened in his body or goods, nor otherwise suffer on account of his religious opinions or beliefs." There remained some vestigial connections between church and state, but their separation was completed by 1802.

The statute was revolutionary because it represented a new trend in Enlightenment thought. The concept of separation of church and state was not part of British political culture, as the British crown was still seen as the head of the Anglican Church. The idea of removing the power of the government from the structure of the church, known as disestablishment, grew up in the British colonies. By 1776 Virginia had incorporated into its Declaration of Rights a provision for religious freedom. Ten years later, Jefferson's wish had been turned into law.

The First Amendment has language that is very similar to that of the Virginia statute. The opening words of the Bill of Rights state: "Congress shall make no law respecting the establishment of religion or prohibiting the free exercise thereof." This language in the First Amendment, known as the Establishment and the Free Exercise Clauses, respectively, create what Jefferson called "a wall of separation between church and state."

Few other states immediately followed Virginia's lead. Office holders under many of the original constitutions were required to be believers in God, Christians, or even Protestants. It was not until 1818 that Connecticut abolished compulsory public support of churches, and not until 1833 was a similar establishment completely eliminated in Massachusetts. The First Amendment to the federal Constitution, which prohibited religious establishment or infringement of religious liberty on the national level, helped to commend the example of Virginia to its sister states.

Thomas Jefferson paid a political price for writing the statute. Partly because of his efforts, Jefferson gained a reputation as an enemy of religion. Thirty years later he wrote that "the priests indeed have ... thought it proper to ascribe to me ... antireligious sentiments. ... They wished him to be thought atheist, deist, or devil, who could advocate freedom from their religious dictations."

VOUCHERS   Vouchers have been one of the most popular, yet controversial, proposals for education reform in recent years. Under such proposals, a voucher is given to parents who may then give it to any public or private school in lieu of tuition. The voucher is redeemed by the school for government funds. One of the best-known voucher proposals that have been implemented has been a Milwaukee program that provides to low-income families vouchers that can be used at any nonsectarian private school.

The concept of school vouchers was first popularized by economist Milton Friedman in his book *Capitalism and Freedom* (1962). The theory underlying voucher plans is that private and parochial schools should be allowed to compete with public institutions in order to infuse the competitive forces of free market economy into the educational system. This would supposedly result in schools that are more diverse, efficient, and effective than schools operating under the current financial structure. Under many of these plans, vouchers would be used for students to attend parochial or sectarian schools, raising the question of whether such plans are constitutional in light of the Establishment Clause of the First Amendment.

Widespread discontent with public schools has precipitated demands that parents be given some choice about which school their children will attend. Several states have adopted laws affording parents some choice among public schools in their area. These laws have attracted few constitutional attacks. Many people argue that choice plans should be broadened to offer parents government vouchers redeemable at any accredited school, public or private, including religious schools. Supporters of this approach cite as a model the GI Bill, under which the federal government pays certain expenses of military veterans to attend any accredited college.

Proponents contend that vouchers will produce better education, especially for poor and minority students who often fair poorly in public schools. They cite the superior performance of private school students. They also believe that public schools would be shaken out of the complacency induced by their monopoly on state funding and prodded to do better by competition from private schools. Further, proponents want parents to be able to choose for their children an education consistent with their values, whether religiously based or not.

Opponents of vouchers deny that private schools generally provide a better education; they ascribe any superior performance to private schools "skimming the cream" by taking better students. They also question whether public schools would benefit from increased competition. They feel that vouchers would lead to further deterioration of the public schools, by leaving public schools to handle the most difficult students and by eroding the tax base of public schools.

Critics further assert that voucher plans would be unconstitutional.

They fear that vouchers would worsen racial segregation in violation of equal protection as interpreted in *Brown v. Board of Education* (U.S. 1954, 1955). Moreover, to be effective vouchers would have to be available to pay a large percentage of the tuition at private schools in order to actually allow the poor to participate. Many voucher programs proposed would offer up so little money toward tuition that they would in effect benefit only the rich, who would see tuition costs go down for them, while the poor still would not be able to afford the private schooling. Critics also argue that vouchers redeemed at parochial schools would constitute government aid to religious institutions and an unconstitutional establishment of religion.

Opponents to vouchers also argue that the Supreme Court has long articulated that there is a substantial difference between higher education and primary and secondary schools, including the fact that students at the higher levels of education are less likely to be easily inculcated with religious doctrine, as they are more able to think for themselves and to discern efforts to indoctrinate them. [*See McCollum v. Board of Education* (U.S. 1948); *Grand Rapids School District v. Ball* (U.S. 1985); *Tilton v. Richardson* (U.S. 1971); and *Hunt v. McNair* (U.S. 1973)]

Defenders respond that vouchers would not worsen school segregation, which is already widespread, but that if they did, this effect would result from individual choices, not from state action, which is necessary to invoke the Fourteenth Amendment. Moreover, segregative effects could be avoided by requiring participating schools to meet certain standards of racial composition in admissions procedures. Defenders also deny that vouchers would establish religion. Pointing again to the GI Bill, they see vouchers as merely giving parents a choice in obtaining a service that the government subsidizes for secular reasons: any benefit to religious institutions would be incidental and thus of no constitutional concern. Critics reply that even an indirect benefit is an unlawful establishment.

Although school voucher legislation that included religious schools was enacted in Wisconsin and Ohio, strict separationists such as People for the American Way helped defeat legislative voucher proposals in several other states.

No state has yet adopted a true voucher program, although a few have proposed limited programs for low-income children. Confused and conflicting Supreme Court pronouncements on aid to religious schools preclude any prediction of how the Court would handle the issue. Quite possibly, vouchers could be upheld for the same reasons that the GI Bill is considered constitutional, especially if steps were taken to avoid racial segregation. Some kind of voucher program might even be necessary to accommodate children with religious objections to what is taught in public schools.

W

"WALL OF SEPARATION" METAPHOR   In 1802 President Thomas Jefferson wrote a letter to a congregation of Baptists in Danbury, Connecticut, in which he asserted that the First Amendment was introduced to build "a wall of separation between Church and State." It remains the most famous statement concerning the proper relationship of religion and government in the United States. The letter has animated the Supreme Court's interpretation of both the Free Exercise Clause [*Reynolds v. United States* (U.S. 1879)], and the Establishment Clause [*Everson v. Board of Education* (U.S. 1947)].

In *Reynolds v. United States* (U.S. 1879), a case involving the Mormon practice of polygamy, Chief Justice Waite writing for the Court interpreted the phrase as "almost an authoritative declaration of the scope and effect of the [First] Amendment."

In its first attempts to adjudicate challenges to state programs on religious grounds, the Supreme Court relied on Jefferson's metaphor for substantial guidance. In *Everson v. Board of Education* (1947) all of the justices' separate opinions agreed that the test of the Establishment Clause is separation of church and state, and all suggested that Jefferson's metaphor of the "wall of separation" is appropriate to deciding these cases. Further, all relied almost exclusively on the history of disestablishment in Virginia, and in particular, James Madison's *Memorial and Remonstrance,* in interpreting the language of the First Amendment. [See also *McCollum v. Board of Education* (U.S. 1948); *West Virginia State Board of Education v. Barnette* (U.S. 1943); *Zorach v. Clausen* (U.S. 1952)]

In *Lemon v. Kurtzman* (U.S. 1971), Chief Justice Burger remarked that "the line of separation, far from being a 'wall,' is a blurred, indistinct and variable barrier depending on all the circumstances of a particular relationship."

Justice Hugo Black cited Jefferson's phrase in the 1962 decision of *Engel v. Vitale* (U.S. 1962), which outlawed the mandated recitation in the public schools of a government-composed prayer. Many opponents of Black's opinion criticized his use of the metaphor and attempted to rebut the Court's understanding of it. Justice Potter Stewart, in his dissent in *Engel*, wrote that, "I think that the Court's task ... is not responsibly aided by the uncritical invocation of metaphors like the 'wall of separation,' a phrase nowhere to be found in the Constitution."

Justice William Rehnquist in his dissent in *Wallace v. Jaffree* (1985) claimed that the Supreme Court's understanding of the metaphor was lacking in historical foundation, useless in guiding the Court's interpretation of the Establishment Clause, and should be abandoned. He noted that Jefferson was in Paris when the religion clauses were adopted by Congress in 1789. Rehnquist, however, apparently overlooked the fact that there were 36 letters exchanged between Jefferson and James Madison from 1787 to 1789. Much of that correspondence dealt with whether there should be a Bill of Rights, with Jefferson seeking to convince Madison of the necessity of such a document. Finally, passage of Jefferson's Virginia Statute on Religious Freedom was accomplished by Madison in 1786. The "separation" phrase was not unique to Jefferson. Madison's voluminous writings affirm the same sentiment, especially in a letter to Robert Walsh in 1819: "[T]he number, the industry, and the morality of the Priesthood, and the devotion of the people have been manifestly increased by the total separation of the Church from the State."

Other Supreme Court decisions invalidated a Connecticut statute that allowed employees an absolute right to observe their chosen Sabbath and an Alabama law allowing for a moment of silent prayer in public schools, both of which invoked the "wall of separation" metaphor. [*Estate of Thornton v. Calder* (U.S. 1986); *Wallace v. Jaffree* (U.S. 1985)]

Lower federal courts have also invoked the separation of church and state doctrine in both Arkansas and Louisiana to strike down state laws passed in 1981 that allowed for the teaching of creationism in public schools. [*McLean v. Arkansas Board of Education* (E.D. Ark. 1982); *Edwards v. Aguillard* (U.S. 1987)]

Because of the weight the Supreme Court and other courts have given to Jefferson's letter, its importance has been discussed among academic and religious commentators. Some believe the letter was an offhand reply to political supporters, meaning little in terms of constitutional jurisprudence. Other scholars have read the letter as a clear statement of Jefferson's views.

Some Christian fundamentalists believe that the "separation of church and state" is an erroneous concept because America developed as a Christian society and nation, the term "separation of church and state" does not appear in the Constitution, and important court cases suggest the legal prominence of Christianity, especially in the nineteenth century.

▦ *WALLACE V. JAFFREE* **(U.S. 1985)**   This case arose from constitutional challenges to three Alabama statutes. The first statute, enacted in 1978 by the Alabama legislature, established a "period of silence not to exceed one minute in duration, that should be observed for meditation." The Supreme Court did not have to rule on this statute because the persons who attacked the statute in the lower court abandoned the claim that the law was unconstitutional in their argument before the U.S. Supreme Court. The second statute passed by Alabama in 1981 authorized a period of silence for "meditation or voluntary prayer." The third statute was enacted in 1982, and stated that any teacher "in any educational institution within the state of Alabama, recognizing that the Lord God is one, at the beginning of any homeroom or any class" could lead a legislatively prescribed prayer. There was no significant issue on the constitutionality of the third statute, which was invalid on the basis of the Court's previous rulings on government-prescribed prayer. Thus, the only significant issue facing the Court was the constitutionality of the period of silence for "meditation or voluntary prayer" statute.

The Court in *Jaffree* was called upon to overturn a district court opinion that would have allowed the state not only to have a moment of silence for silent prayer or meditation, but also a separate statute that would have authorized teachers to lead "willing students" in legislatively prescribed prayer. The federal district court reached this decision by determining that the U.S. Supreme Court had misinterpreted the meaning of the First and Fourteenth Amendments that, in the district judge's opinion, would not prohibit state-sponsored school prayer.

The U.S. Supreme Court invalidated the Alabama law requiring a minute of silence in public schools for "meditation or silent prayer." The Court decided by a six-to-three vote that the statute violated the Establishment Clause of the First Amendment. Justice John Paul Stevens, who wrote the Court's opinion, said that the clause requires governmental neutrality and that this statute failed the three-part *Lemon* test [from *Lemon v. Kurtzman* (U.S. 1971)] because it did not have a secular purpose. The Supreme Court found that religious concerns were the sole motivation for the statute, which was enacted to convey to Alabamans that the legislature endorsed prayer at school. The Supreme Court majority in *Jaffree* reaffirmed its longstanding view of the applicability of the religion clauses to the states in upholding its previous decisions on school prayer. Regarded as another significant "purposes prong case," *Wallace v. Jaffree* found that religious concerns were the sole motivation for an Alabama statute requiring a minute of silence in public schools for meditation or voluntary prayer. Alabama already had a required moment of silence in which those who were so inclined could silently pray if they chose. The new law amended the previous statute to encourage the use of that time specifically for voluntary prayer as opposed to meditation or quiet reflection. As this was the only change to the statute's text, and as new legislation is presumed to be an attempt to change existing law, the Supreme Court construed the changes as the manifestation of the state's intent "to characterize prayer as a favored practice." The Alabama statute thus failed the purpose prong of the *Lemon* test [from *Lemon v. Kurtzman* (U.S. 1971)], which invalidates legislation having a religious, rather than secular, purpose. The Alabama statute therefore violated the First Amendment of the Constitution.

The fact that the challenged law permitted no new actions clued the Court in to the exclusively religious purpose of the Alabama statute. School children in that state already had the right to a moment of silence for use in whatever manner they chose. Adding "voluntary prayer" to the list of possible uses did not make that use suddenly and newly available, but only underscored the state's approval and encouragement of the moment of silence for that use. By this example, if a law grants no new powers or abilities, that law is likely a symbol of support for some cause that may or may not be appropriate, and thus warrants close scrutiny.

Two justices, Lewis Powell and Sandra Day O'Connor, supported the decision while suggesting that some state moment of silence laws might be constitutional. Three dissenting justices indicated dissatisfaction with the *Lemon* test precedent followed in the opinion of the Court. The Court also warned against government-sponsored religious activities directed at impressionable children.

WALZ V. TAX COMMISSION (U.S. 1970)   In this case the U.S. Supreme Court by a vote of eight to one, upheld the universal practice of exempting churches from paying either property or sales taxes. The case addressed the question of whether tax exemptions for religious property are compatible with the Establishment Clause of the First Amendment. The exemption authorized by the state law included "real or personal property used exclusively for religious, educational, or charitable purposes as defined by law and owned by any corporation or association organized or conducted exclusively for one or more such purposes and not operating for profit." Frederick Walz, a property owner and taxpayer, contended that the exemption indirectly compelled him financially to support religious organizations owning exempted properties.

Separationists supported Walz's position, asserting that the Supreme Court's decision in *Everson v. Board of Education* (U.S. 1947) insisted that an impenetrable "wall of separation" exist between church and state, and that the government must maintain "strict neutrality" with regard to religion.

The Supreme Court upheld the exemption over the dissent of Justice William O. Douglas. In the majority opinion Chief Justice Warren Burger asserted that the First Amendment "will not tolerate either governmentally established religion or governmental interference with religion." If those proscribed acts are avoided, "there is room for play in a benevolent neutrality which will permit religious exercise to exist without sponsorship and without interference." Evaluation of policies using the religion clauses rests on "whether particular acts in question are intended to establish or interfere with religious beliefs and practices or have the effect of doing so." The legislative purpose served here is legitimate, Burger said. The tax exemptions in question were historical, common exemptions that recognized the "beneficial and stabilizing influences" of nonprofit groups as a reason to reward them fiscally. The Court noted that churches were one of several types of nonprofit institutions that enjoy tax exemptions. On that basis, the Court concluded that the New York law being challenged was secular in both purpose and effect—the two tests required under existing Establishment Clause doctrine. The policy also responded to the "latent danger inherent in the imposition of property taxes. . . . What New York is doing is simply sparing the exercise of religion from the burden of property taxation levied on private profit institutions." On considering the primary effect of the exemption, the Court introduced the entanglement criterion, which would become decisive in many later establishment cases: whether the exemption resulted in an excessive involvement of the government in religious activities. The chief justice argued that government involvement with religion existed with or without the exemption. Indeed, "elimination of the exemption would tend to expand the involvement of government by giving rise to tax valuation of church property, tax liens, tax foreclosures, and the direct confrontations and conflicts that follow in the train of those legal processes." Although some indirect economic benefits and some involvements result from granting the exemption, they are lesser involvements than collecting the property tax. Finally, the Court rejected any "nexus between tax exemption and establishment of religion." The tax exemption is clearly not "sponsorship since the government does not transfer part of its revenue to churches but simply abstains from demanding that the church support the state." Thus Burger concluded that, while taxation of churches posed a risk of entanglement, the tax exemption created "only a minimal and remote involvement between church and state."

▥ **WAR**   See CONSCIENTIOUS OBJECTOR

▥ *WATSON V. JONES* **(U.S. 1872)**   This was the first
Supreme Court case involving internal ecclesiastical dissension, and was decided on common law principles rather than a constitutional basis. With jurisdiction based on diversity of citizenship, the federal courts were required to decide which of two contesting groups
would be deemed to lawfully control the property of the Walnut Street
Presbyterian Church of Louisville, Kentucky. A state court had awarded
the local elders and trustees control of the church property, although they
had been replaced by an edict of the highest council of the Presbyterian
Church in the United States.

The Supreme Court held that the state courts were required to follow
the edicts of the highest ecclesiastical tribunal. Although the First
Amendment had not yet been made applicable to the states, the decision
is now recognized as reflecting the values of the First Amendment's religion clauses. The majority found three general rules applicable to civil
court resolution of internal ecclesiastical disputes. First, if a property is
given to a congregation with an express condition in the terms of the
grant that it shall be used only to support a specific purpose, the civil
courts could order a return of the property if it is no longer used for that
purpose. Second, when property has been given to the general use of an
independent religious group the property must be used as determined by
a majority of the society or by another manner that the group has previously established for this purpose. Third, where property has been acquired by a society or group that forms a part of a general religious organization, the established tribunals of that organization must be deferred
to by civil courts. The right to church property as far as it is dependent on
questions of religious doctrine or ecclesiastical law must be settled by the
highest tribunal or authority of the religious organization.

Since the *Watson* decision, the authority of a civil court to resolve questions of "departure from purpose" involving church property has been
limited in the light of the principles of the First Amendment. The principles of deference to a congregational polity or hierarchical authority have
been strengthened by later decisions. The U.S. Supreme Court rendered
two other decisions on church disputes before it applied the First Amendment to the states. In *Bouldin v. Alexander* (U.S. 1872) the Court held that
a civil court could declare who was entitled to control the property of an
independent congregational church. In this case a minority of the congregation had met and expelled the majority of the members and the
trustees in whom the title to the church property was formally vested.
The Court found that civil courts must follow the will of the majority of

this church to decide the question of legal title. Although it is not clear whether this decision was based on First Amendment principles, it is the only case in which the Supreme Court was presented with a dispute over the property of a clearly independent local congregation, and it follows the principles stated in *Wilson*.

WELSH V. UNITED STATES (U.S. 1970)   Elliott A. Welsh was convicted of refusing to submit to induction into the armed forces despite his claim for conscientious objector status under § 6(j) of the Universal Military Training and Service Act. That provision exempts from military service persons who because of "religious training and belief" are conscientiously opposed to war in any form, that term being defined in the Act as "belief in a relation to a Supreme Being involving duties superior to those arising from any human relation" but not including "essentially political, sociological, or philosophical views or a merely personal code." In his exemption application, Welsh stated that he could not affirm or deny belief in a "Supreme Being," and struck the words "my religious training and" from the form. He affirmed that he held deep conscientious scruples against participating in wars. The court of appeals, while noting that Welsh's beliefs were "held with the strength of more traditional religious convictions," concluded that those beliefs were not sufficiently "religious" to meet the requirements of § 6(j), and affirmed the conviction.

On appeal Welsh contended that the Act violated the First Amendment's prohibition of establishment of religion, and that his conviction should be set aside based on the ruling in *United States v. Seeger* (U.S. 1965), which held that the test of religious belief under § 6(j) is whether it is a sincere and meaningful belief occupying in the life of its possessor a place parallel to that filled by the God of those admittedly qualified for the exemption. The Supreme Court agreed.

Justice Black, joined by Justices Douglas, Brennan, and Marshall, concluded that this case was controlled by *Seeger*, to which it is factually similar. Under *Seeger*, § 6(j) is not limited to those whose opposition to war is prompted by orthodox or parochial religious beliefs. A draft registrant's conscientious objection to all war is "religious" within the meaning of § 6(j) if this opposition is based on the registrant's moral, ethical, or religious beliefs about what is right and wrong and these beliefs are held with the strength of traditional religious convictions. In view of the broad scope of the word "religious," a registrant's characterization of his or her beliefs as "nonreligious" is not a reliable guide to those administering the exemption.

The Court found that the language of § 6(j) cannot be construed (as it was in *Seeger* and as it is in the prevailing opinion) to exempt from military service all individuals who in good faith oppose all war, it being clear from both the legislative history and textual analysis of that provision that Congress used the words "because of religious training and belief" to limit religion to its theistic sense, and to confine it to formal, organized worship or shared beliefs by a recognizable and cohesive group.

The Court also found that § 6(j) contravened the Establishment Clause of the First Amendment by exempting those whose conscientious objection claims are founded on a theistic belief, while not exempting those whose claims are based on a secular belief. To comport with that clause, an exemption must be "neutral" and include those whose belief emanates from a purely moral, ethical, or philosophical source.

West Virginia State Board of Education v. Barnette (U.S. 1943)

This case was another involving laws mandating salute of the nation's flag. Here the West Virginia state board of education required all children in the public schools to salute the flag and pledge allegiance by extending the right arm, palm upward, and declaring, "I pledge allegiance to the flag of the United States of America and to the Republic for which it stands; one Nation, indivisible, with liberty and justice for all." Children who refused to comply with the law were expelled from school. Their absence thereby became "unlawful," which in turn subjected them and their parents or guardians to criminal sanctions. The case was appealed by the state from a district court that enjoined the enforcement of the regulation as a violation of the students' rights to free exercise of their religious beliefs protected by the First Amendment.

In deciding this case, the U.S. Supreme Court overruled a three-year-old precedent established in *Minersville School District v. Gobitis* (U.S. 1940), which found that a law requiring students at public schools to salute the flag did not unconstitutionally restrict freedom of religion. In *Gobitis,* Justice Felix Frankfurter, writing for all but one member of the Court, argued that religious freedom had to be balanced against the state's rational interest in national unity, and claimed that the Court was no more qualified to perform this balancing act than was the school board. The *Gobitis* decision surprised the public and was widely criticized.

In *Barnette,* the plaintiff argued that the requirement of reciting the pledge violated the Free Exercise Clause of the First Amendment because as Jehovah Witnesses, his children could not say the pledge without violating the religious prohibition against worshipping a graven image. Members of the Jehovah's Witnesses argued that the law unconstitutionally infringed on the separation of church and state guaranteed by the First Amendment.

The Court's majority opinion, written by Justice Robert Jackson, however, stated that the most fundamental question at stake was free expression, and that religious freedom was a secondary issue. (The free exercise of religion issue was given more weight in concurrences by Justices William O. Douglas, Hugo Black, and Frank Murphy, who argued that the state could only interfere with religious freedom for reasons that were "imperative" or "necessary.") The Supreme Court found that the Fourteenth Amendment protects against state action, including state action that violates the First and Fourteenth Amendments, and struck down the law.

In dissent, Justice Felix Frankfurter argued that the West Virginia statute did not mandate accepting particular religious dogma, but simply intended to pursue the secular goal of good citizenship, which according to Frankfurter, falls well within the police powers of the state.

WIDMAR V. VINCENT (U.S. 1981)

In this case the U.S. Supreme Court held that a state-supported school's policy of allowing religious groups to use its facilities does not violate the Establishment Clause of the First Amendment, provided the policy is truly neutral as between religious and nonreligious groups. The case involved a state university that prohibited the use of its facilities for purposes of worship by student-run religious groups, but allowed all nonreligious student groups to use them. After finding this policy unconstitutional on free speech grounds, the Court rejected the university's claim that an equal-access policy would have violated the Establishment Clause.

It was precisely the fact that the facilities were also available to nonreligious groups that distinguished the situation in *Widmar* from the use of school facilities for religious purposes in *McCollum v. Board of Education* (U.S. 1948). Here, equal access would not "confer any imprimatur of state approval on religious acts or practices," and the advancement of religion would not be the "primary effect" of such a policy.

The majority in *Widmar*, however, put aside the issue of whether a different result would be required if there were evidence that religious groups would dominate the use of facilities under an open-access scheme. Arguably, such dominance would cause the scheme to clash with the requirement that the state not pursue policies the "primary effect" of which is to advance religion.

WISCONSIN V. YODER (U.S. 1972)

In this decision the U.S. Supreme Court held that adherents of traditional religious groups that provide an alternative way of life for members cannot be required to send children to school beyond the eighth grade. Members of the Old Order Amish and Conservative Amish Mennonite Church had been convicted of violating a Wisconsin law requiring all children to attend school until they were 16 years old. The Amish parents had removed their children from the public schools after the eighth grade, preferring to train their them in an informal, vocational manner. They claimed that public education was dangerous to their way of life and a threat to their children's salvation and their own.

Yoder reaffirmed the principle that the Free Exercise Clause, at times, constitutionally requires an exemption from general law. The U.S. Supreme Court, per Chief Justice Burger, recognized the First Amendment claim of the Amish that they were entitled to an exemption from the general school attendance law.

Unlike previous cases, the burden on the religious practices of the Amish was severe and inescapable: "[T]he Wisconsin law affirmatively compels them, under threat of criminal sanction, to perform acts undeniably at odds with fundamental tenets of their religious belief." This was the kind of objective danger the Free Exercise Clause was designed to prevent. The Amish must either abandon their beliefs and suffer assimilation or leave Wisconsin. Although acknowledging the Establishment Clause danger of creating "an exception from a general obligation of citizenship on religious grounds," Chief Justice Burger concluded that an exception was required in Yoder.

Yoder set forth a standard of review that may be interpreted as employing the compelling state interest or strict scrutiny analysis. In fact, however, the Yoder decision spoke more obliquely: "[O]nly those interests of the highest order and those not otherwise served can overbalance legitimate claims to the free exercise of religion." The state's asserted interest in developing educated citizens capable of participating in democratic society and in preparing self-reliant and self-sufficient individuals did not justify the burdens on the Amish. The chief justice stressed the success of the Amish in developing productive and law-abiding members of society. The possibility that Amish children might someday be illequipped to enter the larger world as a result of exempting them from the Wisconsin law was deemed to be speculative. Nor was there any evidence that recognizing the primary right of the parents to make decisions on their children's education would jeopardize the health and safety of the children or impose any significant social burden.

Burger's opinion set forth three criteria against which the claims of the Amish and similar claims in the future should be weighed: (1) the sincerity of religious beliefs; (2) the fundamental nature of the outlawed beliefs to the religion; and (3) the adequacy of the substitute measures that the religion proposed to achieve the goals of the law.

The invocation of strict scrutiny does not necessarily mean that an exemption from a general law will always be constitutionally required. At times, the state is able to prove that a compelling justification for denying such an exemption exists. Despite *Yoder*, for example, the Amish have not secured a permanent exemption from general laws. In *United States v. Lee* (U.S. 1982), the Court upheld the federal government against the refusal, based on free exercise grounds, of an Amish employer to provide Social Security coverage for his employees.

The *Yoder* test became part of what became known as the *Sherbert-Yoder* analysis for examining government actions that allegedly violated the Free Exercise Clause. The *Sherbert-Yoder* precedent was broken by the Supreme Court in *Smith v. Employment Division* (U.S. 1990). There, the Supreme Court found that the Constitution does not require a religiously based exemption from laws of general applicability (a law governing the conduct of all persons). Thus, *Yoder* stands out as the one instance in which the Court required the government to grant an exemption from a law of general applicability to persons who would not comply with the law due to their religious beliefs.

WITTERS V. WASHINGTON DEPARTMENT OF SERVICES (U.S. 1986)

Suffering from a progressive eye condition, Larry Witters sought state financial assistance to attend a Bible college to prepare himself for a career as a minister, missionary, or youth director. The Washington State Commission for the Blind, a government agency, generally provided aid to visually handicapped persons seeking education or training for careers so that they could be self-supporting. Nevertheless, the state denied Witters aid, citing the Washington State constitution's prohibition of public aid to religion. The state supreme court upheld the denial on Establishment Clause grounds, holding that aid to Witters would advance religion as its primary effect and thus violate the second prong of the *Lemon* test [from *Lemon v. Kurtzman* (U.S. 1971)]. The U.S. Supreme Court unanimously reversed.

Writing the opinion of the Court, Justice Thurgood Marshall said it would be inappropriate to view the funds ultimately flowing to the Bible college in this case as the result of state action to aid religion. Marshall noted that the financial assistance "is paid directly to the student who transmits it to the educational institution of his or her choice. Any aid provided under Washington's program that ultimately flows to religious institutions does so only as a result of the genuinely independent and private choices of aid recipients." Marshall further emphasized that the program "is in no way skewed toward religion" and "creates no financial incentive for students to undertake sectarian education." Finally, Marshall stressed that nothing indicated any significant proportion of state money provided under the program would flow to religious institutions if Witters's claim was granted.

That last reason was not dispositive for a majority of justices, five of whom joined concurring opinions that noted the applicability of *Mueller v. Allen* (U.S. 1983) to *Witters*. In *Mueller*, the Court had upheld general tax deductions for certain school expenses, despite the fact that more than 90 percent of these tax benefits went to those who sent their children to religious schools.

WOLMAN V. WALTER (U.S. 1977)   In a complicated statutory program, Ohio attempted to aid private schools, which were primarily Catholic schools. This program consisted of six types of aid for all nonpublic elementary and secondary schools: (1) a secular text book program like the ones approved in prior cases; (2) the provision of funds to distribute and score standardized educational tests; ((3) diagnostic services with state personnel testing the individual children for specified health and educational problems; (4) therapeutic services for health and educational disabilities provided by state personnel at sites outside of the parochial school; (5) loans to students of instructional materials and equipment; and (6) funds for commercial transportation, or the use of state school buses for field trips. The program was challenged on the grounds that such aid violated the Establishment Clause of the First Amendment.

The U.S. Supreme Court held that the program was constitutional, with the exception of those portions providing instructional materials and equipment, and field trip services, because the latter could be used for inculcating religious doctrines.

The rulings on these provisions were consistent with earlier cases, and basic tests remained the same, but the Court showed itself hopelessly fragmented in *Wolman*. The Court continued to adhere to the three part test from *Lemon v. Kurtzman* (U.S. 1971), although fewer justices had wanted to employ that test in the school aid area. The *Wolman* opinion by Justice Blackmun was a majority opinion in part and a plurality opinion in part. The opinion applied the *Lemon* test in a straightforward manner and the results are best understood in the terms of this opinion.

The textbook program was upheld by a vote of six to three on the basis of *Mueller v. Allen* (U.S. 1983). The testing and scoring provisions, by a six-to-three vote, was upheld because, unlike *Levitt v. Committee for Public Education* (U.S. 1973), these were standard educational tests prepared by state employees and designed to ensure that private school students are, in fact, being properly educated. The diagnostic services were upheld by a vote of eight to one, as there was an important secular goal of caring for children and no possible religious effect. The therapeutic services were upheld by a vote of seven to two, as the removal of the services from the school eliminated the danger of religious permeation of the program. The instructional materials program was held invalid, by a six- to-three vote, on precisely the same basis as was the similar program in *Meek v. Pittenger* (U.S. 1975). The provision of transportation aid was held invalid, by a five-to-four vote, on an aid-to-the-religious-enterprise concept quite similar to the *Meek* rationale.

The reason for the differing votes in *Wolman* was that the justices were evenly split between three positions. Chief Justice Burger and Justices White and Rehnquist would allow the state to help the education of all children so long as there was no clear aid to religion. Justices Stewart, Blackmun, and Powell believed that an independent application of the three-part test would allow the state to promote secular education without impermissibly fostering religion. Justices Brennan, Marshall, and Stevens were committed to the position that the First Amendment was designed to prohibit any aid to religion, although only Justice Brennan could follow this position when voting on the diagnostic services.

WORKPLACE RELIGIOUS FREEDOM ACT   In work-places across the country, religious employees are often forced to make a difficult choice between practicing their faiths and keeping their jobs. In keeping with the aim of protecting people of all beliefs from religious discrimination, the Workplace Religious Freedom Act (WRFA) was introduced in the 105th Congress in 1997.

The WFRA would require employers to make reasonable accommodation for an employee's religious observance, provided that this would not impose an undue hardship on the employer. Though current law contains a similar provision, the courts have interpreted the law so narrowly that it provides little restraint on an employer's ability to refuse such an accommodation. If enacted, the WRFA would eliminate the conflict between their jobs and their faith that many employees face. For instance, an employee may need to leave work early on Fridays due to religious obligations. If the employee is willing to work late without overtime earlier in the week to make up for the hours missed on Friday, the WFRA would require the employer to grant such accommodation unless this would present an "undue hardship" for the employer. "Undue hardship" is defined in the bill as a situation that imposes "significant difficulty or expense" upon the employer, taking into account both the number of employees seeking accommodation and the employer's operating costs and size. The WRFA also provides protection to employers in that they are not required to provide an accommodation that will result in an employee's inability to perform the essential functions of his or her job.

Senators John Kerry (D-Mass) and Dan Coats (R-Ind) introduced the WRFA in the Senate in July 1997, and Representative Bill Goodling (R-Pa) introduced the House's version of the bill in November 1997. The bill was not enacted.

Z

ZOBREST V. CATALINA FOOTHILLS SCHOOL DISTRICT (U.S. 1993) This case involved whether the Arizona school district of Catalina Foothills should provide a deaf high school student who attended a religious school with a state-funded interpreter. When the school district refused to provide a deaf child with a signing interpreter for classes at a Catholic high school, the parents brought suit, alleging that the federal Individuals with Disabilities Education Act (IDEA) and the Free Exercise Clause of the First Amendment required the school district to provide the interpreter and that such provision did not violate the Establishment Clause.

The U.S. Supreme Court ruled five to four that the Establishment Clause was not violated by the Individuals with Disabilities Education Act, because it was the student, not the religious school, that would be the beneficiary of the state support. Thus, state funding would not constitute a "direct subsidy" to the school and would not violate the Establishment Clause. Writing for the court, Chief Justice William Rehnquist said, "Government programs that neutrally provide benefits to a broad class of citizens defined without reference to religion are not readily subject to an Establishment Clause challenge just because sectarian institutions may also receive an attenuated financial benefit." As a result, the school district was required to provide an interpreter to the student. The decision marked the first time that the U.S. Supreme Court had approved the use of a public employee to aid instruction at a religious elementary or secondary school.

The majority held that the provision of the interpreter resulted from the decision of the student's parents and not from a decision by the state. Therefore, it did not unconstitutionally entangle the government with religion.

Justices Byron White, Antonin Scalia, Anthony Kennedy, and Clarence Thomas joined the majority opinion.

Justice Harry Blackmun issued a dissenting opinion that was joined by Justice David Souter. Blackmun wrote that the "interpreter's every gesture would be infused with religious significance." Thus, the provision of the interpreter "necessarily entails governmental participation in the school's inculcation of religion."

Justices John Stevens and Sandra Day O'Connor dissented on the grounds that the case could have been decided without considering issues of church and state.

▥ ZONE OF PERMISSIBLE ACCOMMODATION   Harvard Professor Lawrence Tribe suggests that the Supreme Court's cases recognize a "zone of permissible accommodation," a zone that the Free Exercise Clause of the First Amendment creates out of the Establishment Clause for permissible accommodation of religious interests. Thus, the government may "accommodate its institutions and programs to the religious interests of the people." [Lawrence L. Tribe. *American Constitutional Law*. § 14–4, at p. 819–823. 2d ed, 1988). Under this view, if any governmental action is "arguably compelled" by the Free Exercise Clause, then that action is not forbidden by the Establishment Clause. Thus wherever an action might violate the Free Exercise Clause and a contrary action might violate the Establishment Clause, it will always be safe for the government to elect the course in which the threat is to the Establishment Clause. In other words, "[t]he free exercise principle should be dominant in any conflict with the anti-establishment principle." [Tribe 1988]

In a continuous chain of U.S. Supreme Court decisions, it has been commonly assumed that there is zone of permissible accommodation, which is understood to be the "breathing space" between the two religion clauses. [*Abington School District v. Schempp* (U.S. 1963)(Justice Goldberg concurring opinion); *Edwards v. Aguillard* (U.S. 1987)(Justice Scalia's opinion)]

▥ ZONING   Zoning refers to the setting aside of certain sections of land within city limits for specific uses. Through zoning, the state's interest in promoting the orderly development of land is fulfilled. The zoning regulations pertain to the land and the buildings and structures on the land. This function falls within the police power of the state to promote order, safety, health, morals, and general welfare. The U.S. Supreme Court has allowed local governments to use zoning to protect public interests. The Court first held zoning laws constitutional in *Euclid v. Ambler Realty Co.* (U.S. 1926).

Issues involving zoning restrictions on religious properties and activities have arisen in recent years, as municipalities have increasingly sought to limit or regulate church property as a legitimate exercise of police power via the authority vested in them by state zoning enabling acts. Churches and other religious uses present a complex zoning problem because, on the one hand, they are believed to contribute to the public welfare and are protected by the First Amendment right to the free exercise of religion, and on the other hand, they can, especially if they are broadly defined, harm a residential neighborhood by creating extra traffic, noise, and litter, and by shifting the property tax burden to other landowners.

The power of a municipality to limit the use of property for religious use is not necessarily a violation of the Free Exercise Clause of the First Amendment because, while this clause guarantees unrestrained freedom to believe, it does not imply unlimited freedom to act. Because every use of church property, whether as a place of worship, a meeting place, or a recreation facility, is a form of religious conduct, rather than belief, the conduct is not free from regulation.

Although a city has the right of police power to determine zoning restrictions, it may not do so arbitrarily. To regulate religious activities, the municipality must overcome the presumption of a religious organization's First Amendment right of free exercise. The ordinance must be reasonable and achieve a legitimate end relating to health, safety, morals, or public welfare.

Not only does the First Amendment protect religious groups from arbitrary zoning restrictions; the due process clause of the Fourteenth Amendment requires moderation in state action. The municipality may not exert unfair application of zoning ordinances against a religious organization.

Ordinances that totally exclude churches or other religious uses from a municipality have been consistently invalidated, and according to most of the courts, ordinances totally excluding such uses from certain (usually residential) districts are also invalid. Thus, zoning ordinances typically list churches, religious uses, or the like, among those uses permitted in residential district, either absolutely or as a special exception if they meet specified requirements.

Because zoning ordinances can limit the use of land to residences, the permissible extent of zoning regulation of church buildings is controversial. Several courts have held zoning regulations that exclude churches violate constitutional provisions on religious liberty. Zoning ordinances were declared unconstitutional in *City of Sherman v. Simms* (Tex. 1944); *Lake Drive Baptist Church v. Village of Bayside Board of Trustees* (Wis. 1961); *Church of Christ v. Metropolitan Board of Zoning Appeals* (Ind. App. Ct. 1978).

Cases upholding the zoning ordinance as opposed to the church include: *Corporation of Presiding Bishop v. City of Porterville* (Cal. 1949) and *Miami Beach United Lutheran Church of the Epiphany v. City of Miami Beach* (Fla. 1955).

Generally, the majority view has been that churches, by their nature, are in conformity with the ends of zoning because they promote public morals and the general welfare. Attempts to exclude churches from residential areas have been especially scrutinized. Churches have, thus, been included within residential districts, although required to conform to building requirements. The zoning authority might attempt to dress up exclusions under the need to protect against hazards of traffic congestion that might threaten the reasonable welfare of a residential neighborhood, but the traditional disposition of the courts has been to strike down such ordinances.

Increasingly, zoning determinations excluding churches from residential areas have been upheld by some courts. More recent decisions have been more deferential to land use regulations, and move away from the traditional deference accorded to church property. The reason for this may be the changing perception of the value of churches in communities. In some cases, residents may oppose the construction of churches because of concerns that they contribute to congested traffic, bring a large number of children into the area, and contribute additional noise to the community. In *Congregation of Jehovah's Witnesses, Inc. v. City of Lakewood* (6th Cir.), the court upheld a zoning ordinance that restricted the construction of religious structures that comprised only 10 percent of the total land area of the city.

Land use and its effect on religion is controversial in contemporary America. The intersection where religious practice meets zoning regulation is marked by contentious litigation. Religion and land use conflicts are occurring throughout the United States, involving both mainstream and nontraditional churches. For example, 10 percent of the Presbyterian churches that applied for permits or zoning variances from government authorities between 1992 and 1997 reported "significant conflict" with city/county staff, neighbors, commission members, or others.

In 1993 the Religious Freedom Restoration Act was enacted by Congress. It stated that, "Governments should not substantially burden religious exercise" without a "compelling interest."

One of the first religious leaders to invoke the RFRA in a land-use dispute was Patrick F. Flores, Archbishop of San Antonio. In 1993 the city of Boerne, Texas, had turned down a request for an addition to St. Peter the Apostle Roman Catholic Church because the expansion would radically alter the exterior of the Spanish Mission-style building, which is the centerpiece of the city's mile-long downtown historic district. Flores argued that the RFRA exempted St. Peter's from landmark designation; the city argued that the RFRA was unconstitutional because Congress had infringed on the long-settled authority of the courts to protect religious freedom. The U.S. Supreme Court agreed with the city and in June 1997 declared the RFRA unconstitutional.

This case, however, has not given planning and zoning commissions a clear advantage in land-use conflicts. Three states—Connecticut, Rhode Island, and Massachusetts—have passed their own versions of the RFRA, and many others have begun considering similar bills.

State court decisions on zoning and religious organizations have varied widely. The Washington Supreme Court has ruled in favor of churches protesting designations as historic landmarks. The court held that the rule designating a church as a landmark under a city ordinance and placing specific controls on the church's ability to alter the structure's exterior violated the church's free exercise rights under both the federal and state constitutions. [*First Covenant Church v. City of Seattle* (Wash. 1990, *vacated* U.S. 1990)]. New York state courts have consistently upheld the regulators. [*Ethical Culture v. Spatt* (N.Y. 1980); *St. Bartholomew's Church v. City of New York* (2d Cir. 1990)].

Religious rights advocates have sought to draft a "RFRA II," a tentative draft of which asks zoning decision makers to equate religious institutions with other places where large numbers of people assemble, like movie theaters and community centers. They hope to prohibit cities from denying access of churches to areas where they allow commercial enterprises.

Prior to the U.S. Supreme Court declaring the RFRA unconstitutional, several courts have ruled on the question of whether the zoning regulations violated their rights to free exercise of religion. The following courts found that the zoning law had in fact violated their rights under RFRA: *Brown v. Borough of Maheffey* (3d Cir., 1994)(regarding borough's action in deliberately erecting fence and locking gate between public park and property church uses for revival meetings); *Western Presbyterian Church v. Board of Zoning Adjustment* (D. D.C. 1995, *motion dismissed on other grounds*)(on church's program for feeding homeless). The courts that found that the plaintiff religious groups' rights to free exercise of religion were not substantially burdened and that defendants established that their zoning regulations were justified by compelling government interests using the least restrictive means under RFRA, include: *Thirty v. Carlson* (10th Cir. 1996)(suit brought by Quakers and Native Americans challenging proposed highway project because it would have required removal of stillborn's daughter's grave and prevented prayer services at site).

Zoning controversies in the future may arise when petitions come from nontraditional religious groups, from congregations wanting to build very large churches, or from established churches that want to expand their missions by feeding the homeless or establishing day care centers.

ZORACH V. CLAUSEN (U.S. 1952)   In this case, the U.S. Supreme Court upheld a New York state statute permitting released-time programs, that permitted public school students, on the written requests of their parents, to leave school premises during regular school hours so they could attend religious centers for religious instruction or devotional exercises. The instructors for these programs were paid from private funds in facilities managed by participating religious societies. The same statute made school attendance compulsory. Students not released from school could stay in the classrooms, and the churches reported to the schools the names of children released from public schools who failed to report for religious instruction. The program involved neither religious instruction in public schools nor the expenditure of public funds. New York's highest court (the New York Court of Appeals) sustained the statute and the regulations thereunder permitting absence of students from the public schools for religious observance and education, against the claim that the program violated the federal Constitution. The U.S. Supreme Court affirmed the New York holding, finding that the released-time program did not violate the First Amendment, made applicable to the states by the Fourteenth Amendment. Thus, the court "distinguished" or differentiated, this case from *McCollum v. Board of Education* (U.S. 1948), in which the Supreme Court ruled that public schools could not allow religious teachers to offer religious instruction within school buildings.

The Court found that the New York statute had neither inhibited the free exercise of religion nor made a law "respecting an establishment of religion" within the meaning of the First Amendment.

The Court also found that there was no evidence that the system involved the use of coercion to force public school students to attend religious classes.

Table of Cases

Table of Statutes

Adolescent Family Life Act of 1981, 95 Stat. 578 (1981), 42 U.S.C. § 300 et seq.

American Indian Religious Freedom Act of 1978, 92 Stat. 469 (1978), 42 U.S.C. § 1996

Anti-Arson Act of 1982, 96 Stat. 1319 (1982), 18 U.S.C. §§ 841 note, 844

Asylum, 8 U.S.C. § 1158(b)

Child Abuse Prevention and Treatment Act of 1974, 88 Stat. 5 (1974) 42 U.S.C. §§ 5105–5116

Civil Rights Act of 1964, 78 Stat. 241 (1964), 42 U.S.C §§ 1971, 1975a to 1975d, 2000a to 2000h-6

Comstock Act of 1873, 17 Stat. 599 (1873), 18 U.S.C. § 1461

Defense of Marriage Act of 1996, 110 Stat. 2419 (1996) 28 U.S.C. 1738C

Edmunds Act of 1882, 22 Stat. 30 (1882); amended 1887, repealed 1909

Edmunds-Tucker Act of 1887, 24 Stat. 635 (1887), 48 U.S.C. § 1480a

Elementary and Secondary School Act of 1965, 79 Stat. 27 (1965), 20 U.S.C. §§ 236 to 244, 331 to 332b, et seq.

Equal Access Act of 1984, 98 Stat. 1302 (1984), 20 U.S.C. §§ 4071, note, 4072 to 4074

Fair Housing Act of 1968, 82 Stat. 81 (1981), 42 U.S.C. § 3601 et seq.

Fair Labor Standards Act of 1938, 52 Stat. 1060 (1938), 29 U.S.C. § 201–212

Family Planning Services and Population Research Act of 1970, 84 Stat. 1504 (1970), 33 U.S.C. § 763c; 42 U.S.C. § 201 note, § 211a, § 212

For Further Reading

ARTICLES

Abraham, Henry J. "Religion, Medicine, and the State: Reflections on Some Contemporary Issues." *Journal of Church and State* 22 (Autumn 1980): 423–436.

———. "The Status of the First Amendment's Religion Clauses: Some Reflections on Lines and Limits." *Journal of Church and State* 22 (Spring 1980): 215–231.

Adams, Andrew A. "Cleveland, School Choice, and 'Laws Respecting an Establishment of Religion.'" *Texas Review of Law & Politics* 2 (Fall 1997): 165.

Adams, Arlin M., and Charles J. Emmerich. "A Heritage of Religious Liberty." *University of Pennsylvania Law Review* 137 (May 1989): 1559–1671.

Adams, Arlin M., and Sarah Barringer Gordon. "The Doctrine of Accommodation in the Jurisprudence of the Religion Clauses." *DePaul Law Review* 37 (Spring 1988): 317–345.

Adams, Arlin M., and William R. Hanlon. "*Jones v. Wolf*: Church Autonomy and the Religion Clauses of the First Amendment." *University of Pennsylvania Law Review* 128 (June 1980): 409–426.

Ahlstrom, Sydney E. "Religion, Revolution and the Rise of Modern Nationalism: Reflections on the American Experience." *Church History* 44 (December 1975): 492–504.

———. "The Traumatic Years: American Religion and Culture in the '60s and '70s." *Theology Today* 36 (1980): 504–522.

———. "Aid to Parochial Schools: A Free Exercise Perspective." *Santa Clara Law Review* 21 (Spring 1983): 587–605.

Akins, Nancy. "New Direction in Sacred Land Claims." *Natural Resources Journal* 29 (Spring 1989): 593–605. Case note on *Lyng v. Northwest Indian Cemetery Protective Association*.

Alley, Robert S. "Public Education and the Public Good," in "Symposium: How Much God in the Schools?" *William and Mary Bill of Rights Journal* 4 (Summer 1995): 277.

Amar, Akhil Reed. "The Bill of Rights and the Fourteenth Amendment." *Yale Law Journal* 100 (March 1991): 1131–1210.

Anastaplo, George. "Church and State: Explorations." *Loyola University of Chicago Law Journal* 19 (Fall 1987): 61–193.

Andres, Greg D. "Private School Voucher Remedies in Education Cases." *University of Chicago Law Review* 62 (Spring 1995): 795–823.

Anthony, Dick, and Thomas Robbins. "Negligence, Coercion, and the Protection of Religious Belief." *Journal of Church and State* 37 (Summer 1995): 509–536.

Araujo, Robert J., S. J. "Christian Social Thought and American Public Policy: A

Dialogue Between the Laity and the American State." *Journal of Church and State* 35 (Autumn 1993): 751–780.

Are, D. Gareth. "Beyond *Mergens:* Balancing a Student's Free Speech Right Against the Establishment Clause in Public High School Equal Access Cases." *William and Mary Law Review* 32 (Fall 1990): 127–160.

Arons, Stephen. "The Separation of School and State: *Pierce* Reconsidered." *Harvard Educational Review* 46 (1976):76.

Atkinson, Rob. "Theories of the Federal Income Tax Exemption for Charities: Thesis, Antithesis, and Synthesis." *Stetson Law Review* 27 (Fall 1997): 395.

Ayres, T. D. "*Widmar v. Vincent:* The Beginning of the End of the Establishment Clause." *Journal of College and University Law* 8 (Fall 1981): 511–517.

Baer, Richard A., Jr. "The Supreme Court's Discriminatory Use of the Term 'Sectarian.'" *The Journal of Law and Politics* 6 (Spring 1990): 449–468.

Baker, Brent. "The Special Immigrant Exception for Religious Ministers: An Establishment Clause Analysis." *Boston College Third World Law Journal* 7 (Winter 1987): 97–108.

Balitzer, Alfred. "Some Thoughts About Civil Religion." *Journal of Church and State* 16 (Winter 1974): 31–50.

Ball, William Bentley. "The Fault Is Not in the Laws." *Report from the Capital* 45 (June 1990): 7.

Barfield, Daniel A. "Note, Better to Give Than to Receive: Should Nonprofit Corporations and Charities Pay Punitive Damages?" *Valparaiso University Law Review* 29 (Summer 1995): 1193–1250.

Basil, Robert J. "Note, Clergy Malpractice: Taking Spiritual Counseling Conflicts Beyond Intentional Tort Analysis." *Rutgers Law Journal* (Winter 1988): 419–450.

Bauer, Janine G. "The Constitutionality of Student Fees for Political Student Groups in the Campus Public Forum: *Galda v. Bloustein* and the Right to Associate." *Rutgers Law Journal* 15 (September 1983): 135–184.

Becker, William H. "Creationism: New Dimensions of the Religion Democracy Relation." *Journal of Church and State* 27 (Spring 1985): 315–333.

Bedig, Laurel A. "The Supreme Court Narrows an Employer's Duty to Accommodate an Employee's Religious Practices Under Title VII." *Brooklyn Law Review* 53 (Spring 1987): 245–269.

Bellah, Robert N. "Civil Religion in America." *Daedalus* 96 (Winter 1967): 1–21.

Benjamin, Walter W. "Separation of Church and State: Myth and Reality." *Journal of Church and State* 1 (Winter 1969): 93–110.

Bennet, L. Leslie, Jr., and David E. Sumler. "Ethical Policymaking in Higher Education: State Regulation of Religious Colleges in Maryland." *Journal of Church and State* 35 (Summer 1993): 547–557.

Beredy, George Z. F. "Values, Education and the Law." *Mississippi Law Journal* 48 (Summer 1977): 585–619.

Bereiter, Carl. "Schools Without Education." *Harvard Education Review* 42 (1972): 391.

Berg, Thomas C. "What Hath Congress Wrought? An Interpretative Guide to the Religious Freedom Restoration Act." *Villanova Law Review* 39 (1994): 1.

Berger, Raoul. "Standing to Sue in Public Actions: Is It a Constitutional Requirement?" *Yale Law Journal* 78 (April 1969): 816–840.

Berman, Harold J. "Religious Freedom and the Challenge of the Modem State." *Emory Law Journal* 65 (Winter 1990): 149–164.

Bernardin, Joseph Cardinal. "The Role of the Religious Leader in the Development of Public Policy." *DePaul Law Review* 34 (Fall 1984): 3–21.

Bertonneau, Brian. "*Estate of Thornton v. Caldor, Inc.*: Defining Sabbath Rights in the Workplace." *Hastings Constitutional Law Quarterly* 15 (Spring 1988): 513–532.

Beschle, Donald L. "The Conservative as Liberal: The Religion Clauses, Liberal Neutrality, and the Approach of Justice O'Connor." *Notre Dame Law Review* 62 (Spring 1987): 151–191.

———. "Catechism or Imagination: Is Justice Scalia's Judicial Style Typically Catholic?" *Villanova Law Review* 37 (October 1992): 1329–1359.

Best, James. "*Lynch v. Donnelly*: The Rebirth of the Supreme Court's Attitude Towards the Establishment Clause." *Southern University Law Review* 12 (Fall 1987): 97–105.

BeVier, Lillian R. "The Free Exercise Clause: A View from the Public Forum." *William and Mary Law Review* 27 (1987): 963–974.

Bird, Wendell R., and George K. Rahdert. "The Exemption of Nonprofit Organizations from Federal Income Taxation." *Yale Law Journal* 87 (January 1978): 515–570.

Bird, Wendell R., and Thomas O. Koutouc. "Exempt Religious Organizations Have Strict Limits." *Taxation for Accountants* 48 (April 1992): 207–215.

Birkby, Robert. "The Supreme Court and the Bible Belt: Tennessee Reaction to the *Schempp* Decision." *Midwest Journal of Political Science* 10 (August 1966): 304–319.

Bittker, Boris I. "Churches, Taxes, and the Constitution." *Yale Law Journal* 78 (1969): 1285.

Bjorklun, Eugene C. "The Rites of Spring: Prayers at High School Graduation." *Educational Law Report* 61 (August 30, 1990):1–9.

———. "Commentary, Condom Distribution in the Public Schools: Is Parental Consent Required?" *Educational Law Reporter* 91 (1994): 11.

Blischak, Matthew P. "*O'Lone v. Estate of Shabazz*: The State of Prisoners' Religious Free Exercise Rights." *American University Law Review* 37 (Winter, 1988): 453–486.

Block, Sharon I. "Note, The Establishment Clause in Public Schools: A Model for Future Analysis." *Georgetown Law Journal* 79 (October 1990): 121–140.

Bloostein, Marc J. "The 'Core'-'Periphery' Dichotomy in First Amendment Free Exercise Clause Doctrine: *Goldman v. Weinberger, Bowen v. Roy,* and *O'Lone v. Estate of Shabazz*." *Cornell Law Review* 72 (May 1987): 827–855.

Bohner, Robert J., Jr. "Religious Property Disputes and Intrinsically Religious Evidence: Towards a Narrow Application of the Neutral Principles Approach." *Villanova Law Review* 35 (September 1990): 949–981.

Boles, Donald E. "Church and State and the Burger Court: Recent Developments Affecting Parochial Schools." *Journal of Church and State* 18 (Winter 1976): 21–38.

———. "Religion and the Public Schools in Judicial Review." *Journal of Church and State* 26 (Winter 1984): 55–71.

Bolton, S. Charles, and Cal Ledbetter, Jr. "Compulsory Bible Reading in Arkansas and the Culture of Southern Fundamentalism." *Social Science Quarterly* 64 (September 1983): 670–676.

Boothby, Lee, and R. W. Nixon. "Religious Accommodation: An Often Delicate Task." *The Notre Dame Lawyer* 57 (June 1982): 797–808.

Boston, Rob. "The Day 'Sherbert' Melted." *Church and State* 43 (June 1990): 4–6.

Bowden, Henry Warner. "A Historian's Response to the Concept of American Civil Religion." *Journal of Church and State* 17 (Autumn 1975): 495–505.

Bradley, Gerald V. "Dogmatomachy—A 'Privitization' Theory of the Religion Clause Cases." *Saint Louis University Law Journal* 30 (March 1986): 275–330.

———. "The No Religious Test Clause and the Constitution of Religious Liberty: A Machine That Has Gone of Itself." *Case Western Law Review* 37 (Summer 1987): 674–747.

———. "Church Autonomy in the Constitutional Order: The End of Church and State." *Louisiana Law Review* 49 (May 1989): 1057–1087.

———. "Beguiled: Free Exercise Exemptions and the Siren Song of Liberalism." *Hofstra Law Review* 20 (Winter 1991): 245–319.

Braveman, Daan. "The Establishment Clause and the Course of Religious Neutrality." *Maryland Law Review* 45 (Spring 1986): 352–386.

Brown, Bruce P. "The Establishment Clause Jurisprudence of Chief Justice Warren Burger." *Oklahoma Law Review* 45 (Spring 1992): 33–56.

Byers, David E. "Title VII and Sectarian Institutions of Higher Education: Congress Shall Make No Law Prohibiting Free Exercise of Religion." *Cumberland Law Review* 14 (Summer 1984): 597–641.

Calabresi, Steven G., and Kevin H. Rhodes. "The Structural Constitution: Unitary Executive, Plural Judiciary." *Harvard Law Review* 105 (April 1992): 1153–1216.

Carmella, Angela C. "Houses of Worship and Religious Liberty: Constitutional Limits to Landmark Preservation and Architectural Review." *Villanova Law Review* 36 (April 1991): 401–515.

———. "State Constitutional Protection of Religious Exercise: An Emerging Post-*Smith* Jurisprudence." *Brigham Young University Law Review* 1993 (Winter 1993): 275–325.

Carpenter, James G. "State Regulation of Religious Schools." *Journal of Law and Education* 14 (April 1985): 229–249.

Carroll, Anne Berrill. "Religion, Politics, and the IRS: Defining the Limits of Tax Law Controls on Political Expression by Churches." *Marquette Law Review* 76 (Fall 1992): 217–263.

Carroll, William A. "The Constitution, the Supreme Court, and Religion." *American Political Science Review* 61 (September 1967): 657–674.

Carter, Stephen L. "Evolutionism, Creationism, and Treating Religion as a Hobby." *Duke Law Journal* 1987 (December 1987): 977–996.

———. "The Religiously Devout Judge." *Notre Dame Law Review* 64 (Winter 1989): 932–944.

———. "Comment: The Resurrection of Religious Freedom?" *Harvard Law Review* 107 (November 1993): 118–142.

Casad, Robert C. "Note, Compulsory High School Attendance and the Old Order Amish: A Commentary on *State v. Garber*." *University of Kansas Law Review* 16 (April 1968): 423–436.

Case, David W. "Resolving the Conflict Between Chapter 13 of the Bankruptcy Code and the Free Exercise Clause—*In Re Green*: A Step in the Wrong Direction." *Mississippi Law Journal* 57 (April 1987): 163–184.

Casino, Bruce J. "'I Know It When I See It': Mail-Order Ministry Tax Fraud and the Problem of a Constitutionally Acceptable Definition of Religion." *American Criminal Law Review* 25 (Summer 1987): 113–164.

Cavanaugh, William T., Jr. "The United States Military Chaplaincy Program: Another Seam in the Fabric of Our Society?" *Notre Dame Law Review* 59 (1983): 181–223.

Chase, Jonathan B. "Litigating a Nativity Scene Case." *St. Louis University Law Journal* 24 (September 1980): 237–271.

Choper, Jesse H. "Religion in the Public Schools: A Proposed Constitutional Standard." *Minnesota Law Review* 47 (January 1963): 329–416.

———. "The Religion Clauses of the First Amendment: Reconciling the Conflict." *University of Pittsburgh Law Review* 41 (Summer 1980): 673–701.

———. "Defining 'Religion' in the First Amendment." *University of Illinois Law Review* 1982 (Summer 1982): 579–613.

———. "The Free Exercise Clause: A Structural Overview and an Appraisal of Recent Developments." *William and Mary Law Review* 27 (1986): 943–961.

———. "The Establishment Clause and Aid to Parochial Schools—An Update." *California Law Review* 75 (January 1987): 5–14.

———. "Separation of Church and State: 'New' Directions by the 'New' Supreme Court." *Journal of Church and State* 34 (Spring 1992): 363–375.

Chopko, Mark. "Ascending Liability of Religious Entities for the Actions of Others." *American Journal of Trial Advocacy* 17 (Fall 1993): 289–350.

Clark, Elias. "Charitable Trusts and the Fourteenth Amendment and the Will of Stephen Girard." *Yale Law Journal* 66 (June 1957): 979–1015.

Clark, J. Morris. "Guidelines for the Free Exercise Clause." *Harvard Law Review* 83 (December 1969): 327–365.

Clements, Ben. "Defining 'Religion' in the First Amendment: A Functional Approach." *Cornell Law Review* 74 (March 1989): 532–558.

Cline, Christopher P. "Pursuing Native American Rights in International Law Venues: A Jus Cogens Strategy After *Lyng v. Northwest Indian Cemetery Protective Association*." *Hastings Law Journal* 42 (January 1991): 591–633.

Clune, William H. "Educational Adequacy: A Theory and Its Remedies." *University of Michigan Journal of Law Reform* 28 (Spring 1995): 481–491.

Cohen, Cynthia Price. "Introductory Note: United Nations Convention on the Rights of the Child." *International Legal Materials* 28 (November 1989): 1448–1476.

Collins, Camala. "No More Religious Protection: The Impact of *Lyng v. Northwest Indian Cemetery Protection Association*." *Washington University Journal of Urban and Contemporary Law* 38 (Summer 1990): 369–384.

Conkin, Paul. "The Church Establishment in North Carolina, 1765–1776." *North Carolina Historical Review* 32 (1955): 1.

Conkle, Daniel. "Toward a General Theory of the Establishment Clause." *Northwestern University Law Review* 82 (Summer 1988): 1113–1194.

Connolly, John W., III. "*Mueller v. Allen*: A New Standard of Scrutiny Applied to Tax Deductions for Educational Expenses." *Duke Law Journal* 1994 (November 1994): 983–1001.

Connor, M. Colleen. "The Constitutionality of Religious Symbols on Government Property: A Suggested Approach." *Journal of Church and State* 37 (Spring 1995): 385–411.

"The Constitutional Dimensions of Student-Initiated Religious Activity in Public High Schools." *Yale Law Journal* 92 (December 1982): 499–519.

"Constitutional Law—Legislative Prayer and the Establishment Clause: An Exception to the Traditional Analysis—*Marsh v. Chambers.*" *Creighton Law Review* 17 (1983/1984): 157–185.

"Constitutional Law—The Clash Between the Free Exercise of Religion and the Military's Uniform Regulations—*Goldman v. Secretary of Defense.*" *Temple Law Quarterly* 58 (Spring 1985): 195–219.

Cook, Theresa. "The Peyote Case: A Return to *Reynolds.*" *Denver University Law Review* 68 (Winter 1991): 91–103.

Cooper, Charles L. "Stare Decisis: Precedent and Principle in Constitutional Adjudication." *Cornell Law Review* 73 (January 1988): 401–410.

Copilevitz, Errol. "The Historical Role of the First Amendment in Charitable Appeals." *Stetson Law Review* 27 (Fall 1997): 457–472.

Cord, Robert L., and Howard Ball. "Church-State Separation: Restoring the 'No Preference' Doctrine of the First Amendment." *Harvard Journal of Law and Public Policy* 9 (Winter 1986): 129–172.

———. "The Separation of Church and State: A Debate." *Utah Law Review* 1987 (Fall 1987): 895–925.

Cordes, Mark W. "Where To Pray? Religious Zoning and the First Amendment." *University of Kansas Law Review* 35 (Summer 1987): 697–762.

Cornelius, William J. "Church and State: The Mandate of the Establishment Clause: Wall of Separation or Benign Neutrality?" *St. Mary's Law Journal* 16 (Winter 1984): 1–39.

Corwin, Edward S. "The Supreme Court as National School Board." *Law and Contemporary Problems* 14 (Winter 1949): 3–22.

Cote, Denise. "Establishment Clause Analysis of Legislative and Administrative Aid to Religion." *Columbia Law Review* 74 (October 1974): 1175–1202.

Cover, Robert. "Foreward: Nomos and Narrative." *Harvard Law Review* 97 (November 1983): 4–68.

Crabb, Kelly C. "Religious Symbols, American Traditions and the Constitution." *Brigham Young University Law Review* 1984 (Fall 1984): 509–562.

Crane, Linda R. "Family Values and the Supreme Court." *Connecticut Law Review* 25 (Winter 1993): 427–469.

Crockenberg, Vincent A. "An Argument for the Constitutionality of Direct Aid to Religious Schools." *Journal of Law and Education* 13 (January 1984): 1–18.

Croney, Vance M. "Secondary Right: Protection of the Free Exercise Clause Reduced by *Oregon v. Smith.*" *Willamette Law Review* 27 (Winter 1991): 173–196.

Crumpler, M. Greg. "Constitutional Law—Legislative Chaplaincy Program Held Not to Violate the Establishment of Religion Clause—*Marsh v. Chambers.*" *Campbell Law Review* 6 (Spring 1984): 143–161.

Cuomo, Mario. "Religious Belief and Public Morality: A Catholic Governor's Perspective, Address at the University of Notre Dame (Sept. 13, 1994)." *Notre Dame Journal of Law, Ethics, and Public Policy* 13 (Fall 1984): 755–756.

Curriden, Mark. "Defenders of the Faith." *ABA Journal* 80 (December 1994): 86.

Curry, David P. "The Constitution in the Supreme Court: Civil Rights and Liberties, 1930–1941." *Duke Law Journal* 1987 (November 1987): 800–830.

———. "The Constitution in the Supreme Court: The Preferred-Position Debate, 1941–1946." *Catholic University Law Review* 37 (Fall 1987): 39–71.

Curry, Patricia E. "James Madison and the Burger Court: Converging Views of Church-State Separation." *Indiana Law Journal* 56 (Summer 1981): 615–636.

"Daily Moments of Silence in Public Schools: A Constitutional Analysis." *New York University Law Review* 58 (May 1983): 364–408.

Dane, Perry. "Religious Exemptions Under the Free Exercise Clause: A Model of Competing Authorities." *Yale Law Journal* 90 (December 1980): 350–378.

Dankanich, Michael D. "Constitutional Law—State May Ban Religious Solicitation in Public Sports Complex, Since Complex Is Not A Public Forum—*International Society For Krishna Consciousness, Inc. v. New Jersey Sports & Exposition Authority*, 691 F.2D 155 (3d Cir. 1982)." *Temple Law Review* 57 (1984): 119–133.

Danzig, Richard. "How Questions Begot Answers in Felix Frankfurter's First Flag Salute Opinion." *Supreme Court Review* 1977 (1977): 257–274.

———. "Justice Frankfurter's Opinions in the Flag Salute Cases: Blending Logic and Psychologic in Constitutional Decisionmaking." *Stanford Law Review* 36 (February 1984): 675–723.

Darling, Webster. "*Mozert v. Hawkins County Board of Education:* The Struggle to Balance Constitutional Interests in the Public School Curricula." *Arkansas Law Review* 42 (Spring 1989): 519–548.

Davis, Derek H. "Editorial: Rebuilding the Wall: Thoughts on Religion and the Supreme Court Under the Clinton Administration." *Journal of Church and State* 35 (Winter 1993): 7–17.

———. "Editorial: Religious Pluralism and the Quest for Unity in American Life." *Journal of Church and State* 36 (Spring 1994): 245–259.

———. "Editorial: Religious Dimensions of the Declaration of Independence: Fact and Fiction." *Journal of Church and State* 36 (Summer 1994): 469–482.

———. "Editorial: Religion and the American Revolution." *Journal of Church and State* 36 (Autumn 1994): 709–724.

———. "Editorial: Assessing the Proposed Religious Equality Amendment." *Journal of Church and State* 37 (Summer 1995): 493–508.

———. "Editorial: A Commentary on the Proposed 'Religious Equality/Liberties' Amendment." *Journal of Church and State* 38 (Winter 1996): 5–23.

de Andrade, David. "The Equal Access Act: The Establishment Clause v. The Free Exercise and Free Speech Clauses." *New York Law School Law Review* 33 (Fall 1988): 447–468.

Dean, James J. "Ceremonial Invocations at Public High School Events and the Establishment Clause." *Florida State University Law Review* 16 (Spring 1989): 1000–1031.

Delgado, Richard. "Religious Totalism: Gentle and Ungentle Persuasion Under the First Amendment." *Southern California Law Review* 51 (November 1977): 1–98.

———. "The Inward Turn in Outsider Jurisprudence." *William and Mary Law Review* 31 (Spring 1993): 741–768.

Dellinger, Walter. "The Sound of Silence: An Epistle on Prayer and the Constitution." *Yale Law Journal* 95 (July 1986): 1631–1646.

Denbeaux, Mark P. "The First Word of the First Amendment." *Northwestern University Law Review* 80 (Spring 1986): 1156–1220.

"Developments in the Law—Privileged Communications—I.V. Medical and Counseling Privileges." *Harvard Law Review* 98 (May 1985): 1530–1563.

Devins, Neal, and Charles O. Galvin. "State Regulation of Christian Schools." *Journal of Legislation* 10 (Summer 1983): 351–381.

———. "A Tax Policy Analysis of *Bob Jones University v. United States*." *Vanderbilt Law Review* 36 (November 1983): 1353–1382.

————. "Religious Symbols and the Establishment Clause." *Journal of Church and State* 27 (Winter 1985): 19–46.

Dodge, Joseph M., II. "The Free Exercise of Religion: A Sociological Approach." *Michigan Law Review* 67 (February 1969): 679–728.

————. "Does the Wall Still Stand?: Separation of Church and State in the United States." *Baylor Law Review* 37 (Summer 1985): 755–775.

Donahue, Mary Jo. "Note, First Amendment Rights in the Military Context: What Deference Is Due?" *Creighton Law Review* 20 (Fall 1986): 85–110.

Douglas, William O. "Stare Decisis." *Columbia Law Review* 49 (June 1949): 735–758.

Dow, David R. "Toward a Theory of the Establishment Clause." *University of Missouri-Kansas City Law Review* 56 (Spring 1988): 491–513.

Doyle, Denis. "A Den of Inequity: Private Schools Reconsidered." *American Education* 18 (1982): 11–18.

Drakeman, Donald L. "Antidisestablishmentarianism: The Latest (and Longest) Word from the Supreme Court in *Marsh v. Chambers*." *Cardozo Law Review* 5 (Fall 1983): 153–181.

————. "Religion and the Republic: James Madison and the First Amendment." *Journal of Church and State* 25 (Autumn 1983): 427–445.

Dreisbach, Daniel L. "Thomas Jefferson and Bills Number 82–86 of the Revision of the Laws of Virginia, 1776–1786: New Light on the Jeffersonian Model of Church-State Relations." *North Carolina Law Review* 69 (November 1990): 159–211.

Drennan, William A. "Religion and the Republic: James Madison and the First Amendment." *Journal of Church and State* 25 (Autumn, 1983): 427–445.

————. "Prayer in the Schools: Is New Jersey's Moment of Silence Constitutional?" *Rutgers Law Review* 35 (Winter 1983): 341–359.

————. "Note, For Whom Will the Bell Toll" *St. Louis University Law Journal* 29 (March 1985): 561–596.

Driggs, Kenneth David. "The Mormon Church-State Confrontation in Nineteenth-Century America." *Journal of Church and State* 30 (Autumn 1988): 273–289.

Drinan, Robert F., S.J. "State and Federal Aid to Parochial Schools." *Journal of Church and State* 7 (Winter 1965): 67–77.

Drinan, Robert F., S.J., and Jennifer I. Huffman. "Religious Freedom and the *Oregon v. Smith* and *Hialeah* Cases." *Journal of Church and State* 35 (Winter 1993): 19–35.

Drucker, Margo R. "*Bowen v. Kendrick*: Establishing Chastity at the Expense of Constitutional Prophylactics." *New York University Law Review* (November 1989): 1165–1210.

Dunsford, John E. "Prayer in the Well: Some Heretical Reflections on the Establishment Syndrome." *Utah Law Review* 1984 (Winter 1984): 1–44.

Durham, W. Cole, Jr. "Religious Liberty and the Call of Conscience." *De Paul Law Review* 42 (Fall 1992): 71–88.

Durrant, Matthew B. "Accrediting Church-Related Schools: A First Amendment Analysis." *Journal of Law and Education* 14 (April 1985): 147–179.

Durso, Keith E. "The Voluntary School Prayer Debate: A Separationist Perspective." *Journal of Church and State* 36 (Winter 1994): 79–96.

Dwyer, James G. "Parent's Religion and Children's Welfare: Debunking the Doctrine of Parents' Rights." *California Law Review* 82 (December 1994): 1371.

Edwards, John Evan. "Democracy and Delegation of Legislative Authority: *Bob Jones University v. United States.*" *Boston College Law Review* 26 (May 1985): 745–778.

Eisgruber, Christopher L. "Madison's Wager: Religious Liberty in the Constitutional Order." *Northwestern University Law Review* 89 (Winter 1995): 347–410.

Eisgruber, Christopher L., and Lawrence G. Sager. "The Vulnerability of Conscience: The Constitutional Basis for Protecting Religious Conduct." *University of Chicago Law Review* 61 (Fall 1994): 1245–1316.

Elifson, Kirk, and C. Kirk Hadaway. "Prayer in Public Schools: When Church and State Collide." *Public Opinion Quarterly* 49 (Fall 1985): 317–329.

Ericsson, Samuel E. "Clergy Malpractice: Constitutional and Political Issues." *The Center for Law and Religious Freedom* (May 1981): 1–32.

Esbeck, Carl H. "The Establishment Clause and Liquor Sales: The Supreme Court Rushes in Where Angels Fear to Tread—*Larkin v. Grendel's Den.*" *Washington Law Review* 59 (1983–1984): 87–101.

———. "Establishment Clause Limits on Governmental Interference with Religious Organizations." *Washington and Lee Law Review* 41 (Spring 1984): 347–420.

———. "Toward a General Theory of Church-State Relations and the First Amendment." *Public Law Forum* 4 (Spring 1985): 325–354.

———. "Religion and a Neutral State: Imperative or Impossibility?" *Cumberland Law Review* 15 (Winter 1985): 67–88.

———. "Five Views of Church-State Relations in Contemporary American Thought." *Brigham Young University Law Review* 1986 (Spring 1986): 371–404.

———. "Tort Claims Against Churches and Ecclesiastical Officers: The First Amendment Considerations." *West Virginia Law Review* 89 (Fall 1986): 1–114.

———. "The *Lemon* Test: Should It Be Retained, Reformulated or Rejected?" *Notre Dame Journal of Law, Ethics & Public Policy* 4 (Fall-Winter 1990): 513–548.

———. "Government Regulation of Religiously Based Social Services: The First Amendment Considerations." *Hastings Constitutional Law Quarterly* 19 (Winter 1992): 343–412.

———. "A Restatement of the Supreme Court's Law of Religious Freedom: Coherence, Conflict, or Chaos?" *Notre Dame Law Review* 70 (January 1995): 581–650.

Evans, Bette Novit. "Evolution and Creationism in the Public Schools." *Journal of Contemporary Law* 9 (1983): 81–126.

———. "Contradictory Demands on the First Amendment Religion Clauses: Having It Both Ways." *Journal of Church and State* 30 (Autumn 1988): 463–481.

Evans, Daniel. "Note, Another Brick in the Wall: Denominational Preferences and Strict Scrutiny Under the Establishment Clause." *Nebraska Law Review* 62 (Spring 1983): 359–383.

Fallon, Richard H., Jr. "Two Senses of Autonomy." *Stanford Law Review* 46 (April 1994): 875–905.

Fava, Eileen M. "Desegregation and Parental Choice in Public Schooling: A Legal Analysis of Controlled Choice Student Assignment Plans." *Boston College Third World Law Journal* 11 (Winter 1991): 83–105.

Feder, Benjamin D. "And a Child Shall Lead Them: Justice O'Connor, The Principle of Religious Liberty and Its Practical Application." *Pace Law Review* 8 (Spring 1988): 249–302.

Feigenson, Neal R. "Political Standing and Governmental Endorsement of Religion: An Alternative to Current Establishment Clause Doctrine." *DePaul Law Review* 40 (Fall 1990): 53–114.

Fellman, David. "Religion, the State, and the Public University." *Journal of Church and State* 26 (Winter 1984): 73–90.

Felsen, David. "Developments in Approaches to Establishment Clause Analysis: Consistency for the Future." *American University Law Review* 38 (Winter 1989): 395–428.

Fielder, David A. "Serving God or Caesar: Constitutional Limits on the Regulation of Religious Employers." *Missouri Law Review* 51 (Summer 1986): 779–791.

Fisher, Barry A. "Comment on the Free Exercise Clause: A Structural Overview and an Appraisal of Recent Developments." *William and Mary Law Review* 27 (1987): 975–984.

Fisher, Louis A. "The Curious Belief in Judicial Supremacy." *Suffolk Law Review* 25 (Spring 1991): 85–116.

Flowers, Ronald B. "The Supreme Court's Three Tests of the Establishment Clause." *Religion in Life* 45 (Spring 1976): 41–52.

———. "The Supreme Court's Interpretation of the Free Exercise Clause." *Religion in Life* 49 (Fall 1980): 322–335.

———. "Withholding Medical Care for Religious Reasons." *Journal of Religion and Health* 23 (Winter 1984): 268–282.

———. "Can Churches Discipline Members and Win in Court?" *Journal of Church and State* 27 (Autumn 1985): 483–498.

———. "Government Accommodation of Religious-Based Conscientious Objection." *Seton Hall Law Review* 24 (Spring 1994): 695–735.

Fordham, Jefferson B. "The Implications of the Supreme Court Decisions Dealing with Religious Practices in the Public Schools." *Journal of Church and State* 6 (Winter 1964): 44–60.

Fox, Richard P. "Conscientious Objection to War: The Background and a Current Appraisal." *Cleveland State Law Review* 31 (Winter 1982): 77–106.

Freed, Mayer G., and Daniel D. Polsby. "Race, Public Policy, and *Bob Jones University.*" *Supreme Court Review* (1983): 1–31.

Freeman, Brian A. "The Supreme Court and First Amendment Rights of Students in the Public School Classroom: A Proposed Model of Analysis." *Hastings Constitutional Law Quarterly* 12 (September 1984): 1–70.

Freeman, George C., III. "The Misguided Search for the Constitutional Definition of 'Religion.'" *Georgetown Law Journal* 71 (August 1983): 1519–1665.

Freund, Paul A. "Public Aid to Parochial Schools." *Harvard Law Review* 82 (June 1969): 1680–1692.

Friedland, Jerod A. "Constitutional Issues in Revoking Religious Tax Exemptions: *Church of Scientology of California v. Commissioner.*" *University of Florida Law Review* 37 (Tax 1985): 565–589.

Frohlich, David. "Note, Will Courts Make Change for a Large Denomination? Problems of Interpretation in an Agency Analysis in Which a Religious Denomination Is Involved in an Ascending Liability Tort Case." *Iowa Law Review* 72 (July 1987): 1377–1399.

Funston, C. Eric. "Comment, Made Out of Whole Cloth? A Constitutional Analysis of the Clergy Malpractice Concept." *California Western Law Review* 19 (Summer 1983): 507–544.

Gaffney, Edward M., Jr. "Political Divisiveness Along Religious Lines: Entanglement of the Court in Sloppy History and Bad Public Policy." *St. Louis University Law Journal* 24 (September 1980): 205–236.

———. "Biblical Religion and American Politics: Some Historical and Theological Reflections." *Journal of Law and Religion* 1 (Summer 1983): 171–186.

Galanter, Marc. "Religious Freedoms in the United States: A Turning Point?" *Wisconsin Law Review* 1966 (Spring 1966): 217–296.

Galligan, Michael William. "Judicial Resolution of Intrachurch Disputes." *Columbia Law Review* 83 (December 1983): 2007–2038.

Galloway, Russell W. "Basic Free Exercise Clause Analysis." *Santa Clara Law Review* 29 (Fall 1989): 865–878.

Garrett, James Leo. "The 'Free Exercise' Clause of the First Amendment: Retrospect and Prospect." *Journal of Church and State* 17 (Autumn 1975): 393–398.

Garrett, W. Barry. "IRS Proposal Scored." *Church and State* 29 (June 1976): 10–11.

Garvey, John H. "Free Exercise and the Values of Religious Liberty." *Connecticut Law Review* 14 (1981): 193–221.

———. "Freedom and Equality in the Religion Clauses." *Supreme Court Review* 1981 (1981): 193–221.

———. "Churches and the Free Exercise of Religion." *Notre Dame Journal of Law, Ethics, and Public Policy* 4 (Fall/Winter 1990): 567–589.

Gaustad, Edwin Scott. "A Disestablished Society: Origins of the First Amendment." *Journal of Church and State* 11 (Autumn 1969): 409–426.

Gavin, Charles O., and Neal Devins. "A Tax Policy Analysis of *Bob Jones University v. United States.*" *Vanderbilt Law Review* 36 (November 1983): 1353–1382.

Gay, John. "Note, *Bowen v. K:* Establishing a New Relationship Between Church and State." *American University Law Review* 38 (Spring 1989): 953–992.

Gedicks, Frederick M. "Motivation, Rationality, and Secular Purpose in Establishment Clause Review." *Arizona State Law Journal* 1985 (Summer 1985): 677–726.

———. "Public Life and Hostility to Religion." *Virginia Law Review* 78 (April 1992): 671–696.

Gedicks, Frederick M., and Robert Hendrix. "Democracy, Autonomy, and Values: Some Thoughts on Religion and Law in Modern America." *Southern California Law Review* 60 (September 1987): 1579–1619.

Gerardi, Donald F. "Zephaniah Swift and Connecticut's Standing Order: Skepticism, Conservatism, and Religious Liberty in the Early Republic." *New England Quarterly* 67 (1994): 234.

Gershon, Richard. "Tax-Exempt Entities: Achieving and Maintaining Special Status under the Watchful Eye of the Internal Revenue Service." *Cumberland Law Review* 16 (Spring 1986): 301–327.

Gey, Steven G. "Why is Religion Special?: Reconsidering the Accommodation of Religion under the Religion Clauses of the First Amendment." *University of Pittsburgh Law Review* 52 (Fall 1990): 75–187.

Geyer, Thomas E. "Free Exercise Jurisprudence: A Comment on the Heightened Threshold and the Proposal of the 'Burden Plus' Standard." *Ohio State Law Journal* 50 (October 1989): 1035–1057.

Giannelial, Donald A. "Religious Liberty, Nonestablishment, and Doctrinal Development. Part 1. The Religious Liberty Guarantee." *Harvard Law Review* 80 (May 1967): 1381–1431.

———. "*Lemon* and *Tilton:* The Bitter and Sweet of Church-State Entanglement." *Supreme Court Review* 147 (1971): 147–200.

Glendon, Mary Ann, and Raul Yanes. "Structural Free Exercise." *Michigan Law Review* 90 (December 1991): 477–550.

Goff, J. Edward. "Constitutional Law—First Amendment—A State Statute that Permits a Tax Deduction for Public as Well as Non-Public School Tuition and Related Expenses Does Not Violate the Establishment Clause of the First Amendment—*Mueller v. Allen.*" *Villanova Law Review* 29 (April 1984): 505–534.

Goodwin, Glenn. "Would Caesar Tax God? The Constitutionality of Governmental Taxation of Churches." *Drake Law Review* 35 (1986): 383–404.

Gordon, James D., III. "Free Exercise on the Mountaintop." *California Law Review* 79 (January 1991): 91–116.

Gordon, Sarah B. "Indian Religious Freedom and Governmental Development of Public Lands." *Yale Law Journal* 94 (May 1985): 1447–1471.

Gottlieb, Stephen E. "Compelling Governmental Interests: An Essential but Unanalyzed Term in Constitutional Adjudication." *Boston University Law Review* 68 (November 1988): 917–978.

———. "Compelling Governmental Interests and Constitutional Discourse." *Albany Law Review* 55 (Spring 1992): 549–560.

———. "The Paradox of Balancing Significant Interests." *Hastings Law Journal* 45 (April 1994): 825–866.

Gould, Diane Brazen. "Government Neutrality and Separation of Church and State: Tuition Tax Credits." *Harvard Law Review* 92 (January 1979): 696–717.

———. "The First Amendment and the American Indian Religious Freedom Act: An Approach to Protecting Native American Religion." *Iowa Law Review* 71 (March 1986): 869–891.

Govert, Gary R. "Something There Is That Doesn't Love a Wall: Reflections on the History of North Carolina's Religious Test for Public Office." *North Carolina Law Review* 64 (June 1986): 1071–1098.

Grabiner, Judith V., and Peter D. Miller. "Effects of the Scopes Trial." *Science* 185 (September 6, 1974): 832.

Graham, David. "Balancing the Free Religious Exercise Right Against Governmental Interests." *Hamline Law Review* 9 (July 1986): 649–699.

Graham, John Remington. "A Restatement of the Intended Meaning of the Establishment Clause in Relation to Education and Religion." *Brigham Young University Law Review* 1981 (Spring 1981): 333–359.

Grant, Harriet. "Note, The Disappearing Wall." *North Carolina Law Review* 63 (April 1985): 782–793.

Green, Steven K. "The Misnomer of Equality Under the Equal Access Act." *Vermont Law Review* 14 (Winter 1990): 369–400.

———. "Evangelicals and the Becker Amendment: A Lesson in Church-State Moderation." *Journal of Church and State* 33 (Summer 1991): 541–567.

———. "The Blaine Amendment Reconsidered." *American Journal of Legal History* 36 (Summer 1992): 38–73.

———. "The Legal Argument Against Private School Choice." *University of Cincinnati Law Review* 62 (Summer 1993): 37–73.

Greenawalt, Kent. "All or Nothing at All: The Defeat of Selective Conscientious Objection." *Supreme Court Review* 1971 (1971): 31.

———. "Religion as a Concept in Constitutional Law." *California Law Review* 72 (September 1984): 753–816.

———. "The Role of Religion in a Liberal Democracy: Dilemmas and Possible Resolutions." *Journal of Church and State* 35 (Summer 1993): 503–519.

———. "The Use of Religious Convictions by Legislators and Judges." *Journal of Church and State* 36 (Summer 1994): 541–555.

———. "The Participation of Religious Groups in Political Advocacy." *Journal of Church and State* 36 (Winter 1994): 143–160.

Greene, Abner S. "The Political Balance of the Religion Clauses." *Yale Law Journal* 102 (May 1993): 1611–1644.

Griggs, Walter S., Jr. "The Selective Conscientious Objector: A Vietnam Legacy." *Journal of Church and State* 21 (Winter 1979): 91–107.

Grossman, Thomas E. "Constitutionality of Student-Initiated Religious Meetings on Public School Grounds." *University of Cincinnati Law Review* 50 (Fall 1981): 740–785.

Hafen, Bruce C. "*Hazelwood School District* and the Role of First Amendment Institutions." *Duke Law Journal* 1988 (September 1988): 685–705.

Hall, Timothy L. "Note, The Sacred and the Profane: A First Amendment Definition of Religion." *Texas Law Review* 61 (August 1982): 139–173.

———. "Religion, Equality, and Difference." *Temple Law Review* 65 (Spring 1992): 1–89.

Hamburger, Philip A. "A Constitutional Right of Religious Exemption: An Historical Perspective." *George Washington Law Review* 60 (April 1992): 915–948.

Hamilton, Marci. "The Religious Freedom Restoration Act: Letting the Fox Into the Henhouse Under Cover of Section 5 of the Fourteenth Amendment." *Cardozo Law Review* 16 (December 1994): 357–398.

Hammett, Harold D. "Separation of Church and State: By One Wall or Two?" *Journal of Church and State* 7 (Spring 1965): 190–206.

Hammond, Phillip E., and Eric M. Mazur. "Church, State and the Dilemma of Conscience." *Journal of Church and State* 37 (Summer 1995): 555–571.

Hancock, Ralph C. "Religion and the Limits of Limited Government." *Review of Politics* 50 (Fall 1988): 682–703.

Hanrahan, E. M. "Constitutionality of Legislation Denying Tax-Exempt Status to Racially Discriminatory Schools." *The Catholic Lawyer* 28 (Spring 1983): 137–143.

Hansmann, Henry. "The Rationale for Exempting Nonprofit Organizations from Corporate Income Taxation." *Yale Law Journal* 91 (November 1981): 54–100.

Harkins, James C. "Of Textbooks and Tenets: *Mozert v. Hawkins County Board of Education* and the Free Exercise of Religion." *American Review* 37 (Spring 1988): 985–1012.

Harpaz, Leora. "Justice Jackson's Flag Salute Legacy: The Supreme Court Struggles to Protect Intellectual Individualism." *Texas Law Review* 64 (February 1986): 817–914.

Harris, David J. "Respect for the Living and Respect for the Dead: Return of Indian and Other Native American Burial Remains." *Washington University Journal of Urban & Contemporary Law* 39 (Spring 1991): 195–224.

Hayes, B. Douglas. "Secular Humanism in Public School Textbooks: Thou Shalt

Have No Other God (Except Thyself)." *Notre Dame Law Review* 63 (Summer 1988): 358–379.

Head, Neil W. "Property-Neutral Principles Approach in Interchurch Property Disputes—Presbytery of Beaver-Butter of the United Presbyterian Church in the *United States v. Middlesex Presbyterian Church.*" *Temple Law Review* 59 (Summer 1986): 789–806.

Heady, Brian D. "Constitutional Law: What Offends a Theist Does Not Offend the Establishment Clause." *San Diego Law Review* 25 (Fall 1988): 153–174.

———. "First Americans and the First Amendment: American Indians Battle for Religious Freedom." *Southern Illinois University Law Journal* 13 (Summer 1989): 945–974.

Healy, Peggy. "Note, A Form-Over Effect Standard for the Free Exercise Clause." *Loyola University of Chicago Law Journal* (Fall 1988): 171–196.

Heise, Michael. "State Constitutions, Education Finance, and Legal Impact: An Empirical Analysis." *University of Cincinnati Law Review* 63 (Summer 1995): 1735–1765.

Hess, Danielle A. "The Undoing of Mandatory Free Exercise Accommodation— *Employment Division, Department of Human Resources v. Smith.*" *Washington Law Review* 66 (April 1991): 587–603.

Hill, Alexander D., and Chi-Dooh Li. "A Current Church-State Battleground: Requiring Clergy to Report Child Abuse." *Journal of Church and State* 32 (Autumn 1990): 795–811.

———. "Religious Speech in Public Schools: A Case Study in Contradictions." *Journal of Church and State* 37 (Summer 1995): 623–640.

Hilton, Jim. "Note, Local Autonomy, Educational Equity, and Choice: A Criticism of a Proposal to Reform America's Educational System." *Boston University Law Review* 72 (November 1992): 973–989.

Hitchcock, James. "The Supreme Court and Religion: Historical Overview and Future Prognosis." *St. Louis University Law Journal* 24 (September 1980): 183–204.

Hodson, Trevor. "The Religious Employer Exemption Under Title VII: Should a Church Define its Own Activities?" *Brigham Young University Law Review* 1994 (Summer 1994): 571–599.

Hogue, William M. "The Civil Disability of Ministers of Religion in State Constitutions." *Journal of Church and State* 36 (Spring 1994): 329–355.

Holland, Robert A. "A Theory of Establishment Clause Adjudication: Individualism, Social Contract, and the Significance of Coercion in Identifying Threats to Religious Liberty." *California Law Review* 80 (December 1992): 1595–1694.

Hopkins, Steven. "Comment, Is God a Preferred Creditor? Tithing as an Avoidable Transfer in Chapter 7 Bankruptcies." *University of Chicago Law Review* 62 (Summer 1995): 1139–1160.

Horn, Carl, III "Secularism and Pluralism in Public Education." *Harvard Journal of Law and Public Policy* 7 (Winter 1984): 177–183.

Horner, Timothy, and Hugh M. Makens. "Securities Regulation of Fundraising Activities of Religious and Other Nonprofit Organizations." *Stetson Law Review* 27 (Fall 1997): 473–528.

Hostetter, John A. "The Amish and the Law: A Religious Minority and Its Legal Encounters." *Washington and Lee Law Review* 41 (Winter 1984): 33–47.

Howarth, Don, and William D. Connell. "Student Rights to Organize and Meet for Religious Purposes in the University Context." *Valparaiso Law Review* 16 (Fall 1981): 103–143.

Hughes, Richard W. "Indian Law." *New Mexico Law Review* 18 (Winter 1988): 403–467.

Hughson, Thomas, S. J. "From James Madison to William Lee Miller: John Courtney and Baptist Theory of the First Amendment." *Journal of Church and State* 37 (Winter 1995): 15–37.

Hyde, Henry. "Keeping God in the Closet: Some Thoughts on the Exorcism of Religious Values from Public Life, Address at Notre Dame (September 24, 1984)." *Notre Dame Journal of Law, Ethics, and Public Policy* 1 (Fall 1984): 33–51.

Idleman, Scott C. "The Religious Freedom Restoration Act: Pushing the Limits of Legislative Power." *Texas Law Review* 73 (December 1994): 247–334.

Ignani, Joseph A. "Explaining and Predicting Supreme Court Decision Making: The Burger Court's Establishment Clause Decisions." *Journal of Church and State* 36 (Spring 1994): 301–327.

Ingber, Stanley. "Religion or Ideology: A Needed Clarification of the Religion Clauses." *Stanford Law Review* 41 (January 1989): 233–333.

Ivers, Gregg. "Organized Religion and the Supreme Court." *Journal of Church and State* 32 (Autumn 1990): 775–793.

Jamars, Steven D. "This Article Has No Footnotes: An Essay on RFRA and the Limits of Logic in the Law." *Stetson Law Review* 27 (Fall 1997): 559–587.

Johnson, Phillip E. "Concepts and Compromise in First Amendment Religious Doctrine." *California Law Review* 72 (September 1984): 817–846.

Jones, Harry W. "The Constitutional Status of Public Funds for Church-Related Schools." *Journal of Church and State* 6 (Winter 1964): 61–73.

Jones, Richard H. "Judicial Intervention in Disputes Over the Use of Church Property." *Harvard Law Review* 75 (1962): 1142–1186.

———. "Accommodationist and Separationist Ideas in Supreme Court Establishment Decisions." *Journal of Church and State* 28 (Spring 1986): 193–223.

Juster, Sara A. "Note, Free Exercise—Or the Lack Thereof?" *Creighton Law Review* 24 (December 1990): 239–265.

Kannar, George. "The Constitutional Catechism of Antonin Scalia." *Yale Law Journal* 99 (April 1990): 1297–1357.

Kaplan, Julie B. "Military Mirrors on the Wall: Nonestablishment and the Military Chaplaincy." *Yale Law Journal* 95 (May 1986): 1210–1236.

Katz, Wilber, and Harold P. Southertand. "Religious Pluralism and the Supreme Court." *Daedalus* 96 (Winter 1967): 180–192.

Kauper, Paul G. "Note, Church Autonomy and the First Amendment: The Presbyterian Church Case." 1969 *The Supreme Court Review* (1969): 347–378.

———. "*Everson v. Board of Education*: A Product of the Judicial Will." *Arizona Law Review* 15 (1973): 307–326.

Kauper, Paul G., and Stephen C. Ellis. "Religious Corporations and the Law." *Michigan Law Review* 71 (1973): 1499–1576.

Kelley, Dean M. "A Primer for Pastors: What to Do When the FBI Knocks." *Christianity and Crisis* 37 (May 2, 1977): 86–92.

Kemper, Keith. "Freedom of Religion vs. Public School Reading Curriculum." *University of Puget Sound Law Review* (Spring 1989): 405–449.

Kerley, John E. "Constitutional Law—Christian Science Malpractice—Illinois Ap-

pellate Court Commands: Thou Shalt Not Interfere with Faith Healers."
Southern Illinois University Law Journal 13 (Winter 1989): 411–427.

Killitea, Alfred G. "Privileging Conscientious Dissent: Another Look at *Sherbert v. Verner.*" *Journal of Church and State* 16 (Spring 1974): 194–216.

Kirby, James C., Jr. "*Everson* to *Meek* and *Roemer:* From Separation to Detente in Church-State Relations." *North Carolina Law Review* 55 (April 1977): 563–575.

Kliever, Lonnie D. "Academic Freedom and Church-Affiliated Universities." *Texas Law Review* 66 (June 1988): 1477–1480.

Klinkhamer, Marie Carolyn. "The Blaine Amendment of 1875: Private Motives for Political Action." *Catholic Historical Review* 42 (1955): 15.

Knight, Barbara B. "Religion in Prison: Balancing the Free Exercise, No Establishment, and Equal Protection Clauses." *Journal of Church and State* 26 (Autumn 1984): 437–454.

Knight, Catherine M. "Comment, Must God Regulate Religious Corporations? A Proposal for Reform of the Religious Corporations Provisions of the Revised Model Nonprofit Corporation Act." *Emory Law Journal* 42 (Spring 1993): 721–746.

Kurland, Philip B. "Of Church and State and the Supreme Court." *University of Chicago Law Review* 29 (Autumn 1961): 1–96.

———. "The Irrelevance of the Constitution: The Religion Clauses of the First Amendment and the Supreme Court." *Villanova Law Review* 24 (November 1978): 3–27.

———. "The Religion Clauses and the Burger Court." *Catholic University Law Review* 34 (Fall 1984): 1–19.

———. "The Origins of the Religion Clauses of the Constitution." *William and Mary Law Review* 27 (1986): 839–862.

Kushner, James A. "Toward the Central Meaning of Religious Liberty: Non-Sunday Sabbatarians and the Sunday Closing Cases Revisited." *Southwestern Law Journal* 35 (June 1981): 557–584.

Kuznicki, Joseph M. "Section 170, Tax Expenditures, and the First Amendment: The Failure of Charitable Religious Contributions for the Return of a Religious Benefit." *Temple Law Review* 61 (Summer 1988): 443–487.

Lam, Eddie. "*Employment Division, Department of Human Resources of Oregon v. Smith:* The Limits of the Free Exercise Clause." *Thurgood Marshall Law Review* 16 (Spring 1991): 377–397.

Lambert, Frank. "God—and a Religious President . . . Or Jefferson and No God: Campaigning for a Voter-Imposed Religious Test in 1800." *Journal of Church and State* 39 (Autumn 1997): 769.

Lardner, Lynford A. "How Far Does the Constitution Separate Church and State?" *American Political Science Review* 45 (March 1951): 110–132.

Latham, Bill. "*Valley Forge Christian College v. Americans United for Separation of Church and State:* Taxpayer Standing and the Establishment Clause." *Baylor Law Review* 34 (Fall 1982): 748–762.

Lavi, Terri Jane. "Free Exercise Challenges to Public School Curricula: Are States Creating Enclaves of Totalitarianism Through Compulsory Reading Requirements?" *George Washington Law Review* 57 (December 1988): 301–327.

Lawless, James J., Jr. "*Roy v. Cohen:* Social Security Number and the Free Exercise Clause." *American University Law Review* 36 (Fall 1986): 217–242.

Laycock, Douglas. "The Religious Freedom Restoration Act." *Brigham Young University Law Review* 1993 (1993): 221–258.

———. "Free Exercise and the Religious Freedom Restoration Act." *Fordham Law Review* 62 (February 1994): 883–904.

———. "RFRA, Congress, and the Ratchet." *Montana Law Review* 56 (Winter 1995): 145–170.

Laycock, Douglas, and Oliver S. Thomas. "Interpreting the Religious Freedom Restoration Act." *Texas Law Review* 73 (December 1994): 209–245.

Laycock, Douglas, and Susan E. Waelbroeck. "A Survey of Religious Liberty in the United States." *Ohio State Law Journal* 47 (1986): 409–451.

———. "'Nonpreferential' Aid to Religion: A False Claim About Original Intent." *William and Mary Law Review* 27 (1986): 875–923.

———. "Academic Freedom and the Free Exercise of Religion." *Texas Law Review* 66 (June 1988): 1455–1475.

———. "Peyote, Wine and the First Amendment." *The Christian Century* 106 (October 4, 1989): 876–880.

———. "Text, Intent, and the Religion Clauses." *Notre Dame Journal of Law, Ethics, and Public Policy* 4 (Fall/Winter 1990): 683–697.

———. "Formal, Substantive, and Disaggregated Neutrality Toward Religion." *DePaul Law Review* 39 (Summer 1990): 993–1018.

———. "'Noncoercive' Support for Religion: Another False Claim About the Establishment Clause." *Valparaiso University Law Review* 26 (Fall 1991): 37–69.

———. "The Remnants of Free Exercise." *The Supreme Court Review* 1991 (1991): 1–68.

Leavy, Edward N. and Eric A. Raps. "The Judicial Double Standard for State Aid to Church-Affiliated Educational Institutions." *Journal of Church and State* 21 (Spring 1979): 209–222.

Lee, Rex E. "The Legal Relationship of Conscience to Religion: Refusals to Bear Arms." *University of Chicago Law Review* 38 (Spring 1971): 583–611.

———. "The Religion Clauses: Problems and Prospects." *Brigham Young University Law Review* (Spring 1986): 337–347.

Leitch, David G. "The Myth of Religious Neutrality by Separation in Education." *Virginia Law Review* 71 (February 1985): 127–172.

Leventhal, David. "The Free Exercise Clause Gets a Costly Workout in *Employment Division, Department of Human Resources v. Smith.*" *Pepperdine Law Review* 18 (December 1990): 163–212.

Levinson, Sanford. "The Confrontation of Religious Faith and Civil Religion: Catholics Becoming Justices." *DePaul Law Review* 39 (Summer 1990): 1047–1081.

Levit, Nancy. "Creationism, Evolution and the First Amendment: The Limits of Constitutionally Permissible Scientific Inquiry." *Journal of Law and Education* 14 (April 1985): 211–227.

Levy, Tracey. "Comment, Rediscovering Rights: State Courts Reconsider the Free Exercise Clauses of Their Own Constitutions in the Wake of *Employment Division v. Smith.*" *Temple Law Review* 67 (Fall 1994): 1017–1050.

Linder, Robert D. "Civil Religion in Historical Perspective: The Reality That Underlies the Concept." *Journal of Church and State* 17 (Autumn 1975): 399–421.

Lines, Patricia M. "The Entanglement Prong of the Establishment Clause and the

Needy Child in the Private School: Is Distributive Justice Possible?" *Journal of Law and Education* 17 (Winter 1988): 1–33.

Linford, Orma. "The Mormons and the Law: The Polygamy Cases." *Utah Law Review* 9 (1964–1965): 308.

Little, David. "Thomas Jefferson's Religious Views and Their Influence on the Supreme Court's Interpretation of the First Amendment." *Catholic University Law Review* 26 (Fall 1976): 57–72.

Little, Sandra Morgan. "Counsel By Clergy: Is It Privileged?" *Family Advocate* 10 (Summer 1987): 24–27.

Lively, Donald E. "The Establishment Clause: Lost Soul of the First Amendment." *Ohio State Law Journal* (June 1989): 681–699.

Loewy, Arnold H. "School Prayer, Neutrality, and the Open Forum: Why We Don't Need a Constitutional Amendment." *North Carolina Law Review* 61 (October 1982): 141–156.

Long, Leonard J. "Religious Exercise as Credit Risk." *Bankruptcy Developments Journal* 10 (Fall-Spring 1992/93): 119–170.

Louisell, David W., and John H. Jackson. "Religion, Theology and Public Higher Education." *California Law Review* 50 (December 1962): 751–799.

Lovin, Robin W. "Rethinking the History of Church and State: The Believer and the Powers that Are." *California Law Review* 76 (October 1988): 1185–1198.

Lowry, Bruce E., Jr. "The New Discrimination in America: In Defense of the Religious Equality Amendment." *St. Louis University Public Law Review* 16 (1996): 205.

Lupu, Ira C. "Free Exercise Exemption and Religious Institutions: The Case of Employment Discrimination." *Boston University Law Review* 67 (May 1987): 391–442.

———. "Home Education, Religious Liberty, and the Separation of Powers." *Boston University Law Review* 67 (November 1987): 971–990.

———. "Where Rights Begin: The Problem of Burdens on the Free Exercise of Religion." *Harvard Law Review* 102 (March 1989): 933–990.

———. "Reconstructing the Establishment Clause: The Case Against Discretionary Accommodation of Religion." *University of Pennsylvania Law Review* 140 (December 1991): 555–612.

Maddigan, Michael M. "The Establishment Clause, Civil Religion and the Public Church." *California Law Review* 81 (January 1993): 293–349.

Magan, Virginia C. "*Employment Division, Department of Human Resources of Oregon v. Smith:* Does the Constitutionally Compelled Free Exercise Exemption Have a Prayer?" *Pacific Law Journal* 22 (July 1991): 1415–1453.

Manion, Maureen D. "Parental Religious Freedom, the Rights of Children and the Role of the State." *Journal of Church and State* 34 (Winter 1992): 77–92.

Mansfield, John H. "The Religion Clauses of the First Amendment and the Philosophy of the Constitution." *California Law Review* 72 (September 1984): 847–907.

Marin, Kenneth. "*Marsh v. Chambers:* The Supreme Court Takes a New Look at the Establishment Clause." *Pepperdine Law Review* 11 (March 1984): 591–611.

———. "The Supreme Court Alters the State of Free Exercise Doctrine." *American University Law Review* 40 (Summer 1991): 1431–1476.

Marshall, Brent E. "The Unseen Regulator: The Role of Characterization in First Amendment Free Exercise Cases." *Notre Dame Law Review* 59 (Summer 1984): 978–1004.

Marshall, William P. "In Defense of *Smith* and Free Exercise Dilemma: Free Exercise as Expression." *Minnesota Law Review* 67 (1983): 545–594.

———. "Solving the Free Exercise Dilemma: Free Exercise as Expression." *Minnesota Law Review* 67 (Fall 1983): 545–594.

———. "'We Know It When We See It': The Supreme Court and Establishment." *Southern California Law Review* 59 (March 1986): 495–550.

———. "The Case Against the Constitutionally Compelled Free Exercise Exemption." *Case Western Reserve Law Review* 40 (Spring 1990): 357–412.

Marshall, William P., and Douglas C. Blomgren. "Regulating Religious Organizations Under the Establishment Clause." *Ohio State Law Journal* 47 (Spring 1986): 293–331.

Martin, Aric. "Comment, Chapter 13 and the Tithe: Is God a Creditor?" *Ohio State Law Journal* 56 (February 1995): 307–328.

Martin, Christina. "Student-Initiated Religious Expression after *Mergens* and *Weisman*." *University of Chicago Law Review* 61 (Fall 1994): 1565–1595.

Marty, Martin E. "On a Medial Moraine: Religious Dimensions of American Constitutionalism." *Emory Law Journal* 39 (Winter 1990): 9–20.

Mauney, Constance. "Religion and First Amendment Protections: An Analysis of Justice Black's Constitutional Interpretation." *Pepperdine Law Review* 10 (January 1983): 377–420.

Mawdsley, Alice S. "Has *Wisconsin v. Yoder* Been Reversed? Analysis of *Employment Division v. Smith*." *West's Education Law Reporter* 63 (December 1990): 11–22.

Mawdsley, Ralph D., and Alice L. Mawdsley. "Religious Freedom and Public Schools: Analysis of Important Policy Areas." *West's Education Law Reporter* 47(1988): 15–43.

McBride, James. "Capital Punishment as the Unconstitutional Establishment of Religion: A Guardian Reading of the Death Penalty." *Journal of Church and State* 37 (Spring 1995): 263–287.

McCaffrey, C. Grace. "Note, Clergy Malpractice—A Threat to Both Liberty and Life." *Pace Law Review* II (Fall 1990): 137–166.

McCarthy, Martha M. "Student Religious Expression: Mixed Messages from the Supreme Court." *West's Education Law Reporter* 64 (1991): 1–13.

McClamorack, David H. "The First Amendment and Public Funding of Religiously Controlled or Affiliated Higher Education." *Journal of College and University Law* 17 (Winter 1991): 381–428.

McConnell, Michael W. "Accommodation of Religion." *Supreme Court Review* 1985 (1985): 1–59.

———. "Neutrality Under the Religion Clauses." *Northwestern University Law Review* 81 (Fall 1986): 146–167.

———. "The Religion Clauses of the First Amendment: Where Is the Supreme Court Heading?" *Catholic Lawyer* 32 (Summer 1988): 187–202.

———. "The Origins and Historical Understanding of Free Exercise of Religion." *Harvard Law Review* 103 (May 1990): 1410–1517.

———. "Religious Freedom: A Surprising Pattern. An Analysis of the Court's Religious Freedom Decisions of the Last Decade." *Quarterly—Christian Legal Society* (Spring 1990): 4–8.

———. "Free Exercise Revisionism and the *Smith* Decision." *The University of Chicago Law Review* 57 (Fall 1990): 1109–1153.

——. "A Response to Professor Marshall." *University of Chicago Law Review* 58 (Winter 1991): 329–332.

——. "Religious Freedom at a Crossroads." *University of Chicago Law Review* 59 (Winter 1992): 115–194.

McConnell, Michael W., and Richard A. Posner. "An Economic Approach to Issues of Religious Freedom." *University of Chicago Law Review* 1 (Winter 1989): 1–60.

McCoy, Thomas R., and Gary A. Kurtz. "A Unifying Theory for the Religion Clauses of the First Amendment." *Vanderbilt Law Review* 39 (March 1986): 249–274.

Meiklejohn, Donald. "Religion in the Burger Court: The Heritage of Mr. Justice Black." *Indiana Law Review* 10 (1977): 645–674.

Merel, Gail. "The Protection of Individual Choice: A Consistent Understanding of Religion Under the First Amendment." *University of Chicago Law Review* 45 (Summer 1978): 805–843.

Mermann, Debra Ann. "Free Exercise: A 'Hollow Promise' for the Native American in *Employment Division, Department of Human Resources of Oregon v. Smith.*" *Mercer Law Review* 42 (Summer 1991): 1597–1622.

Michaelsen, Robert S. "Is the Miner's Canary Silent? Implications of the Supreme Court's Denial of American Indian Free Exercise of Religion Claims." *Journal of Law and Religion* 6 (1988): 97–114.

Middleton, Michael A. "Challenging Discriminatory Guesswork: Does Impact Analysis Apply?" *Oklahoma Law Review* 42 (Summer 1989): 187–241.

Miles, Judith C. "Beyond *Bob Jones:* Toward the Elimination of Governmental Subsidy of Discrimination by Religious Institutions." *Harvard Women's Law Journal* 8 (Spring 1985): 31–58.

"Military Ban on Yarmulkes: *Goldman v. Weinberger.*" *Harvard Law Review* 100 (November 1986): 163–172.

Miller, Nicholas P., and Nathan Sheers. "Religious Free Exercise under State Constitutions." *Journal of Church and State* 34 (Spring 1992): 303–323.

Mills, Samuel A. "Parochiaid and the Abortion Decisions: Supreme Court Justice William J. Brennan, Jr. versus the U.S. Catholic Hierarchy." *Journal of Church and State* 34 (Autumn 1992): 751–773.

Mirsky, Yehudah. "Civil Religion and the Establishment Clause." *Yale Law Journal* 95 (May 1986): 1237–1257.

Mitchell, Mary Harter. "Must Clergy Tell? Child Abuse Reporting Requirements Versus the Clergy Privilege and Free Exercise of Religion." *Minnesota Law Review* 71 (February 1987): 723–825.

——. "Secularism in Public Education: The Constitutional Issues." *Boston University Law Review* 67 (July 1987): 603–746.

Moen, Matthew C. "School Prayer and the Politics of Lifestyle Concern." *Social Science Quarterly* 65 (December 1984): 1065–1071.

Monopoli, Paula A. "Allocating the Costs of Parental Free Exercise: Striking a New Balance Between Sincere Religious Belief and a Child's Right to Medical Treatment." *Pepperdine Law Review* 18 (January 1991): 319–352.

Monsma, Stephen V. "Justice Potter Stewart on Church and State." *Journal of Church and State* 36 (Summer 1994): 557–576.

Moody, Lizabeth A. "The Who, What, and How of the Revised Model Nonprofit Corporation Act." *Northern Kentucky Law Review* 16 (Winter 1989): 251–283.

Moore, Juliana S. "The *Edwards* Decision: The End of Creationism in Our Public Schools?" *Akron Law Review* 21 (Fall 1987): 255–267.

Morgan, John. "Values Clarification and Religious Neutrality in the Public Schools: The *Smith v. Board of School Commissioner* Constitutional Challenge." *Houston Law Review* (October 1988): 1137–1177.

Morken, Paul J. "Church Discipline and Civil Tort Claims: Should Ecclesiastical Tribunals Be Immune?" *Idaho Law Review* 28 (Winter 1992): 93–165.

Mott, Kenneth F. "The Supreme Court and the Establishment Clause: From Separation to Accommodation and Beyond." *Journal of Law and Education* 14 (April 1985): 111–145.

"*Mueller v. Allen:* The Continued Weakening of the Separation Between Church and State." *New England Law Review* 19 (1983/1984): 459–485.

"*Mueller v. Allen:* Tuition Tax Relief and the Original Intent." *Harvard Journal of Law and Public Policy* 7 (Fall 1984): 551–579.

Neal, Patrick. "Religion Within the Limits of Liberalism Alone?" *Journal of Church and State* 39 (Autumn 1997): 697–722.

Nelson, John Stuart. "Native American Religious Freedom and the Peyote Sacrament: The Precarious Balance Between State Interests and the Free Exercise Clause." *Arizona Law Review* 31 (Spring 1989): 423–446.

Noonan, John T., Jr. "The Constitution's Protection of Individual Rights: The Real Role of the Religion Clauses." *University of Pittsburgh Law Review* 49 (Spring 1988): 717–722.

Noone, Michael F. "Rendering Unto Caesar: Legal Responses to Religious Nonconformity in the Armed Forces." *St. Mary's Law Journal* 18 (Spring 1987): 1233–1294.

Nordin, Virginia Davis, and William Lloyd Turner. "Tax Exempt Status of Private Schools: *Wright, Green,* and *Bob Jones.*" *West's Education Law Reporter* 35 (1986): 329–349.

Note. "Adjudicating What *Yoder* Left Unresolved: Religious Rights for Minors After *Danforth* and *Carey.*" *University of Pennsylvania Law Review* 126 (May 1978): 1135–1170.

Note. "Judicial Intervention in Disputes Over the Use of Church Property." *Harvard Law Review* 75 (1962): 1142.

Note. "*Lynch v. Donnelly:* Our Christmas Will Be Merry Still." *Mercer Law Review* 36 (Fall 1984): 409–420.

Note. "McLean v. Arkansas Board of Education: Finding the Science in 'Creation Science.'" *Northwestern University Law Review* 77 (October 1982): 374–402.

Note. "Reinterpreting the Religion Clauses: Constitutional Construction and Conceptions of the Self." *Harvard Law Review* 97 (April 1984): 1468–1486.

Note. "Toward a Constitutional Definition of Religion." *Harvard Law Review* 91 (March 1978): 1056–1089.

Note. "The Unconstitutionality of State Statutes Authorizing Moments of Silence in the Public Schools." *Harvard Law Review* 96 (June 1983): 1874–1893.

Nowak, John E. "The Supreme Court, the Religion Clauses and the Nationalization of Education." *Northwestern University Law Review* 70 (January-February 1976): 883–909.

Nuger, Kenneth P. "The Religion of Secular Humanism in Public Schools: *Smith v. Board of School Commissioners.*" *West's Education Law Reporter* 38 (1987): 871–879.

Oaks, Dallin H. "Separation, Accommodation and the Future of Church and State." *DePaul Law Review* 35 (Fall 1985): 1–22.

O'Connor, Sandra Day. "Conference on Compelling Governmental Interests: The Mystery of Constitutional Analysis." *Albany Law Review* 55 (Spring 1992): 535–547.

O'Hara, Julie U. "State Aid to Sectarian Higher Education." *Journal of Law and Education* 14 (April 1985): 181–209.

Okamoto, Duane E. "Religious Discrimination and the Title VII Exemption for Religious Organizations: A Basic Values Analysis for the Proper Allocation of Conflicting Rights." *Southern California Law Review* 60 (July 1987): 1375–1427.

O'Reilly, James M., and Joann Strasser. "Clergy Sexual Misconduct: Confronting the Difficult Constitutional and Institutional Liability Issues." *St. Thomas Law Review* 7 (Fall 1994): 31–73.

Page, Ellen Adair. "The Scope of the Free Exercise Clause: *Lyng v. Northwest Indian Cemetery Protective Association.*" *North Carolina Law Review* 68 (January 1990): 410–422.

Patric, Gordon. "The Impact of a Court Decision: Aftermath of the *McCollum* Case." *Journal of Public Law* 6 (Fall 1967): 455–465.

Paulsen, Michael S. "Religion, Equality, and the Constitution: An Equal Protection Approach to Establishment Clause Adjudication." *Notre Dame Law Review* 61 (1986): 311–371.

Paviischek, Keith J. "John Courtney Murray, Civil Religion, and the Problem of Political Neutrality." *Journal of Church and State* 34 (Autumn 1992): 729–750.

Pavis, John J. "Compulsory Medical Treatment and Religious Freedom: Whose Law Shall Prevail?" *University of San Francisco Law Review* 10 (Summer 1975): 1–15.

Pawa, Matt. "When the Supreme Court Restricts Constitutional Rights, Can Congress Save Us? An Examination of Section 5 of the Fourteenth Amendment." *University of Pennsylvania Law Review* 141 (December 1992): 1029–1101.

Pearlman, Kenneth. "Zoning and the Location of Religious Establishments." *Catholic Lawyer* 31 (1988): 314–345.

Pepper, Stephen L. "*Reynolds, Yoder* and Beyond: Alternatives for the Free Exercise Clause." *Utah Law Review* 1981 (Spring 1981): 309–378.

———. "The Case of the Human Sacrifice: In the Supreme Court of the New States: Spring 2382: *State v. Williams.*" *Arizona Law Review* 23 (Summer 1981): 897–934.

———. "The Conundrum of the Free Exercise Clause: Some Reflections on Recent Cases." *Northern Kentucky Law Review* 9 (1982): 265–303.

———. "Taking the Free Exercise Clause Seriously." *Brigham Young University Law Review* 1986 (Spring 1986): 299–336.

Peterson, Walfred H. "The Thwarted Opportunity for Judicial Activism in Church-State Relations: Separation and Accommodation in Precarious Balance." *Journal of Church and State* 22 (Autumn 1980): 437–458.

Pfeffer, Leo. "Freedom and/or Separation: The Constitutional Dilemma of the First Amendment." *Minnesota Law Review* 64 (March 1980): 561–584.

———. "The Deity in American Constitutional History." *Journal of Church and State* 23 (Spring 1981): 215–239.

———. "Workers' Sabbath, Religious Belief and Employment." *Civil Liberties Review* 4 (November-December 1977): 52–56.

Phenix, Philip H. "Religion in Public Education: Principles and Issues." *Journal of Church and State* 14 (Autumn 1979): 415–430.

Piele, Philip K., and Stephen M. Pitt. "The Use of School Facilities by Student Groups for Religious Activities." *Journal of Legal Education* 13 (April 1984): 197–207.

Pochop, Sandra Ashton. "Note, Religious Peyotism and the 'Purposeful' Erosion of Free Exercise Protections." *South Dakota Law Review* 36 (Summer 1991): 358–381.

Polifka, John C. "Use of the *Lemon* Test in the Review of Public School Curricular Decisions Concerning 'Secular Humanism' Under the Establishment Clause." *South Dakota Law Review* 33 (1987–1988): 112–130.

"Political Entanglement as an Independent Test of Constitutionality Under the Establishment Clause." *Fordham Law Review* 52 (May 1984): 1209–1241.

Pollak, Louis H. "Public Prayers in Public Schools." *Harvard Law Review* 77 (November 1963): 62–78.

Porth, William C., and Robert P. George. "Trimming the Ivy: A Bicentennial Re-Examination of the Establishment Clause." *West Virginia Law Review* 90 (Fall 1987): 109–170.

Posner, Ethan M. "Public Prayer and the Constitution." *Michigan Law Review* 86 (May 1988): 1294–1301.

Post, Robert C. "Cultural Heterogeneity and Law: Pornography, Blasphemy, and the First Amendment." *California Law Review* 76 (March 1988): 297–335.

Prevost, Robert. "Clergy Malpractice After *Oregon v. Smith.*" *Journal of Church and State* 34 (Spring 1992): 279–301.

Price, Donald R., and Mark C. Rahdert, "Distributing the First Fruits: Statutory and Constitutional Implications of Tithing in Bankruptcy." *University of California Law Review* 26 (Summer 1993): 853–934.

Pritchard, J. Brett. "Conduct and Belief in the Free Exercise Clause: Developments and Deviations in *Lyng v. Northwest Indian Cemetery Protective Association.*" *Cornell Law Review* 76 (November 1990): 268–296.

"Protecting Religious Exercise: The First Amendment and Legislative Responses to Religious Vandalism." *Harvard Law Review* 97 (December 1983): 547–563.

"Public School Prayer and the First Amendment: Reconciling Constitutional Claims." *Duquesne Law Review* 22 (Winter 1984): 465–478.

Pushaw, Robert J. "Labor Relations Board Regulation of Parochial Schools: A Practical Free Exercise Accommodation." *Yale Law Journal* 97 (November 1987): 135–155.

Rains, Rebecca. "Can Religious Practice Be Given Meaningful Protection after *Employment Division v. Smith?*" *University of Colorado Law Review* 62 (1991): 687–710.

Ratz, Lucy V. "Caesar, God and Mammon: Business and the Religion Clauses." *Gonzaga Law Review* 22 (June 1987): 327–364.

Raucher, Alan. "Sunday Business and the Decline of Sunday Closing Laws: A Historical Overview." *Journal of Church and State* 36 (Winter 1994): 13–33.

Rawlings, Tom C. "*Employment Division, Department of Human Resources of Oregon v. Smith:* The Supreme Court Deserts the Free Exercise Clause." *Georgia Law Review* 25 (Winter 1991): 567–593.

Redlich, Norman. "Separation of Church and State: The Burger Court's Tortuous Journey." *Notre Dame Law Review* 60 (Fall 1985): 1094–1149.

"Reinterpreting the Religion Clauses: Constitutional Construction and Conceptions of the Self." *Harvard Law Review* 97 (April 1984): 1468–1486.

"Religion and the Law." *Hastings Law Journal* 29 (July 1978): (entire issue devoted to this topic).

"Religion and the State." *Harvard Law Review* 100 (May 1987): 1607–1781.

"Religious Expression in the Public School Forum: The High School Student's Right to Free Speech." *Georgia Law Journal* 72 (October 1983): 135–160.

"Religious Liberty in the Public High School: Bible Study Clubs." *The John Marshall Law Review* 17 (Summer 1981): 933–967.

"Rethinking the Incorporation of the Establishment Clause: A Federalist View." *Harvard Law Review* 105 (May 1992): 1700–1719.

Reutter, E. Edmund, Jr. "Unclear Signals On Free Exercise Clause: *Bowen v. Roy.*" *West's Education Law Reporter* 37 (1987): 1–10.

Rice, Mark G. "The Constitutionality of the Equal Access Act: *Board of Westside Community School District v. Mergens.*" *Educational Law Report* 64 (1991): 609–621.

Rice, Terry. "Re-Evaluating the Balance Between Zoning Regulations and Religious and Educational Uses." *Pace Law Review* 81 (Winter 1988): 1–61.

Richardson, James T. "Cult/Brainwashing Cases and Freedom of Religion." *Journal of Church and State* 33 (Winter 1991): 55–74.

Richardson, James T., and John Dewitt. "Christian Science Spiritual Healing, the Law, and Public Opinion." *Journal of Church and State* 34 (Summer 1992): 549–561.

Riggs, Robert E. "Judicial Doublethink and the Establishment Clause: The Fallacy of Establishment by Inhibition." *Valparaiso University Law Review* 18 (Winter 1984): 285–330.

Ripple, Kenneth F. "The Entanglement Test of the Religion Clauses—A Ten Year Assessment." *UCLA Law Review* 27 (August 1980): 1195–1239.

Ross, William G. "The Need for an Exclusive and Uniform Application of 'Neutral Principles' in the Adjudication of Church Property Disputes." *St. Louis University Law Journal* 32 (Winter 1987): 263–316.

Rostain, Tanina. "Note, Permissible Accommodations of Religion: Reconsidering the New York Get Statute." *Yale Law Journal* 96 (April 1987): 1147–1171.

Rotstein, Andrew. "Good Faith? Religious-Secular Parallelism and the Establishment Clause." *Columbia Law Review* 93 (November 1993): 1763–1806.

Rotz, Brenda J. "Note, The Christmas Cross." *Chicago-Kent Law Review* 63 (Spring 1987): 369–389.

Rouse, Kelly Beers. "Clergy Malpractice Claims: A New Problem for Religious Organizations." *North Kentucky Law Review* 16 (Winter 1989): 383–396.

Ruegger, MaryAnn Schlegel. "An Audience for the Amish: A Communication-Based Approach to the Development of Law." *Indiana Law Journal* 66 (Summer 1991): 801–823.

Rugg, Janet V., and Andria A. Simone. "The Free Exercise Clause: Inexplicable Departure from the Strict Scrutiny Standard." *St. John's Journal of Legal Commentary* 6 (Spring 1990): 117–141.

Salomone, Rosemary C. "From *Widmar* to *Mergens:* The Winding Road of First Amendment Analysis." *Hastings Constitutional Law Quarterly* 18 (Winter 1991): 295–323.

Schachner, Elliot M. "Religion and the Public Treasury after Taxation with Representation of *Washington, Mueller,* and *Bob Jones."* *Utah Law Review* 1984 (May 1984): 275–312.

Schaeffer, Sherri. "Note, Creation Science and Evolution—The Fall of Balanced Treatment Acts in the Public Schools." *San Diego Law Review* (September-October 1988): 829–855.

Schimmel, David. "Religious Freedom and the Public School Curriculum: An Analysis of *Mozert* and *Hawkins."* *West's Education Law Reporter* 42 (1988): 1047–1057.

Schmid, Peter D. "Religion, Secular Humanism and the First Amendment." *Southern Illinois University Law Journal* 13 (Winter 1989): 357–393.

Schwartz, Jordan G. "Note, Toward a Constitutional Definition of Religion." *Harvard Law Review* 91 (March 1978): 1056–1089.

Sciarrino, Alfred J. "'Free Exercise' Footsteps in the Defamation Forest: Are 'New Religions' Lost?" *The American Journal of Trial Advocacy* 7 (Summer 1984) 517–565.

———. *"United States v. Sun Myung Moon:* Precedent for Tax Fraud Prosecution of Local Pastors?" *Southern Illinois University Law Journal* 1984 (Summer 1984): 237–281.

Senn, Stephen. "The Prosecution of Religious Fraud." *Florida State University Law Review* 17 (Winter 1990): 325–352.

Serritella, James A. "Tangling with Entanglement: Toward a Constitutional Evaluation of Church-State Contacts." *Law and Contemporary Problems* 44 (Spring 1981): 143–167.

Shaffer, Thomas L. "Erastian and Sectarian Arguments in Religiously Affiliated American Law Schools in Symposium on Civic and Legal Education." *Stanford Law Review* 45 (July 1993): 1859–1879.

Shapiro, Robert N. "'Mind Control' or Intensity of Faith: The Constitutional Protection of Religious Beliefs." *Harvard Civil Rights-Civil Liberties Law Review* 13 (Summer 1978): 751–797.

———."Of Robots, Persons, and the Protection of Religious Beliefs." *Southern California Law Review* 56 (Spring 1983): 1277–1318.

Sheffer, Martin S. "The Free Exercise of Religion and Selective Conscientious Objection: A Judicial Response to a Moral Problem." *Capital University Law Review* 9 (1979): 7–29.

———. "The U. S. Supreme Court and the Free Exercise Clause: Are Standards of Adjudication Possible?" *Journal of Church and State* 23 (Autumn 1981): 533–549.

Sherry, Suzanna. *"Lee v. Weisman:* Paradox Redux." *Supreme Court Review* 1992 (1992): 123–153.

Shobe, Kiply S. "Public Education in Shreds: Religious Challenges to Curricular Decisions." *Indiana Law Journal* 64 (Winter 1988): 111–153.

Shortt, Bruce Nevin. "The Establishment Clause and Religion-Based Categories: Taking Entanglement Seriously." *Hastings Constitutional Law Quarterly* 10 (Fall 1982): 145–185.

Silbiger, Sara L. "Heaven Can Wait: Judicial Interpretation of Title VII's Religious Accommodation Requirement Since *Trans World Airlines v. Hardison."* *Fordham Law Review* 5 (March 1985): 839–861.

Silverman, Debra. "Note, Defining the Limits of Free Exercise: The Religion Clause Defenses in *United States v. Moon."* *Hastings Constitutional Law Quarterly* 12 (Spring 1985): 515–528.

Simon, Harry. "Rebuilding the Wall Between Church and State: Public Sponsorship of Religious Displays Under the Federal and California Constitutions." *Hastings Law Journal* 37 (January 1986): 499–534.

Simon, Karla W. "The Tax Exempt Status of Racially Discriminatory Religious Schools." *Tax Law Review* 36 (Summer 1981): 477–516.

Simonetti, Louis F., Jr. "The Constitutionality of State Labor Relations Board Jurisdiction over Parochial Schools: *Catholic High School Association v. Culvert.*" *Catholic Lawyer* 30 (Spring 1986): 162–176.

Simson, Gary J. "The Establishment Clause in the Supreme Court: Rethinking the Court's Approach." *Cornell Law Review* 72 (July 1987): 905–935.

Singleton, Marvin K. "Colonial Virginia as First Amendment Matrix: Henry, Madison, and the Establishment Clause." *Journal of Church and State* 8 (Autumn 1966): 344–364.

Sirico, Louis J., Jr. "Church Property Disputes: Churches as Secular and Alien Institutions." *Fordham Law Review* 55 (December 1986): 335–362.

———. "The Secular Contribution of Religion to the Political Process: The First Amendment and School Aid." *Missouri Law Review* 50 (Spring 1985): 321–376.

Slack, Reed D. "The Mormon Belief of an Inspired Constitution." *Journal of Church and State* 36 (Winter 1994): 35–56.

Slye, Terry L. "Rendering Unto Caesar: Defining 'Religion' for Purposes of Administering Religion-Based Tax Exemptions." *Harvard Journal of Law and Public Policy* 6 (Summer 1983): 219–294.

Smart, James M. "*Widmar v. Vincent* and the Purposes of the Establishment Clause." *Journal of College and University Law* 9 (Fall 1982): 469–483.

Smith, Michael C. "The Pastor on the Witness Stand: Toward a Religious Privilege in the Courts." *Catholic Lawyer* 29 (Winter 1984): 1–21.

Smith, Michael E. "The Special Place of Religion in the Constitution." *The Supreme Court Review 1983* (1983): 83–123.

Smith, Michael R. "Emerging Consequences of Financing Private Colleges with Public Funds." *Valparaiso University Law Review* 9 (Summer 1973): 561–610.

Smith, Norman B. "Constitutional Rights of Students, Their Families, and Teachers in the Public Schools." *Campbell Law Review* 10 (Summer 1988): 353–409.

Smith, Rodney K. "Getting Off on the Wrong Foot and Back On Again: A Reexamination of the History of the Framing of the Religion Clauses of the First Amendment and a Critique of the *Reynolds* and *Everson* Decisions." *Wake Forest Law Review* 20 (Fall 1984): 569–642.

Smith, Steven D. "Symbols, Perceptions, and Doctrinal Illusions: Establishment Neutrality and the 'No Endorsement' Test." *Michigan Law Review* 86 (November 1987): 266–332.

———. "Separation and the 'Secular': Reconstructing the Disestablihment Decision." *Texas Law Review* 67 (April 1989): 955–1031.

Smith, W. F. "Some Observations on the Establishment Clause." *Pepperdine Law Review* 11 (March 1984): 457–471.

Spiro, Daniel A. "The Creation of a Free Marketplace of Religious Ideas: Revisiting the Establishment Clause After the Alabama Secular Humanism Decision." *Alabama Law Review* 39 (Fall 1987): 1–71.

Stacy, Tom. "Death, Privacy, and the Free Exercise of Religion." *Cornell Law Review* 77 (March 1992): 490–595.

Starr, Kenneth W. "The Establishment Clause." *Oklahoma Law Review* 41 (Fall 1988): 477–487.

Steffey, Matthew S. "Redefining the Modern Constraints of the Establishment Clause: Separable Principles of Equality, Subsidy, Endorsements, and Church Autonomy" in "Symposium, Redefining the Modern Constraints of the Establishment Clause." *Marquette Law Review* 75 (Summer 1992): 903–974.

Steinberg, David E. "Church Control of a Municipality: Establishing a First Amendment Institutional Suit." *Stanford Law Review* 38 (May 1986): 1363–1409.

———. "Religious Exemptions as Affirmative Action." *Emory Law Journal* 40 (Winter 1991): 77–139.

Stern, Nat. "State Action, Establishment Clause, and Defamation: Blueprints for Civil Liberties in the Rehnquist Court." *University of Cincinnati Law Review* 57 (Spring 1989): 1175–1242.

Stevens, John V., Sr., and John G. Tulio. "Casenote *United States v. Lee,* A Second Look." *Journal of Church and State* 26 (Autumn 1984): 455–472.

Stone, Geoffrey R. "In Opposition to the School Prayer Amendment." *University of Chicago Law Review* 50 (Spring 1983): 823–848.

Strossen, Nadine. "'Secular Humanism' and 'Scientific Creationism': Proposed Standards for Reviewing Curricular Decisions Affecting Students' Religious Freedom." *Ohio State Law Journal* 47 (Spring 1986): 333–407.

Sullivan, Dwight H. "The Congressional Response to *Goldman v. Weinberger.*" *Military Law Review* 121 (Summer 1988): 125–152.

Sullivan, Kathleen. "Religion and Liberal Democracy." *University of Chicago Law Review* 59 (Winter 1992): 195–223.

Swift, Joel H. "To Insure Domestic Tranquility: The Establishment Clause of the First Amendment." *Hofstra Law Review* (Winter 1988): 301–327.

Tager, Evan M. "The Supreme Court, Effect Inquiry, and Aid to Parochial Education." *Stanford Law Review* 37 (November 1984): 219–251.

Tarr, G. Alan. "Church and State in the States." *Washington Law Review* 64 (January 1989): 73–110.

Taylor, Timothy B. "Redemption Song: An Update on the Rastafarians and the Free Exercise Clause." *Whittier Law Review* 9 (Winter 1988): 663–682.

Terrar, Edward. "Was There a Separation Between Church and State in Mid-17th-Century England and Colonial Maryland?" *Journal of Church and State* 35 (Winter 1993): 61–82.

"Their Life Is in the Blood: Jehovah's Witnesses, Blood Transfusions, and the Courts." *Northern Kentucky Law Review* 10 (Spring 1983): 281–304.

Tillotson, David B. "Free Exercise in the 1980s: A Rollback of Protection." *University of San Francisco Law Review* 24 (Spring 1990): 505–540.

Tipton, Steven M. "Republic and Liberal State: The Place of Religion in an Ambiguous Policy." *Emory Law Journal* 39 (Winter 1990): 191–202.

Torres, Maximilian B. "Free Exercise of Religion." *Harvard Journal of Law and Public Policy* 14 (Winter 1991): 282–292.

Treinan, David. "Religion in the Public Schools." *Northern Kentucky Law Review* 9 (1982): 229–263.

Tribe, Laurence H. "Revising the Rule of Law." *New York University Law Review* (June 1989): 726–731.

Tushnet, Mark V. "The Constitution of Religion." *Connecticut Law Review* 18 (Summer 1986): 701–738.

———. "Reflections on the Role of Purpose in the Jurisprudence of the Religion Clauses." *William and Mary Law Review* 27 (1986): 997–1009.

———. "The Emerging Principle of Accommodation of Religion (Dubitante)." *Georgetown Law Journal* 76 (June 1988): 1691–1714.

———. "The Rhetoric of Free Exercise Discourse." *Brigham Young University Law Review* 1993 (Winter 1993): 117–140.

Underwood, Julie K., and W. W. Sparkman. "School Finance Litigation: A New Wave of Reform." *Harvard Journal of Law and Public Policy* 14 (Spring 1991): 517–544.

Unmack, Fred. "Equality Under the First Amendment: Protecting Native American Religious Practices on Public Lands." *Public Land Law Review* 8 (1987): 165–176.

Valauri, John T. "The Concept of Neutrality in Establishment Clause Doctrine." *University of Pittsburgh Law Review* 48 (Fall 1986): 83–151.

Van Alstyne, William W. "Constitutional Separation of Church and State: The Quest for a Coherent Position." *American Political Science Review* 57 (December 1963): 865–882.

———. "Trends in the Supreme Court: Mr. Jefferson's Crumbling Wall—A Comment on *Lynch v. Donnelly*." *Duke Law Journal* 1984 (September 1984): 770–787.

———. "What Is 'An Establishment of Religion'?" *North Carolina Law Review* 65 (June 1987): 909–916.

Van Meter-Drew, Linn. "*Stein v. Plainwell Community Schools* -The American Civil Religion and the Establishment Clause." *Hastings Constitutional Law Quarterly* 15 (Spring 1988): 533–547.

Van Patten, Jonathan. "In the End Is the Beginning: An Inquiry into the Meaning of the Religion Clauses." *St. Louis University Law Journal* 27 (Fall 1983): 1–93.

Vanden Berge, Douglas P. "The Establishment Clause: Historical Analysis and Current Application to Public Education." *Williamette Law Review* 24 (Spring 1988): 503–524.

Veltri, Stephen. "Nativism and Nonpreferentialism: A Historical Critique of the Current Church and State Theme." *University of Dayton Law Review* 13 (Winter 1988): 229–265.

Venable, Giovan Harbour. "Courts Examine Congregationalism." *Stanford Law Review* 41 (February 1989): 719–749.

Walker, Robert S. "What Constitutes a Religious Use for Zoning Purposes?" *The Catholic Lawyer* 27 (Spring 1982): 129–183.

"*Wallace v. Jaffree:* The *Lemon* Test Sweetened." *Houston Law Review* 22 (October 1985): 1273–1292.

Ward, Scott J. "Reconceptualizing Establishment Clause Cases as Free Exercise Class Action." *Yale Law Journal* 98 (June 1989): 1739–1759.

Washington, James M. "The Crisis in the Sanctity of Conscience in American Jurisprudence." *De Paul Law Review* 42 (Fall 1992): 11–60.

Way, Frank, and Barbara J. Burt. "Religious Marginality and the Free Exercise Clause." *American Political Science Review* 77 (September 1983): 652–665.

Weber, T. J. "Constitutional Law—Establishment Clause Supreme Court Upholds Direct Noncategorical Grants to Church-Affiliated Colleges." *Fordham Law Review* 45 (March 1977): 979–992.

Weiss, Jonathon. "Privilege, Posture and Protection: Religion in the Law." *Yale Law Journal* 73 (March 1964): 593–623.

Wellons, Gregory D. "Note, The Melting of *Sherbert* Means a Chilling Effect on Religion." *University of San Francisco Law Review* 26 (Fall 1991): 149–173.

West, Ellis. "The Case Against a Right to Religion-Based Exemptions." *Notre Dame Journal of Law, Ethics, and Public Policy* 4 (Fall/Winter 1990): 591–638.

Whitehead, John W. "Accommodation and Equal Treatment of Religion: Federal Funding of Religious Affiliated Child Care Facilities." *Harvard Journal on Legislation* 26 (Summer 1989): 573–590.

———. "Avoiding Religious Apartheid: Affording Equal Treatment for Student-Initiated Religious Expression in Public Schools." *Pepperdine Law Review* 16 (1989): 229–258.

———. "Tax Exemption for Religious Organizations: A Historical and Constitutional Analysis." *Cumberland Law Review* 22 (1992): 521–594.

Wickham, Douglas A. "Prisoner's Rights." *Georgia Law Review* 74 (February 1986): 973–997.

Williams, David C., and Susan H. Williams. "Volitionism and Religious Liberty." *Cornell Law Review* 76 (1991): 769–926.

Williams, J. D. "The Separation of Church and State in Mormon Theory and Practice." *Journal of Church and State* 9 (Spring 1967): 238–262.

Wilson, John K. "Religion Under the State Constitutions, 1776–1800." *Journal of Church and State* 32 (Autumn 1990): 753–773.

Witte, John, Jr. "Tax Exemption of Church Property: Historical Anomaly or Valid Constitutional Practice?" *Southern California Law Review* 64 (January 1991): 363–415.

———. "The Theology and Politics of the First Amendment Religion Clauses: A Bicentennial Essay." *Emory Law Journal* 40 (Spring 1991): 489–507.

Wolman, Benson A. "Separation Anxiety: Free Exercise Versus Equal Protection." *Ohio State Law Journal* 47 (Spring 1986): 453–474.

Wood, James E., Jr. "Church-State Relations in the United States Since 1940." *Affirmation* 2 (Fall 1989): 37–69.

———. "Abridging the Free Exercise Clause." *Journal of Church and State* 32 (Autumn 1990): 741–752.

———. "Editorial: Ceremonial Prayers at Public School Graduations: *Lee. v. Weisman*." *Journal of Church and State* 34 (Winter 1992): 7–14.

Worthing, Sharon L. "The Internal Revenue Service as a Monitor of Church Institutions: The Excessive Entanglement Problem." *Fordham Law Review* 45 (March 1977): 929–948.

———. "'Religion' and 'Religious Institutions' under the First Amendment." *Pepperdine Law Review* 7 (Winter 1980): 313–353.

———. "The State and the Church School: The Conflict Over Social Policy." *Journal of Church and State* 26 (Winter 1984): 91–104.

Yarbrough, Tinsley E. "Church, State, and the Rehnquist Court: A Brief for *Lemon*." *Journal of Church and State* 38 (Winter 1996): 59–85.

Yellin, Jacob C. "The History and Current Status of the Clergy-Penitent Privilege." *Santa Clara Law Review* 23 (Winter 1983): 95–156.

Yerby, Winton E., III. "Toward Religious Neutrality in the Public School Curriculum." *University of Chicago Law Review* 56 (Spring 1989): 899–934.

Young, L. Benjamin, Jr. "Justice Scalia's History and Tradition: The Chief Nightmare in Professor Tribe's Anxiety Closet." *Virginia Law Review* 78 (March 1992): 581–622.

Young, David J., and Steven W. Tigges. "Discovery and Use of Church Records by Civil Authorities." *Catholic Lawyer* 30 (Autumn 1986): 198–217.

———. "Into the Religious Thicket—Constitutional Limits on Civil Court Jurisdiction over Ecclesiastical Disputes." *Ohio State Law Journal* 47 (Spring 1986): 475–499.

Zamora, Omar. "Discriminatory Religious Services: The Exception to Practices Prohibited by Civil Rights Statutes." *American Journal of Trial Advocacy* 10 (Summer 1986): 141–156.

Zerangue, Clare. "Sabbath Observance and the Workplace: Religion Clause Analysis and Title VII's Reasonable Accommodation Rule." *Louisiana Law Review* 46 (July 1986): 1265–1288.

Ziegler, Carol L., and Nancy M. Lederman. "Essay, School Vouchers: Are Urban Students Surrendering Rights for Choice?" *Fordham Urban Law Journal* 19 (Spring 1992): 813–831.

"Zoning Ordinances Affecting Churches: A Proposal for Expanded Free Exercise Protection." *University of Pennsylvania Law Review* 132 (June 1984): 1113–1162.

Zuckert, Michael P. "Completing the Constitution: The Fourteenth Amendment and Constitutional Rights." *Publius* 22 (Spring 1992): 69–91.

Zwicker, Laura. "The Politics of Toleration: The Establishment Clause and the Act of Toleration Examined." *Indiana Law Journal* 66 (Summer 1991): 773–799.

BOOKS

Aaron, Henry J., Thomas E. Mann, and Timothy Taylor. *Values and Public Policy.* Washington, DC: Brookings Institution, 1994.

Abraham, Henry J. *Justices and Presidents: A Political History of Appointments to the Supreme Court.* 2d ed. New York: Oxford University Press, 1985.

———. *The Judicial Process: An Introductory Analysis of the Courts of the United States, England, and France.* 5th ed. New York: Oxford University Press, 1986.

———. *Freedom and the Court: Civil Rights and Liberties in the United States.* 5th ed. New York: Oxford University Press, 1988.

Ackerman, Bruce. *Social Justice in the Liberal State.* New Haven, CT: Yale University Press, 1980.

Adams, Arlin M., and Charles J. Emmerich. *A Nation Dedicated to Religious Liberty: The Constitutional Heritage of the Religion Clauses.* Philadelphia: University of Pennsylvania Press, 1990.

Adams, James L. *The Growing Church Lobby in Washington.* Grand Rapids, MI: Eerdmans, 1970.

Ahlstrom, Sidney E. *A Religious History of the American People.* New Haven, CT: Yale University Press, 1973.

Albanese, Catherine L. *Sons of the Fathers: The Civil Religion of the American Revolution.* Philadelphia: Temple University Press, 1976.

Alfs, Matthew. *The Evocative Religion of Jehovah's Witnesses.* Minneapolis, MN: Old Theology Book House, 1991.

Alley, Robert S. *School Prayer: The Court, the Congress, and the First Amendment.* Buffalo, NY: Prometheus Books, 1994.

———. *Without a Prayer: Religious Expressions in Public Schools.* Buffalo, NY: Prometheus Books, 1996.

Alley, Robert S., ed. *So Help Me God: Religion and the Presidency, Wilson to Nixon.* Richmond, VA: John Knox Press, 1972.

——. *James Madison and Religious Liberty.* Buffalo, NY: Prometheus Books, 1985.

——. *The Supreme Court on Church and State.* New York: Oxford University Press, 1988.

——. *James Madison on Religious Liberty.* Buffalo, NY: Prometheus Books, 1989.

Allitt, Patrick. *Catholic Intellectuals and Conservative Politics in America: 1950–1985.* Ithaca, NY: Cornell University Press, 1993.

Allport, Gordon W. *The Individual and His Religion.* New York: Macmillan, 1962.

American Association of School Administrators. *Religion in the Public Schools.* New York: Harper & Row, 1964.

Antieau, Chester J., Arthur T. Downey and Edward C. Roberts. *Freedom from Federal Establishment.* Milwaukee, WI: Bruce Publishing, 1964.

Arnold, O. Carroll. *Religious Freedom on Trial.* Valley Forge, PA: Judson Press, 1978.

Arrington, Leonard J., and Davis Britton. *The Mormon Experience: A History of the Latter Day Saints.* New York: Knopf, 1979.

Askew, Thomas A., and Peter W. Spellman. *The Churches and the American Experience: Ideals and Institutions.* Grand Rapids, MI: Baker Book House, 1984.

Atkins, Stanley, and Theodore McConnell, eds. *Churches on the Wrong Road.* Lake Bluff, IL: Gateway Editions, 1986.

Auerbach, Jerold S. *Rabbis and Lawyers: The Journey from Torah to Constitution.* Bloomington, IN: Indiana University Press, 1993.

Bailyn, Bernard. *The Ideological Origins of the American Revolution.* Cambridge, MA: Belknap Press of Harvard University Press, 1967.

Baker, John W., ed. *Taxation and the Free Exercise of Religion: Papers and Proceedings of the Sixteenth Religious Liberty Conference.* (Washington, DC, 3–5 October 1977) Washington, DC: Baptist Joint Committee on Public Affairs, 1978.

Balk, Alfred. *The Religion Business.* Richmond, VA: John Knox Press, 1968.

Ball, William Bentley. "Religious Liberty in Our Time: What Has the Supreme Court Said?" In *Freedom of Religion Clauses of the First Amendment: What Do They Mean Today?* Pennsylvania Catholic Conference, 23–24. Erie, PA: Pennsylvania Catholic Conference, 1990.

Ball, William Bentley, ed. *In Search of a National Morality: A Manifesto for Evangelicals and Catholics.* Grand Rapids, MI: Ignatius Press, 1992.

Barker, Lucius J., and Twiley W. Barker, Jr., eds. *Civil Liberties and the Constitution: Cases and Commentaries.* Englewood Cliffs, NJ: Prentice-Hall, 1970.

Barker, Sir Ernest. *Church, State and Education.* Ann Arbor, MI: University of Michigan Press, 1957.

Barr, David L., and Nicholas Piediscalzi, eds. *The Bible in American Education: From Source Book to Textbook.* Philadelphia: Fortress Press, 1982.

Barrett, Patricia. *Religious Liberty and the American Presidency: Study in Church-State Relations.* New York: Herder and Herder, 1963.

Barron, Bruce. *Heaven on Earth? The Social and Political Agendas of Dominion Theology.* Grand Rapids, MI: Zondervan Publishing House, 1992.

Barth, Karl. *Community, State, and Church.* Garden City, NY: Doubleday, 1960.

Bates, Stephen. *Battleground: One Mother's Crusade, the Religious Right, and the Struggle for Control of Our Classrooms.* New York: Poseidon Press, 1993.

Beach, Bert B. *Bright Candle of Courage.* Boise, ID: Pacific Press Publishing Association, 1989.

Becker, Theodore L., and Malcolm M. Feeley. *The Impact of Supreme Court Decisions*. New York: Oxford University Press, 1973.

Beggs, David W., III., and R. Bruce McQuigg, eds. *America's Schools and Churches, Partners in Conflict*. Bloomington, IN: Indiana University Press, 1965.

Bell, Sadie. *The Church, the State, and Education in Virginia*. New York: Arno Press, 1969.

Bellah, Robert N. *The Broken Covenant. American Civil Religion in Time of Trial*. New York: Seabury Press, 1975.

Bellah, Robert N., and Phillip E. Hammond. *Varieties of Civil Religion*. New York: Harper & Row, 1980.

Bems, Walter. *The First Amendment and the Future of American Democracy*. New York: Basic Books, 1976.

Benavides, Gustavo, and M. W. Daly, eds. *Religion and Political Power*. Albany, NY: State University of New York Press, 1989.

Benson, Peter L., and Dorothy L. Williams. *Religion on Capitol Hill: Myths and Realities*. San Francisco: Harper & Row, 1982.

Berger, Peter L. *The Noise of Solemn Assemblies: Christian Commitment and the Religious Establishment in America*. Garden City, NY: Doubleday, 1961.

Berman, Harold J. *The Interaction of Law and Religion*. Nashville, TN: Abingdon Press, 1974.

———. *Faith and Order*. Atlanta, GA: Scholars Press, 1993.

Berra, Tim M. *Evolution and the Myth of Creationism: A Basic Guide to the Facts in the Evolution Debate*. Lexington, KY: University of Kentucky Press, 1990.

Beth, Loren P. *The American Theory of Church and State*. Gainesville, FL: University of Florida Press, 1958.

Blackwell, Victor V. *O'er the Ramparts They Watched*. New York: Carlton Press, 1976.

Blakely, William, ed. *American State Papers and Related Documents on Freedom of Religion*. 4th rev. ed. Washington, DC: Published for the Religious Liberty Association by the *Review and Herald*, 1949.

Blanchard, Paul. *Religion and the Schools: The Great Controversy*. Boston: Beacon Press, 1963.

Blau, Joseph L. *Cornerstones of Religious Freedom in America*. Rev. ed. New York: Harper & Brothers, 1964.

Blum, Virgil C. *Freedom in Education: Federal Aid for All Children*. Garden City, NY: Doubleday, 1965.

Boles, Donald E. *The Bible, Religion, and the Public Schools*. Ames, IA: Iowa State University Press, 1961, 1964.

———. *The Two Swords: Commentaries and Cases in Religion and Education*. Ames, IA: Iowa State University Press, 1967.

Borden, Morten. *Jews, Turks, and Infidel*. Chapel Hill, NC: University of North Carolina Press, 1984.

Boyd, Julian P., ed. *The Papers of Thomas Jefferson*. 20 vols. Princeton, NJ: Princeton University Press, 1950–.

Bradley, Gerard V. *Church-State Relationships in America*. New York: Greenwood Press, 1987.

Bradley, Martha Sontagg. *Kidnapped From that Land: The Government Raids on the Short Creek Polygamists*. Salt Lake City, UT: The University of Utah Press, 1993.

Brady, Joseph H. *Confusion Twice Confounded: The First Amendment and the Supreme Court*. South Orange, NJ: Seton Hall University Press, 1954.

Brauer, Jerald C., ed. *The Lively Experiment Continued*. Macon, GA: Mercer University Press, 1987.

Brauer, Jerald C., Sidney E. Mead and Robert N. Bellah. *Religion in the American Revolution*. Philadelphia: Fortress Press, 1976.

Breslauer, S. Daniel. *Judaism and Civil Religion*. Atlanta, GA: Scholars Press, 1993.

Brickman, William, and Stanley Lehrer, eds. *Religion, Government, and Education*. New York: Society for the Advancement of Education, 1961.

Brock, Peter. *Pacifism in the United States: From the Colonial Era to the First World War*. Princeton, NJ: Princeton University Press, 1968.

Bromley, David G., and Anson Shupe, eds. *And Strange Gods: The Great American Cult Scare*. Boston: Beacon Press, 1982.

———. *New Christian Politics*. Macon, GA: Mercer University Press, 1984.

Bromley, David G., and James T. Richardson, eds. *The Brainwashing/Deprogramming Controversy: Sociological, Psychological, Legal, and Historical Perspectives*. Lewiston, NY: The Edwin Mellen Press, 1983.

Brown, Nicholas C., ed. *The Study of Religion in the Public Schools: An Appraisal*. Washington, DC: American Council on Education, 1958.

Brown, Robert McAfee. *Saying Yes and Saying No: On Rendering to God and Caesar*. Philadelphia: Westminster Press, 1986.

———. *Liberation Theology: An Introductory Guide*. New York: Paulist Press, 1993.

Bruce, Steve. *The Rise and Fall of the New Christian Right: Conservative Protestant Politics in America, 1978–1988*. New York: Oxford University Press, 1990.

Bryk, Anthony S., Valerie E. Lee and Peter B. Holland. *Catholic Schools and the Common Good*. Notre Dame, IN: University of Notre Dame, 1992.

Bryson, Joseph, and Samuel H. Houston, Jr. *The Supreme Court and Public Funds for Religious Schools: The Burger Years, 1969–1986*. Jefferson, NC: McFarland and Company, 1990.

Burstein, Abraham. *Law Concerning Religion in the United States*. 2d ed. Dobbs Ferry, NY: Oceana, 1966.

———. *Religion, Cults, and the Law*. Rev. 2d ed. Dobbs Ferry, NY: Oceana, 1980.

Butts, R. Freeman. *The American Tradition in Religion and Education*. Boston: Beacon Press, 1950.

Buzzard, Lynn R. *Schools: They Haven't Got a Prayer*. Elgin, IL: David C. Cook, 1982.

———. *With Liberty and Justice: A Look at Civil Law and the Christian*. Wheaton, IL: Victor Books, 1984.

Buzzard, Lynn R., and Samuel Ericsson. *The Battle for Religious Liberty*. Elgin, IL: David C. Cook, 1982.

Buzzard, Lynn R., ed. *Freedom and Faith: The Impact of Law on Religious Liberty*. Westchester, IL: Crossway Books, 1982.

Byrnes, Lawrence. *Religion and Public Education*. New York: Harper & Row, 1975.

Byrnes, Timothy, and Mary C. Segers, eds. *The Catholic Church and the Politics of Abortion*. Boulder, CO: Westview Press, 1992.

Cady, Linell E. *Religion, Theology and American Public Life*. Albany, NY: State University of New York Press, 1993.

Callahan, Daniel, ed. *Federal Aid and Catholic Schools*. Baltimore, MD: Helicon Press, 1964.

Capps, Walter H. *The New Religious Right: Piety, Patriotism, and Politics.* Columbia, SC: University of South Carolina Press, 1990.

Carey, George W., and James V. Shall, eds. *Essays on Christianity and Political Philosophy.* Lanham, MD: University Press of America, 1984.

Carmody, Denise Lardner, and John Tully Carmody. *The Republic of Many Mansions: Foundations of American Religious Thought.* New York: Paragon House, 1990.

Carper, James C., and Thomas C. Hunt, eds. *Religious Schooling in America.* Birmingham, AL: Religious Education Press, 1984.

Carter, Lief. *An Introduction to Constitutional Interpretation: Cases in Law and Religion.* New York: Longman, 1991.

Carter, Paul A. *Politics, Religion and Rockets.* Tucson, AZ: The University of Arizona Press, 1991.

Carter, Stephen L. *The Culture of Disbelief. How American Law and Politics Trivialize Religious Devotion.* New York: Basic Books, 1993.

Castelli, Jim. *A Plea for Common Sense: Resolving the Clash Between Religion and Politics.* San Francsico: Harper & Row, 1988.

Catterall, James S. *Tuition Tax Credits: Fact and Fiction.* Bloomington, IN: Phi Delta Kappa Education Foundation, 1983.

Chambers, Robert R. *Political Theory and Societal Ethics.* Buffalo, NY: Prometheus Books, 1992.

Chapman, Audrey R. *Faith, Power, and Politics: Political Ministry and Transformation in Mainline Churches.* New York: Pilgrim Press, 1991.

Cherry, Conrad, ed. *God's New Israel: Religious Interpretations of American Destiny.* Englewood Cliffs, NJ: Prentice-Hall, 1971.

Chidester, David. *Patterns of Power: Religion and Politics in American Culture.* Englewood Cliffs, NJ: Prentice-Hall, 1988.

Chubb, John E., and Terry M. Moe. *Politics, Markets, and America's Schools.* Washington, DC: Brookings Institution, 1990.

Church, Robert L., and Michael W. Sedlak. *Education in the United States: An Interpretive History.* New York: Free Press, 1976.

Clark, Henry B., II., ed. *Freedom of Religion in America: Historical Roots, Philosophical Concepts, and Contemporary Problems.* New Brunswick, NJ: Transaction Books, 1982.

Clark, Stephen R. L. *God's World and the Great Awakening.* Oxford, UK: Clarendon Press, 1991.

Clayton, A. Stafford. *Religion and Schooling: A Comparative Study.* Waltham, MA: Blaisdell, 1969.

Cobb, Sanford H. *The Rise of Religious Liberty in America.* New York: Macmillan, 1902.

Cogdell, Gaston D. *What Price Parochiaid?* Washington, DC: Americans United for Separation of Church and State, 1970.

Cogley, John, ed. *Religion in America: Original Essays on Religion in a Free Society.* New York: Meridian Books, 1958.

Cohen, Richard. *Sunday in the Sixties.* New York: Public Affairs Committee, 1962.

Colombo, Furio. *God in America: Religion and Politics in the United States.* New York: Columbia University Press, 1984.

Colombo, John D., and Mark A. Hall. *The Charitable Tax Exemption.* Boulder, CO: Westview Press, 1995.

Conway, Flo, and Jim Siegelman. *Holy Terror: The Fundamentalist War on America's Freedom in Religion, Politics, and Our Private Lives*. Garden City, NY: Doubleday, 1982.

Cookston, Peter, Jr. *School Choice: The Struggle for the Soul of American Education*. New Haven, CT: Yale University Press, 1994.

Coons, John E., and Stephen D. Sugarman. *Education by Choice: The Case for Family Control*. Berkeley, CA: University of California Press, 1978.

Cord, Robert L. *Separation of Church and State: Historical Fact and Current Fiction*. New York: Lambeth Press, 1982.

Cornell, Julian. *The Conscientious Objector and the Law*. New York: John Day, 1943.

Costanzo, Joseph T., S.J. *This Nation Under God: Church, State and Schools in America*. New York: Herder and Herder, 1964.

Couser, Richard B. *Ministry and the American Legal System: A Guide for Clergy, Lay Workers, and Congregations*. Minneapolis, MN: Fortress/Augsburg Press, 1993.

Cousins, Norman, ed. *'In God We Trust': The Religious Beliefs and Ideas of the American Founding Fathers*. New York: Harper & Row, 1958.

———. *The Republic of Reason: The Personal Philosophies of the Founding Fathers*. San Francisco: Harper & Row, 1988.

Coutin, Susan Bibler. *The Culture of Protest: Religious Activism and the U.S. Sanctuary Movement*. Boulder, CO: Westview Press, 1993.

Cox, Archibald. *The Role of the Supreme Court in American Government*. New York: Oxford University Press, 1976.

Craig, Robert H. *Religion and Radical Politics: An Alternative Christian Tradition in the United States*. Philadelphia: Temple University Press, 1992.

Cromartie, Michael, ed. *No Longer Exiles: The Religious New Right in American Politics*. Washington, DC: Ethics and Public Policy Center, 1992.

Curry, Thomas J. *The First Freedoms: Church and State in America to the Passage of the First Amendment*. New York: Oxford University Press, 1985.

Dalcho, F. *History of the Episcopal Church in South Carolina*. Charleston, SC: N.p., 1820.

Daum, Annette. *Assault on the Bill of Rights*. New York: Union of American Hebrew Congregations, 1982.

Davis, Derek. *Original Intent: Chief Justice Rehnquist and the Course of American Church-State Relations*. Buffalo, NY: Prometheus Books, 1991.

Dawson, Joseph M. *America's Way in Church, State, and Society*. New York: Macmillan, 1953.

Dewey, John. "My Pedagogic Creed." In *My Pedagogic Creed* by Professor John Dewey. Chicago: E. L. Kellogg, c 1897. Reprinted Washington, DC: Progressive Education Association, 1929.

———. *Theory of the Moral Life*. New York: Holt, Rinehart, & Winston, c. 1960.

Dierenfield, R. H. *Religion in American Public Schools*. Washington, DC: Public Affairs Press, 1962.

Doerr, Edd, and Albert J. Menendez. *Church Schools and Public Money*. Buffalo, NY: Prometheus Books, 1991.

Dolbeare, Kenneth M., and Philip E. Hammond. *The School Prayer Decisions: From Court Policy to Local Practice*. Chicago: University of Chicago Press, 1971.

Dorsen, Norman, ed. *Religion, the Courts, and Public Policy*. New York: McGraw-Hill, 1963.

————. *The Rights of Americans: What They Are and What They Should Be.* New York: Pantheon, 1971.

Douglas, William O. *The Bible and the Schools.* Boston: Little, Brown & Co., 1966.

Drakeman, Donald L. *Church-State Constitutional Issues: Making Sense of the Establishment Clause.* New York: Greenwood Press, 1991.

Drazin, Israel, and Cecil B. Currey. *For God and Country: The History of a Constitutional Challenge to the Army Chaplaincy.* New York: KTAV, 1995.

Dreisbach, Daniel L. *Real Threat and Mere Shadow: Religious Liberty and the First Amendment.* Westchester, IL: Crossway Books, 1987.

Dreisbach, Daniel L., ed. *Religion and Politics in the Early Republic: Jasper Adams and the Church-State Debate.* Lexington, KY: University Press of Kentucky, c. 1936.

Drinan, Robert F., S.J. *Religion, the Courts, and Public Policy.* New York: McGraw-Hill, 1963.

————. *God and Caesar on the Potomac.* Wilmington, DE: Michael Glazier, 1986.

Duker, Sam. *The Public Schools and Religion: The Legal Context.* New York: Harper & Row, 1966.

Dunn, Charles W., ed. *American Political Theology: Historical Perspectives and Theoretical Analysis.* New York: Praeger, 1984.

————. *Religion in American Politics.* Washington, DC: CQ Press, 1988.

Dunn, Gerald T. *Justice Joseph Story and the Rise of the Supreme Court.* New York: Simon & Schuster, 1970.

————. *Hugo Black and the Judicial Revolution.* New York: Simon & Schuster, 1977.

Dutile, Fernand N., and Edward McGlynn Gaffney, Jr. *State and Campus: State Regulation of Religiously Affiliated Higher Education.* Notre Dame, IN: University of Notre Dame Press, 1984.

————. *Stories from the American Soul: A Reader in Ethics and American Policy for the 1990s.* Chicago: Loyola University Press, 1990.

Dworkin, Ronald. *Life's Dominion.* New York: Knopf, 1993.

Eastland, Terry, ed. *Religious Liberty in the Supreme Court: The Cases That Define the Debate over Church and State.* Grand Rapids, MI: Eerdmans, 1995.

Ebersole, Luke Eugene. *Church Lobbying in the Nation's Capital.* New York: Macmillan, 1951.

Edel, Wilbur. *Defenders of the Faith: Religion and Politics from the Pilgrim Fathers to Ronald Reagan.* New York: Praeger, 1987.

Edwards, Newton. *The Courts and the Public Schools.* Chicago: University of Chicago Press, 1971.

Eidsmore, John. *Christian Legal Advisor.* Milford, MI: Mott Media, 1984.

————. *Christianity and the Constitution: The Faith of Our Founding Fathers.* Grand Rapids, MI: Baker House, 1987.

Elliot, Jonathan, ed. *The Debates in the Several State Conventions on the Adoption of the Federal Constitution.* 2d ed. 5 vols. Philadelphia: J. P. Lippincott Company, 1891.

Ellis, John Tracy. *Catholics in Colonial America.* Baltimore, MD: Helicon, 1965.

Ellison, Tamara. *Religion and the Public Schools: Guidelines for a Growing and Changing Phenomenon for K-12.* New York: Anti-Defamation League of B'nai B'rith, 1992.

Emerson, Ralph Waldo. *Essays: Second Series.* Reprinted in *The Collected Works of Ralph Waldo Emerson; Essays: Second Series,* vol. 3. Cambridge, MA: Belknap Press of Harvard University Press, 1984.

Engel, David E. *Religion in Public Education.* New York: Paulist Press, 1974.

Epstein, Richard A. *Bargaining with the State.* Princeton, NJ: Princeton University Press, 1993.

Erickson, Donald A., ed. *Public Controls for Nonpublic Schools.* Chicago: University of Chicago Press, 1969.

Ervin, Sam J., Jr. *Preserving the Constitution.* Charlottesville, VA: The Michie Co., 1985.

Esposito, John L. *The Islamic Threat: Myth or Reality?* New York: Oxford University Press, 1992.

Evans, J. Edward. *Freedom of Religion.* Minneapolis, MN: Lemer Publications, 1990.

Fackre, Gabriel. *The Religious Right and Christian Faith.* Grand Rapids, MI: Eerdmans, 1982.

Farber, Daniel A., and Suzanna Sherry. *A History of the American Constitution.* St. Paul, MN: West, 1990.

Farrand, Max. *Records of the Federal Convention.* Rev. ed. 3 vols. New Haven, CT: Yale University Press.

Feldman, Egal. *Dual Destinies: The Jewish Encounter with Protestant America.* Chicago: University of Illinois Press, 1990.

Feliman, David. *Religion in American Public Law.* Boston: Boston University Press, 1974.

Fenwick, Lynda Beck. *Should the Children Pray?: A Historical, Judicial, and Political Examination of Public School Prayer.* Waco, TX: Baylor University Press, 1989.

Ferguson, Thomas P. *Catholic and American: The Political Theology of John Courtney Murray.* Kansas City, MO: Sheed and Ward, 1993.

Fetzer, Joel. *Selective Prosecution of Religiously Motivated Offenders in America: Scrutinizing the Myth of Neutrality.* Lewiston, NY: Edwin Mellen Press, 1989.

Finke, Roger, and Rodney Starke. *The Churching of America, 1776–1990: Winners and Losers in Our Religious Economy.* New Brunswick, NJ: Rutgers University Press, 1992.

Finn, James D., ed. *A Conflict of Loyalties: The Case for Selective Conscientious Objection.* New York: Pegasus, 1968.

Fisher, Louis. *American Constitutional Law.* 2d ed. New York: McGraw-Hill, 1995.

Fisher, Wallace E. *Politics, Poker, and Piety: A Perspective on Cultural Religion in America.* Nashville, TN: Abingdon Press, 1972.

Fishman, James, and Stephen Schwartz. *Nonprofit Organizations: Cases and Materials.* Westbury, NY: Foundation, 1995.

Flowers, Ronald B. *Religion in Strange Times: The 1960s and 1970s.* Macon, GA: Mercer University Press, 1984.

———. *That Godless Court?: Supreme Court Decisions on Church-State Relationships.* Louisville, KY: Westminster John Knox Press, 1995.

Forcinelli, Joseph. *The Democratization of Religion in America: A Commonwealth of Religious Freedom by Design.* Lewiston, ME: Edwin Mellen Press, 1990.

Ford, Paul L., ed. *The Works of Thomas Jefferson.* New York, London: G.P. Putnam's Sons, 1904–1905.

Forell, George W., and William H. Lazareth. *God's Call to Public Responsibility.* Philadelphia: Fortress Press, 1978.

Fowler, Robert Booth. *A New Engagement: Evangelical Political Thought, 1966–1976.* Grand Rapids, MI: Eerdmans, 1982.

———. *Religion and Politics in America.* Metuchen, NJ: Scarecrow Press, 1986.

Frankel, Marvin E. *Faith and Freedom.* New York: Hill and Wang, 1994.

Freund, Paul A., and Robert Utich. *Religion and the Public Schools.* Cambridge, MA: Harvard University Press, 1965.

Friedman, Murray. *The Utopian Dilemma: American Judaism and Public Policy.* Washington, DC: Ethics and Public Policy Center, 1985.

Frommer, Arthur, ed. *The Bible and the Public Schools.* New York: Liberal Arts Press, 1963.

Frost, J. William. *A Perfect Freedom: Religious Liberty in Pennsylvania.* Westport, CT: Greenwood, 1990.

Gaffney, Edward McGlynn, Jr. *Private Schools and the Public Good: Policy Alternatives for the Eighties.* Notre Dame, IN: University of Notre Dame Press, 1981.

Gaffney, Edward McGlynn, Jr., and Philip C. Sorensen. *Ascending Liability in Religious and Other Nonprofit Organizations.* Macon, GA: Mercer University Press, 1984.

Gaffney, Edward McGlynn, Jr., and Philip R. Motts. *Government and Campus: Federal Regulation of Religiously Affiliated Higher Education.* Notre Dame, IN: University of Notre Dame Press, 1982.

Garvey, John H., Jr. *What Are Freedoms For?* Cambridge, MA: Harvard University Press, 1996.

Gaustad, Edwin Scott. *Religious Issues in American History.* New York: Harper & Row, 1968.

———. *Dissent in American Religion.* Chicago: University of Chicago Press, 1973.

———. *Faith of Our Fathers: Religion and the New Nation.* San Francisco: Harper & Row, 1987.

———. *Liberty of Conscience: Roger Williams in America.* Grand Rapids, MI: Eerdmans, 1995.

Gedicks, Federick Mark.*The Rhetoric of Church and State: A Critical Analysis of Religion Clause Jurisprudence.* Durham, NC: Duke University Press, 1995.

Gedicks, Federick Mark, and Roger Hendrix. *Choosing the Dream: The Future of Religion in American Public Life.* New York: Greenwood Press, 1991.

Geisler, Norman L., A. F. Brooke II and Mark J. Keough. *The Creator in the Courtroom: "Scopes II."* Milford, MI: Mott Media, 1982.

Gellhorn, Walter, and R. Kent Greenawalt. *The Sectarian College and the Public Press.* Dobbs Ferry, NY: Oceana, 1970.

Giannelia, Donald A., ed. *Religion and the Public Order, No. 5.* Ithaca, NY: Cornell University Press, 1969.

Gibson, William. *Church, State, and Society.* New York: St. Martin's Press, 1992.

Gilkey, Langdon. *Creationism on Trial: Evolution and God at Little Rock.* Minneapolis, MN: Winston Press, 1985.

Ginsberg, Benjamin. *The Fatal Embrace: Jews and the State.* Chicago: University of Chicago Press, 1993.

Goldberg, George. *Reconsecrating America.* Grand Rapids, MI: Eerdmans, 1984.

Goldwin, Robert A., and Art Kaufman, eds. *How Does the Constitution Protect Religious Freedom?* Washington, DC: American Enterprise Institute, 1988.

Gordis, Robert. *Religion and the Schools.* New York: Fund for the Republic, 1959.

Grant, Daniel R. *The Christian and Politics.* Nashville, TN: Broadman Press, 1968.

Green, John C., James L. Guth, Corwin E. Smidt and Lyman Kellstedt. *Religion and the Culture Wars: Dispatches from the Front.* Lanham, MD: Rowman & Littlefield, 1966.

Greenawalt, Kent. *Conflicts of Law and Morality*. New York: Oxford University Press, 1987.

———. *Religious Convictions and Political Choice*. New York: Oxford University Press, 1988.

Greene, Evarts B. *Religion and the State: The Making and Testing of an American Tradition*. Ithaca, NY: Cornell University Press, 1959.

Greene, M. Louise. *The Development of Religious Liberty in Connecticut*. Boston: Houghton, Mifflin, 1905. Reprinted New York: DaCapo Press, Inc., 1970.

Griffin, Leslie, ed. *Religion and Politics in the American Milieu*. Notre Dame, IN: Review of Politics, 1989.

Griffith, Carol Friedley. *Christianity and Politics: Catholic and Protestant Perspectives*. Washington, DC: Ethics and Public Policy Center, 1981.

Griffiths, William E. *Religion, the Courts, and the Public Schools: A Century of Litigation*. Cincinnati, OH: W. H. Anderson, 1966.

Groh, John E. *Facilitators of the Free Exercise of Religion: Air Force Chaplains, 1981–1990*. Washington, DC: Office of the Chief of Chaplains, USAF, 1991.

Guinness, Os. *The American Hour: A Time of Reckoning and the Once and Future Role of Faith*. New York: The Free Press, 1993.

Haddon, Jeffrey K., and Anson Shupe, eds. *Prophetic Religions and Politics: Religion and the Political Order*. New York: Paragon House Publishers, 1986.

Hamilton, Alexander. *The Federalist, No. 78*. Edited by Clinton Rossiter. New York: New American Library, 1961.

Hamilton, Otto Templar. *The Courts and the Curriculum*. Unpublished Ph.D. Thesis: Columbia University, 1927.

Hammar, Richard R. *Pastor, Church, and Law*. 2d ed. Matthews, NC: Christian Ministry Resources, 1991.

Hammond, Phillip E. *Religion and Personal Autonomy: The Third Disestablishment in America*. Columbia, SC: University of South Carolina Press, 1992.

Handy, Robert T. *A Christian America: Protestant Hopes and Historical Realities*. 2d ed. Oxford, UK: Oxford University Press, 1984.

———. *Undermined Establishment: Church-State Relations in America, 1880–1920*. Princeton, NJ: Princeton University Press, 1991.

Hanley, *Their Rights and Liberties*. Westminster, MD: Newman Press, 1959.

Hansen, Klaus J. *Mormonism and the American Experience*. Chicago: University of Chicago Press, 1981.

Hardy, B. Carmon. *Solemn Covenant: The Mormon Polygamous Passage*. Urbana, IL: University of Illinois Press, 1992.

Harper, Fowler V. *Justice Rutledge and the Bright Constellation*. Indianapolis, IN: Bobbs-Merrill, 1965.

Hart, Stephen. *What Does the Lord Require?: How American Christians Think About Justice*. New York: Oxford University Press, 1992.

Hayes, Carlton J. H. *Nationalism: A Religion*. New York: Macmillan, 1960.

Healey, Robert M. *Jefferson on Religion in Public Education*. New Haven, CT: Yale University Press, 1962.

Hefley, James C., and Edward E. Plowman. *Christians and the Corridors of Power*. Wheaton, IL: Tyndale House, 1975.

Henig, Jeffrey R. *Rethinking School Choice: Limits of the Market Metaphor*. Princeton, NJ: Princeton University Press, 1993.

Herberg, Will. *Protestant, Catholic, Jew: An Essay in American Religious Sociology.* Rev. ed. Garden City, NY: Doubleday, 1960.

Hertzke, Allen D. *Representing God in Washington: The Role of Religious Lobbies in the American Polity.* Knoxville, TN: The University of Tennessee Press, 1988.

———. *Echoes of Discontent: Jesse Jackson, Pat Robertson, and the Resurgence of Populism.* Washington, DC: CQ Press, 1993.

Heslep, Robert D. *Thomas Jefferson and Education.* New York: Random House, 1969.

Hessel, Dieter, ed. *The Church's Public Role: Retrospect and Prospect.* Grand Rapids, MI: Eerdmans, 1993.

Hoekema, Anthony A. *The Four Major Cults: Christian Science, Jehovah's Witnesses, Mormonism, Seventh-Day Adventists.* Grand Rapids, MI: Eerdmans, 1963.

Hoffer, Peter Charles. *The Law's Conscience: Equitable Constitutionalism in America.* Chapel Hill, NC: University of North Carolina Press, 1990.

Hogan, John C. *The Schools, the Courts, and the Public Interest.* Lexington, MA: Lexington Books, 1985.

Honeywell, Roy J. *The Educational Work of Thomas Jefferson.* Cambridge, MA: Harvard University Press, 1963.

Hook, Sidney. *Religion in a Free Society.* Lincoln, NE: University of Nebraska Press, 1967.

Hopkins, Bruce R. *The Law of Tax-Exempt Organizations.* 6th ed. New York: John Wiley & Sons, 1992.

Hostetler, John A. *Amish Society.* Rev. ed. Baltimore, MD: Johns Hopkins University Press, 1968.

Howard, A. E. Dick. *State Aid to Private Higher Education.* Charlottesville, VA: The Michie Co., 1977.

Howe, Mark DeWolfe, ed. *Cases of Church and State in the United States.* Cambridge, MA: Harvard University Press, 1952.

———. *The Garden and the Wilderness: Religion and the Government in American Constitutional History.* Chicago: University of Chicago Press, 1965.

Hudson, Winthrop S. *The Great Tradition of the American Churches.* New York: Harper & Brothers, 1953.

———. *Religion in America.* New York: Scribner, 1992.

Hughson, Thomas, S.J. *The Believer as Citizen: John Courtney Murray in a New Context.* New York: Paulist Press, 1993.

Hunt, Robert P., and Kenneth L. Grasso, eds. *John Courtney Murray and the American Civil Conversation.* Grand Rapids, MI: Eerdmans, 1992.

Hunter, James Davison. *Culture Wars: The Struggle to Define America.* New York: Basic Books, 1991.

Hunter, James Davison, and Os Guinness, eds. *Articles of Faith, Articles of Peace–The Religious Liberty Clauses and the American Public Philosophy.* Washington, DC: Brookings Institution, 1990.

Hutcheson, Richard G., Jr. *God in the White House–How Religion Has Changed the Modern Presidency.* New York: Macmillan, 1989.

Isaac, Rhys. *The Transformation of Virginia, 1740–1790.* Chapel Hill, NC: University of North Carolina Press, 1999.

Ivers, Gregg. *Lowering the Wall: Religion and the Supreme Court in the 1980s.* New York: Anti-Defamation League, 1991.

————. *Redefining the First Freedom: The Supreme Court and the Consolidation of State Power.* New Brunswick, NJ: Transaction Publishers, 1992.

Jackson, Robert H. *The Supreme Court in the American System of Government.* New York: Harper & Row, 1955.

James, Thomas, and Henry M. Levin, eds. *Public Dollars for Private Schools: The Case of Tuition Tax Credits.* Philadelphia: Temple University Press, 1983.

Jelen, Ted G. *The Political Mobilization of Religious Beliefs.* New York: Praeger Publishers, 1991.

Jelen, Ted G., and Clyde Wilcox. *Public Attitudes Toward Church and State.* Armonk, NY: M.E. Sharpe, 1995.

Johnson, Alvin W. *The Legal Status of Church-State Relationships in the United States with Special Reference to the Public Schools.* Minneapolis, MN: University of Minnesota Press, 1934.

Johnson, Alvin W., and Frank H. Yost. *Separation of Church and State in the United States.* Minneapolis, MN: University of Minnesota Press, 1948.

Johnson, F. Ernest, ed. *American Education and Religion: The Problem of Religion in the Schools.* New York: Harper & Row, 1952.

Johnson, James Turner, ed. *The Bible in American Law, Politics, and Political Rhetoric.* Philadelphia: Fortress Press, 1985.

Johnson, Richard M. *The Dynamics of Compliance: Supreme Court Decision-Making from a New Perspective.* Evanston, IL: Northwestern University Press, 1967.

Jorstad, Erling. *Evangelicals in the White House: The Cultural Maturation of Born Again Christianity, 1960–1981.* New York: Edwin Mellon Press, 1981.

————. *The Politics of Moralism: The New Christian Right in American Life.* Minneapolis, MN: Augsburg, 1981.

————. *Being Religious in America: The Deepening Crisis Over Public Faith.* Minneapolis, MN: Augsburg, 1986.

Katz, Wilber G. *Religion and American Constitutions.* Evanston, IL: Northwestern University Press, 1963.

Kelley, Dean M., ed. *Government Intervention in Religious Affairs.* New York: Pilgrim Press, 1986.

Kennedy, John F. "Remarks on Church and State." In *Church and State in American History.* 2nd ed. Edited by John F. Wilson and Donald L. Drakeman. Boston: Beacon Press, 1987.

Kolbenschlag, Madonna, ed. *Between God and Caesar: Priests, Sisters, and Political Office in the United States.* New York: Paulist Press, 1985.

Kommers, Donald P., and Michael Wahoske, eds. *Freedom and Education: Pierce v. Society of Sisters Reconsidered.* Notre Dame, IN: Center for Civil Rights, University of Notre Dame Law School, 1978.

La Noue, George R., ed. *Educational Vouchers: Concepts and Controversies.* New York: Teachers College, Columbia University Press, 1972.

Lannie, Vincent P. *Public Money for Parochial Education.* Cleveland, OH: Case Western Reserve University Press, 1968.

Larson, Martin, and C. Stanley Lowell. *Praise the Lord for Tax Exemption: How the Churches Grow Rich, While the Cities and You Grow Poor.* Washington, DC: Robert B. Luce, 1969.

————. *The Religious Empire: The Growth and Danger of Tax-Exempt Property in the United States.* Washington, DC: Robert B. Luce, 1976.

Laubach, John H. *School Prayers: Congress, the Courts, and the Public*. Washington, DC: Public Affairs Press, 1969.

Lee, Francis G., ed. *All Imaginable Liberty: The Religious Liberty Clauses and the First Amendment*. Lanham, MD: University Press of America, 1995.

Levy, Leonard Williams, ed. *Blasphemy in Massachusetts: Freedom of Conscience and the Abner Kneeland Case: A Documentary Record*. New York: Da Capo Press, 1973.

———. *Blasphemy: Verbal Offense Against the Sacred, From Moses to Salman Rushdie*. New York: Knopf, 1993.

———. *The Establishment Clause: Religion and the First Amendment*. New York: Macmillan, 1989.

Liebman, Robert C., and Robert Wuthnow, eds. *The New Christian Right: Mobilization and Legitimation*. New York: Aldine, 1983.

Lienesch, Michael. *Redeeming America: Piety and Politics in the New Christian Right*. Chapel Hill, NC: University of North Carolina Press, 1995.

Lincoln, C. Eric. *The Black Muslims in America*. Boston: Beacon Press, 1973.

Linder, Robert D., and Richard V. Pierard. *Politics: A Case for Christian Action*. Downers Grove, IL: Inter-Varsity Press, 1973.

Lingley, Charles Ramsdell. *The Transition in Virginia from Colony to Commonwealth*. New York: AMS Press, 1967.

Littell, Franklin Hamlin. *The Church and the Body Politic*. New York: Seabury Press, 1969.

———. *From State Church to Pluralism: A Protestant Interpretation of Religion in American History*. New York: Macmillan, 1971.

Loder, James E. *Religion and the Public Schools*. New York: Association Press, 1965.

Lovin, Robin W. *Religion and American Public Life: Interpretations and Explorations*. Mahwah, NJ: Paulist Press, 1986.

Lunceford, Lloyd J. *The Religion Clauses of the First Amendment*. Baton Rouge, LA: L. J. Lunceford, 1988.

Lunger, Harold L. *A Citizen Under God*. St. Louis, MO: Christian Board of Publication, 1973.

Lynn, Barry, Marc D. Stern and Oliver S. Thomas. *The Right to Religious Liberty: The Basic ACLU Guide to Religious Rights*. Carbondale, IL: Southern Illinois University Press, 1995.

Maddox, Robert L. *Separation of Church and State: Guarantor of Religious Freedom*. New York: Crossroad Books, 1987.

Malbin, Michael J. *Religion and Politics: The Intentions of the Authors of the First Amendment*. Washington, DC: American Enterprise Institute, 1978.

Malony, H. Newton, Thomas L. Neeham and Samuel Southard, eds. *Clergy Malpractice*. Philadelphia: Westminster, 1986.

Manwaring, David R. *Render Unto Caesar: The Flag Salute Controversy*. Chicago: University of Chicago Press, 1962.

———. *Religion, Liberty, and the State*. Indianapolis, IN: Bobbs-Merrill, 1971.

Marnell, William H. *The First Amendment: The History of Religious Freedom in America*. Garden City, NY: Doubleday, 1964.

Marsden, George. *The Soul of the American University: From Protestant Establishment to Established Nonbelief*. New York: Oxford University Press, 1994.

Marty, Martin E. *The New Shape of American Religion*. New York: Harper & Row, 1959.

———. *The Pro & Con Book of Religious America: A Bicentennial Argument.* Waco, Texas: Word Incorporated, 1975.

———. *The Public Church: Mainline Evangelical-Catholic.* New York: Crossroad Books, 1981.

———. *Pilgrims in Their Own land: 500 Years of Religion in America.* Boston: Little, Brown & Co., 1984.

———. *Religion and Republic: The American Circumstance.* Boston: Beacon Press, 1987.

McBrien, Richard P. *Caesar's Coin: Religion and Politics in America.* New York: Macmillan, 1987.

McCarthy, Martha M. *A Delicate Balance: Church, State, and the Schools.* Bloomington, IN: Indiana University Press, 1983.

McCarthy, Rockne M., James W. Skillen and William A. Harper. *Disestablishment a Second Time: Genuine Pluralism for American Schools.* Grand Rapids, MI: Christian University Press, 1982.

McClellan, James. *Joseph Story and the American Constitution.* Norman, OK: University of Oklahoma Press, 1971.

McCluskey, Neil G. *Catholic Viewpoint on Education.* Rev. ed Garden City, NY: Image Books, 1962.

———. *Catholic Education in America.* New York: Teachers College, Columbia University Press, 1964.

McCollister, John. *So Help Me God: The Faith of America's Presidents.* Louisville, KY: John Knox Press, 1991.

McCollum, Vashti C. *One Women's Fight.* Boston: Beacon Press, 1951; Madison, WI: Freedom from Religion Foundation, 1993.

McCuen, Gary E. *Religion and Politics: Issues in Religious Liberty.* Hudson, WI: G. E. McCuen Publications, 1989.

McGrath, Joseph H., ed. *Church and State in American Law.* Milwaukee, WI: Bruce, 1962.

McManus, Edgar J. *Law and Liberty in Early New England: Criminal Justice and Due Process.* Amherst, MA: The University of Massachusetts Press, 1993.

McMillan, Richard C. *Religion in the Public Schools: An Introduction.* Macon, GA: Mercer University Press, 1984.

Mead, Sidney E. *The Lively Experiment: The Shaping of Christianity in America.* New York: Harper & Row, 1963.

———. *The Nation with the Soul of a Church.* New York: Harper & Row, 1975.

———. *The Old Religion in the Brave New World: Reflections on the Relation Between Christendom and the Republic.* Berkeley, CA: University of California Press, 1977.

Mechling, Jay, ed. *Church, State, and Public Policy: The New Shape of the Church-State Debate.* Washington, DC: American Enterprise Institute, 1978.

Meixner, Linda L. *The Bible in Literature Courses: Successful Lesson Plans.* New York: Praeger, 1991.

Melton, J. Gordon. *The Encyclopedia of American Religions.* 2 vols. Wilmington, NC: McGrath, 1978.

Menendez, Albert J. *Religious Conflict in America: A Bibliographic Guide.* New York: Garland, 1984.

———. *School Prayer and Other Issues in American Public Education: An Annotated Bibliography.* New York: Garland, 1984.

——. *Religion and the U.S. Presidency: A Bibliography.* New York: Garland, 1986.

——. *The December Dilemma: Christmas in American Public Life.* Silver Spring, MD: Americans United for Separation of Church and State, 1988.

——. *Visions of Reality: What Fundamentalist Schools Really Teach.* Buffalo, NY: Prometheus Books, 1993.

——. *Evangelicals at the Ballot Box.* Buffalo, NY: Prometheus Books, 1996.

Menendez, Albert J., and Edd Doerr, eds. *The Great Quotations of Religious Freedom.* Long Beach, CA: Centerline Press, 1991.

——. *Religion and Public Education: Common Sense and the Law.* Long Beach, CA: Centerline Press, 1991.

Meyer, Jacob C. *Church and State in Massachusetts from 1740 to 1833.* Cleveland, OH: Western Reserve University Press, 1930.

Michaelson, Robert. *Piety in the Public School: Trends and Issues in Relationship between Religion and the Public School in the United States.* New York: Macmillan, 1970.

Michnik, Adam. *The Church and the Left.* Chicago: University of Chicago Press, 1993.

Miller, Glenn T. *Religious Liberty in America: History and Prospects.* Philadelphia: Westminster Press, 1976.

Miller, Perry. *Roger Williams: His Contribution to the American Tradition.* Indianapolis, IN: Bobbs-Merrill, 1953.

Miller, Richard B. *Interpretations of Conflict: Ethics, Pacifism, and the Just-War Tradition.* Chicago: University of Chicago Press, 1991.

Miller, William L. *The First Liberty: Religion and the American Republic.* New York: Alfred A. Knopf, 1986.

Miller, William L., Robert Bellah, Martin Marty, and Arlin Adams. *Religion and the Public Good: A Bicentennial Forum.* Macon, GA: Mercer University Press, 1989.

Monti, Daniel J. *A Semblance of Justice.* Columbia, MO: University of Missouri Press, 1985.

Mooney, Christopher F. *Public Virtue: Law and the Social Character of Religion.* Notre Dame, IN: Notre Dame Press, 1986.

Morgan, Edmund S. *The Puritan Dilemma: The Story of John Winthrop.* New York: HarperCollins, 1958.

——. *Roger Williams: The Church and the State.* New York: Harcourt, Brace & World, 1967.

Morgan, Richard E. *The Politics of Religious Conflict: Church and State in America.* New York: Pegasus, 1968. Reprint Washington: University Press of America, 1980.

——. *The Supreme Court and Religion.* New York: Free Press, 1972.

Neuhaus, Richard John. *The Naked Public Square: Religion and Democracy in America.* Grand Rapids, MI: Eerdmans, 1984.

Newmyer, R. Kent. *Supreme Court Justice Joseph Story: Statesman of the Old Republic.* Chapel Hill, NC: University of North Carolina Press, 1985.

Noll, Mark A. *One Nation Under God? Christian Faith and Political Action in America.* San Francisco: Harper & Row, 1988.

Noonan, John T., Jr. *The Believer and the Powers That Are.* New York: Macmillan, 1987.

O'Brien, F. William, S.J. *Justice Reed and the First Amendment: The Religion Clauses.* Washington, DC: Georgetown University Press, 1958.

Office of Legal Policy, United States Department of Justice. *Report to the Attorney General: Religious Liberty Under the Free Exercise Clause.* Washington, DC: Government Printing Office, 1986.

Oleck, Howard L. *Nonprofit Corporations, Organizations, and Associations.* 5th ed. Englewood Cliffs, NJ: Prentice-Hall, 1988.

O'Neill, James M. *Catholicism and American Freedom.* New York: Harper, 1952.

Pennock, J. Roland, and John W. Chapman, eds. *Religion, Morality, and the Law.* New York: New York University Press, 1988.

Perry, Michael. *Morality, Politics, and Law.* New York: Oxford University Press, 1988.

Peterson, Merill, ed. *Democracy, Liberty, and Property: The State Constitutional Conventions of the 1820's.* Indianapolis, IN: Bobbs-Merrill, 1966.

Pfeffer, Leo. *Church, State, and Freedom.* Rev. ed. Boston: Beacon Press, 1967.

———. *Religion, State, and the Burger Court.* Buffalo, NY: Promoetheus Books, 1984.

Pfeffer, Leo. "The Future of the Bill of Rights: Church-State Relations." In *The Future of Our Liberties: Perspectives on the Bill of Rights.* Edited by Stephen C. Halpern, 111–129. Westport, CT: Greenwood Press, 1982.

Phillips, Harlan. *Felix Frankfurter Reminisces.* New York: Reynal, 1960.

Plunkett, Dudley. *Secular and Spiritual Values.* London, New York: Routledge, 1990.

Power, Edward J. *Religion and the Public Schools in Nineteenth-Century America: The Contribution of Orestes A. Brownson.* New York: Paulist Press, 1996.

Pratt, John Webb. *Religion, Politics, and Diversity: The Church-State Theme in New York History.* Ithaca, NY: Cornell University Press, 1967.

Prucha, Francis Paul. *The Churches and the Indian Schools, 1888–1912.* Lincoln, NE: University of Nebraska Press, 1979.

Ravitch, Diane. *The Great School Wars.* New York: Basic Books, 1974.

Reichley, A. James. *Religion in American Public Life.* Washington, DC: Brookings Institute, 1985.

Religion and the Public Good: A Bicentennial Forum. Foreword by John F. Wilson. Macon, GA: Mercer University Press, 1988.

Richman, Sheldon. *Separating School and State: How to Liberate America's Families.* Fairfax, VA: Future of Freedom Foundation, 1994.

Robbins, Thomas, and Roland Robertson, eds. *Church-State Relations: Tensions and Transitions.* New Brunswick, NJ: Transaction Books, 1987.

Robbins, Thomas, W. Shepherd, and J. McBride, eds. *Cults, Culture, and the Law: Perspectives on New Religious Movements.* Chico, CA: Scholars Press, 1985.

Robinson, John A. T. *Honest to God.* Philadelphia: Westminster Press, 1963.

Rutynas, Richard, and John W. Kuehl, eds. *Conceived in Conscience: An Analysis of Contemporary Church-State Relations.* Norfolk, VA: Donning Company, 1983.

Sahliyeh, Emile, ed. *Religious Resurgence and Politics in the Contemporary World.* Albany, NY: State University of New York Press, 1990.

Sampson, William. *The Catholic Question in America.* New York: Edward Gillespay, 1813. Reprint Ann Arbor, MI: Xerox Microfilms, 1976.

Sandeen, Ernest R., ed. *The Bible and Social Reform.* Philadelphia: Fortress Press, 1982.

Sanders, Thomas G. *Protestant Concepts of Church and State: Historical Backgrounds and Approaches for the Future.* New York: Holt, Rinehart & Winston, 1964.

Sandoz, Ellis. *A Government of Laws: Political Theory, Religion, and the American Founding*. Baton Rouge, LA: Louisiana State University Press, 1990.

———. *Political Sermons of the American Founding Era*. Indianapolis, IN: Liberty Press, 1990.

Sanford, Charles B. *The Religious Life of Thomas Jefferson*. Charlottesville, VA: University of Virginia Press, 1984.

Savage, David G. *Turning Right: The Making of the Rehnquist Supreme Court*. New York: John Wiley & Sons, 1992.

Schwehn, Mark. *Exiles from Eden: Religion and the Academic Vocation in America*. New York: Oxford University Press, 1993.

Semonche, John E. *Religion and Constitutional Government in the United States: A Historical Overview with Sources*. Carrboro, NC: Signal Books, 1986.

Sheldon, Garrett Ward. *Religion and Politics: Major Thinkers on the Relation of Church and State*. New York: Peter Lang, 1990.

Shepherd, William C. *To Secure the Blessings of Liberty: American Constitutional Law and the New Religious Movements*. New York: Crossroad Books and Scholars Press, 1985.

Sherwood, Carlton. *Inquisition: The Persecution and Prosecution of the Reverend Sun Myung Moon*. Washington, DC: Regnery Gateway, 1991.

Sibley, Mulford Q. *The Obligation to Disobey: Conscience and the Law*. New York: Council on Religion and International Affairs, 1970.

Sibley, Mulford Q., and Philip E. Jacob. *Conscription of Conscience: The American State and the Conscientious Objector, 1940–1947*. Ithaca, NY: Cornell University Press, 1952.

Simon, Arthur. *Christian Faith and Public Policy: No Grounds for Divorce*. Grand Rapids, MI: Eerdmans, 1987.

Sine, Tom. *Cease Fire: Searching for Sanity in America's Culture Wars*. Grand Rapids. MI: Eerdmans, 1995.

Sizer, Theodore R., ed. *Religion and Public Education*. Boston: Houghton, Mifflin, 1967; Lanham, MD: University Press of America, 1982.

Skillen, James W. *The Scattered Voice: Christians At Odds in the Public Square*. Grand Rapids, MI: Zondervan, 1990.

Smith, Elwyn A. *Church and State in Your Community*. Philadelphia: Westminster Press, 1963.

———. *Religious Liberty in the United States: The Development of Church-State Thought since the Revolutionary Era*. Philadelphia: Fortress Press, 1972.

Smith, Elwyn A., ed. *The Religion of the Republic*. Philadelphia: Fortress Press, 1971, 1980.

Smith, H. Shelton, Robert T. Handy, and Lefferts A. Loetscher. *American Christianity: An Historical Interpretation with Representative Documents*. 2 vols. New York: Charles Scribner's Sons, 1960.

Smith, Rodney K. *Public Prayer and the Constitution: A Case Study in Constitutional Interpretation*. Wilmington, DE: Scholarly Resources, 1987.

Smith, Steven D. *Foreordained Failure: The Quest for a Constitutional Principle of Religious Freedom*. New York: Oxford University Press, 1995.

Sorauf, Frank. *The Wall of Separation: The Constitutional Politics of Church-State*. Princeton, NJ: Princeton University Press, 1976.

Spicer, George W. *The Supreme Court and Fundamental Freedom*. New York: Appleton Century-Crofts, 1959.

Stanmeyer, William A. *Clear and Present Danger: Church and State in Post-Christian America.* Ann Arbor, MI: Servant Books, 1983.

Stedman, Murray S. *Religion and Politics in America.* New York: Harcourt, Brace & World, 1964.

Stokes, Anson Phelps. *Church and State in the United States.* 3 vols. New York: Harper & Brothers, 1950.

Stokes, Anson Phelps, and Leo Pfeffer. *Church and State in the United States.* Rev. ed. New York: Harper & Row, 1964.

Stone, Ronald H., ed. *Reformed Faith and Politics: Essays Prepared for the Advisory Council on Church and Society of the United Presbyterian Church in the USA and the Council on Theology and Culture of the Presbyterian Church in the USA.* Washington, DC: University Press of America, 1983.

Storing, Herbert J., ed. *The Complete Anti-Federalist.* Chicago: University of Chicago Press, 1981.

Story, Joseph. *The Commentaries on the Constitution.* Boston: Hilliard, Gray, 1833. Reprint Littleton, CO: F. B. Rothman, 1991.

Strickland, Reba Carolyn. *Religion and the State in Georgia in the Eighteenth Century.* New York: Columbia University Press, 1939.

Stroup, Herbert H. *The Jehovah's Witnesses.* New York: Columbia University Press, 1945.

Strout, Cushing. *The New Heavens and the New Earth: Political Religion in America.* New York: Harper & Row, 1974.

Sullivan, Winnifred Fallers. *Paying the Words Extra: Religious Discourse in the Supreme Court of the United States.* Cambridge, MA: Harvard University Press, 1994.

Swancara, Frank. *Obstruction of Justice by Religion.* San Diego: Superior Books, 1936.

Swanson, Wayne R. *The Christ Child Goes to Court.* Philadelphia: Temple University Press, 1990.

Swartley, Williard M., ed. *The Bible and Law.* Elkhart, IN: Institute of Mennonite Studies, 1982.

Sweet, William W., ed. *Religion in Colonial America.* New York: Charles Scribner's Sons, 1942.

Swisher, Carl Brent. *Stephen J. Field: Craftsman of the Law.* Washington, DC: Brookings Institution, 1930.

Swomley, John M., Jr. *Religion, the State, and the Schools.* New York: Pegasus, 1968.
———. *Religious Liberty and the Secular State: The Constitutional Context.* Buffalo, NY: Prometheus Books, 1987.

Talparar, Morris. *The Sociology of Colonial Virginia.* 2d rev. ed. New York: Philosophical Library, 1968.

Tanner, Kathryn. *The Politics of God: Christian Theologies, and Social Justice.* Minneapolis, MN: Fortress Press, 1992.

Tarr, B. Alan. *Judicial Impact and State Supreme Courts.* Lexington, MA: D. C. Heath, 1977.

Thernstrom, Abigail. *School Choice in Massachusetts.* Boston: Pioneer Institute for Public Policy Research, 1991.

Thiemann, Ronald F. *Religion in Public Life: A Dilemma for Democracy.* Washington, DC: Georgetown University Press, 1996.

Thorpe, Francis Newton. *The Federal and State Constitutions.* 7 vols. Washington,

DC: Government Printing Office, 1909. Reprint St. Clair Shores, MI: Scholarly Press, 1977.

Tiemann, William Harold, and John C. Bush. *The Right to Silence: Privileged Clergy Communication and the Law.* Nashville, TN: Abingdon Press, 1989.

Tinder, Glenn. *The Political Meaning of Christianity: A Prophetic Stance.* San Francisco: HarperCollins, 1991.

Tinker, George. *Missionary Conquest: The Gospel and Native American Cultural Genocide.* Minneapolis, MN: Augsburg Fortress Press, 1993.

Torpey, William G. *Judicial Doctrines of Religious Rights in America.* Chapel Hill, NC: University of North Carolina Press, 1948.

Tribe, Laurence H. *American Constitutional Law.* Mineola, NY: The Foundation Press, 1978.

———. *The Constitutional Protection of Individual Rights: Limits on Government Authority.* Mineola, NY: The Foundation Press, 1978.

———. *God Save This Honorable Court: How the Choice of Supreme Court Justices Shapes Our History.* New York: Random House, 1985.

———. *American Constitutional Law.* 2d ed. Mineola, NY: The Foundation Press, 1988.

Tribe, Laurence H. "Church and State in the Constitution." In *Government Intervention in Religious Affairs.* Edited by Dean M. Kelley, 31–40. New York: The Pilgrim Press, 1982.

Trimble, Bruce R. *Chief Justice Waite.* Princeton, NJ: Princeton University Press, 1938.

Tucker, Henry St. George. *Commentaries on the Laws of Virginia.* 1837.

Tushnet, Mark V. *Red, White, and Blue: A Critical Analysis of Constitutional Law.* Cambridge, MA: Harvard University Press, 1988.

Tussman, Joseph, ed. *The Supreme Court on Church and State.* New York: Oxford Press, 1962.

Twomley, Dale E. *Parochiaid and the Courts.* Perrier Springs, MI: Andrews University Press, 1981.

Utley, Robert M. *The Lance and the Shield.* New York: Henry Holt, 1993.

Vaux, Kenneth L. *Ethics and the Gulf War: Religion, Rhetoric, and Righteousness.* Boulder, CO: Westview Press, 1992.

Veit, Helen, ed. *Creating the Bill of Rights: The Documentary Record from the First Federal Congress.* Baltimore, MD: Johns Hopkins Press, 1991.

Vetterlil, Richard, and Gary Bryner. *In Search of the Republic: Public Virtue and the Roots of American Government.* Totowa, NJ: Rowman & Littlefield, 1987.

Wald, Kenneth D. *Religion and Politics in the United States.* New York: St. Martin's Press, 1987.

Walter, Erich A., ed. *Religion and the State University.* Ann Arbor, MI: University of Michigan Press, 1964.

Walters, Kerry S. *The American Deists: Voices of Reason and Dissent in the Early Republic.* Lawrence, KS: University Press of Kansas, 1992.

Ward, Hiley H. *Space-Age Sunday.* New York: Macmillan, 1960.

Watts, Tim J. *Church and Court—Settling Religious Disputes with Secular Law.* Monticello, IL: Vance Bibliographies, 1988.

Webb, George E. *The Evolution Controversy in America.* Lexington, KY: University Press of Kentucky, 1994.

Weber, Paul J., ed. *Equal Separation: Understanding the Religion Clauses of the First Amendment.* Westport, CT: Greenwood Press, 1990.

Weber, Paul J., and Dennis A. Gilbert. *Private Churches and Public Money: Church-Government Fiscal Relations.* Westport, CT: Greenwood Press, 1981.

Weeks, Stephen B. *Church and State in North Carolina.* Baltimore, MD: Johns Hopkins Press, 1893.

Weigel, George, and Robert Royal, eds. *A Century of Catholic Social Thought: Essays on "Rerum Novarum" and Nine Other Key Documents.* Washington, DC: Ethics and Public Policy Center, 1991.

Wells, Guy Fred. *Parish Education in Colonial Virginia.* New York: Arno Press, 1969.

Wells, Ronald A., ed. *The Wars of America: Christian Views.* Macon, GA: Mercer University Press, 1991.

Wells, Ronald A., and Thomas A. Askew, eds. *Liberty and Law: Reflections on the Constitution in American Life and Thought.* Grand Rapids, MI.: Eerdmans, 1987.

Wenz, Peter S. *Abortion Rights as Religious Freedom.* Philadelphia: Temple University Press, 1992.

White, Ronald C., and Albright G. Zimmerman, eds. *An Unsettled Arena: Religion and the Bill of Rights.* Grand Rapids, MI: Eerdmans, 1990.

Whitehead, John W. *The Separation Illusion: A Lawyer Examines the First Amendment.* Milford, MI: Mott Media, 1977.

———. *The Rights of Religious Persons in Public Education.* Wheaton, IL: Crossway Books, 1991.

———. *The Second American Revolution.* Elgin, IL: David C. Cook, 1982.

Wills, Garry. *Under God: Religion and American Politics.* New York: Simon & Schuster, 1990.

Wilson, John F. *Public Religion in American Culture.* Philadelphia: Temple University Press, 1979.

Wilson, John F., ed. *Church and State in American History.* Boston: D. C. Heath, 1965.

———. *Church and State in America: A Bibliographical Guide.* Vol. 1: *The Colonial and Early National Period,* 1986; Vol. 2: *The Civil War to the Present Day.* Westport, CT: Greenwood Press, 1987.

Wilson, John F., and Donald L. Drakeman, eds. *Church and State in American History: The Burden of Religious Pluralism.* 2d ed. Boston: Beacon Press. 1987.

Wogaman, Philip. *Protestant Faith and Religious Liberty.* Nashville, TN: Abingdon Press, 1967.

Wolf, Donald J., S.J. *Toward Consensus: Catholic-Protestant Interpretations of Church and State.* Garden City, NY: Doubleday, 1968.

Wood, James E., Jr. *Religion and Politics.* Waco, TX: J. M. Dawson Institute of Church-State Studies, Baylor University Press, 1983.

———. *Religion and the State: Essays in Honor of Leo Pfeffer.* Waco, TX: Baylor University Press, 1985.

———. *The First Freedom: Religion and the Bill of Rights.* Waco, TX: J. M. Dawson Institute of Church-State Studies, Baylor University, 1990.

———. *The Role of Religion in the Making of Public Policy.* Waco, TX: J. M. Dawson Institute of Church-State Studies, Baylor University, 1991.

Wood, James E., Jr., ed. *Religion, the State, and Education.* Waco, TX: Baylor University Press, 1984.

———. *Ecumenical Perspectives on Church and State: Protestant, Catholic, and Jewish.*

Waco, TX: J. M. Dawson, Institute of Church-State Studies, Baylor University, 1988.

Wood, James E., Jr., and Derek Davis, eds. *The Role of Government in Monitoring and Regulating Religion in Public Life.* Waco, TX: J. M. Dawson Institute of Church-State Studies, Baylor University Press, 1993.

Wood, James E., Jr., Robert T. Miller, and E. Bruce Thompson, eds. *Church and State in Scripture, History, and Constitutional Law.* Waco, TX: Baylor University Press, 1958.

Woodford, Howard J., Jr. *Mr. Justice Murphy: A Political Biography.* Princeton, NJ: Princeton University Press, 1968.

Worton, Stanley N. *Freedom of Religion.* Rochelle Park, NJ: Hayden, 1975.

Wunder, John R. *"Retained by the People": A History of American Law and the Bill of Rights.* New York: Oxford University Press, 1994.

Wuthnow, Robert. *The Restructuring of American Religion.* Princeton, NJ: Princeton University Press, 1988.

———. *The Struggle for America's Soul.* Grand Rapids, MI: Eerdmans, 1989.

Yandian, Bob. *One Nation Under God: The Rise or Fall of a Nation.* Tulsa, OK: Harrison House, 1988.

Zaretsky, I. I., and M. P. Leone, eds. *Religious Movements in Contemporary America.* Princeton, NJ: Princeton University Press, 1974.

Zetterbert, J. Peter, ed. *Evolution versus Creationism: The Public Education Controversy.* Phoenix, AZ: Oryx Press, 1983.

Zolliman, Carl F. *American Church Law.* St. Paul, MN: West, 1933.

Index

Christopher Thomas Anglim has an M.A. in history from Arizona State University, an M.L.S. from the University of Arizona, and a J.D. from the Arizona State University College of Law. He works as a reference law librarian at the University of St. Thomas in Houston, Texas; the government documents librarian at Lee College in Baytown, Texas; and a reference librarian at the Houston Community College. He is the author of ABC-CLIO's *Labor, Employment, and the Law: A Dictionary* (1997) as well as other books, articles, and a special-collections catalog.